D0840221

Justice and Beauty in Muslim Marriage

Justice and Beauty in Muslim Marriage

Towards Egalitarian Ethics and Laws

Edited by Ziba Mir-Hosseini,
Mulki Al-Sharmani, Jana Rumminger
and Sarah Marsso

ONEWORLD
ACADEMIC

Oneworld Academic

An imprint of Oneworld Publications

Published by Oneworld Academic in 2022

Copyright © Ziba Mir-Hosseini, Mulki Al-Sharmani,
Jana Rumminger and Sarah Marsso 2022

All rights reserved
Copyright under Berne Convention
A CIP record for this title is available from the British Library

ISBN 978-0-86154-447-9
eISBN 978-0-86154-448-6

Typeset by Geethik Technologies
Printed and bound in Great Britain by Clays Ltd, Elcograf S.p.A.

Oneworld Publications
10 Bloomsbury Street
London WC1B 3SR
England

Stay up to date with the latest books,
special offers, and exclusive content from
Oneworld with our newsletter

Sign up on our website
oneworld-publications.com

MIX
Paper from
responsible sources
FSC® C018072

Contents

ISLAMIC LEGAL THEORY AND ETHICS

LAW AND PRACTICE

Foreword

I grew up in the 1960s and 70s with an utter faith in a just God and a just Islam. God cannot be God if God is unjust. It was as simple as that.

But by the 1980s, things began to change. The rise of political Islam globally and in my home country, Malaysia, saw the inclusive and compassionate Islam I grew up with slowly evolve into a dogmatic, patriarchal and punitive religion that made no sense to the realities of my life.

Islamist political leaders and preachers over radio, television and in private homes were dominating the public discourse on Islam and women's rights: 'Men are superior to women'; 'A man has a right to four wives'; 'A husband has a right to beat his wife'; 'He has a right to demand obedience from his wife'; 'He has a right to have sex with his wife on demand and the wife has no right to say no'; 'Hell is full of women who have disobeyed their husbands'. The worst was a so-called hadith that said even if a woman has licked the pus oozing from her husband from head to toe, she still would not have done enough to be obedient to him. What kind of Islam could preach this injustice and harm to women?

At the same time, women were facing difficulties such as getting a divorce if the husband objected, husbands taking second wives without the first wives' knowledge, religious department officials telling women to go home and be good obedient wives when they reported domestic violence. Women felt they were pushed around like a ball, kicked from pillar to post in their search for solutions to end their misery.

The obvious question before us was this: Where is the justice and beauty of Islam in pronouncements and actions that cause harm to women and families? These assertions in the name of Islam went completely against my belief. I went to religious school for five years. None of my religious teachers ever talked of God and Islam in these unkind ways or used Islam to justify patriarchy and women's subordination. The Islam I learned in school and lived was about a kind and compassionate God, a just God, and our duties to be good human beings who are honest, kind and respectful. Not about male superiority, or even men's and women's rights and responsibilities.

So, to be assaulted as an adult with a religious discourse that was unjust was simply an affront to my faith. I was outraged that the God and the Islam I grew up with were abused in order to justify men's bad behaviour. Something must be done. Instead of turning my back on the religion, I decided to reread the Qurʾan once again to find out if God really did sanction such misogynistic behaviour towards women. This led me and the founding members of Sisters in Islam to meet every week to study the Qurʾan in search of the promised justice of Islam.

There were many eureka moments in this process. The Qurʾan says: '... marry only one, that will be best to prevent you from doing injustice' (4:3); 'men and women are protectors of one another' (9:71); 'men and women are garments for one another' (2:187); 'be you male or female, you are members, one of another' (3:195); 'God puts between your hearts, love and compassion' (30:21).

What happened to these beautiful egalitarian messages of the Qurʾan? Why didn't this language of justice, equality, reciprocity and compassion become the source of jurisprudence governing marriage and family relations? Obviously, men in authority who interpreted the Qurʾan and deduced the laws decided that these verses should be silent and silenced, and instead their favourite verse on supposed 'male authority' (4:34) should be the basis of marriage. This maintained men's power and privilege over women.

We felt we could no longer remain silent or be silenced. In the context of rising political Islam in many Muslim countries and the consequent attacks on gains women had made over the decades, we felt compelled to produce and disseminate knowledge that demonstrates the necessity and possibility of equality and justice for women in Islam.

With knowledge comes courage. From the pioneering work of Sisters in Islam in Malaysia to the global movement Musawah, it has been a long and exciting journey for us to challenge this patriarchal terrain of Islam and to embark on a new path that we feel represents the beauty and justice of Islam. We wanted to build new feminist knowledge in Islam, to unearth the gems within our *tafsīr* and *fiqh* traditions, to open the public space for debate and for a new public discourse to emerge on Islam and women's rights.

As a founding member and founding Executive Director of Musawah, I am proud to see these efforts brought to fruition in this book, *Justice and Beauty in Muslim Marriage: Towards Egalitarian Ethics and Laws.*

We have always believed that the egalitarian and compassionate Qur'anic ethos and the many sophisticated Islamic legal concepts could lead us to a new ethical and legal framework for Muslim marriages. The classical legal (*fiqh*) framework that regarded women as inferior to men and established rules that led to the control and subjugation of women can no longer be the basis for regulating marriage and divorce in the twenty-first century. This man-made classical juristic construct of the providing, protecting husband and the submissive wife has no relevance to the contemporary experiences and ethical values of today. In fact, it is harmful to individuals, families and societies. Musawah's knowledge building work – including the scholarship presented in this book – bridges the disconnect between ethics, law and contemporary lived realities to enable Muslims to build an understanding of marriage based on ethics of justice, equality, beauty and goodness.

We hope the chapters in this book will empower readers to translate the new ideas, concepts, ways of thinking and approaches to the tradition into practical ways of transforming the model for Muslim marriage into one that cultivates nourishing forms of love and partnership. During the Covid-19 pandemic, Musawah hosted public webinars in which our scholars shared their works in progress. The excitement they engendered with their research and enlightening ideas and the questions raised and responses we received from participants led us to ponder doable ways we can move forward from theory to practice. Some excellent ideas emerged – a new premarital course on how to build a marriage based on equality, justice, spiritual growth, beauty and goodness; *nikāḥ* khutbahs that reflect a more egalitarian aspiration of marriage; a model marriage contract that embodies Qur'anic values; and even mediation services to end marriage with grace and compassion for those who feel they can no longer live together in harmony.

These are all exciting possibilities as Musawah follows through its tradition of bringing together scholarship and activism in building a movement for change. Our Campaign for Justice in Muslim Family Laws is now underway in Asia, the Middle East and North Africa and Sub-Saharan Africa. It is this new knowledge grounded within Islam that will give Musawah advocates the confidence and the courage to build a public voice demanding change.

Musawah is proud to be working with the seventeen scholars who have contributed to the production of this volume. We are grateful to the many who have engaged with Musawah from the very beginning, and the new ones whom we hope find this engagement enriching. Musawah would like to thank all of the scholars for their patience and openness to the exactitudes of the Musawah ways of working and most of all for their generosity in sharing their knowledge and time with us.

We would also like to express our deepest gratitude to the dream team that makes up the Musawah Knowledge Building Working Group. Ziba Mir-Hosseini, who leads this team, holds a special place in our hearts for providing conceptual leadership to the project with clarity, generosity and deep insight, and doing it in egalitarian ways. To Mulki Al-Sharmani, Jana Rumminger and Sarah Marsso, the rigour, meticulousness and dedication that you pour into this work serve as a model for us all.

To those of us who believe in equality, justice, beauty and goodness, this book is a gift to inspire and to drive us to transform how we live our lives in our families and societies in more just and caring ways.

Zainah Anwar
Musawah Founding Executive Director (2009–21)

Acknowledgements

This book arose out of a rich exchange of scholarship and ideas generated through the first three years of Musawah's Research Initiative on 'Reclaiming *'Adl* and *Iḥsān* in Muslim Marriages: Between Ethics and Law'. This incredible journey to unearth ethics of justice, beauty and equality would not have been possible without the inspiration and support of many across the world. We are extremely grateful to each of them for pouring their hearts into this project, especially given the challenges posed by the Covid-19 pandemic and all of our personal life circumstances.

We would like to express our special thanks to the eminent scholar amina wadud, whose groundbreaking scholarship, spiritual mentorship and close friendship played a significant role in shaping this project. She provided critical insights, scholarly advice and support in Musawah workshops and webinars and in personal conversations. Beyond this, amina holds a special place within Musawah and for so many involved in this project for whom she has opened new horizons of thought and motivated the quest for social justice.

This book would not exist without the generosity, patience and goodwill of the seventeen authors who tirelessly shared their knowledge and time, helping to ensure the depth, sincerity and quality of this work. We are immensely grateful for their dedication and engagement in our long participatory process.

We extend our gratitude to the university partners that generously collaborated in hosting conceptual workshops and public seminars in London, Helsinki, Kuala Lumpur and Toronto in 2018 and 2019: the Centre of Islamic and Middle Eastern Law (CIMEL) at SOAS, University of London; the University of Helsinki; the Institute of Islamic Studies and Emmanuel College of Victoria University at the University of Toronto; and particularly Lynn Welchman, Mulki Al-Sharmani, Jana Turk, Anver Emon and Nevin

Reda. These events involved scholars and activists whose insights and expertise were critical to help develop the project's early framework and bring the ideas together into a more cohesive whole. In particular, we wish to thank Annelies Moors, Nadjma Yassari, Samia Bano, Shaheen Sardar Ali, Soroush Dabbagh, Kamala Chandrakirana, Rozana Isa, Sarah Shah, and our friends and fellow Musawah advocates from Rahima in Indonesia and the Canadian Council of Muslim Women, especially Pera Sopariyanti, Andi Nur Fa'izah, Alia Hogben, Nuzhat Jafri, Sabrine Azraq, Zahra Grant, Fathima Hussain, Shaheen Sayed and Nina Karachi-Khaled.

After these productive meetings, the world came to a standstill in early 2020 with the arrival of the Covid-19 pandemic. We quickly pivoted from in-person to online collaboration, implementing a series of public webinars that provided space to share and discuss the knowledge produced under the research initiative with wider and more diverse audiences. We would like to thank all who contributed to the success of these webinars: the speakers, moderators, participants, Musawah's support team, and especially discussants Lena Larsen, Ayesha Royker, Heba Salah, Nada Nashat, Faeeza Vaid, Hadeel Hazim, Noorjehan Safia Niaz and Fatima Seedat.

We have benefited enormously from the generosity, rigour and thoroughness of Dr Randa Aboubakr, who is undertaking the immense task of translating this book into Arabic as she did with *Men in Charge? Rethinking Authority in Muslim Legal Tradition*. The insights she has shared while interrogating word choice and unpacking key concepts have been extremely illuminating. We'd also like to thank Asma Ghelawi and Alaa Mansour for their valuable research assistance.

Our sincere gratitude goes to the Henry Luce Foundation for generously funding this research project as part of their Initiative on Religion in International Affairs, and to Toby Volkman for her enthusiastic support, understanding and flexibility under the pandemic circumstances.

Most of all, we are truly blessed with wonderful support and unceasing encouragement from our dear sisters in the Musawah Secretariat. We wish to thank Rosezaini Mansor, Zamaria Mohamed and Noor Baizura Baharudin, who oversaw the administrative and financial aspects of this project; Marwa Sharafeldin, Suri Kempe, Hyshyama Hamin, Alex McCarthy and Zulaikha Shihab, whose inputs and sense of teamwork, regardless of the hour of the day, have strengthened the project from the beginning; and the newest team members for their enthusiasm and assistance: our two co-directors Zharin Zhafrael Mohamed and Huda Jawad and the programme officers Rasha

Dewedar, Rehema Namukose, Hamizah Adzmi, Fatima Qureshi and Asmaa Gharib.

We remain indebted to Zainah Anwar, founding member and former executive director of Musawah, whose passion, courage and love have inspired and encouraged us throughout this journey.

We are forever grateful for the dedication, love and unwavering support of our spouses and families.

Finally, this book is a collective outcome of Musawah and the Knowledge Building Working Group; we are grateful to God for bringing us together. We have collaborated not only as colleagues and teammates but also as close friends, complementing each other in terms of skills, personalities, demeanours, perspectives and in so many other ways. We have created a beautiful and strong bond between our hearts based on admiration, respect and deep love for one another.

Ziba Mir-Hosseini, Mulki Al-Sharmani,
Jana Rumminger and Sarah Marsso
December 2021

Note on Translation and Transliteration

Translation and transliteration are always tricky issues. Most of the authors provided their own translations of Arabic texts and terms, sometimes with small but significant differences in interpretation. Unless otherwise noted, the translation of Qurʾanic verses and terms follows M. A. S. Abdel Haleem, *The Qurʾan* (2004), occasionally with slight modification by the author(s).

For transliteration, we have standardized the contributors' varied usages by adopting the *International Journal of Middle East Studies* standards with a few modifications. Inconsistencies undoubtedly remain, but readers who are familiar with Arabic should have no trouble recognizing the terms.

Introduction: Towards Marriage as a Partnership of Equals

Ziba Mir-Hosseini, Mulki Al-Sharmani,
Jana Rumminger and Sarah Marsso

Every Friday, in mosques across the world, worshippers hear a recitation of Qur'anic verse 16:90 before they start the communal prayer: 'God commands *'adl* (justice) and *iḥsān* (goodness and beauty), and generosity towards relatives, and forbids what is shameful, blameworthy and oppressive. God teaches you, so that you may take heed.' This verse is a reminder of two core ethical principles: *'adl* and *iḥsān*.

How have these principles informed norms and laws that guide gender relations and rights, particularly in relation to marriage? The model of marriage constructed in classical Islamic jurisprudence (*fiqh*) rests on patriarchal ethics that deny gender equality and privilege men. This worldview persists in many contemporary Muslim family laws that are drawn from *fiqh*, notwithstanding reforms introduced in different codes over the past decades, and in gender norms in various Muslim contexts. Yet the current realities of gender roles in Muslim families and their changing needs show the limitations of such patriarchal ethics and laws. Addressing these limitations is not only crucial for the well-being of spouses, children and families in general, but also to maintain the egalitarian ethos of Islam.

This volume explores how the dominant conception of Muslim marriage can be shifted from a contract that requires a woman's obedience in exchange for a man's protection and maintenance, to a partnership grounded in equality, justice and mutual well-being. It brings together twelve chapters that engage with a series of interconnected questions: How should we reconsider the patriarchal ethics that have informed Muslim marriages, as articulated in classical *fiqh* rulings and many modern Muslim family laws? What insights can we garner from the Qur᾽an, prophetic tradition and Muslim legal tradition to construct a new ethical and legal discourse on Muslim marriage as a partnership of equals and a relationship of mutual spiritual growth and well-being? How can historical practices inform contemporary debates on advancing gender equality in Muslim family laws? And, more broadly, how do we challenge the dominant patriarchal religious discourse from within and create an alternative discourse that cherishes beauty, goodness and justice?

BUILDING KNOWLEDGE FROM WITHIN

This book grew out of a research project titled 'Reclaiming *ʿAdl* and *Iḥsān* in Muslim Marriages: Between Ethics and Law', which was initiated by Musawah in 2018.[1] Musawah ('equality' in Arabic) is a global movement that brings together scholars and activists advocating for equality and justice in Muslim families. Musawah brings new perspectives on Islamic teachings by reinserting women's lived realities and voices in the production of religious knowledge. It does so by facilitating access to existing knowledge about gender in Islam and creating new multidimensional knowledge about Muslim gender norms and rights.

The project that informs this book builds on an earlier Musawah 'Knowledge Building Initiative on *Qiwamah* and *Wilayah*' (2010–18).[2] This initiative culminated in several publications, among which is the edited volume *Men in Charge? Rethinking Authority in Muslim Legal Tradition* (Oneworld, 2015).[3]

[1] The research project is led within Musawah by the Knowledge Building Working Group, which supports, advises and assists the Musawah Secretariat in developing work plans, building resources and implementing knowledge building activities. The team currently comprises the four editors of this volume, who are situated in different countries with various educational and research backgrounds.

[2] This first initiative in turn built on the insights of an Oslo Coalition of Freedom of Religion or Belief research project to which key members of Musawah contributed, and which resulted in the edited volume *Gender and Equality in Muslim Family Law: Justice and Ethics in Islamic Legal Tradition* (Mir-Hosseini et al., 2013).

[3] Other publications resulting from the *Qiwamah* and *Wilayah* initiative include Musawah (2016a; 2016b7; 2018), and a series of Knowledge Building Briefs explaining core concepts.

The aim of the earlier project was to trace and deconstruct the underlying discursive foundation for gender inequality in Muslim marriages. This was done through a multifaceted inquiry into two key concepts in Islamic jurisprudence, namely *qiwāma*, which is commonly understood as a husband's legal obligation as a provider and his authority over his wife, and *wilāya*, commonly understood as a man's authority within the family as guardian over his children or their dependent female relatives.

Several key insights emerged from this initiative. First, male authority over women (as encapsulated in the two key concepts) can no longer be supported on religious grounds. *Qiwāma* and *wilāya*, in the sense of placing women under male authority and guardianship, are not Qur'anic concepts. Rather they are juristic constructs that in time became the building blocks of patriarchy in Muslim legal tradition. Second, these two concepts function as 'legal postulates' as defined by Japanese legal scholar Masaji Chiba.[4] That is, they act as value principles or systems that shape the construction of marriage and gender rights in *fiqh* and codified family laws. Finally, such a patriarchal construct poses a crisis for Muslims on multiple levels. On one level, it highlights the wide gap that exists between contemporary notions of justice and gender rights and classical notions that underpin juristic rulings and continue to be the source of Muslim family laws. On another level, gender roles as constructed by jurists are divorced from the realities of marriage and family relations as lived by many Muslims today.

While the previous initiative analysed the roots of gender inequality in Muslim legal tradition, the aim of this second research initiative is to investigate ethical and legal frameworks that conceptualize how Muslim marriages can be grounded in equality, justice and mutual spiritual growth and well-being. In other words, this project takes up the work of reconstruction.

The project rests on three premises. The first is that existing Muslim marriage norms, laws and practices are no longer in line with contemporary notions of justice. They are informed by legal and religious frameworks developed by classical scholars in contexts where justice did not include the notion of gender equality.

The *Musawah Vision for the Family* (2016a) was a prototype for the current 'Reclaiming *'Adl* and *Iḥsān*' project, providing arguments for why and how to rethink family relationships, structures and norms in a way that recognizes equality and ensures the well-being of all.

[4] Lynn Welchman introduced the conceptualization of *qiwāma* and *wilāya* as legal postulates – using 'postulate' in the sense defined by Chiba (1986, p. 7): 'A value system that simply exists in its own right' – during a Musawah workshop in Amman, Jordan, in 2011, and then in her chapter in *Men in Charge?* (Welchman, 2015, p. 132).

The second premise is that there are ways and reasons for approaching the subject of marriage and gender relations within Islamic textual tradition and from an egalitarian perspective. The ethical worldview and message of the Qurʾan affirm the equal worth of all humans, and call for social relations (including gender relations) that reflect core Qurʾanic ethical principles such as justice (*ʿadl*), goodness and beauty (*iḥsān*), and doing what is commonly known to be good (*maʿrūf*). While these values have multiple meanings that evolve according to different contexts and circumstances, the research project is based on an understanding of *ʿadl* as encompassing values of transformative justice and equality; and *iḥsān* as a call to pursue beauty, goodness and care in individual and broader social relations. The prophetic Sunna – as reflected in the exemplary life of Prophet Muhammad and his collated sayings and deeds in Hadith compilations – can also provide strong foundations to inspire egalitarian gender relations within the family. Similarly, Islamic legal tradition and early Muslim social and legal practices offer conceptual and methodological building blocks for rethinking the *fiqh* model of marriage.

The third premise is that we live in a world in which there is a plurality of 'ethical frameworks,' 'norms' or 'laws' through which contemporary social relations – in this case Muslim gender relations and rights in the family domain – are regulated, negotiated and transformed. The legal trajectories in different contemporary Muslim contexts can serve as another rich and diverse source for constructing a new legal foundation for Muslim marriages based on a model of equal partnership.

Working from these premises, the Musawah Knowledge Building Working Group developed a framework to build an understanding of marriage as a partnership of equals in a way that is rooted within Muslim legal tradition. Central to the inquiry is the aim of systematically mapping out ethical values such as *ʿadl* and *iḥsān* and considering how they can be implemented in laws and family relations.

The first phase of research consisted of studies conducted by scholars from a variety of disciplines on the Qurʾan, the *sīra* (biography) of Prophet Muhammad, Hadith, Islamic legal tradition, social history of Muslim marriages in selected contexts, and contemporary Muslim family law reform processes. These studies represent authors from diverse disciplines and divergent perspectives engaging in conversation with Islamic interpretive tradition towards the goal of providing new approaches that reclaim justice and beauty in marital relationships.

Musawah, in collaboration with several universities, held conceptual workshops to develop the project in London (May 2018), Helsinki (November 2018), Kuala Lumpur (June 2019) and Toronto (December 2019).[5] These workshops provided spaces in which authors and women's rights activists could discuss the ideas and later the working papers in depth. The Covid-19 pandemic and ensuing restrictions on travel, however, prevented further face-to-face roundtables and workshops. Therefore, the project pivoted into extensive and sometimes intense discussions (virtual and email) between the Knowledge Building Working Group and individual authors on their papers, along with a series of public webinars in which the authors shared their works-in-progress with a moderator from Musawah and a discussant who is engaged in activism work on the ground. The webinar conversations aimed to highlight key arguments from the individual chapters; methodological contributions; how the paper speaks to the larger goal of the research initiative; and how the ideas can inform specific challenges and efforts towards legal, religious or societal reform. The fact that the webinars were public provided an opportunity to share, discuss and consolidate the knowledge being produced with wider and more diverse audiences. It also created a digital space for interdisciplinary discussions around questions of gender and family relations in Muslim tradition.

Musawah embarks on the second phase of the project involving multi-sited empirical research in multiple Muslim contexts in 2023. The empirical research will investigate how diverse actors from the domains of advocacy, policy making, the religious establishment and public discourse and Muslim individuals and couples in their daily lives are creating language, ideas, practices and modalities for egalitarian marriages.

A HOLISTIC APPROACH

Musawah celebrates the inherent diversity and plurality within Muslim tradition. In line with new trends of Islamic reformist thought, Musawah contends that Islam's textual sources are open to interpretation and compatible with modern ideas such as gender equality. We build our claim to gender equality

---

[5] Musawah collaborated with the following universities in hosting conceptual workshops and developing early background paper ideas: University of Helsinki; Centre of Islamic and Middle Eastern Studies, SOAS, University of London; Institute of Islamic Studies, University of Toronto. The project was generously funded from 2019–21 by the Henry Luce Foundation.

and our arguments for reform using a holistic approach that combines Islamic teachings, international human rights standards, national laws and constitutional guarantees of equality and non-discrimination, and the lived realities of Muslim families.[6] We understand 'equality' to mean substantive and transformative equality that seeks meaningful change of institutions and systems to ensure women have equal and full decision-making power in their families, societies and states.[7] We ground our claim to equality and arguments for reform within the intersections of the four corners of this framework.

Musawah's approach intersects with the work of the legal scholars Masaji Chiba and Werner Menski.[8] Chiba argues that all systems of law are plural and are linked to culture. He also divides the structure of the law into 'official law' (state law), 'unofficial law' (not recognized by the state but authoritative in practice), and 'legal postulate', a value principle or value system that relates to either official or unofficial law and provides legitimacy for it (1986, pp. 5–6). Werner Menski further develops Chiba's three-pronged structure of law into a four-cornered image of 'law as a flying kite' (2011, 2012). In line with other legal pluralists, Menski argues that law, as it functions and is experienced in the lived realities of people, is plural, consisting of multiple entities. Each entity is characterized by its own internal plurality. He calls this 'living law', or 'law in context.' According to Menski, this 'living law,' similar to a kite, consists

[6] This approach is outlined in the 2009 'Musawah Framework in Action' (www.musawah.org/resources/musawah-framework-for-action/). Musawah takes a critical feminist perspective that works from within the tradition of Islamic legal thought. As such, we invoke several distinctions that give us the conceptual tools to argue for gender equality from within the tradition. The first is between Shariʿa as God's will as revealed to the Prophet Muhammad and *fiqh* as Islamic jurisprudence, the process and the methodology for interpreting the Shariʿa and extracting legal rules from the sacred sources. 'Islamic' laws are the result of *fiqh*; like any other human system of jurisprudence, *fiqh* is mundane, temporal and local. The second distinction is between the two main categories of legal rulings (*aḥkām*): *ʿibādāt*, ritual/spiritual acts that regulate relations between God and the believer and thus offer limited scope for change, and *muʿāmalāt*, social/contractual acts that regulate relations among humans and remain open to change. Most rulings concerning women and gender relations belong to the second category. The Framework also notes that diversity of opinion (*ikhtilaf*) has always been a basic premise in *fiqh*; there has never been a single, unitary 'Islamic law'.

[7] See Musawah Knowledge Building Brief 'Islam and the Question of Gender Equality' (www.musawah.org/resources/knowledge-building-brief-3-islam-and-the-question-of-gender-equality-en/).

[8] The chapter by Welchman, Jouirou and Sharafeldin in this volume explores this in more detail, along with application to the field of law reform. As noted above, Lynn Welchman introduced these concepts to Musawah in the context of *qiwāma* and *wilāya*, drawing attention to the parallels between Menski's kite and Musawah's four-pronged Framework.

of four poles representing overlapping entities, namely: religious/ethical/moral laws; social norms and lived realities; state laws; and international law. Menski argues that the ways in which actors understand and use these entities are often dynamic and fluid. Actors also contest and negotiate the meanings within each entity. Hence, the relationships between the different entities are often in dialectic tension and interaction.

Menski's quadripartite structure of law parallels Musawah's four-pronged approach to all its work, that is, Islamic teachings, international human rights standards, constitutional and legislative guarantees of equality and non-discrimination and lived realities in Muslim contexts. The image of 'law as a flying kite' is helpful in thinking about the different 'norms', 'laws' and political and socio-economic forces at play in debating and reforming gender rights in Muslim family relations. Laws are created and revised within this context of multi-dimensional religious, social and political forces that ebb and flow on their own and in interaction with each other. For instance, Islamic teachings are plural, and include patriarchal and egalitarian ethics which constantly interact with one another. Similarly, the lived realities of Muslim families are plural, evolving and contrasting according to different backgrounds (class, race, age, etc.) and contexts. Actors negotiating the meanings within this entity include conservative, reformist and/or feminist Muslims whose positions also shift depending on the context and dominant influences at any given time. The kite model allows us to think holistically about the ways in which political, religious, and socio-economic forces can shape debates and the ultimate destiny of reform, sometimes acting like gusts of wind that blow the kite out of the control of the handler. One of the key objectives in Musawah from the outset has been to better understand the shaping of norms, laws and power relations in each of the four poles, and to balance them against patriarchal forces and towards the development of egalitarian family relations.

Central to the vision of Musawah, and related to the four poles of Musawah's 'Framework for Action', are the intertwined arenas of scholarship and activism. The knowledge produced within Musawah is intended to inform and be informed by multifaceted activism that is undertaken by the movement (for example, legal advocacy, raising awareness, creating spaces for constructive dialogues with relevant actors). This knowledge-building process happens simultaneously with actions on the ground, such as campaigns for law reform, capacity building workshops, policy briefs, etc., and the methodologies and concepts developed are directly tested against the challenges faced by women's rights groups in different contexts. Muslims' contemporary lived realities and experiences and the dialectal relationship between the text and the context are at the heart of all of its work, including this volume.

ETHICS, LAW AND GENDER

Islamic reformist thinkers have often critiqued the hegemony of *fiqh* in Islamic textual tradition and the fact that Islamic ethics has not been systematically conceptualized and formulated.[9] But it was left to feminist scholars to reveal and engage with problems in the relations between ethics, law and lived realities of contemporary Muslims, which are most evident in issues related to gender.[10] For instance, the classical *fiqh* notion of marriage, as mentioned above, was modelled on a contract of sale in which a husband offers financial security and protection in exchange for his wife's obedience and submission. This model was based on patriarchal and fixed ideas of gender roles and rights, and as a result led to asymmetrical relationships between the spouses. The effects of this model are reflected in the lived realities of contemporary Muslim families. Women have unequal legal rights in marriage, divorce, child custody and inheritance, while men face pressures and anxiety when they are unable to fulfil their roles as providers. Moreover, this model stands in contrast with the Qurʾanic ethical principles guiding spousal and family relationships, such as *mawadda* (love), *raḥma* (compassion), *tashāwur* (consultation), *sakīna* (tranquillity), *tarāḍī* (mutual consent). Above all, this model and the laws and norms that are still influenced by it are no longer in line with the ethos of the Shariʿa.

How can we bridge the disconnect between ethics, laws and contemporary lived realities of Muslims to build an understanding of marriage based on ethics of justice, equality, beauty and goodness as understood today? The authors contributing to this volume engage with the central question of ethics and its relationship to gender laws and norms. Each individual chapter explores the ethical and legal foundations for marriages of equality, justice and beauty from its own perspective, whether the starting point is the Qurʾan, Sunna, Islamic legal theory, historical Muslim marriage practices or contemporary Muslim family law reform processes. While the authors probe

---

[9] See, for example, Rahman (1966; 1982), Moosa (2000; 2020), Abou El Fadl (2001; 2014), Abu Zayd (2006) and Sajoo (2018).

[10] There are many scholars who explore the intersections of gender, Islamic law and ethics. Among them are Wadud (1999; 2006), Barlas (2002), Mir-Hosseini (2003), Ali (2006), Abou-Bakr and Al-Sharmani (2020) and the authors featured in Mir-Hosseini et al. (2015).

a variety of themes from divergent perspectives, their interrelated ideas speak to one another and all work to address the larger question guiding this edited volume. They show that the solution lies not in simply reforming individual juristic rulings and/or their modern-day manifestations in state laws, but rather requires a shift in the philosophy behind marriage and gender relations to enable spouses to realize their full potential. This must include a substantive transformation in how we conceptualize marriage: from domination to a partnership of equals.

The chapters are grouped into broad themes that focus on key textual genres in Islamic tradition, but they also speak to one another across the themes. They deconstruct methodologies and ideological frameworks that produced patriarchal interpretations and explore ways in which egalitarian ethics can be reclaimed and subsequently inform Muslim family laws and lived realities.

REREADING THE QUR᾽AN

The first section of the book concentrates on the Qur᾽an and its exegesis, with scholars reimagining Muslim norms on gender and family relations through a perspective that is grounded in the Qur᾽an's ethical worldview. They make the case for moving beyond pre-modern interpretations of the Qur᾽an that perpetuate patriarchal ethics and instead centring the Qur᾽anic worldview of justice, beauty and goodness, in line with realities of the twenty-first century. In doing so, they offer different approaches to bridge the gap between the Qur᾽anic ethics of marriage and the norms that shape our contemporary family relations.

In 'Qur᾽anic Ethics of Marriage', Omaima Abou-Bakr, Asma Lamrabet and Mulki Al-Sharmani map out the key methodological and hermeneutic gaps in *tafsīr* tradition, such as its atomistic approach and its lack of close and systematic attention to Qur᾽anic ethics. They then propose, explain and implement an interpretive approach towards reading the Qur᾽an that is holistic, thematic, intra-textual, linguistic and ethically-oriented. They show how the Qur᾽an's egalitarian ethics of marriage is formulated within three interconnected concentric discursive circles. The first affirms the ontological equality of all human beings and their equal responsibility of *taqwā*.[11] The second discur-

[11] The authors choose not to translate the Qur᾽anic term *taqwā* because it is not possible to capture in English its layered meanings of God-consciousness, devotion to God, self-reflective piety, commitment to justice and an ethical life.

sive circle constructs marriage as a solemn bond (*mīthāq ghalīẓ*) highlighting first and foremost its spiritual significance. The third establishes the key ethical pillars of marriage, namely: affection (*mawadda*), resting abode (*sakan*), and compassion (*raḥma*). They explore how these circles connect with one another, and how this Qur'anic ethical framework can be applied to different dimensions of spousal relations. The authors argue that this Qur'anic ethical worldview – in which marital partnerships and family relations are grounded in compassion, affection, equal worth, the protection of the vulnerable, justice, generosity, magnanimity and spiritual growth – can also guide reform of gender norms and rights.

In 'Reading the Qur'an through Women's Experiences', Nur Rofiah puts forward a gender-sensitive, holistic reading of the Qur'an that recognizes how different verses speak to different stages of the unfolding Qur'anic trajectory to gender justice. Her methodology foregrounds women's social experiences of marginalization and the physical experiences which are unique to women. The underlying messages of the Qur'an, according to Nur Rofiah, are to alleviate the historical marginalization of women; to recognize and validate their physical experiences; and to chart a dynamic trajectory towards real gender justice, which she terms '*ḥaqīqī* justice', that is based on equality. Nur Rofiah closes her chapter by reflecting on the implications of this approach in her native Indonesia, and specifically how a council of women ulama applied these messages when issuing a fatwa on child marriage. She uses this example to show how centring women's lived experiences and the needs of the vulnerable can guide us in reshaping Muslim norms on gender and family relations.

Amira Abou-Taleb concludes the section with '*iḥsān*: A Mandate for Beauty and Goodness in Family Relations', which focuses on the concept of *iḥsān* in the Qur'an as a command for believers to exercise moral agency and spiritual growth by enacting goodness and beauty. She applies a close linguistic and intra-textual analysis of *iḥsān* (and its derivatives) in the Qur'an to establish it as an overarching ethical principle that can serve as a guiding framework for family relations at both the individual and the societal level. Abou-Taleb outlines how the call for *iḥsān* creates ripple effects throughout the concentric circles in society that begin with the innermost soul (*nafs*) and expand to include the partner (*zawj*), offspring, extended family, orphans and those who are most vulnerable. More broadly, she argues that the ethics of *iḥsān* should be foregrounded in the process of reviewing and reforming

Muslim family laws. As such, her inquiry connects across the moral message of the Qurʾan, the historical interpretations of this moral message, and the lived realities of present-day Muslim women and men.

LESSONS FROM THE PROPHET

The second section of the volume shifts the lens to the prophetic tradition and how it can inform contemporary reform efforts towards justice and equality in Muslim families. Reformist Islamic scholars, and Islamic feminists in particular, have struggled to engage with Hadith, since Hadith reports are often used to justify discriminatory norms against women. Consequently, many feminist scholars have decided to focus on the Qurʾan and minimalize the prophetic tradition. Yet the Sunna plays an important role for Muslims and informs norms and practices in Muslim contexts, so engagement with these sources is crucial. The chapters in this section look at the prophetic tradition from different lenses that reflect their political and epistemological locations. Their aim is not to provide absolute answers on how to approach the Sunna, nor to resolve issues of authenticity and transmission. Rather, they propose different angles through which prophetic teachings can be read and inform our contemporary needs.

In 'Reclaiming Khadīja and Muhammad's Marriage as an Islamic Paradigm: Towards a New History of the Muslim Present', Shadaab Rahemtulla and Sara Ababneh suggest that the marriage of Prophet Muhammad and Khadīja should be examined and upheld as a model for present day Muslim marriages and spousal relations. They adopt the theoretical framework of the 'history of the present' to question the dominance of certain aspects of the Prophet's marital relationships (such as his marriage to ʿĀʾisha and her age) and the silences in the tradition about other important aspects of the Sunna. They focus on two moments in Khadīja's life – her marriage to the Prophet and her presence during the first Qurʾanic revelations – to show that Khadīja was the more powerful partner in their relationship (in terms of age, resources, wealth, influence, strength, etc.), and that Muhammad was not threatened by this power dynamic but thrived within it. They argue that Khadīja and Muhammad's relationship not only challenges the notion of a male provider and dependent wife, but offers an alternative model for marital relationships built on mutual care, support and love.

Yasmin Amin's '"Your Wife Enjoys Rights Over You" Or Does She? Marriage in the Hadith' takes a discursive journey through a collection of hadith-reports that record the teachings of Muhammad and his example on marriage and spousal relations. Amin shows that the prophetic Sunna can provide egalitarian models of marriage and inform contemporary norms. Her analysis draws out key thematic observations that show that an ideal marriage according to the prophetic tradition is based on mutual care, kindness and trust. Spouses bring joy to one another and are kind and caring to one another. Husbands share the housework with their wives; they respect their wives as full-fledged human beings. Conflicts are resolved with magnanimity. This is in accordance with the vision of marriage articulated in the Qur᾽an, and in stark contrast with jurists' notion of hierarchical spousal roles as laid out in classical *fiqh* rulings.

In the final chapter of this section, entitled '*Qirā᾽a Mubādala*: Reciprocal Reading of Hadith on Marital Relationships', Faqihuddin Abdul Kodir explains and applies his reciprocal (*mubādala*) methodology of reading Hadith. This method aims to identify positive and gender-sensitive meanings and messages from selected hadiths that linguistically can be read as either discriminatory to women or exclusionary of one sex or the other (mostly women). Building on the work of the Islamic scholar ʿAbd al-Ḥalīm Muḥammad Abū Shuqqa, the *mubādala* approach proposes that we read and interpret hadiths beyond their surface meanings and always from the lens of the key ethical principles established by the Qur᾽an. Abdul Kodir's methodology is grounded in the Qur᾽an's central principles of the equality of all human beings and their equal responsibility and accountability to enact *tawḥīd* (oneness and unity of God). Applying this methodology to the selected hadiths, Abdul Kodir understands them to be calling upon both men and women to treat one another justly and lovingly.

ISLAMIC LEGAL THEORY AND ETHICS

The third section of the volume introduces a group of three chapters that address ethics and Islamic legal tradition in theory and practice. Mohsen Kadivar, in 'Rethinking Muslim Marriage Rulings through Structural *Ijtihād*', critiques the traditional theory of *ijtihād*, which he argues remains blindly attached to textual sources, and proposes a bold new approach that he calls 'structural *ijtihād*'. In this method, human reason and intellect play a key role in the construction of ethics, while simultaneously affirming the importance of key Qurʾanic values. Within this new methodology, he holds that all juristic arguments on marriage and the validity of all derived rulings should be tested against four criteria: rationality, justice, ethics and effectiveness, all according to contemporary standards of justice and social realities. He applies structural *ijtihād* to four contested areas of marriage (child marriage, rights and duties in marriage, divorce and polygamy) to demonstrate the implementation of these criteria. Kadivar argues that most classical *fiqh* rulings can no longer be regarded as 'Islamic' because they are not just, reasonable or moral, and they are less functional than other laws. In contrast, applying the structural *ijtihād* approach can preserve principles and standards within the tradition while adequately addressing today's needs, contexts and standards.

In 'Reform of *Uṣūl al-Fiqh* and Marriage: A Spiritually Integrative Approach', Nevin Reda also critically engages with traditional Islamic legal theory by proposing an Islamic feminist, spiritually integrative approach to *uṣūl al-fiqh* (principles of jurisprudence) that builds an understanding of marriage as a site for spiritual growth. Reda respectfully explores the main sources of law-making – Qurʾan, Sunna, consensus (*ijmāʿ*), reason (*qiyās*), showing how each contains problems that contribute to gender injustice. These include the elevated authority that is given to Hadith in elaborating on the Qurʾan; consensus of jurists (*ijmāʿ*) serving as a tool to solidify unjust medieval rulings in *fiqh*; and analogical reasoning (*qiyās*) being applied haphazardly and often to the detriment of women. She then outlines her Qurʾan-centric ethico-legal theory, explains how it addresses these gaps and applies it to the case of marriage and divorce. In her proposed theory, Reda holds that all of the Qurʾan, and not just *āyāt al-aḥkām* (verses with legal signification), should serve as the basis of comprehensive teachings and norms in order to ensure the spiritual, ethical and legal are interconnected. She proposes that reason (*ʿaql*) should rely on traditional tools but also include consideration of justice (*istiʿdāl*) as a new principle. Instead of *ijmāʿ*, she argues that lawmaking should take place through consultation (*shūrā*) of all concerned actors. Within this framework, marriage becomes a spiritual school in which mutual care and support between spouses are part of their striving towards ethical excellence.

The section ends with Mariam Al-Attar's 'Ethics and Gender Equality in Islam: A Constructivist Approach', which provides a philosophical engagement with ethics, focusing on the foundations of moral judgement. Al-Attar first sheds light on how different genres of pre-modern Islamic religious sciences tackled pertinent ethical questions related to moral values, norms and norm-making, cultivation of individual virtues, etc. She notes the piecemeal approach to ethics in Islamic textual tradition and the hegemony of the *fiqh* discourse over other Islamic discourses. Al-Attar underscores how this diverse tradition nonetheless offers concepts and arguments that can be the building blocks for a new and robust understanding of the foundations of moral judgement. She also notes important and relevant modern developments in Islamic intellectual thought such as the centring and systematic study of Qur'anic ethics, and the foregrounding of the constructivist nature of moral judgement that relies on human reasoning as bound by objective and universal principles. She elaborates on this latter approach and explores its relevance to the question of gender.

LAW AND PRACTICE

The focus in the final section shifts from legal theory to laws and practices on the ground in both historical and contemporary times. The authors explore how Muslim marriage norms are developed not just through juristic interpretation but also through the enactment, application, and reform of laws and the ways in which people interact with these laws in specific and time-bound contexts. The chapters eloquently speak to the dynamic interactions of different elements of family law and practice that can come together to create or frustrate equality on the ground – namely, in our homes.

Hoda El Saadi's chapter, 'Historicizing Muslim Marriage Practices in Premodern Islamic Egypt', provides a window into history, drawing the attention of the reader to the marriage and divorce practices in Egypt from the seventh to the sixteenth centuries CE. She examines a variety of historical sources, both traditional and non-traditional – such as court records, marriage contracts, deeds, fatwa collections, traditional biographical dictionaries and chronicles – to help understand marital relations in Islamic jurisprudence (*fiqh*) and in people's lived experiences. The study shows that diversity and dynamism were integral to the implementation and reformulation of *fiqh* rulings according to the changing realities and needs of different Muslim communities. Rather than dictating women's behaviour and gender relations, jurists in pre-modern Egypt in fact reacted and responded to women's lived experiences and needs in ways that supported justice. Her approach also highlights the methodological importance of non-traditional historical sources in the process of understanding how family laws operate on the ground.

In 'Muslim Family Laws: Trajectories of Reform', Lynn Welchman, Zahia Jouirou and Marwa Sharafeldin review three broad types of reforms in contemporary Muslim family laws: substantive reform using multiple frames of reference, procedural reform and indirect reform to family law and practices introduced through other legislation. The authors first explore the complexities and dynamic configurations of Muslim family laws, which reflect the interplay between Muslim legal tradition, human rights, state laws and societal norms. They then shed light on various strategies and arguments used to introduce different types of reforms and their complex outcomes. Underlying these arguments is ethical reasoning shaped by plural sources (textual and non-textual) and the variety of factors that coalesce in any society in debates around social and legal reform (for example, political will, activism of women's rights groups, economic exigencies, etc.). The authors highlight the important role of women's movements in enabling change, noting that the wider the networks, the greater the opportunity for differently placed actors to exchange and together identify short- and longer-term strategic objectives in family law reform.

The book ends with a piece entitled 'Justice, Refinement and Beauty: Reflections on Marriage and Spirituality', in which Sa'diyya Shaikh considers how to pursue spiritual growth and advancement in marriage through rituals, contracts and day-to-day practice. She first considers the nature of the *nikāḥ* (marriage) ceremony and creation of the *nikāḥ* contract, especially in contexts where women are made invisible. To address existing imbalances, she proposes ways to craft a contract and celebration that embody ethics of equality, justice and mercy. She explores dynamics within everyday marital relationships and proposes ways through which couples can spiritually grow together and enact love, justice and beauty within their marriages. She ends with a profound aspirational prayer that can be used within *nikāḥ* ceremonies or throughout relationships to cultivate spiritually nourishing forms of love and marriages of equality, justice and beauty.

*

Collectively, the twelve chapters tackle different types of theological, historical and legal sources in Islamic tradition. These sources constitute the components of the overall discursive tradition within which religious and legal patriarchy and gender inequality have been established. Hence, these chapters together illustrate the holistic approach adopted by Musawah in its scholarly work both through the previous 'Knowledge Building Initiative on *Qiwamah* and *Wilayah*' and the current research project on 'Reclaiming *ʿAdl* and *Iḥsān* in Muslim Marriages'. Furthermore, the chapters individually and together foreground the question of ethics and its role in law-making.

Through the research initiatives, we have learned that to address the root causes of gender inequality in Islamic textual and legal tradition, it is not enough to problematize specific interpretations or rulings or to derive new ones. The work of reconstruction and reform requires that we first trace and shed light on the patriarchal ethics informing discriminatory rulings and laws, then develop ethical foundations for moral values and egalitarian laws that make possible Muslim marriages of equality, justice and beauty.

Yet this latter task is far from straightforward. It entails a multifaceted scholarly endeavour that includes the close study of the aforementioned textual sources, delving into the nature of ethics and ethical reasoning. It also requires application of new methodologies to reinterpret relevant texts and reformulate new discourses that establish gender equality and justice on well-substantiated ethical foundations. Additionally, it involves a process of engaging with and bringing diverse norms, sources and ethical frameworks into constructive dialogue with each other, and with the needs and realities of Muslim contexts today.

REFERENCES

Abou-Bakr, Omaima and Mulki Al-Sharmani. 2020. 'Islamic Feminist *Tafsīr* and Qurʾanic Ethics: Rereading Divorce Verses'. In *Islamic Interpretive Tradition and Gender Justice: Processes of Canonization, Subversion, and Change*, edited by Nevin Reda and Yasmin Amin, pp. 23–66. Montreal and Kingston: McGill-Queen's University Press.

Abou El Fadl, Khaled. 2001. *Speaking in God's Name*. Oxford: Oneworld.

Abou El Fadl, Khaled. 2014. *Reasoning with God: Reclaiming Shariʿah in the Modern Age*. Lanham, MD: Rowman & Littlefield.

Abu Zayd, Nasr Hamid. 2006. *Reformation of Islamic Thought: A Critical Historical Analysis*. Amsterdam: Amsterdam University Press.

Ali, Kecia. 2006. *Sexual Ethics and Islam: Feminist Reflections on Qurʾan, Hadith, and Jurisprudence*. Oxford: Oneworld.

Barlas, Asma. 2002. *Believing Women in Islam: Unreading Patriarchal Interpretations of the Qurʾan*. Austin: University of Texas Press.

Chiba, Masaji. 1986. 'Introduction'. In *Asian Indigenous Law in Interaction with Received Law*, edited by Masaji Chiba, pp. 1–9. London: Kegan Paul International.

Menski, Werner F. 2012. 'Plural Worlds of Law and the Search for Living Law'. In *Rechtsanalyse als Kulturforschung*, edited by Werner Gephart, pp. 71–88. Frankfurt: Vittoria Klostermann.

Mir-Hosseini, Ziba. 2003. 'The Construction of Gender in Islamic Legal Thought and Strategies for Reform'. *Hawwa* 1 (1): pp. 1–28.

Mir-Hosseini, Ziba, Kari Vogt, Lena Larsen and Christian Moe (eds). 2013. *Gender and Equality in Muslim Family Law: Justice and Ethics in Islamic Legal Tradition*. London: I.B. Tauris.

Mir-Hosseini, Ziba, Mulki Al-Sharmani and Jana Rumminger (eds). 2015. *Men in Charge? Rethinking Authority in Muslim Legal Tradition*. London: Oneworld.

Moosa, Ebrahim. 2000. 'Introduction'. In *Revival and Reform in Islam*, by Fazlur Rahman. Oxford: Oneworld.

Moosa, Ebrahim. 2020. 'The Ethical in Shari ʿa Practices: Deliberations in Search of an Effective Paradigm'. In *Pathways to Contemporary Islam: New Trends in Critical Engagement*, edited by Mohamed Nawab Mohamed Osman, pp. 235–64. Amsterdam: Amsterdam University Press.

Musawah. 2016a. *Musawah Vision for the Family*. Kuala Lumpur: Musawah.

Musawah. 2016b. *Women's Stories, Women's Lives: Male Authority in Muslim Contexts*. Kuala Lumpur: Musawah.

Musawah. 2018. *Who Provides? Who Cares? Changing Dynamics in Muslim Families*. Kuala Lumpur: Musawah.

Rahman, Fazlur. 1966. 'The Impact of Modernity on Islam'. *Islamic Studies* 5 (2): pp. 113–28.

Rahman, Fazlur. 1982. *Islam and Modernity: Transformation of an Intellectual Tradition*. Chicago: University of Chicago Press.

Sajoo, Amyn (ed.). 2018. *Sharia: History, Ethics and Law* (Muslim Heritage Series). London: Institute of Ismaili Studies, I.B. Tauris.

Shaikh, Sa ʿdiyya. 2015. 'Islamic Law, Sufism and Gender: Rethinking the Terms of the Debate'. In *Men in Charge? Rethinking Authority in Muslim Legal Tradition*, edited by Ziba Mir-Hosseini, Mulki Al-Sharmani and Jana Rumminger, pp. 106–31. London: Oneworld.

Wadud, Amina. 1999. *Qur ʾan and Woman: Rereading the Text from a Woman's Perspective*. Oxford: Oxford University Press.

Wadud, Amina. 2006. *Inside the Gender Jihad: Women's Reform in Islam*. London: Oneworld.

Welchman, Lynn. 2015. '*Qiwamah* and *Wilayah* as Legal Postulates in Muslim Family Laws'. In *Men in Charge? Rethinking Authority in Muslim Legal Tradition*, edited by Ziba Mir-Hosseini, Mulki Al-Sharmani and Jana Rumminger, pp. 132–62. London: Oneworld.

THE QUR'AN

Qur'anic Ethics of Marriage

Omaima Abou-Bakr, Asma Lamrabet and Mulki Al-Sharmani

The aim of this chapter is to trace the Qur'anic ethics of marriage. We contend that the Qur'an is an important textual source for a universal vision of Muslim marriages that are grounded in equal partnership and mutual care. We shed light on this vision and reflect on its significance for contemporary efforts to legislate Muslim family laws that uphold equality and justice. We note, in particular, the Qur'anic emphasis on moral agency of the involved parties in marriage and the significance of this relationship to the pursuit of spiritual growth and intimacy with the Creator.

Medieval Muslim jurists, theologians, philosophers and scholars of the science of ethics (*'ilm al-akhlāq*) engaged with various ethical questions. Despite rich ethical insights in these different genres, it has been argued that Islamic ethics as such was not developed as a full-fledged coherent field in Islamic history (Ansari, 1989). A notable gap is the lack of a systematic and comprehensive study of the Qur'an as a source of ethical teachings and norms (al-Khaṭīb, 2017).

In modern times, there have been numerous Muslim scholarly efforts to theorize and develop the field of Islamic ethics. For example, Muhammad Draz (2008, originally published in 1951) investigated the ways in which Qur'anic injunctions are shaped by underlying ethical directives constituting a unified Qur'anic ethical system. Japanese scholar Toshihiko Izutsu (1966) traced the Qurʾanic ethical worldview by examining how key Qurʾanic terms and concepts constitute unified semantic fields. Fazlur Rahman (1982) studied the moral themes of the Qurʾan and emphasized the importance of linking the 'ethical' and 'legal' in the process of discerning the normative role of the Qurʾan.

Other notable examples include the works of Taha Abderrahman, Majid Fakhry and Amyn B. Sajoo. Khaled Abou El Fadl (2014) examined the Qurʾanic ethos of moral beauty and goodness and its relevance for different contexts and temporalities. Scholars such as Abdulaziz Sachedina (2005), Jerusha Tanner Lamptey (2014; 2018), Muqtedar Khan (2019) and Ramon Harvey (2018) each approached the Qurʾan with distinct ethical questions around areas such as religious pluralism, governance and the Qurʾanic concepts of *iḥsān* and social justice (see also Abou-Taleb in this volume).

Particularly relevant to our inquiry are the works of a number of Muslim women scholars (Mernissi, 1991; Wadud, 1999; 2006; 2015; Mir-Hosseini, 2003; 2015; Barlas, 2004; Ali, 2006; Shaikh, 2015; Abou-Bakr, 2015; Lamrabet, 2015). These scholars have been re-reading the Qurʾan and authoritative texts in Islamic interpretive tradition to systematically trace the development of dominant patriarchal interpretations and rulings and unpack their hermeneutical, epistemological and ideological foundations. Furthermore, this scholarship, which has been termed 'Islamic feminism', has been concerned with exploring the textual basis for alternative methodologies and readings that make the case for gender equality and justice (Al-Sharmani, 2014).

We situate this study within this Islamic feminist scholarship and the larger Muslim reformist intellectual efforts to provide systematic understanding of the Qurʾan as a source of Islamic ethics. As Muslim women, we believe it is our prerogative to partake in the process of religious meaning making, which thus far for the most part has been dominated by men and more specifically by patriarchal voices and discourses whether from the past or present. Furthermore, we bring to this endeavour our expertise as scholars who are well-versed in the Qurʾan and Islamic interpretive tradition; contemporary Muslim family laws; modern theories of gender; hermeneutics and textual analysis; and anthropological knowledge of Muslim marriage norms and practices in different contexts.

In the first section of the chapter, we present a succinct critique of the *tafsīr* corpus to identify central gaps that we argue resulted in the exegetes' failure to pay systematic attention to the Qurʾanic ethical discourse on marriage. In the second section, we explain our interpretive methodology, which we describe as holistic, thematic, intra-textual, linguistic, historical and ethically oriented. Using this methodology, we trace the Qur'anic ethical framework for marriage through a number of verses that we argue establish this framework. We visualize this framework as consisting of three concentric discursive circles. In the first circle, the Qur'an establishes human relations in general and family relations in particular on these key principles: the equal worth of human beings, as they are created from one self (*al-nafs al-wāḥida*) and in matching equal pairs (*zawj*); and their equal responsibility to enact the moral compass of *taqwā*[1] and compassion in family relations, the latter emphasized through the 'feminine' expression of wombs (*arḥām*). In the second circle, the Qur'an proceeds to define marriage between two ontologically equal human beings as a solemn bond (*mīthāq ghalīẓ*), or a special and strong bond of trust, commitment to each other's well-being and mutual care. This bond is as important as that between prophets and the Creator. In the third circle, the Qur'an lays down three main ethical pillars that sustain this bond, namely a resting abode (*sakan*), affection (*mawadda*) and compassion (*raḥma*), emphasizing that such a bond is one of the signs (*ayāt*) of God. These three discursive circles, we argue, are interconnected and lead into one another: marriage as a solemn bond can only be built on the ontological equality of the couple and their commitment to moral agency. Furthermore, such a bond can only be upheld by the ethics of mutual tranquillity, love and compassion. Then in the third section we explore how this Qur'anic ethical framework can guide our reading of specific aspects of marriage and family relations. Because of the scope of the chapter, we confine our application of the methodology to one thematic example, namely spousal relations. We examine several interconnected dimensions of this theme: dower, sexual intimacy, spousal maintenance, marital discord and polygyny.[2] We conclude with reflections on the implications of the methodology and the reading we propose as an intellectual framework that can inform multidimensional reform of Muslim gender norms and rights.

---

[1] The Qur'anic term *taqwā* has layered meanings of God-consciousness, devotion to God, self-reflective piety, commitment to justice and an ethical life. Since it is not possible to capture these meanings in one singular English word, we will use the Arabic term throughout the chapter to highlight all of these layered meanings.

[2] In a recently published paper, the first and third authors have also presented a comprehensive analysis of the divorce verses using a similar ethically oriented holistic methodology (Abou-Bakr and Al-Sharmani, 2020). Additionally, in a forthcoming paper, the three authors undertake a comprehensive reading of marriage, divorce and parenting.

1. QUR'ANIC EXEGETICAL CORPUS ON MARRIAGE: A CRITIQUE

Given the limited space, we will focus on four general observations that outline the limited approaches of various exegetes and their failure to connect legal and technical aspects of their juristic (*fiqh*) rulings with the ethical imperatives in the Qur'an. First, as part of the recent so-called 'ethical turn' in Islamic studies,[3] it has been observed by scholars (especially in the field of *tafsīr*) that despite the huge diversity and sophistication of this tradition, there has not been a major classical work that uses a systematic ethical approach as a method of interpretation 'even though the sacred text is all about ethics' (Hashas and al-Khaṭīb, 2020, p. 1). Exegetical works have been classified and categorized according to either theological, juristic, philosophical or Sufi schools of thought, on one hand, or according to the method of deduction of meanings and reliance on traditional reports, on the other, but not according to a consistent ethical system. Of course, a variety of theoretical works on the science of ethics do exist in the Islamic tradition. Issues of ethical judgement also permeate within the various Islamic sciences since moral action is an explicit goal of Shariʿa. But this has not occurred as an independent and systematic discipline of applied ethics in the *tafsīr* field.

There has been a revival of interest in twentieth-century scholarship on Qur'an and ethics as evidenced in the works of Draz, Izutsu, Rahman, Omar al-Faruqi and Taha Abderrahman. The scholar Muhammad Abed al-Jabri (2001), for example, argued that ethics has not been systematically engaged within Islamic Arabic thought and that the concept of the good deed (*al-ʿamal al-ṣāliḥ*) is central to Qur'anic ethics. There is also the work of Khaled Abou El Fadl, who argues that the ethicality of the Islamic divine message, the close textual interpretation of particular suras and verses in light of these ideas, or the application of ethical reasoning is not always available (2014, chapter 11).[4] However, none of the works above address the question of gender

[3] See, for example, the 2017 launching issue of the *Journal of Islamic Ethics* and its Introduction by Mohammed Ghaly (2017). See also the 2019 issue with the title 'Contemporary *Ijtihād*, Ethics and Modernity', which seeks to revitalize the link between *ijtihād* and specific ethical issues.

[4] Also, Hashas and al-Khaṭīb (2020) present a useful review of several studies on Qur'anic ethical thought, particularly since the second half of the twentieth century. Additionally, two studies in Arabic (al-Khaṭīb, 2017; Rashwānī, 2017) stand out in the 2017 issue of the *Journal of Islamic Ethics* as especially relevant to this chapter's outlook of prioritizing the ethical lens in interpreting gender issues in the Qur'an.

with a direct focus. Hence, the adoption of an ethical exegetical method that scrutinizes gender verses contributes to narrowing the gap between theorizing and textual interpretation. It can demonstrate a concretization of the Qur'anic ethical outlook or moral vision on the level of practical, lived domestic and social realities and can reveal the divine morally edifying intent. In this regard, Ebrahim Moosa observes: 'The truth is that only a portion of Muslim ethical thinking gives rise to a law requiring a public authority to enforce it' (2020, p. 468), beyond the personal effort to cultivate the ethical self and its *akhlāq*. And despite this recent interest and revival of ethical studies, there is still 'little attempt at the systematization of a Qur'anic ethics per se' (p. 470).

A second observation is that most classical *tafsīr* works tend to move from verse to verse, rarely establishing significant connections in meaning and divine intentionality between verses in different suras (other than the purely philological or the juristic). There is a lack of holistic, intra-textual interpretations to deduce ethical and egalitarian meanings. This is especially true in the case of gender relations. For example, with regard to three well-known, very explicit equality verses (9:71; 3:195; 33:35), exegetes tend to limit themselves to the apparent explication of the verses and the occasion of their revelation, without delving into further discussions of their significance or relation to other verses on women, such as in marriage or divorce (for example, al-Ṭabarī, 1961; al-Rāzī, 1938; al-Baidawī, 1968; al-Qurṭubī, 1967; Ibn Kathīr, n.d.). One brief comment is found in Muḥammad al-Ṭāhir Ibn ʿĀshūr's *tafsīr*, for example, that 33:35 demonstrates that the Shariʿa is not only for men but for both genders, and that 'perhaps by this verse and its likes the principle of equality (*aṣl al-taswiyya*) is sufficiently established, making it unnecessary to draw attention to it in most Qur'anic and sunna statements' (Ibn ʿĀshūr, 1984, vol. 22, p. 20). Hence, the present research fills the gap of this 'hermeneutical silence' on the gendered aspect of the equality verses in classical commentaries, and builds on some rare modern insights with more specific applications and with a wider scope of extension of the basic Qur'anic egalitarian ethos. One of the reasons that perhaps most exegetes did not find such equality verses meriting comment is because they considered them to be applicable only in the spiritual, other-worldly domain with no impact on changing economic rights or a shift in existing hierarchical and power relations between the genders. Therefore, these verses did not contain seeds for the generation of formal legal prohibitions or correctness of specific acts in social reality. As for other marriage/divorce verses that contain ethical commandments and stipulations (as we shall see later), exegetes and jurists also focused only on procedural technicalities that can be controlled by law.

A third observation (and a result of the methodology of the early exegetes) is that there is a disconnect between the ethical and the legal in drawing specific rulings, with jurists overemphasizing and exaggerating the formal correctness of legalistic and procedural details at the expense of inner/spiritual meanings, the principles of fairness, justice and egalitarianism, and the role of conscience. For example, some exegetes played down the role of *niyya* (intent/intention) in legally constructing the ruling itself, such as when there is an unethical intent on the part of a husband to spite and hurt a wife in retracting a divorce. Or they did not discuss the element of free will for women in marriage contracts and divorce except through legal reasoning; they did not employ ethical reasoning.

A specific citation is the exegetical discourse on 2:228, a verse with a clear ethical focus – that of a moral commitment not to harm the other partner, to reform one's intentions, and to exchange rights and duties fairly. The last phrase 'And God is almighty, wise', is not superfluous, but rather the governing precept. Abiding by the guiding spirit of Divine wisdom necessitates the pursuit of egalitarian praxis in this situation. The verse's prohibition of the unethical behaviour of divorced women hiding pregnancies is followed by a commandment that husbands are allowed to revoke the divorce *if* they pursue reform and reconciliation, not for further abuse or for spite. In other words, the verse puts this intention to reform as a *condition* to the husbands' right to take the wives back during the waiting period. Al-Ṭabarī rightly understood this clause as a condition: '... *unless* he wants by the return reforming his and her ways' (1961, vol. 2, p. 614). However, the discussion that follows demonstrates a typically traditional method of deducing a legal ruling without considering ethical stipulations, and of separating the textual aspects of a ruling from its underlying and complementing moral message. Al-Ṭabarī differentiates between the 'ruling' (*ḥukm*) that allows the marriage to be resumed and the intent or conscience of the husband that is 'between God and him'. Thus, if the husband wants to harm the wife by revoking the divorce and not reforming or reconciling, then this is not sanctioned (*ghayr jāʾiz murājaʿatihā*). Yet as a legal determination to be implemented it is considered formally correct, even if he has sinned in his bad intentions: 'If he wants to harm the wife by this return, he can obtain this ruling, though he is sinful (*āthim*) in this deed, undertaking to do what God does not permit him to do, and so God is in charge of punishing him for that.'

Subsequent exegetes also acknowledged the divine urging (*taḥrīḍ*) to reform and to cease harm, but did not see this as a condition or a legal stipulation that can invalidate revocation (for example, al-Zamakhsharī,1948; al-Rāzī,1938; al-Qurṭubī,1967). Al-Rāzī argues:

> If it is said that the word *in* (if) is conditional and that the condition invalidates the ruling when it is absent, meaning that if the will to reform or reconcile is absent then the right of revocation cannot be set, the reply is: human will is an inner motive that is not discerned, so the *shar'* does not hinge the validity of revocation on it. Its correctness between God and him is dependent upon this inner will, so that if he returns her with the intention of harm, he acquires a sin. (1938, vol. 6, p. 81)

Al-Qurṭubī calls the revocation *ṣaḥīḥah* (legally correct) even though he uses a stronger word in describing a husband's behaviour in elongating the waiting period(s) and depriving the wife of her freedom: *muḥarram* (forbidden) (1967, vol. 3, p. 123). Still, he does not spell out the legal implications of this forbidden act when committed by the husband.

A fourth and final observation is that the cultural context of the exegetes shaped the processes of their interpretation. Their assumptions of male authority, paternalism, low opinion of women's nature or status, and gender hierarchical mentality blinded them to the text's implications of equal human worth and the superiority of God alone. Thus, there is a lack of application of Qur'anic egalitarian ethics and fairness to gender relations and marriage specifically. An example of this particular hermeneutical failure is when most exegetes did not discern in verse 2:232 – which admonishes a brother for attempting to ignore his sister's wish in resuming her previous marriage – the principle of recognizing women's will and desire that ought to be generalized throughout all related/similar steps or stages in marriage and divorce. This subtle point was left out by jurists during the law-making process, and thus the significant implication of this verse remained limited and in isolation. Furthermore, in an ingenious interpretive move, they deduced that since the verse addresses the brother with this prohibition in the first place, there is an assumption, especially by Imam Shāfi'ī, that he is already in the position of being a guardian over her and is entitled to the rights of guardianship, constructing a whole legal edifice of *wilāyat al-nikāḥ*, *wilāyat al-ijbār* and the juristic concept of *kafā'a* (Masud,

2013). This is a sad example of how an essential meaning of free will and choice for women and a divine command that implies ethics, respect and compassion can be ingeniously reversed.

The end result is a vision and definition of marriage mostly based on a service/monetary exchange: physical provision in exchange for obedience and legal sexual access, and objectification of women (created for the main purpose of being 'enjoyed', albeit treated kindly, yet from a superior, controlling position towards a lesser human being as in 'benevolent patriarchy'). In other words, it is a conception of marriage that is similar to slavery – a conception at odds with the Qurʾanic vision. This type of juristic discourse, obsessed by technical and formalistic correctness, resulted in legal reasoning overshadowing ethical reasoning in most cases.

In response to the above-mentioned gaps, our study pays close attention to the Qurʾanic ethics of marriage. We approach Qurʾanic ethical principles and teachings on marriage and family relations as comprehensive, interdependent and binding, not superfluous. Our vision is wider and more complex than simply proving strict 'formal gender sameness', as we seek to unearth the very principles of egalitarian justice embedded in the Qurʾan's whole ethos and logic and strive towards their application. While taking into consideration the cultural and historical context of early exegetes and jurists in their different conceptions of justice/equality, their interpretations, we contend, still missed a great deal of the original intended moral message by God in the Qurʾan – that of shaking patriarchal culture and enslavement and putting Muslims on the road to equal human dignity and emancipation.

2. QURʾANIC ETHICAL FRAMEWORK FOR MARRIAGE: A NEW METHODOLOGY AND READING

Our starting point is that the Qurʾan is a sacred text that has a coherent worldview and interconnected theological, ethical and legal teachings. In our engagement with the text, we adopt an interpretive approach that is holistic, thematic, linguistic, intra-textual, historical and ethically oriented.

Applying a holistic thematic reading, we examine closely and in juxtaposition all Qurʾanic verses (sixty in total) on marriage and family life. The majority of these verses occur in *Surat an-Nisāʾ* (chapter 4) and *Surat al-Baqara* (chapter 2). We read these verses in relation to one another and examine how they together constitute a whole, speaking to the overall Qurʾanic ethos of marriage as well as addressing different stages and dimensions of family relations.

We also pay close attention to Qur'anic intra-textuality, that is, the textual context in which these verses occur as well the connections between different verses, concepts and terms. Additionally, we conduct linguistic analysis of key terms in relevant verses. Moreover, we take note of the historical contexts in which certain verses were revealed (*asbāb al-nuzūl*) and the role of historicity in determining the normative significance of different Qur'anic rulings. Furthermore, in a process central to our methodology, we trace and examine carefully the ethical principles guiding marriage and family life according to the Qur'an, and specifically the terms and concepts through which they are articulated.

Our reading shows that Qur'anic ethical concepts/principles found in the verses on marriage, divorce and parenting are neither haphazard nor superfluous. Rather they are deeply meaningful and relevant for different temporalities and contexts. The Qur'an, we argue, frames its vision of marriage and gender relations within three concentric discursive circles, which together constitute the text's overall coherent ethical framework. Read together, the verses on marriage convey a central ethical message: marriage and the resulting family relations are to be grounded in compassion, affection, equal worth, the protection of the vulnerable, justice, generosity, magnanimity and spiritual growth. The historicity of some of the verses is evident where the text assumes that Muslims of seventh-century Arabia will build on some of their existing practices to establish the Qur'anic vision of marriage and family relations. On the other hand, some of the existing marriage norms and practices of those times are corrected by the Qur'an either through prohibition or gradual reform. However, the universal ethical goals of this Qur'anic worldview on marriage are not trapped in the historicity of these verses, but rather the latter becomes the initial context (but not the final or end destination) where the ethical intent of the verse is to be set in motion. In what follows, we examine each of these three circles and how together they constitute the Qur'anic ethical framework for marriage.

2.1 First discursive circle: ontological equality and moral agency

In this first discursive circle, the Qur'an links marriage to the human creation from one soul (*nafs wāḥida*) and its existence as part of a matching pair (*zawj*).

Marriage is also related to *taqwā*, an Arabic term that is hard to translate as it has multiple meanings denoting God consciousness, devotion to God with strength and commitment to justice, and/or self-reflective piety. This ontological and ethical foundation of marriage is captured in *Surat an-Nisāʾ* (chapter 4), one of the longest chapters in the text. Verse 4:1 outlines in some detail the different stages of the creation of humans:

> Oh People, have ***taqwā*** of your Lord, who created you from a single soul, and from it created its mate, and from the pair of them spread countless men and women far and wide; have ***taqwā*** of God, in whose name you ask of one another, and the wombs. Indeed Allah is ever, over you, an Observer.[5]

The verse starts with an injunction to all humans ('Oh People') to have *taqwā* of God. This strongly suggests that the verse is directed to humanity at large, and with a specific emphasis on *taqwā*, which occurs twice in the same verse. Then the verse proceeds to discuss the creation of humankind from one essence (*nafs wāḥida*). Ibn Manẓūr defines the *nafs* as the soul (2005, vol. 6, p. 223).[6] We note that the word for soul (*nafs*) is feminine in Arabic, while the word for mate (*zawj*) is masculine. Such a conceptual interlacing might in itself be symbolic of the reciprocity and interconnectedness in human relationships. Looking at this verse as a whole, we can observe the symbolism of the stages of creation, which starts from one soul and continues to the duality of existence and then to the final stage of multiplicity. The term *nafs wāḥida* signifies that God created human life from one essence, and then from that one essence created the mate (*zawjuha*), then 'dispersed' from this couple 'many men and women' (*rijālan kathīran wa nisāʾn*).

We do not find in this verse or in any other the slightest connotation that Adam, a male human being, is the first human created, nor do we find any reference to a secondary stage of existence for Eve, whose name is not mentioned in the Qurʾan. Indeed, neither this verse nor any other verse in the Qurʾan assigns to Eve a secondary or marginal status of creation, nor talks

[5] For English translation of verses, we generally follow M. A. S. Abdel Haleem with some modifications. For example, we retained the Arabic word *taqwā* as is. We also kept the literal translation of *arḥām* (wombs).

[6] Ibn Abbas also defines *nafs* as follows: 'Every human has two *nafs*, one is the *nafs* of the mind which is responsible for judgment, while the other is the *nafs* of the essence, which is responsible for life' (quoted in Ibn Manẓūr, 2005, vol. 6, p. 235).

about her being created from Adam's crooked rib.[7] The verse is unequivocal in asserting the equal status of the creation of humankind (male and female) from *nafs wāḥida*, whereof God created many men and women. Moreover, the Qur'an does not represent any hierarchical view of men and women. On the contrary, we see that the one soul and its mate are two concepts that denote a neutral category encompassing both sexes. This is evidence that the divine intent is equality in creation. It follows then that since there is one origin of humankind, there should be no room for hierarchy, discrimination or claiming the superiority of one sex over the other, nor of one person over the other.

The concept of the one soul is often linked to *taqwā*, *tafaqquh* (knowledge) and *shukr* (thankfulness) to the Creator. The connection between *taqwā* and human creation from one essence reflects that the former entails solemn devotion and attaining the knowledge of how God created humankind. The connection extends to the quest for justice, as is reflected in verse 5:8: 'Stand firmly for justice, for that is closer to *taqwā*', and in verse 4:135: 'You who believe, uphold justice and bear witness to God, even if it is against yourselves, your parents, or your close relatives.' Having *taqwā* entails being in awe of God's greatness, which leads us to abiding by God's commands and especially that of the establishment of justice.

In addition to 4:1, the phrase *nafs wāḥida* occurs in four other verses (6:98; 7:189; 31:28; 39:6). In these verses, the concept is again linked to human creation. In one of these verses, 7:189, *nafs wāḥida* again occurs in relation to marriage.[8] It describes spousal relations as habitation and dwelling (*sakan*).[9] The message of the verse is that each of the two mates settles with the other, or dwells with one another, thus making of each other an abode. This is a symbolic reference to the intimate relationship between the pair – an interpretation consolidated by the rest of the verse where 'that he might dwell in tranquillity with her' is followed by 'And when he covers her, she carries a light burden.' Covering and carrying a light burden are references to sexual intercourse and its aftermath. It is worthy of note here that the Qur'an describes

[7] As reported in the prophetic Hadith tradition and the other Abrahamic traditions. See Hassan (1999).

[8] Verse 7:189 reads, 'It is He who created you from one soul and created from it its mate that he might dwell in tranquillity with her. And when he covers her, she carries a light burden and continues therein. And when it becomes heavy, they both invoke Allah, their Lord, "If You should give us a good [child], we will surely be among the grateful."'

[9] The concept of *sakan* (dwelling) differs from the concept of *sakīna* (peace and calm) as in verses 9:26 and 9:40.

the act of bonding physically and emotionally between the mates in beautifully delicate words. This might be taken as a reference to the characteristics of beauty and gentleness that should characterize the spousal relationship.

In 4:1 and in most other verses where the concept of the *nafs wāḥida* occurs, it is coupled with another significant concept which is that of 'the two mates' (*zawjiyya*). From the one soul, Allah 'created' or 'made' a mate. The concept of *zawjiyya* is derived from the word 'mate' (*zawj*), which is a noun derived from the root *z-a-j*. The verb *zawwaja* means join things together, while the noun *zawj* means one in a pair of likes or companions. In such cases, the noun is used as both masculine and feminine. The term and its derivatives occur twenty-seven times in the Qur'an.[10] The concept of the *zawj* ('two mates'), which occurs several times in the Qur'an, symbolizes the principle of pairing in the creation of the world, which means that everything is created as a matching pair. This is a general principle that applies to all that is created (humans, plants, fruits, crops), since God says: 'And We created pairs of all things so that you (people) might take note' (51:49). The link between *nafs wāḥida* and the concept of the '*zawj*' found in the previously quoted verses 4:1, 7:189 and 39:6 emphasizes the equality of creation among all humans who proceed from that *nafs wāḥida*, from whom a mate was created.

Thus, the concept of the one *nafs* (soul/being) symbolizes the equality of creation among all of humankind, within the divine plan of universal diversity and variety. It is primarily related to the concept of *taqwā*, which is driven by the pursuit of justice in all matters. Second, it is connected with the concept of *zawj* (pairing), or the relationship between woman and man who are connected through compassion (*raḥma*) as denoted by the word *al-arḥām* (wombs).

Verse 4:1 ends by emphasizing *taqwā* for a second time through a reference to '*arḥām*', which is the plural of '*raḥim*' or 'womb', the place where the foetus is developed in a woman's body. Here the connection the verse draws is between the belief in God (in whose name you ask one another) and the wombs. This is a highly significant discursive choice in a verse that opens a chapter mostly dedicated to giving instructions about the protection and care for women and widows and orphans, especially female orphans. The Qur'an links the creation of human beings to the womb in two other verses: 7:189 in

[10] Among the derivatives are: *zawjayn* (in pairs), *zawjak* (your wife), *zawja* (wife), *zawjaha* ([its] mate), *yuzawwijūhum* (bestows on them male and female offspring), *zawwajnakaha* (we married you to her), *zawjan* (two and two), *zawwajnāhum* (joined them) and *zuwwijat* (joined to their likes).

the context of pregnancy ('she conceives a light burden, going about freely') and 39:6 ('He creates you in your mothers' wombs'). Putting *taqwā* on equal footing with the wombs affirms that there is no coincidence in the creation of humankind. It also stands as proof of the close bond between the Creator, whose name is derived from the word 'mercy' (*al-Raḥmān al-Raḥīm*, the Most Gracious, the Most Merciful), and those wombs designed as a cradle and sanctuary to all humankind.

Thus, the Qur'an bases marriage first and foremost on the ontological truth of the equality of human beings in creation; the existence of creatures in equal matching pairs; the affirmation of human plurality; and the responsibility of *taqwā* expected from every human being.

2.2 Second discursive circle: marriage as a solemn bond

Next, the Qur'an adds a second layer to its discourse on marriage. It constructs marriage as a solemn covenant (*mīthāq ghalīẓ*). Verses 4:19–21 read:

> You who believe, it is not lawful for you to inherit women against their will, nor should you treat your wives harshly, hoping to take back some of the bride-gift you gave them, unless they are guilty of ***fāhisha*** (something outrageous). Live with them in accordance with what is ***ma'rūf*** (fair and kind): if you dislike them, it may well be that you dislike something in which God has put much good. If you wish to replace one with another, do not take any of her bride-gift back, even if you have given her a great amount of gold. How could you take it when this is unjust and a blatant sin? How could you take it when ***afḍā b'aḍukum ilā b'aḍ*** (you have lain with each other) and they have taken a ***mīthāq ghalīẓ*** (solemn bond) from you?

The word *mīthāq* (bond) is derived from the word '*wathaqa*', which means trust and commitment, and from '*muathaqa*', which means authentication and agreement. *Mīthāq ghalīẓ* in this verse means the 'stable bond' or the 'firm commitment' that strongly binds the wife and husband in this life.[11] It can also be taken as a beautiful description of the bond of affection and intimacy

[11] Etymologically, *mīthāq* is a robe or a fetter used to tie captives or cattle. See Ibn Manẓūr (2005, vol. 10, p. 371).

that ties the couple together as body and soul. The use of the term *mīthāq* in this verse is significant. The term is used in other verses to refer to the agreements and commitments that God has taken from the prophets, or as treaties between peoples and individuals.[12] The Qur'an stresses that *mīthāq* as a promise and contract between the married couple is a strong and solemn one (*ghalīẓ*) that enjoys the same gravity as that between God and the prophets. It is, moreover, the only contract that is described in the Qur'an as *ghalīẓ* (solemn). This is testimony to the important and highly significant status of this particular contract in the eyes of God as well as the critical role it plays in the establishment of human society. Of further significance is the phrase 'and they have taken from you a solemn covenant', which means that it is the wife that takes such a covenant from the husband. Conversely, it is the husband who gives her such a solemn ethical covenant, and he is the one to be punished if he betrays or trivializes it, or if he indeed (as with any other contract) does not comply with the terms and regulations to which the two parties agree.

In this unit of verses, the universal and the historical are intertwined. On one hand, the Qur'an establishes the notion of marriage as a solemn bond, a vision that is relevant to all contexts and times; on the other, it addresses particular excesses of the patriarchal practices of seventh-century Arabia. The verses open with a prohibition of inheriting women. The Qur'an uses the phrase 'it is not lawful' with such directness that makes the act manifestly forbidden. Inheriting women had been a tribal norm in pre-Islamic times when women were considered part and parcel of the property to be inherited along with other material possessions. When a man died, those who inherited his wealth would also inherit his wife. This was the common practice in most families at the time.[13] The verse prohibits this discriminatory norm, which violated a woman's dignity and humanity and denied her freedom and the right to her late husband's inheritance.[14]

---

[12] See, for example, verses 2:27, 63, 83–84, 93; 3:81, 187; 4:90, 92, 154–155; 5:7, 12–13, 70; 7:169; 8:72; 12:66, 80.

[13] A widow would be detained at the house of one of the late husband's male relatives (whether a father, brother or close kin) under the claim that from the moment the husband died, she had become their possession, their due debt and their inherited property. The woman would be placed under the guardianship of the late husband's male kin and was not able to move freely, let alone start a new life with another husband. See al-Wahidī al-Naisabūrī (2002, p. 107).

[14] We should point out that such chauvinism and discrimination were not practised against all women in society. Elite women who belonged to the upper classes of the pre-Islamic tribal society, for example, were not subjected to such norms. Those women enjoyed a degree of privilege

The use of restrictive measures aimed at incarcerating women or preventing them from securing their rights is another chauvinistic custom prohibited by the Qur'an in equally repudiatory tones. This practice is called *'aḍl*. The verses under discussion here refer to this cruel custom, which men sometimes used to pressure women to give up what they have given them by way of gift, offering or bestowal. In this respect, the Qur'an uses the phrase 'do not make difficulties for them', which urges men not to prevent or restrict women, except in one case where the wife commits a manifest act of immorality (*fāhisha*). The term denotes any foul and infamous act or utterance that is morally unacceptable. In such exceptional cases, men have the right to take back part of what they have given their wives.

The verses continue to discuss the marital relationship by delineating one of its fundamental principles, which is that of 'living in *ma'rūf*. This Qur'anic principle dictates men's duty to treat women in an ethically upright manner because at the time they had greater power. The verse uses the word '*ma'rūf*, which refers to what has been commonly known to be good according to ethical and rational judgement. What is worthy of note is that the decree of this kind of treatment is required even when there are feelings of aversion and hatred on the part of the husband: 'And live with them in *ma'rūf*. For if you dislike them – perhaps you dislike a thing and Allah makes therein much good.' This is an unequivocal call for the compassionate and fair treatment of women even with the presence of unbearable hatred towards the wife; God might turn this attitude of patience and endurance into a path for much good which only God knows. The verses continue in the same vein of warning men who wish to replace one woman with another – perhaps after divorce – not to take back anything of what they had given her before. That would be an act of injustice and manifest sin.

Subsequent to this warning, the Qur'an focuses on two significant and highly symbolic concepts: *ifḍā'* (going into one another) and *mīthāq ghalīẓ* (solemn covenant). *Ifḍā'* is derived from *faḍā'* (space) and means to arrive at something. Within the context of the verse and the framework of marriage, it provides a solid description of the intimate relationship between men and women, and also reflects the refined style the Qur'an always uses in describing this relationship. The sexual act is portrayed as an attempt on both sides to

---

also granting them the right to accept or reject a marriage proposal and the right to divorce (Ali, 1993, vol. 4, p. 606).

arrive at the shared spiritual and physical space that embraces them.[15] Directly after the discussion of *ifḍā'*, the verse brings in the concept of *mīthāq ghalīẓ* to affirm the presence of that relationship in the shared space.

Both the specific gender practices that are the focus of reform in these verses and the broader notion of marriage as a solemn bond point to the centrality of the ethics of justice, care and intimacy in the Qur'anic vision of marriage. In contrast to this Qur'anic viewpoint of marriage, the legal tradition refers to it as *nikāḥ,* and primarily constructs it as a licit sexual relationship between a man and woman as a result of a marriage contract between them.[16] Interestingly, the word *nikāḥ* in the Qur'an has layered meanings such as: agreement, a general term for marriage, a marriage contract and adulthood and maturity (4:6).[17]

2.3 Third discursive circle: three pillars of marriage

Having first established the ontological equality of women and men and emphasized their equal responsibility of moral agency, and second framed marriage as a solemn bond of trust, commitment and care, the Qur'anic discourse on marriage adds a third circle of ethical principles. It spells out three ethical pillars of this solemn bond. In verse 30:21, which is a focal verse on marriage, there are five noteworthy terms. Furthermore, the verse's place in the context of the unit of verses from 19–25 is highly significant. The verse reads:

> Another of His signs is that He created from ***'anfusikum*** (among yourselves) ***'azwāj*** (spouses) for you to live with in ***litaskunu*** (resting abode). He ordained ***mawadda*** (affection) and ***raḥma*** (mercy) between you. There truly are ***ayāt*** (signs) in this for those who reflect.

The two terms *'anfusikum* and *'azwāj* together point to the foundational principle of equality in creating the essential pair of men and women, as they

[15] The Qur'an uses the following terms to refer to sexual relationships: *al-rafath* (intercourse), *lams* (touching), *libās* (garment), *al-ghisha'* (covering).

[16] The word *nikāḥ* was used by Arabs in pre-Islamic times. According to Ibn Manẓūr, *nikāḥ* is coupling (2005, vol. 14, p. 351).

[17] See 2:235 and 2:237 for *nikāḥ* as agreement; 2:221, 230, 232; 4:25 and 28:27 for *nikāḥ* as a general term for marriage; 33:49 for *nikāḥ* as a marriage contract; and 4:6 for *nikāḥ* as adulthood and maturity.

are clearly related to the notion of *al-nafs al-wāḥida* – the one living soul or common humanity. The new divine address to the Muslim community here is to view women as equally created souls and, hence, as forming equal mates or counterparts (*'azwāj*).

The second set of terms in the verse moves to three fundamental pillars that characterize the marital bond: *sakan*[18] (resting abode), *mawadda* (affection), *raḥma* (mercy). These indicate relational values, meaning attitudes to display or exercise towards the other partner. Men and women are urged by God to seek rest in each other's company, be affectionate and act with mercy and compassion. There exists no implication that one partner only displays this conduct, while another is passive, or that one partner defers to another, or that one has more priority than the other. The divine advice applies to both mates, forming this egalitarian and humane partnership.

Another interpretive aspect to consider is the word *ayāt* (signs), which connects the verse to verses before and after, making the group a thematic unit revolving around God's creation of life and the universe. Almost every verse in this unit comprises a duality in which the two halves are interdependent and equal. Verse 30:19 is about the living and the dead. Verse 30:20 is an apt reminder that all humans (*bashar*) have the same origin of being created out of dust. Verse 30:22 comprises the binary of the earth and the heavens, in addition to the diversity of human beings in languages and colours. This very differentiation among humanity is equated with the miracle of the earth and the heavens, with no hierarchies or degrees of preference. Verse 30:23 follows with the duality of night and day, and verses 30:24 to 30:27 are consecutively about earth and sky, along with God's power of rebirth in this life and resurrection in the afterlife. Verse 30:21 on marriage is embedded within this passage, framed by the descriptions of equal dualities or counterparts in the macrocosm as a sign of God's truth and blessings, in addition to the aspect of 'difference' in humanity. Therefore, the whole thrust of the unit is a confirmation of different, but equal, entities in both the universe (macrocosm) and on the level of the most essential of human relations based on parity, which is marriage (microcosm). Textually, the passage creates a dynamic between God's blessed creations and normative marital relationship, each partaking of the other.

Qur'anic subtle meanings transpire at times through consideration of successive verses and how, together, they form or shape a certain message. This kind of interpretive reflection on 'textual contexts' (or contextual framing) of

[18] Note that the verbal form of *sakan* (i.e., *litaskunu*) is used in verse 30:21.

some individual verses in the middle of whole passages or units that appear to argue for a point is also a manifestation of holistic reading. It is a reading that interweaves the spiritual, the normative and the living because God's speech or message to humanity is all one and whole. Verse 30:21 clearly sets an overarching norm of marriage, constituting one of the concentric circles that provide the overall ethical framework for specific teachings. Draz has called this level 'practical ethics', distinguished from the speculative or theoretical probe into the nature of moral obligation: '*one may be virtuous without being able to define virtue*. We are more in need of being shown virtue than of having it defined for us. *What must I do?* – this is the most universal and urgent question of all; this is the daily bread of the human soul' (Draz, 2008, p. 292).

3. SPOUSAL RELATIONS WITHIN THE QUR'ANIC ETHICAL FRAMEWORK: AN APPLICATION

We have argued that there is an overarching Qur'anic ethical framework for marriage consisting of interconnected ethical principles. It follows then that every aspect of marriage and family life needs to be approached from within this overall framework. For example, any specific Qur'an-deduced norms or rulings on spousal relations, parenting, divorce, etc., need to be true to the key ethical principles that constitute this framework. That is, such rulings need to be grounded in the ontological equality of the involved parties; assume their shared responsibility of *taqwā*; approach marriage as a solemn bond of trust, commitment and mutual care; and centre *sakan*, *mawadda* and *raḥma* as the core pillars on which this union rests. The centrality of the ethics of equality, justice and mutual care in the Qur'anic vision on marriage is further attested in the ethical directives that are frequently located in different verses tackling specific themes. Such directives are captured in key Qur'anic concepts such as: justice (*'adl*); fairness (*qisṭ*); goodness and beauty (*iḥsān*); forgiveness (*'afw*); magnanimity (*faḍl*); reconciliation (*islāḥ*); consultation (*tashāwur*); consent (*tarāḍī*); etc. In what follows, we apply our methodology to the thematic example of spousal relations.

We have chosen this theme because it is an important aspect of marriage and has layered and interconnected dimensions. We focus on the following dimensions of spousal relations: dower, spousal maintenance, sexual intimacy, marital discord, polygyny. By applying our methodology to this theme and its layered aspects, our aim is also to show the importance of an integrated approach that connects different dimensions of marriage as addressed in the Qur'an. In particular, we take note of how the Qur'an on the one hand speaks directly to the specific community and problems of seventh-century Arabia, and on the other establishes an overall universal ethical discourse that crosses the boundaries of time and place.

It is not haphazard that many of the verses on marriage and family life, including the ones we are focusing on in this section, are located in *Surat an-Nisā'* (chapter 4). This chapter starts with verse 4:1, which we have analysed earlier, and which establishes the ontological equality of women and men and their shared responsibility of *taqwā*. Immediately after this foundational verse, the chapter proceeds to address in numerous verses many aspects of marriage and family life such as the protection and rights of orphans and widows; spousal rights such as dower and maintenance; sexual intimacy in marriage; marital discord; polygyny; inheritance; etc. The various verses explicitly tackle a number of practices at the time of revelation that were unjust to vulnerable groups such as women and orphans. It is significant that the chapter is called *an-Nisā'*, that is, 'The Women', perhaps to affirm the importance of addressing these forms of gender-based injustice. But at the same time, these historically situated verses also communicate universal teachings that can be traced back to the overall Qur'anic ethical framework on marriage. We will explicate such teachings through our analysis of the selected dimensions of spousal relations.

3.1 Dower

In Islamic legal tradition, dower is an important element in the marriage contract. It is a legal right due from the husband to the wife. However, it is a right (along with maintenance) that jurists made contingent on the wife's obligation to make herself sexually available to her husband. This gendered construction of spousal rights is still present in many contemporary Muslim family laws (Mir-Hosseini, 2013; Welchman, 2015; Al-Sharmani, 2017).

But how can we understand both the historical role of dower and its underlying ethical (and dynamic) meaning within the Qur'anic ethical framework for marriage? Two factors are important in addressing this question. One is the historical context in which the Qur'anic verses on marriage were revealed when women of seventh-century Arabia were for the most part economically, socially and legally marginalized and suffered different forms of abuse with no insurance net to fall back on. The other factor is the emphasis that the

Qur'an consistently places on the universal ethical principles underlying any of its specific injunctions for marriage. We will elucidate on these points in what follows.

The various verses that discuss dower[19] certainly affirm women's legal right to it. Some verses warn men not to exhort women to give up their dower (for example, 4:19); another verse addresses what is due to the wife from the dower in the case of unconsummated marriage (2:236); some also address the rights of different categories of women at the time (for example, slaves, war captives) to the dower (4:24–25). A recurring theme in all the verses is to protect women's economic rights by affirming their right to the dower. These verses are very much shaped by seventh-century Arabia where women were economically vulnerable and financial assets acquired through marriage such as dower and spousal maintenance provided them with much needed resources and hence some economic protection. However, in none of the verses is dower connected to marital sex or the latter constructed as an obligation incumbent on the wife in exchange for the dower and spousal maintenance. We focus in particular on one verse that tackles dower (4:4). This verse appears in the highly significant textual context of *Surat an-Nisā'*. It says:

> And give the women [upon marriage] their [bridal] gifts graciously. But if they give up willingly to you anything of it, then take it in satisfaction and ease.[20]

The verse is addressed to men and instructs them to give dower (*ṣadāq)* to their wives.[21] This can be read as a legal obligation owed to the wife from the husband. However, the message of the verse goes much deeper than that.

---

[19] It is interesting to note that while the Arabic word *mahr* has become the common one used to refer to the dower, the Qur'an does not use this term. It uses several other terms such as *ṣadāq* (verse 4:4), *ujūr* (verses 4:24–25; 5:5; 33:50; 60:10) and *qinṭār* (verse 4:20). *Ṣadāq* is from the root *ṣadaqa* which means to say the truth and it is also about sincerity, kindness and all that can be related to good acting (*al-'amal al-ṣāliḥ*). *Ujūr* means what is useful, what is given for something in return or as a due. The term *qinṭār* means literally quintal – a hundredweight, or a great amount of wealth.

[20] This is the Ṣaḥeeḥ International translation, which we find to be closest to the meaning we understand in Arabic in terms of giving and accepting gifts graciously.

[21] In pre-Islamic Arabia, a distinction was made between *ṣadāq* and *mahr*. The former was what was given by the husband to the wife, while the latter was what was given to the wife's father. See Ali (1993, vol. 4, p. 608).

Husbands are instructed to approach the giving of dower not simply as obligation but rather to view it as an important gift (*niḥla*) to be given graciously to the wives. The nuance of a 'gracious gift', used directly with the term *ṣadāq*, contradicts the juristic notion of spousal maintenance (*nafaqa*) in exchange for obedience (*ṭā'a* and *tamkīn*), which makes marriage like a commercial deal. At the same time, the text anticipates or implicitly encourages situations where wives may give up this right willingly and graciously, perhaps due to a husband's financial hardships or change of living circumstances where gender roles are not shaped by patriarchal values. In such cases, husbands are encouraged to accept their wives' graciousness not grudgingly or as a wound to their patriarchal pride as male providers but rather joyfully as spouses who share with their partners a relationship of reciprocity and care.

By applying an ethically oriented, historically sensitive reading that also pays close attention to the linguistic analysis of key terms mentioned above, the verse can be understood as having two purposes. The first is proposing a legal ruling for the immediate context of revelation, ensuring women's legal right to dower while at the same time situating this legal ruling within a larger ethical directive where both husband and wife are encouraged to view their spousal obligations and rights within the framework of marriage as a solemn bond of equal care, giving and graciousness. The second could be paving the way for dynamic and changing constructions of spousal obligations and rights beyond that of the husband as the exclusive provider of the dependent wife, at all times.

Also noteworthy is that husbands are the direct addressees of the verse. This is congruent with the context of verses in which 4:4 appears. The preceding verse is also addressed to men, instructing them on how to weigh between two ethical directives: not doing injustice by taking new wives; or entering into polygynous marriages with widowed women and their orphans in order to care for them. Hence, verse 4:4 is part of a pattern of verses aimed at reforming men into God-conscious husbands who are constantly developing and applying their moral integrity (*taqwā*).[22]

3.2 Spousal maintenance

Another financial aspect of spousal relations is spousal maintenance. Like dower, maintenance was stipulated by early exegetes and jurists as a legal duty

[22] For analysis of *taqwā*, see Wadud (2009); Reda (2020); Abou-Bakr (2020).

on the husband in exchange for sexual access to the wife. This reading is based on the exegetes' and jurists' interpretation of the first part of verse 4:34:

> Men are ***qawwāmūn*** (in charge of) women with what Allah ***faḍḍala*** (has given) one over the other and what they spend [for maintenance] from their wealth.

In fact, the exegetical corpus constructed *qiwāma* (the noun form of the adjective *qawwāmūn* in the verse) as a patriarchal concept that not only establishes men's duty to provide but also what is assumed to be their 'inherent' God-given superiority and authority over women.[23] We argue that this dominant reading contravenes the Qur'anic ethical framework on marriage as a whole and the reading of the verse in question when we apply our methodology. The verse begins with what can be read as a descriptive statement that men are *qawwāmūn* in relation to women with what 'God has given/favoured (*faḍḍala*) some over others and with what they spend from their means'. This triggers certain questions: Is the verse prescribing normative roles for husbands and wives for all times and contexts or are these context-related and hence subject to change? Why are the husbands caretakers and providers of their wives? The verse answers: 'with what God has favoured/given some over others and with what they spend from their means'. But what has God given some over others and what is it that they spend from their wealth or means?

An intra-textual ethically oriented reading illuminates several points relevant to these questions. This verse comes after verses 4:32 and 4:33, both of which tackle inheritance rights. Verse 4:32 instructs men and women not to covet what God has given some over others, for 'unto men a share of what they have earned' and 'unto women a share of what they have earned'.[24] The verse ends with a call to both groups to ask God from God's bounty (*faḍl*), perhaps a reminder that these shares are not a privilege or base for superiority but God's blessing. But what are these shares? Verse 4:33 provides the

[23] See Abou-Bakr (2015) for a critical genealogical study of exegetes' interpretation of *qawwāmūn* in 4:34 over ten centuries of *tafsīr*.

[24] The literature of *asbāb al-nuzūl* reports that verse 32 was revealed on the occasion of some of the early Muslim women complaining to Prophet Muhammad about what they saw as inequalities in the rights and rewards given to men versus the women. The women complained that the men were receiving double their share in inheritance and were also privileged with the duty of jihad. The men were also pondering whether they were also going to receive double the reward in the afterworld.

clarification, asserting the importance of fulfilling the inheritance rights of different family relatives. These verses and others that deal with inheritance seem to address an extended patriarchal family where male relatives (fathers/husbands) are obligated to provide for the female relatives (spouses/siblings/mothers). Accordingly, brothers inherit twice as much as sisters as they undertake the financial responsibility of providing for their spouses and the dependent unmarried female relatives.

In fact, the ethical thrust of the whole extended passage from the beginning of *Surat an-Nisā'*, particularly starting with verse 2, conveys a strong warning against financial injustice to orphans by usurping their property (verses 2, 3, 6, 10), or avoiding giving wives their due dower (verse 4), or depriving widows from inheritance (verse 7), or male relatives inheriting women themselves like property (verse 19). In other words, the divine intent is a push towards mitigating patriarchal abuse of and monopoly over resources for men's own selfish interests, and not taking responsibility for the weak, the poor or the disempowered. It is in this textual, ethical context of demonstrating *qisṭ* (fairness) that men's role as *qawwāmūn* towards women in verse 34 occurs. Therefore, verse 34 suggests a model of spousal roles in which men undertake the responsibility of providing for their spouses. It depicts a just arrangement in past (or present) historical contexts, particularly when wives may be preoccupied with their reproductive roles. In addition, the phrase 'some of them over others' in the verse could be read as suggesting that the duty of taking care of or providing for the wife is not assigned in absolute terms to all men in relation to all women, but depends on the situation and circumstances of each family (see chapters by Reda and Kadivar in this volume). The phrase 'some of them over others' could also be read in terms of social privilege necessitating greater responsibility since according to the historical background of the verse some men were privileged socially over others, and in line with Qur'anic substantive equality intent, the verse urges those who are privileged with more wealth and means to provide for and support those who are not.[25] So the verse, while guaranteeing a default safety net for women and teaching husbands to deal fairly with them, does not invalidate otherwise socially sensitive and flexible reconstruction of spousal roles. Yet the juristic construction of hierarchical and fixed spousal roles is at odds with this Qur'anic ethical framework.

[25] The marriage of Prophet Muhammad and his first wife Khadīja demonstrates this ethically oriented construction of spousal roles, with Khadīja being a wealthy woman whose established trade business allowed her to serve as the main provider while Muhammad focused on his prophetic mission (see Rahemtulla and Ababneh in this volume).

Again, applying an ethically oriented and intra-textual reading, we notice that the term *qawwāmūn* appears in two other verses: 4:135 and 5:8. In both verses, people are instructed to be in charge of, attend to, bear witness to upholding justice by implementing fairness (*qisṭ*) even if it means standing against one's own closest relatives, or treating one's enemies fairly. If we consider the use of the same term (*qawwāmūn/qawwāmīn*) in the three verses as not being haphazard and we link the verses together in a holistic reading, then '*qawwāmūn*' in verse 4:34 can be read *not* as male prerogative but rather as a responsibility to do justice by wives and to provide for them (Lamrabet, 2015).

3.3 Sexual intimacy

In contrast to the juristic understanding of marital sex, the Qur᾽an depicts sexual intimacy in marriage as a relationship that is based on equality between the spouses and whose spiritual, emotional and ethical dimensions are intertwined. Key terms regarding this subject matter are *rafath* (intercourse), *mubashara* (sexual relations), *libās* (garment), *ḥarth* (tilth) and *ifḍā᾽* (going into one another), which we have previously analysed in the context of 4:19–21. Here we focus on *libās* and *ḥarth*, as these also contain significant meanings.

Verse 2:187 describes wives and husbands as *libās* (garments) for each other. The word *libās* has several meanings in the Qur᾽an and in Arabic in general, determined according to the context. In the context of this verse, *libās* means that which covers the body, albeit in a symbolic guise. Each of the two spouses covers (and consequently veils and protects) the other. This highly beautiful and poignant metaphor describes the intimate relationship between men and women and confirms the permission of intercourse during the nights of Ramadan. The metaphor used here might also indicate that spouses cover each other (meaning support and protect each other) in such a manner that they become one. This suggestion is corroborated by the fact that *libās* in Arabic is also the thin sheath between the skin and the flesh. It is noteworthy that the verse mentions women before men, as if the wife is the one who takes the initiative of covering and protecting her husband, especially emotionally. Thus, the immaterial connotations of *libās* might be stronger and more important here. This connotation is supported in the Qur᾽an in another verse that also uses the term metaphorically, in which the *libās* of *taqwā* is more significant and benevolent than material garments: 'O children of Adam, We have bestowed upon you clothing to conceal your private parts and as adornment. But the clothing of righteousness – that is best. That is from the signs of Allah that perhaps they will remember. But the raiment of *taqwā*, that is better' (7:26).

The second term germane to the subject of sexual relations is *ḥarth*. Ibn Manẓūr (2005, vol. 2, p. 134) defines it as the sowing of seeds. It is also the act of tilling the land so as to make it arable. Hence, it points to the hard work one does in life to earn later rewards and benefits, and how such acts resemble the tilling of land in preparation for planting the seeds and anticipating good harvest. The verb *ḥaratha* also means to gain knowledge and to exert effort fending for one's children. The term occurs in 2:223: 'Your women are a tilth to you, so go unto your tilth as you will.' It also occurs in other verses connected with cultivation, generosity, wealth, fortune, as well as reward for good deeds, as in 42:20: 'Whoever desires the harvest of the Hereafter – We increase for him/her in his/her harvest. And whoever desires the harvest of this world – We give him/her thereof, but there is not for him/her in the Hereafter any share.' The Qur'anic usage implies positive connotations of plenty, abundance and earned returns.

Kecia Ali (2009, p. 90) views these verses as androcentric, depicting women as 'passive' and men as 'active'. On the surface, this reading is plausible. But we would like to propose an alternative reading. Since the verse was revealed to invalidate fearful superstitious beliefs and unfounded constraints regarding certain sexual positions, it is meant to reassure Muslim spouses and counter the negative image in their minds through a shift in the discourse on marital sexual relations. The implied message could be urging husbands to view their wives as the metaphorical source of plenty, auspicious expectations and prosperity. Moreover, this verse follows one responding to a question about intercourse during menstruation, as if to negate any connotations of essential 'uncleanliness' that can stigmatize women's bodies as a result of menstruation. The positive image of tilth has the effect of validating femininity and women's natural biological functions. The conclusion is that marital sexual relations in the Qur'anic ethos is depicted as a form of sanctioned enjoyable intimacy with emotional (mutual support and protectiveness) and spiritual (resembling the harvest of the Hereafter) dimensions.

3.4 Marital discord

Human relations are not free from conflict and challenges. How does the Qur'an tackle marital conflicts arising from failures or transgressions from either spouse? The second part of verse 4:34, the subsequent 4:35 and 4:128 deal with spousal discord. The second part of 4:34 reads:

> So ***ṣāliḥāt*** (ethical/good) women are ***qanitāt*** (God-conscious), ***hafiẓāt lil-ghayb*** (preserving the unseen). But those [wives] from whom you fear ***nushūz*** – [first] advise them; [then if they persist], forsake them in bed; and [finally], strike them. But if they obey you [once more], seek no means against them. Indeed, Allah is ever Exalted and Grand.

The verse first describes women/wives who are ethical/good (*ṣāliḥāt*). What are the characteristics of these women? They are in deep submission to God (*qanitāt*) and preserve the unseen (*hafiẓāt lil-ghayb*), that is their faith in God and in all the Unseen that belongs to God. Our reading of this part of the verse departs substantively from that of most exegetes who interpret *qanitāt* as obedient to their husbands and *hafiẓāt lil-ghayb* as guarding the honour of their husbands in their absence. This reading is consistent with the Qur'anic principles of the ontological equality of all humans as affirmed in verse 4:1 and the equal responsibility of women and men to enact *taqwā*.

An intra-textual reading of the terms *ṣāliḥāt* and *qanitāt* in this verse and other verses also corroborates this reading. The first term is the female plural form of *ṣāliḥ*, which is used in the Qur'an frequently in conjunction to describe the believer and the good deeds that should accompany their belief in God (*wa aladhina amanū wa 'amilu al ṣāliḥāt*/those who believe and do good deeds). The second term is related to *qunūṭ* (n) or *iqnit* (v), which is used in several contexts in the Qur'an to describe the devotion and submission of believers and spiritual role models such as Mariam, mother of Jesus.[26] Hence, it is unpersuasive to read this verse as denoting the obedience of the wife to the husband. Then the verse proceeds to address the cases of wives who might commit *nushūz*. While *nushūz* is colloquially understood as 'disobedience', the dictionary meaning is elevation from a place, or to change location or place. It can more generally be defined as deviation or going far from the ideals of goodness, devotion to God and faith in the Unseen. The word in its verb forms

[26] Verses 3:43 (in reference to Mariam), 33:35 (in reference to male and female believers), etc.

occurs in two other verses, and it can be viewed differently in each.[27] Why are the measures proposed for the wife's *nushūz* in 4:34 (admonishment, abandoning marital bed and beating) different from that proposed for the husband's *nushūz* in 4:128 (settlement)?

> And if a woman fears from her husband ***nushūz*** or ***'irāḍ***, there is no sin upon them if they make terms of settlement between them – and settlement is best. And present in [human] souls is stinginess. But if you do good and fear Allah – then indeed Allah is ever, with what you do, Acquainted.

Is the *nushūz* of the wife different from that of the husband? Pre-modern and modern exegetical literature attempt to resolve this tension in several ways. For example, 4:128 was interpreted as concerning the case of a polygynous husband's negligence of one of his wives in which case the couple can negotiate a just settlement, while 4:34 was read as referring to some form of transgression on the part of the wife. Some modern exegetes interpreted 4:34 as referring to sexual transgression (short of adultery), and rule that the legal system, not the husband, is to hold the wife accountable (see Abou El Fadl, 2006, chapters 41 and 42; Al-Faruqi, 2000). The husband's sexual transgression (*fāhisha*) is also tackled, according to the interpretation in 4:16 where physical punishment is also proposed. Such interpretations were an attempt to deal with the apparent inequality between husbands and wives in the measures the text suggests for holding them accountable for *nushūz*. What about the measure of beating the wife who commits *nushūz* (*iḍrabuhuna*)? Is that not at odds with Qur'anic ethics of justice and equal human dignity? Pre-modern exegetes tried to address this particular tension by restricting the kind and severity of corporal punishment that a husband can inflict on his wife as a form of disciplining (Chaudhry, 2013). Some scholars proposed a new linguistic reading of the word *iḍrabuhuna*, interpreting it as leaving or going away rather than beating (see Wadud, 2006, pp. 198–9; Reda, 2018; Abu Solayman, 2002).

[27] It occurs in verse 2:259 in the context of God raising bones from the dead and covering them with flesh, thus raising them from ground. It also occurs in verse 58:11 in the context of people sitting in a gathering and being asked to get up and leave, to make room. The meaning of the term in these two verses seems to suggest the meaning of getting up and leaving. See Reda (2019).

The subsequent verse, 4:35, further complicates the picture. It describes a situation where there is discord (*shiqāq*) between a married couple and proposes mediation and arbitration undertaken by trusted family relatives on both sides, to help set either terms of reconciliation or a mutually agreed upon divorce:

> And if you fear discord between the two, send an arbitrator from his people and an arbitrator from her people. If they both desire reconciliation, Allah will cause it between them. (4:35)

The use of the dual referent in 'if *both* desire reconciliation, God will bring about agreement between them' (emphasis ours), emphasizes the role and consent of both partners in this situation and its decisions. It does not prioritize one's will over the other. This verse occurs following 4:34, which supposedly gives husbands permission to beat their wives. This begs the question: How can this peaceful and fair mechanism of arbitration regarding a mere 'breach' or disagreement follow the authorization of beating? As Khaled Abou El Fadl contends, there is a logical inconsistency or a tension in the text: 'Why is the husband entrusted to be the accuser, judge, and enforcer, and after we so entrusted him, we then say, go to arbitration for reconciliation is best!' (2006, p.109). Hence this verse 35 seems to undermine the beating command, and furthermore highlights the equitable ethics in various stages and forms of interaction within marriage. Even the two families of both spouses are given fair and equal representation in their involvement. If a reconciliation fails and a divorce is under way, the Qur'an puts forth extensive ethical guidelines.

We recognize the unresolved tensions in verses 4:34 and 4:128 in the treatment of a wife's *nushūz* versus a husband's *nushūz*, as well as the text's proposal of beating as one of the measures to deal with a wife's *nushūz*. Applying Abou El Fadl's interpretive approach of conscientious pause (2014), we argue that the overall ethical, egalitarian thrust of the Qur'an and its interlinked gender verses – which emphasize justice, dignity and ending forms of abuse and disempowerment of women – would favour a reading that prohibits spousal violence, hierarchy and patriarchal moral authority. Towards that goal, we could assume that *nushūz* in 4:34 means something different from 4:128. In 4:34, it could refer to some form of transgression on the part of the wife; whereas in 4:128 it is concerned with husbands who neglect their wives. The measures suggested to address each case, in particular, need to be understood in relation to the historical context of the revelation where injustice and domestic violence against women was a common practice justified by strong patriarchal norms. Thus, we propose: Could the verses be read as part of a Qur'anic message of gradual reform of seventh-century Arabia and its staunch norms of gender injustice?[28] Hence the physical punishment mentioned in the verse (*iḍrabuhuna*) is much less of a recommended last resort measure than one that is meant to be avoided. This reading is also congruent with the ending of the verse, which sternly reminds the addressee not to abuse women and to be mindful of God's power and sovereignty (*ina allaha kān 'aliyan kabīran*). It is plausible that the addressee is the husband or the legal system. Still, we note that the challenge remains for this particular verse: How do we go beyond its specific measures and their contestations and foreground the underlying ethical message of justice? We continue to search for the best of meanings as the Qur'an instructs us.[29]

3.5 Polygyny

Another important and contested issue in relation to spousal relations is polygyny. It is often argued that the Qur'an condones polygyny. This is justified on the basis of 4:3, which seems to sanction marrying 'two, three, four wives'. Is this a valid reading? How does polygyny fit into the Qur'an's ethical vision of marriage and family relations? Applying our intra-textual ethically oriented reading, we note that 4:3 can only be properly understood within its textual context, that is, as part of a unit of verses consisting of 4:1–4:4, as well as 4:127 and 4:129. Verse 4:3 says:

> If you fear that you will not ***tuqsiṭū*** (deal fairly) with the orphans, then marry such women as ***mā ṭāba lakum*** (seem good to you): two, three, or four at the same time. But if you fear that you will not ***ta'dilū*** (deal justly), then only one, or those whom your right hands possess.

It is not haphazard that verse 4:3 is preceded by 4:1 and 4:2. Verse 4:1, as we noted earlier, is foundational and addresses all people (*nās*), affirming their shared ontological existence: that is, being created from one soul (*nafs wāḥida*)

[28] See Nur Rofiah's chapter in this volume and her argument about the three types of Qur'anic verses.

[29] Verse 39:18 instructs readers to search for the best of meanings in the text. For insightful analysis of Qur'an-informed interpretive approach, see Barlas (2004, p. 16).

and as equal pairs who are called to lead a life of *taqwā*. This is followed by 4:2, which commands the addressees to give the orphans (*yatāmā*) in their care their money with which they have been entrusted and warns them that betraying this trust is great injustice (*ḥūban kabīran*). Then comes verse 4:3, which underscores fairness (*qisṭ*) to orphans, and yet also emphasizes justice (*ʿadl*) for co-wives. The addressee in verses 4:2 and 3 can be inferred to be male guardians/husbands. In the former verse they are to honour the trust of managing the property of the (female and male) orphans under their care; and in the latter they must weigh carefully between two ethical directives: not doing injustice either towards female orphans, or to their co-wives.

But what is the connection between the fairness demanded for orphans and the justice also expected for co-wives in verse 4:3? The historical context of seventh-century Arabia may shed some light. According to literature on the occasions of revelation, 4:3 was revealed when the early Muslim community lost large numbers of men in the battle of Uhud against the army of Quraysh of Mecca, resulting in many early Muslim women becoming widowed and their children fatherless (for instance Umm Salama, who later married the Prophet). Equally relevant are some of the customs and social ills of seventh-century Arabia that caused injustice to women. These included the unchecked polygyny of men as they took countless number of wives, sometimes up to ten, and the male guardians' abuse of power and control over dependent orphaned women under their care by seizing the property of the latter through coerced marriage or denying them marriage to other men (see Ali, 1993, p. 936).

Based on this historical context, two common readings of this verse have been prevalent among early exegetes. One reading posits that if men fear that they may do injustice to their female wards by appropriating their money if they marry them, then they should refrain from taking them as wives and marry instead other women as they wish, up to four, as long as they can be just to their co-wives. This is an unconvincing reading. It raises the question: Why is it relevant to sanction polygyny if the focus of the verse is to prohibit doing injustice against orphaned women who are under the care of male relatives/guardians? Why could not the proposed solution for these men be to marry *one* other woman rather than two or three or four? In other words, it seems illogical that taking four wives would shield these men from coveting the property of the female wards under their care.

Another posited reading is that men should avoid injustice to the orphaned women under their care just as they should fear being unjust to their co-wives. The gap in this reading is the lack of clarity of the connection between two forms of injustice. In addition, what is the function of the conditional structure (if) in the verse? And why would the verse suggest that men marry two, three, four women whom they find favourable (*mā ṭāba*)?[30]

We put forward another reading of 4:3 that is more persuasive and compatible with the overall Qur'anic ethical vision of marriage and family life. At times of war when women and their children lose their husbands/providers, an act of justice could be that men of the community through polygynous marriages (with up to four women including these widows) take on the responsibility of their maintenance and protection. But this needs to be weighed carefully against possible injustice that may be done to any of the wives in these marriages. This reading, far from normalizing polygyny, sees it as a difficult but perhaps possible option in exceptional contexts where it could be a way to provide welfare for vulnerable parties. This is illustrated, for example, by the use of conditional structures: If you fear injustice to the widowed women and their orphans, enter into polygynous marriages with them and others up to four, but if you fear you will not do justice to all your wives, then remain monogamous to your wife or female slave. Thus, the verse acknowledges and reminds the addressee (the men/husbands) of the challenges of ethically weighing the implications of either solution. This reading is bolstered by verses 4:127 and 4:129. In the former, men are urged not to deny vulnerable women whom they have married (widowed, orphaned women) their lawful right to dower because of their vulnerability. Meanwhile, 4:129 explicitly reminds men that being equally just to all co-wives is almost an unattainable goal for men (*lan taʿdilū*), hence implying the desirability of monogamy so as not to put oneself in a situation where a man may favour one wife over another.

What is also noteworthy is that verse 4:3 is framed to emphasize that men themselves would be internally seeking the most ethical union and be fearing and wanting to avoid injustice (If you fear ... if you fear ...). This is significant, as it underscores that the Qur'an first and foremost presents an ethical worldview, an overall vision of marriage and family life that speaks to seventh-century Arabian society in its own cultural terms (polygyny, slavery, patriarchy) and also transcends this temporal and geographical context by emphasizing the universal values of fairness and justice, and appealing to human conscience and *taqwā*, the initial key of the whole sura.

---

[30] In a recent fascinating study of the verse, the scholar Nevin Reda (2020) interpreted the phrase *mā ṭāba* to mean women who are favourably disposed to the men, suggesting that the verse is also underscoring the importance of the involved women's consent to polygyny. She substantiates this linguistic explanation by the subsequent verse 4:4, which talks about women willingly (*ṭibn lakum*) giving up for the men some of (or all) of their dower.

In short, in examining Qur'anic teachings on spousal relations, it is important to consider several intertwined dimensions: the central ethical principles that constitute the overall Qur'anic discourse on marriage; the context of revelation and its specific social problems that the Qur'an seeks to address; the specific ethical directives that are aimed at the issue in question; and their universal relevance beyond seventh-century Arabia. In other words, the Qur'an is creating a paradigm shift in thinking about women in marriage and effecting an ethical transformation.

CONCLUSION: LESSONS FOR PRESENT TIMES

We have argued that the Qur'an presents a coherent ethical framework for marriage and family relations. This framework consists of three concentric circles. The first locates marriage within the key Qur'anic message of the equality of all human beings in creation *(nafs wāḥida)* and their equal responsibility of living a life of *taqwā* in a world whose intrinsic features are duality (*zawaj*) and plurality. The implication is that marrying couples aspiring to live by this Qur'anic ideal are to strive for a relationship that reflects this ontological reality of human equality and interconnectedness. The second discursive circle constructs marriage as a solemn bond (*mīthāq ghalīẓ*). This means that marriage has significant spiritual and ethical dimensions. Therefore, marrying couples are to approach their relationship as part of their spiritual quest and their endeavour to fulfil the trust (*amana*) that they have undertaken towards God to uphold *ʿadl* (justice) and *iḥsān* (beauty and goodness) (see Abou-Taleb in this volume). In the third circle, the Qur'an lays down three specific pillars that constitute the purpose of marriage, namely, resting abode (*sakan*), affection (*mawadda*) and compassion (*raḥma*). Different aspects of marriage and family life are to be guided by this ethical framework. Furthermore, within specific units of verses dealing with specific aspects of the marital relationship, the Qur'an abounds with ethical directives such as maintaining one's marriage relationship with *maʿrūf*; purifying one's intention and reforming one's behaviour at times of marital conflict through *taqwā*; severing the marital bond with *iḥsān*; enacting *ʿafw* and *faḍl* in post-divorce financial settlement.

On one level, this Qur'anic vision of marriage targets the marrying couple, but it is not limited to individual reform. It also has significant legal implications. Deducing injunctions that regulate marriage and divorce rights from the Qur'an, we contend, cannot be divorced from its overall ethical framework for gender relations. Authoritative juristic rulings on marriage and gender roles and rights within the family are at odds with this Qur'anic vision. Hence, to enact Qur'anic ethics of marriage, we need to revisit many juristic rulings such as the construction of marital sex as primarily a husband's right that is tied to financial responsibilities such as spousal maintenance and dower; the curtailing of women's autonomous right in entering into and ending their marriage unions, etc. The Qur'an sought to correct some of the abusive marriage and divorce practices at the time of revelation such as male relatives depriving their daughters or sisters from having a say in their marriages or husbands marrying endless number of women and divorcing them repeatedly at whim. The text repeatedly addresses men (and the community of that time), as they were the target of reform. But the Qur'anic vision of marriage is not simply about reforming marriage and divorce practices of seventh-century Arabia. It is also about charting the way to multiple trajectories to *'adl* and *iḥsān* that would be suitable for different contexts and times.

We have applied an approach that reads and interprets the Qur'an holistically and thematically, paying attention to its intra-textual connections on the level of language, concepts and key messages. In particular we have paid close attention to the text's ethical principles and directives, and their functions within individual verses and thematically grouped units of verses. The importance of this approach extends beyond addressing the question of gender inequality in Islamic legal tradition. It is also germane to the larger question of how to study and approach the Qur'an as a source of Islamic ethics for contemporary Muslims.

In conclusion, this chapter is an earnest endeavour of three Muslim women to understand and apply the Qur'an's ethical worldview and teachings to the question of gender and marriage. It is an intellectual, spiritual and feminist endeavour. In these efforts, we follow the example of many past and present-day Muslim women who seek equality and justice – a search that is integral to their faith-based journey on this earth.

REFERENCES

Abou-Bakr, Omaima. 2015. 'The Interpretive Legacy of *Qiwamah* as an Exegetical Construct'. In *Men in Charge? Rethinking Authority in Muslim Legal Tradition*, edited by Ziba Mir-Hosseini, Mulki Al-Sharmani and Jana Rumminger, pp. 44–64. London: Oneworld.

Abou-Bakr, Omaima. 2020. '*Al Manhaj al Niswi fi Tadabur al Qur'an al Karim: Fahm Khitab al Qisṭ Namuthagan*' ('The Feminist Methodology in Understanding the Qur'an: Understanding the *Qisṭ* Discourse as an Example'). In Al-Misbar Center for Studies and Research. *Sijilat Nisweya fi al-Adyan al-Ibrahimeya: al-Tariq wa-l-Manahij (Feminist Contestations in Abrahamic Religions: The History and Methodologies)*, pp. 219–33. Abu Dhabi, UAE: Al-Mutahida for Publishing, Arabic Publication.

Abou-Bakr, Omaima, and Al-Sharmani, Mulki. 2020. 'Islamic Feminist *Tafsīr* and Qur'anic Ethics: Rereading Divorce Verses'. In *Islamic Interpretive Tradition and Gender Justice: Processes of Canonization, Subversion, and Change*, edited by Nevin Reda and Yasmin Amin, pp. 23–66. Montreal and Kingston: McGill-Queen's University Press.

Abou El Fadl, Khaled. 2006. *The Search for Beauty in Islam*. Lanham, MD: Rowman & Littlefield.

Abou El Fadl, Khaled. 2014. *Reasoning with God: Reclaiming Shari'ah in the Modern Age*. Lanham, MD: Rowman & Littlefield.

Abu Solayman, Abdel Hamid. 2002. *Darb al-Mar'ah (Is Beating a Means for Resolving Marital Problems?)*. Damascus: Dar al-Fikr.

Al-Faruqi, Maysam. 2000. 'Women's Self-Identity in the Qur'an and Islamic Law'. In *Windows of Faith: Muslim Women Scholar-Activists in North America*, edited by Gisela Webb, pp. 72–101. Syracuse, NY: Syracuse University Press.

Ali, Jawad. 1993. *Al-Mufassal fi Tarikh al-Arab Qabl al-Islam*. 2nd edn. Baghdad: Baghdad University Press.

Ali, Kecia. 2006. *Sexual Ethics and Islam*. Oxford: Oneworld.

Ali, Kecia. 2009. 'Timeless Texts and Modern Morals – Challenges in Islamic Sexual Ethics'. In *New Directions in Islamic Thought: Exploring Reform and Muslim Tradition*, edited by Kari Vogt, Lena Larsen and Christian Moe, pp. 89–99. London and New York: I.B. Taurus.

Amin, Yasmin. 2020. 'Revisiting the Issue of Minor Marriages: Multidisciplinary *Ijtihad* on Contemporary Ethical Problems'. In *Islamic Interpretive Tradition and Gender Justice: Processes of Canonization, Subversion, and Change*, edited by Nevin Reda and Yasmin Amin, pp. 314–54. Montreal and Kingston: McGill-Queen's University Press.

Ansari, Abdul-Haq. 1989. 'Islamic Ethics: Concept and Prospect'. *The American Journal of Islamic Social Sciences* 6 (1): pp. 81–91.

Al-Baidawī. 1968. *Anwār al-Tanzīl wa Asrār al-Ta'wīl*. Cairo: Matba'at al-Bābī al-Ḥalabī.

Barlas, Asma. 2004. *Believing Women in Islam: Un-reading Patriarchal Interpretations of the Qur'an*. Austin: University of Texas Press.

Chaudhry, Ayesha. 2013. *Domestic Violence and Islamic Tradition: Ethics, Law, and the Muslim Discourse on Gender*. Oxford: Oxford University Press.

Draz, Muhammad. 2008. *The Moral World of the Qur'an*. London and New York: I.B. Taurus.

Ghaly, Mohammed (ed.). 2016. *Islamic Perspectives on the Principles of Biomedical Ethics*. London: World Scientific Publishing.

Ghaly, Mohammed. 2017. 'A Pressing Demand and a Promising Field'. *Journal of Islamic Ethics* 1 (1–2): pp. 1–5.

Hassan, Rifaat. 1999. 'Feminism in Islam'. In *Feminism and World Religions*, edited by Arvind Sharma and Katherine K. Young, pp. 248–78. Albany, NY: State University of New York Press.

Harvey, Ramon. 2018. *The Qur'an and the Just Society*. Edinburgh: Edinburgh University Press.

Hashas, Mohammed and Mutaz al-Khaṭīb (eds). 2020. *Islamic Ethics and the Trusteeship Paradigm: Taha Abderrahmane's Philosophy in Comparative Perspectives*. Leiden: Brill.

Ibn 'Āshūr, Muḥammad al-Ṭāhir. 1984. *Al-Tahrīr wa-l-Tanwīr*. 30 vols. Tunis: al-Dar al-Tunisiyya.

Ibn Kathīr, Isma'il ibn Umar. n.d. *Tafsīr al-Qur'an al-'Azīm*. 4 vols. Cairo: Dar Ihya' al-Kutub al-'Arabiya.

Ibn Manẓūr. 2005. *Lisān al-'Arab*. Beirut: Dar Sadir.

Izutsu, Toshihiko. 1959. *The Structure of the Ethical Terms in the Qur'an*. Tokyo: Keio Institute for Philological Studies.

Al-Jabri, Muhammad Abed. 2001. *Al-'Aql al-'Arabi Al-Akhlāqī* (*The Arabi Ethical Reason*). Center for Studies of Arab Unity.

Khan, M.A. Muqtedar. 2019. *Islam and Good Governance: A Political Philosophy of Ihsan*. Newark: Palgrave.

Al-Khaṭīb, Mutaz. 2017. '*Āyāt al-Akhlāq: Su'āl al-Akhlāq 'inda al-Mufassirīn*' ('Verses on Ethics: The Question of Ethics Among the Qur'an Exegetes'). In *Journal of Islamic Ethics* 1 (1–2): pp. 83–121.

Lamptey, Jerusha. 2014. *Never Wholly Other: A Muslima Theology of Religious Pluralism*. Oxford: Oxford University Press.

Lamptey, Jerusha. 2018. *Divine Words, Female Voices: Muslima Explorations in Comparative Feminist Theology*. Oxford: Oxford University Press.

Lamrabet, Asma. 2015. 'An Egalitarian Reading of the Concepts of *Khilafah*, *Wilayah* and *Qiwamah*'. In *Men in Charge? Rethinking Authority in Muslim Legal Tradition*, edited by Ziba Mir-Hosseini, Mulki Al-Sharmani and Jana Rumminger, pp. 65–87. London: Oneworld.

Lamrabet, Asma. 2016. 'Do Muslim Women Have the Right to Contract their Marriage in the Absence of a Guardian/Wali?' www.asma-lamrabet.com/articles/do-muslim-women-have-the-right-to-contract-their-own-marriage-in-the-absence-of-a-guardian-or-wali/

Masud, Muhammad Khalid. 2013. 'Gender Equality and the Doctrine of *Wilaya*'. In *Gender and Equality in Muslim Family Law: Justice and Ethics in Muslim Legal Tradition*, edited by Ziba Mir-Hosseini, Kari Vogt, Lena Larsen and Christian Moe, pp. 127–52. London: I.B. Taurus.

Mernissi, Fatima. 1991. *The Veil and the Male Elite: A Feminist Interpretation of Women's Rights in Islam*. New York: Basic Books.

Mir-Hosseini, Ziba. 2003. 'The Construction of Gender in Islamic Legal Thought: Strategies for Reform'. *Hawwa* 1 (1): pp. 1–28.

Mir-Hosseini, Ziba. 2013. 'Muslim Family Laws, Justice and Equality: New Ideas, New Prospects'. In *Gender and Equality in Muslim Family Law: Justice and Ethics in the Islamic Legal Tradition*, edited by Ziba Mir-Hosseini, Kari Vogt, Lena Larsen and Christian Moe, pp. 7–34. London: I.B. Tauris.

Mir-Hosseini, Ziba. 2015. 'Muslim Legal Tradition and the Challenge of Gender Equality'. In *Men in Charge? Rethinking Authority in Muslim Legal Tradition*, edited by Ziba Mir-Hosseini, Mulki Al-Sharmani and Jana Rumminger, pp. 13–43. London: Oneworld.

Moosa, Ebrahim. 2020. 'Qur'anic Ethics'. In *The Oxford Handbook of Qur'anic Studies*, edited by Mustafa Shah and Muhammad Abdel Haleem, pp. 464–71. Oxford: Oxford University Press.

Al-Qurṭubī. 1967. *Jāmi' li-Ahkām al-Qur'an*. 20 vols. Cairo: Dar al-Kutub al-Misriya.

Rahman, Fazlur. 1982. *Islam and Modernity: Transformation of Intellectual Tradition*. Chicago: Chicago University Press.

Rashwānī, Samir. 2017. '*Al-Dars al-Akhlāqī fī al-Qur'ān: Qirā'a fī Ba'ḍ al-Muqārabāt al-Ḥadītha*' ('The Ethical Lesson of the Qur'ān: Review of Some Modern Approaches'). *Journal of Islamic Ethics* 1 (1–2): pp. 158–94.

Al-Rāzī, Muhammad ibn ʿUmar Fakhr al-Dīn. 1938. *Al-Tafsīr al-Kabīr*. 32 vols. Cairo: al-Matbaʿat al-Bahiyya al-Misriya.

Reda, Nevin. 2019. 'The Qurʾan and Domestic Violence: An Islamic Feminist, Spiritually Integrative Reading of Verse 4:34'. *International Journal of Practical Theology* 23 (2): pp. 257–73.

Reda, Nevin. 2020. '*Tafsīr*, Tradition, and Methodological Contestations: The Case of Polygamy'. In *Islamic Interpretive Tradition and Gender Justice: Processes of Canonization, Subversion, and Change*, edited by Nevin Reda and Yasmin Amin, pp. 67–99. Montreal and Kingston: McGill-Queen's University Press.

Sachedina, Abdulaziz. 2005. 'The Nature of Scriptural Reasoning in Islam'. *Journal of Scriptural Reasoning* 5 (1).

Shaikh, Saʿdiyya. 2015. 'Islamic Law, Sufism, and Gender: Rethinking the Terms of the Debate'. In *Men in Charge? Rethinking Authority in Muslim Legal Tradition*, edited by Ziba Mir-Hosseini, Mulki Al-Sharmani and Jana Rumminger, pp. 106–31. London: Oneworld.

Al-Sharmani, Mulki. 2014. 'Islamic Feminism: Transnational and National Reflections'. In *Approaching Religion* 4 (2): pp. 83–94.

Al-Sharmani, Mulki. 2017. *Gender Justice and Legal Reform in Egypt: Negotiating Muslim Family Law*. Cairo: American University in Cairo Press.

Sonbol, Amira. 2001. 'Rethinking Women and Islam'. In *Daughters of Abraham: Feminist Thought in Judaism, Christianity, and Islam*, edited by Yvonne Haddad and John Esposito, pp. 108–46. Gainesville: University Press of Florida.

Al-Ṭabarī, Abu Jaʿfar Muḥammad ibn Jarīr. 1961. *Jāmiʿ al-Bayān ʿan Taʾwīl al-Qurʾan*, edited by Mahmud Muhammad Shakir and Ahmad Muhammad Shakir. 16 vols. Cairo: Dar al-Maʾarīf.

Wadud, Amina. 1999. *Qurʾan and Woman: Rereading the Text from a Woman's Perspective*. Oxford: Oxford University Press.

Wadud, Amina. 2006. *Inside the Gender Jihad: Women's Reform in Islam*. London: Oneworld.

Wadud, Amina. 2009. 'Islam Beyond Patriarchy Through Gender Inclusive Qurʾanic Analysis'. In *Wanted: Equality and Justice in the Muslim Family*, edited by Zainah Anwar, pp. 95–112. Petaling Jaya, Malaysia: Musawah.

Wadud, Amina. 2015. 'The Ethics of *Tawhid* over the Ethics of *Qiwamah*'. In *Men in Charge? Rethinking Authority in Muslim Legal Tradition*, edited by Ziba Mir-Hosseini, Mulki Al-Sharmani and Jana Rumminger, pp. 256–74. London: Oneworld.

Al-Wahidī al-Naisabūrī, Abul Hassan. 2002. *Asbāb al-Nuzūl*, verified and introduced by Said Mahmud Aqil. Beirut: Dar al-Jabal.

Al-Zamakhsharī, Mahmud ibn ʿUmar. 1948. *Al-Kashshāf ʿan Haqaʾiq Ghawāmīd al-Tanzil*. 3 vols. Cairo: al-Matbaʿat al-Bābī al-Ḥalabī.

Reading the Qur᾽an Through Women's Experiences

Nur Rofiah

> For men and women who are devoted to God – believing men and women, obedient men and women, truthful men and women, steadfast men and women, humble men and women, charitable men and women, fasting men and women, chaste men and women, men and women who remember God often – God has prepared forgiveness and a rich reward.
>
> Qur᾽an 33:35

'Why are we (women) not mentioned in the Qur᾽an in the same manner as men?' When Umm Salama, the wife of the Prophet Muhammad (pbuh), raised this question, Allah responded with verse 33:35 (al-Ṭabarī, 1971, 33:35). In explicitly noting both masculine and feminine linguistic forms for each of the believers' ethical characteristics, this verse removes any ambiguity about the audience addressed. The Qur᾽an is speaking to all humans who are 'devoted to God', regardless of their gender, class or race.

Umm Salama set a precedent by bringing women's experiences with the text to the conversation. This conversation was carried forward throughout the revelation, with an emphasis on taking different experiences and lived realities into account. However, the dynamic relationship between the text and its context eventually gave way to a male-centred rigid interpretive tradition. As a result, in our contemporary times, women often struggle with how verses are interpreted and used in ways that do not uphold Qurʾanic ethical values of justice, equality and care.

How can we reshape Muslim norms on gender and family relations through an approach towards the Qurʾan that is grounded in both lived realities and the Qurʾanic trajectory towards real, actual justice – or *ḥaqīqī* justice[1] – for women? This chapter addresses this question through an analysis of the ways in which the Qurʾan's ethical worldview gradually unfolded to address gender injustices from the time of the revelation until today. It proposes a methodology that centres women's experiences as a lens for interpreting the sacred text, with the aim of achieving *ḥaqīqī* justice that fully acknowledges women's bodily and social experiences. The chapter also illustrates how this approach has been successfully adopted in activism around Muslim family law reform in the Indonesian context.

My research is situated within Islamic feminist scholarship and grounded in the Indonesian grassroots movement for gender justice. Growing up within the Indonesian *pesantren* (Islamic boarding school) education system and then studying *tafsīr* and Hadith at university level, I received knowledge that was produced through male lenses and did not speak to my lived experiences. However, I had neither the tools nor the language to address this discomfort. After receiving my doctorate degree in Turkey, I became a lecturer at the Institute for Qurʾanic Studies in Jakarta. This was an eye-opening experience, as for the first time I was in a position of authority, and was a woman teaching a classroom of male students. This gave me the agency to question gender-biased Qurʾanic interpretations and to open conversations about our different locations while reading the text of the Qurʾan.

Moving from a position of receiving knowledge to one of constructing knowledge[2] that is grounded in lived experiences, I became involved in several women's grassroots and activist spaces in Indonesia. My engagement as a scholar activist played a key role in shaping my approach to the Qurʾan and the Islamic tradition at large. For instance, as a board member of Rahima, an organization that supports female religious leaders, preachers and teachers, and Alimat, a coalition that advocates for Muslim family law reform in Indonesia, I became increasingly aware of the gap between the beauty of

---

[1] This is the term that I use in Indonesia to signify a layered justice that is real and authentic to women because it takes into account their unique experiences and realities.

[2] These are two of the five knowledge positions in the process of cognitive development known as 'women's ways of knowing' (Belenky, Clinchy, Goldberger and Tarule, 1997).

Islamic teachings and the striking violence, suffering and daily injustices that women face on the ground. These two institutions, along with the Fahmina Institute, helped initiate the Kongres Ulama Perempuan Indonesia (Congress of Indonesian Women Ulama or 'KUPI'). In 2017, KUPI brought together gender-sensitive religious scholars ('*ulama perempuan*') and facilitated women taking the lead in issuing fatwas (religious opinions) for the first time. KUPI is the culmination of more than thirty years of effort to create spaces and mechanisms for the inclusion of female scholars in the production of religious knowledge in Indonesia.

In this chapter, and as part of the KUPI process, I propose a *tafsīr* methodology that allows for women's agency in reading the Qur᾽an in ways that uphold *ḥaqīqī* justice. I also explore the significance of this methodology and the KUPI experience for reform of Muslim family norms and rights.

The chapter is divided into three sections. First, I map out the Qur᾽an's ethical trajectory towards *ḥaqīqī* justice and shed light on how the trajectory gradually unfolds in line with the verses on gender issues. Through a critical analysis of different textual contexts and how they intersect with patriarchal ethics and egalitarian ethics of justice, I argue that based on the concept of *tawḥīd*, men and women as humans can be servants only of Allah, not of each other, and that both are also Allah's vicegerents (*khalīfa*) that have a mandate to create goodness on earth. As Muslims, their value depends entirely on how they could prove their *tawḥīdic* commitment by creating goodness on earth. Muhammad, as the Prophet of Islam, was sent with a message of mercy and blessings to the universe (*raḥmatan lil ʿālāmīn*),[3] including women. The foundation of Islamic teachings is to complete humanity's noble character (*li utamima makārim al-akhlāq*).[4]

Second, I propose an approach that centres women's experiences as a lens for reading the Qur᾽an. The Qur᾽an's ethical trajectory has been curtailed by patriarchal interests to sustain male privileges and exclude women from shaping understandings of individual and collective well-being (*maṣlaḥa*[5]). This

[3] According to verse 21:107 ('And We have not sent you [O Muhammad], except as a mercy to the worlds.'), '*lil ʿālāmīn*' includes everybody, regardless of gender, religion, etc. This is an important Qur᾽anic concept in Indonesia – a plural society – as it emphasizes that the teachings of Islam, as sent to the Prophet Muhammad, bring blessings, inclusivity, and moderation.

[4] Abū Hurayra reported that the Messenger of Allah, may Allah bless him and grant him peace, said, 'I was sent to perfect good character' (*Musnad al-Bazzar*, p. 364, https://shamela.ws/book/12981/8782; see also *Ṣaḥīḥ al-Bukhārī*, 2000, Book 14, no. 273).

[5] I distinguish my understanding of '*maṣlaḥa*' from the *fiqhi* one, which confines it to Qur᾽anic verses of legal competences (*āyāt al-aḥkām*). I understand '*maṣlaḥa*' as a concept that denotes an

methodology offers a way to overcome textual dilemmas related to gender issues by reclaiming women's bodily and social experiences and voices both within the Qur᾿anic text and in relationship with the text. To illustrate my argument, I apply this approach to a set of selected verses on gender relations in marriage.

Finally, I reflect on the implications of this approach on Muslim family law reform efforts in the Indonesian context. Through the example of KUPI and its fatwa on child marriage, I highlight the importance of women's agency in inhabiting the spaces in which religious knowledge is produced. By producing religious knowledge and condemning the harmful practice of child marriage, the women behind KUPI are following and furthering the Qur᾿an's trajectory towards *ḥaqīqī* justice: they stand for the well-being (*maṣlaḥa*) of the vulnerable, young women and girls in this case, and those on the margins.

1. THE QUR᾿ANIC TRAJECTORY TOWARDS *ḤAQĪQĪ* JUSTICE

Although the Qur᾿an was revealed in a specific time and context, namely in the Arabian Peninsula from 611–634 CE, its ethical worldview encompasses humanity at large. The Qur᾿an says in verse 21:107: 'And We have not sent you [O Muhammad], except as a mercy to the worlds.' Behind each of the Qur᾿an's contextual teachings, we can unearth an all-embracing ethical lesson.

Several contemporary Muslim reformist scholars have attempted to theorize this relationship between the ethical intent of the Qur᾿anic text and the derivation of context-specific norms and rules. They proposed different interpretive methods such as historical contextualization, intra-textual analysis focusing on language and themes, or the holistic ethical worldview of the sacred text. Among these reformist scholars is Mahmoud Mohamed Taha (1987), who revisited the concept of *naskh* (abrogation) to prioritize the Meccan verses (upholding universal ethical values) over the Medinan ones (recommending context-specific norms). Another key reformist scholar is Fazlur Rahman (1982), who introduced the 'double movement theory'. He suggested a dynamic reading that overcomes the atomistic approach of conventional *tafsīr* methodologies and highlights the underlying ethical teachings of

all-encompassing goodness for all creatures in the universe, which is true to the core message of the Qur᾿an (which Indonesian scholars call '*maqāṣid al-Qur᾿an*').

the Qur᾿an. This movement 'from the present situation to Qur᾿anic times, then back to the present' (1982, p. 5) allows the reader to better grasp the trajectory of the Qur᾿anic teachings and its relevance to the different audiences across times.

These reformist methodologies have been important in addressing the challenges faced by those whose voices and interests have been silenced within the patriarchal and slavery systems in Muslim contexts. The merit of these modernist scholars is that they have changed our ways of viewing and understanding the verses of the Qur᾿an without disregarding their significance. At the same time, for many of these scholars the verses about women are still seen as stand-alone verses not connected with each other or with universal principles such as *tawḥīd*, *maṣlaḥa* and justice. In addition, women's issues are still often seen as themes in their work, rather than as perspectives of women themselves, and women are still seen as objects rather than subjects in the religious knowledge system. If this is the case, the modernist thinking does not actually affect women's realities. I therefore choose to build on these reformist approaches in a way that centres women's experiences and views the world from women's perspectives.

Here the work of Muslim feminist scholars such as amina wadud and Faqihuddin Abdul Kodir has a significant impact. The theologian and Qur᾿an scholar amina wadud (1999; 2006; 2009) has offered ways to unpack the tensions between patriarchal and egalitarian ethics of the Qur᾿an through a holistic reading centred on the principle of *tawḥīd*, an umbrella concept which encompasses Allah's oneness and how Allah unites all in creation. The idea of oneness in creation implies a horizontal relationship of reciprocity between individual humans who are all equal before Allah's eyes (2009). amina wadud's theory of the 'tawhidic paradigm' and its inherent principles of equality and reciprocity provides a theological basis for reading the Qur᾿anic trajectory to *ḥaqīqī* justice for women: anything that stands against the horizontal and reciprocal relationship between all humans contravenes the concept of *tawḥīd*, and thus needs to be condemned and removed.

In line with amina wadud's work, the Indonesian scholar Faqihuddin Abdul Kodir developed a hermeneutical methodology grounded in an ethics of reciprocity that he calls *Qirā᾿a Mubādala* (see Abdul Kodir, 2019, along with his chapter in this volume). This new method of interpretation, which can be applied to both the Qur᾿an and Hadith traditions, builds on three ethical concepts that apply to all people without distinction: *tawḥīd* (unicity of God that foregrounds reciprocal relationships between humans), *karāma* (human dignity) and *maṣlaḥa* (collective well-being).

In this chapter, I use these approaches to map out the Qur'an's trajectory towards *ḥaqīqī* justice, or real and authentic justice for women. I understand the term '*ḥaqīqī* justice' as embracing the full humanity of all people while taking into account the different locations, privileges, and other factors that play an important role in advantaging or disadvantaging some humans over others. This includes experiences that many women face but men do not, including bodily experiences like menstruation, pregnancy, giving birth, puerperium (*nifās*) and breastfeeding. These experiences are more complex, of longer duration, and feature greater pain than bodily and reproductive experiences of men. Whereas menstruation, pregnancy, giving birth, recovering from birthing and breastfeeding can be incredibly painful and last from days to years, men's ejaculation of sperm is generally pleasurable and lasts only minutes. In addition, women face social experiences that men do not, such as being seen as the property of men and thus socially stigmatized, marginalized, subordinated or subject to violence and double burdens. My main focus therefore lies in shedding light on the Qur'an's ethos of *ḥaqīqī* justice for women and girls in a way that honours their full humanity.

Throughout the twenty-three years of revelation, the Qur'anic message included a clear intention to improve the situation of women and girls within seventh-century Arabian society. While stressing their full human dignity and equal position before the eyes of God, in creation, and in the Hereafter, the revelation adopted a gradual approach to achieving gender justice in society. Hence, like all trajectories towards social change, the Qur'anic trajectory towards gender justice has a starting point, an intermediary stage and a final objective. According to this Qur'anic didactic approach, we can identify three types of verses which reflect different locations within the trajectory towards justice when it comes to addressing women's issues.

The first type of verses mark the starting point of the Qur'anic trajectory towards *ḥaqīqī* justice. These verses convey a picture of the social fabric and systems of Arab society at the time of the revelation, which viewed women as inferior and dependent on men. These verses therefore address a context-specific audience and cannot be read without considering the circumstances of their revelation. The teachings behind these verses are starting points that do not reflect and cannot be applied to today's requirements of gender justice. Examples of these verses include 2:223: '["]Your wives are your fields, so go into your fields whichever way you like, and send [something good] ahead for yourselves. Be mindful of God: remember that you will meet Him" [Prophet], give good news to the believers.' Or verses 56:35–40: 'We have specially created – virginal, loving, of matching age – for those on the Right, many from the past and many from later generations.' Through these verses we can clearly see the tensions between the patriarchal and egalitarian ethics of the Qur'an. If we read this type of verse literally, without taking into account their socio-historical and linguistic context, we have trouble seeing the trajectory towards women's *ḥaqīqī* justice. But by categorizing them as 'starting point verses', these verses have only a didactic purpose: to help us grasp the scope of the Qur'anic message, where it starts and where it can potentially take us in different times and circumstances. For instance, as a starting point message, the wife is described as a place of cultivation, but the moral foundation and eternal messages relate to husbands putting forth righteousness for all people, and to the connection between sexual behaviour and *taqwā* (God-consciousness).

The second type of verse reflects an intermediary stage in the Qur'anic trajectory towards women's *ḥaqīqī* justice. These verses take a step forward and plant the seeds for reforming discriminatory norms and practices against women. However, true to the Qur'an's gradual approach, these verses still speak to an audience for which women's full human dignity and equality were not a given. Hence, these verses call for social justice within the patriarchal and slavery social system of the seventh century, and thus still value women as one quarter, one third, one half of men. The teachings behind these verses are strongly embedded within the social fabric of that time, which is not aligned with our contemporary understandings of justice. Examples of these verses include 4:3: 'If you fear that you will not deal fairly with orphan girls, you may marry whichever [other] women seem good to you, two, three or four. If you fear that you cannot be equitable [to them], then marry only one ...' Or verse 2:282: '... Call in two men as witnesses. If two men are not there, then call one man and two women out of those you approve as witnesses, so that if one of the two women should forget the other can remind her ...' Many other verses, including some related to marriage and inheritance matters, fall under this intermediate category. While they aim at upholding social justice, the scope is limited by the strong political, economic and social barriers of that time. As for the category above, these verses play an important didactic role in the Qur'anic ethical trajectory towards *ḥaqīqī* justice. These verses bring women to the table after they had been completely excluded from the economic and political vision of that time. Yet, this new position is still not an equal one, but one that is subjected to men's maintenance and protection. That is why these verses need to be taken forward.

Verses in the third category focus on the final goal of the Qur'anic trajectory, which is a system that is a blessing for the universe, provides *ḥaqīqī* justice for all people, including women, and values women equally with men. These verses are the compass that guides us towards finding our better selves. They transcend different times and contexts and address humanity at large. Through these verses, the Qur᾽an reminds us of the foundations of its ethical message: justice, equality, human dignity, beauty and compassion. In order to achieve this final objective, women and men, as well as all people at the margins, are to be treated as equals. Anything that stands against these foundations, such as injustices, discriminatory norms, and practices and violence perpetrated against women, constitutes an obstacle to achieving the Qur᾽anic ethical end-goal. Examples of these verses include 9:71: 'The believers, both men and women, support each other; they order what is right and forbid what is wrong; they keep up the prayer and pay the prescribed alms; they obey God and His Messenger. God will give His mercy to such people: God is almighty and wise.' Or verse 3:195: 'Their Lord has answered them: "I will not allow the deeds of any one of you to be lost, whether you are male or female, each is like the other [in rewards] ..."' There are many other verses that integrate this approach and foreground the Qur᾽anic ethical worldview towards justice.[6] These verses play a critical role in taking forward the Qur᾽an's movement for social change. They provide the overarching lenses through which all the verses need to be read and interpreted in order to speak to today's requirements of justice.

The three types of verse outlined above mirror three different social systems in which the recognition of women's equality and full humanity ranges from non-existent to fully enhanced: 'hard patriarchies', 'soft patriarchies' and 'gender just societies'. Like 'justice', how we define 'human' must be true to all humans. Yet for centuries, the patriarchal systems – across cultures, religions and geographical spaces – have put forward a male-centred definition of humanity that excludes the experiences of those on the margins, such as women. As a result, their dignity and human rights have been violated, and their access to justice hindered. The social systems can be explained as follows:

- **Hard patriarchies** establish structures of domination of men over women. The most powerful men in these societies impose their will

[6] Other verses include, for example, verse 4:3. This verse is often used to justify polygynous marriage, but its ending ('If you fear that you cannot be equitable [to them], then marry only one ...') clearly emphasizes the call for justice and hence the final goal of the Qur᾽an to promote monogamous marriages. Verse 4:3 and other verses like 4:11 and 24:6–10 include elements that fall both in the second and third category and need to be interpreted in light of the overarching Qur᾽anic trajectory towards *ḥaqīqī* justice.

and their definition of what it means to be human, which exclusively serves their interests. In such social systems, women are considered to be passive objects and deficient human beings. Hence, their experiences, needs and demands are not considered in measuring and achieving the collective well-being (*maṣlaḥa*). Within hard patriarchies, only the *maṣlaḥa* of men exists.

- **Soft patriarchies** sustain existing forms of male domination while putting in place a system of protection and care for those who are subjected to this domination. Women are now included in the definition of what it means to be human, but as second-class human beings with no regard for their experiences, needs and demands. Instead, they are subjected to a male standard of what it means to be human and what is needed to achieve well-being. Under soft patriarchies, women's human dignity and rights are still not fully honoured and they cannot access real justice. In soft patriarchies, only the same experiences, needs and demands of men and women are considered in determining *maṣlaḥa*, and not needs and experiences that differ between them.
- **Gender just societies** aim to prevent, counteract and redress the consequences of patriarchal domination. These social systems represent the final objective in the trajectory towards *ḥaqīqī* justice for all, including women. All human beings and their distinctive experiences and locations are taken into account, equally, in the measure of what it means to be human and the contours of the collective well-being (*maṣlaḥa*). Women's physical experiences like menstruation, pregnancy, giving birth, puerperium (*nifās*) and breastfeeding, and social experiences such as stigmatization, subordination, marginalization, violence and double burdens, are taken into account and addressed to eliminate any pain they may bring, whether physically or psychologically. The goal of such societies is to humanize all people as active subjects who equally belong to Allah.

These three categories of verses and social systems also reflect a change in the concepts of *qiwāma* (male authority) and *wilāya* (guardianship). In the hard patriarchal system and starting point verses, the social context was that women were owned by men during their lifetimes: first by fathers, then husbands, and then sons or other male relatives. The intermediary stage and soft patriarchal system, which mostly serve as a paradigm in existing Muslim laws, is that women are under men's protection and care: before marriage they are under the care of their fathers, and after marriage their husbands. The third stage, the gender just society that is the final goal of marriage in Islam, is that women and men are equal and both are full and active subjects of marriage. They are protectors and carers one of another. The second section of this chapter will draw on this type of verse to understand the Qur᾽anic framework and final objectives for marital relations.

Reading the Qur᾽an in context implies a deep understanding of the social systems in which it was revealed; the social systems in which the exegetes lived; and the present social systems in which we, contemporary readers, live. This contextualization guides us in mapping the Qur᾽an's ethical trajectory. It allows us to distinguish the verses and their locations from the starting point to the intermediary stages, and then to the final aspirations. Following this Qur᾽anic didactic approach, we can identify ways to overcome the tensions between the patriarchal and egalitarian ethics of the text.

All in all, I view the Qur᾽an as a system and a direction to continually work to ensure that lived realities can be closer to its mission. As a system, the Qur᾽an contains three important levels of teachings. The top level is teachings on the ultimate mission, which is to bring compassion (*raḥma*) to the universe, including to women. The intermediate level is teachings on the moral foundation that includes the overarching ethical concepts of *tawḥīd*, *maṣlaḥa*, justice, love, humanity, natural sustainability and other universal positive values and principles in which all are seen as equal beings, and the best interests of all people and things are considered in the collective well-being. The lowest level is teachings on the strategy or method of how to proceed from the lived realities at the time of revelation to be closer to the mission based on an Islamic moral foundation. We cannot alter the first and second levels of this system, but we can address the third level. If social changes mean that the textual meaning of the Qur᾽anic verses begins to contradict its moral foundation and hinder its mission, we must reject the textual meaning and move to the contextual ones.

As part of the process, we must always identify the kind of verses (starting point, intermediary or final goal verses) and the contexts at the time of revelation and present society (hard patriarchal, soft patriarchal or gender just social system). We can use the present lived realities to move from starting point to final goals and from hard patriarchal to gender just social systems. We may still need the intermediary verses if the lived realities of society are still hard patriarchy, but we do not need them if the society is operating as a gender-just system or is already practising the final goal verses.

I argue that we should centre women's experiences in reading the Qur'an and view it as both a system and a continuing process. This will help ensure that lived realities reflect the mission of Islam to bring mercy and blessings (*raḥma*) to the universe, including to women. If the Qur'an speaks to all times, all circumstances and all humans, then women's experiences must be taken into account in understanding its message.

2. CENTRING WOMEN'S EXPERIENCES IN READING THE QUR'AN

When Umm Salama asked the Prophet Muhammad why women are not mentioned in the Qur'an, she touched upon a critical dimension of the Qur'anic text: Who is the audience? If women are considered full and equal humans, as well as equal believers, then their experiences need to be explicitly acknowledged by the sacred text. Umm Salama was fully aware of the patriarchal structure of the Arabic language in which the masculine form takes precedence over the feminine form. Yet she still requested that the Qur'an address both males and females equally. We can fairly say that Umm Salama laid the foundation for the linguistic interpretive methods that emerged centuries later.

The gendered structure of the Arabic language has several other consequences related to women's experiences of the text. How do we know if a statement is intended for all human beings or addresses only men? Why are women sometimes explicitly addressed (in feminine forms) and other times included within a masculine 'generic' form? Coming from a culture with a gender-neutral language (Bahasa Indonesia), I was surprised to find so many gender markers in the Arabic language. Nasr Hamid Abu Zayd (1999) explains how the gendered structure of Arabic language can lead to social assumptions and norms about gender. For instance, in Arabic every noun is gendered and takes a masculine (*mudhakar*) or feminine (*mu'annath*) form. There is no neutral category, unlike in some other languages. Even Allah, who is genderless – neither male nor female (verse 112:1–4) – is nevertheless mentioned in the Qur'an with a masculine form. Furthermore, nouns are male by default, and female nouns are generally formed from existing male nouns with the addition of a marker, such as *muslima* (female believer) from the word *muslim* (male believer). This reflects the idea that males are primary while females are secondary. The term for a group made up primarily of women with just one man present would take the masculine form. This reflects the idea that one man is more valuable than any number of women. In addition, the plural masculine (*jam῾ mudhakar*) can include women, while the plural feminine (*jam῾ mu᾿annath*) can never include men. This reflects a perspective of men as active subjects who can incorporate women into their midst and women as passive objects who stand apart. How do we address the shortcomings of a gender-specific language when we are trying to uncover a universal Qur᾿anic ethical message?

The scholar amina wadud proposed a hermeneutical approach that combines analysis of the social context, grammatical composition and the ethical worldview of the Qur᾿anic text. In her book *Qur᾿an and Woman* (1999, p. 7) she writes:

> Although each word in Arabic is designated as masculine or feminine, it does not follow that each use of masculine or feminine persons is necessarily restricted to the mentioned gender – from the perspective of universal Qur᾿anic guidance. A divine text must overcome the natural restrictions of the language of human communication.

Just as the Qur᾿an had to grapple with the constraints of the social system in which it was revealed, it also had to deal with the limits of the human language in which it was conveyed. According to wadud, one needs to transcend the human restrictions of the Arabic language and focus on its ethical worldview. As such every reading of the Qur᾿an is informed by the ethical intent of the text and what she calls the 'prior text', or the language and cultural context in which the text is read. For the Qur᾿an, this 'prior text' is the male-centred Arabic language and culture, which has significant implications related to gender perspectives. Hence, it is important to keep in mind the limits and consequences of this 'prior text' in efforts to uncover women's voices and experiences of the Qur᾿an in its trajectory towards justice.

Throughout the past centuries and until today, women's experiences have been excluded from what are considered 'authoritative' sources of knowledge. Building on patriarchal assumptions and dichotomies such as 'rationality' (deemed to be a masculine value) versus 'emotionality' (deemed to be a feminine value), 'objective' versus 'subjective', or 'conceptual' versus 'empirical', women's experiences have been relegated to the backstage and regarded as informal and inadequate sources of knowledge. These patriarchal biases in knowledge production and sharing have impacted the ways in which male exegetes have interpreted the Qur'an: that is, through their own standards and experiences, which were viewed as rational, objective and relevant to all. Yet the conventional readings of the Qur'an reflect the positionality and privileges of a dominant faction in society and exclude women and other marginalized people from a direct relationship with the Qur'anic text.

Despite the patriarchal societal and linguistic limits, the Qur'an makes a point of directly speaking to all human beings regardless of their class, gender, race or social position. Therefore, when we put aside the 'prior text' and the male-centred conventional readings of the Qur'an, we can begin to pay closer attention to the instances in which the Qur'an embodies women's experiences. One example can be found in the verses on breastfeeding and parental duties, such as verse 31:14, in which Allah says: 'We have commanded people to be good to their parents: their mothers carried them, with strain upon strain, and it takes two years to wean them. Give thanks to Me and to your parents – all will return to Me.' Here the Qur'an acknowledges women's experience of pregnancy, childbirth, puerperium (*nifās*) and breastfeeding in which the process is not only lengthy (more than two years) but is also painful – '*wahnan 'ala wahnin*' (hardship upon hardship). By emphasizing the difficulty of this motherly experience, the Qur'an aims to shift the reader's perspective from one that sees motherhood as 'degrading' or a reason to discriminate against women to one that values and celebrates the strength and perseverance of women who are undertaking this task. In addition, the verse not only addresses mothers but also includes them in the parental unit, emphasizing the shared responsibility of both parents. This is significant when we think of seventh-century Arab society in which mothers were considered second-class parents under the authority of their husband and even sons. In this verse, while raising awareness about the parents' different locations (and the hardships experienced by the mother), the Qur'an puts both parents on equal footing who both deserve care, respect and gratitude from their children.

In fact, the Qur'an even goes a step further in acknowledging women's physical and social experiences by raising the question of breastfeeding and other maternal labour in verse 2:233:

> Mothers suckle [breastfeed] their children for two whole years, if they wish to complete the term, and clothing and maintenance must be borne by the father in a fair manner. No one should be burdened with more than they can bear: no mother shall be made to suffer harm on

> account of her child, nor any father on account of his. The same duty is incumbent on the father's heir. If, by mutual consent and consultation, the couple wish to wean [the child], they will not be blamed, nor will there be any blame if you wish to engage a wet nurse, provided you pay as agreed in a fair manner. Be mindful of God, knowing that He sees everything you do.

In this verse, the Qur᾽an put an emphasis on women's agency in shaping their physical and social experience of motherhood. They may choose to breastfeed for whatever period they see fit, but they also may choose not to breastfeed for whatever reason or circumstances they are facing. Here there is a recognition of the heterogeneity of women's experiences as well as the difficulty of the nursing task, which again is not taken for granted. The Qur᾽an is extremely sensitive to the mother's lived experiences and removes all feelings of guilt: 'No one should be burdened with more than they can bear: no mother shall be made to suffer harm on account of her child, nor any father on account of his' (2:233). Instead, the Qur᾽an suggests that different arrangements, which do not harm any of the parties, are possible. Furthermore, fathers are called upon to take their share and responsibility by providing maintenance and care for the nursing mother. It was a common Meccan practice to send babies to wet nurses in the Bedouin tribes. Since these wet nurses were paid for their services, it is only logical to value the same service provided by the breastfeeding mother. Again, in this verse the Qur᾽an is raising awareness about women's physical experiences of nursing, which can be extremely painful, alongside with their social experiences – that they may use wet nurses, or in contemporary times use formula, or may choose to breastfeed but with an 'acceptable' compensation for their efforts. Furthermore, the context for this verse was in cases of divorce, which demonstrates that a former husband should respect the opinions and choices of a former wife. We can infer from this that the opinions and wishes of an existing wife should be equally respected. The last part of the verse mentions *taqwā* as the only standard of humans' qualification in the eyes of Allah. It means that the way former spouses treat each other in nurturing their baby determines their quality as humans in the eyes of Allah.

The verses analysed above are only a few examples of the ways in which the Qur᾽an speaks to different human experiences, constantly reminding the reader of the different locations and resulting privileges or injustices. This awareness is essential to our understanding of the Qur᾽anic ethical trajectory both at the time of the revelation and in the present. Yet, conventional methods of *tafsīr* have failed to include non-male locations in the meaning-making of the Qur'anic text. To address this gap when it comes to gender hierarchies, I propose approaching the Qur'an first and foremost through the contemporary lived experiences of women. Here the work of Sa'diyya Shaikh and her concept of '*tafsīr* of praxis' is particularly relevant:

> I focus on how ordinary women engage, interpret, contest, and redefine the dominant understandings of Islam and how their engagement can inform some of the ethical quandaries that emerge from ahistorical interpretations of the Qur'anic text. I argue that this often invisible community of the text, through its explicitly experiential grappling with Qur'anic ethics, offers us a '*tafsir* through praxis'. (Shaikh, 2007, p. 70)

This '*tafsīr* of praxis' provides a way to shift the focus from hegemonic male-centred interpretations to ones that include the 'invisible community of the text' – that is women's lived interactions with and interpretations of the Qur'an.

Within Indonesian religious grassroots spaces, it is obvious that ordinary women struggle with the disconnect between their lived realities and dominant interpretations of the Qur'an. If a woman is experiencing sexual abuse at the hands of her husband, she suffers another level of violence if she is told that the Qur'an (supposedly) enjoins her to bear it with patience and fulfil her husband's sexual desires. Such patriarchal interpretations stand in stark contrast to the sensitivity we find in the Qur'an regarding women's experiences of pain and hardship.

In order to address these discrepancies, it is important to shift the focus to the ethical intent of the text and how it speaks to women's lived experiences. One metaphor that has proven useful in engagement with grassroots communities has been to imagine that we all wear a type of eyeglasses while we read the Qur'an. A 'privileged man' wears glasses shaped by his lived experiences of positive social interactions, sexual pleasure, decision-making in the family and in the public space, etc. These glasses necessarily impact the ways in which the privileged man reads and understands the Qur'anic verses. Hence, his interpretation of the text does not speak to those whose glasses are shaped by different and marginalizing experiences.

While recognizing that women are a heterogeneous group with different experiences, which the Qur'an also acknowledges, I argue that women's eyeglasses and way of seeing the world are mainly shaped by two categories of experiences: physical and social experiences. Women's physical or bodily experiences include menstruation, pregnancy, childbirth, puerperium (*nifās*) and breastfeeding. These experiences may differ from one woman to another; can range in duration from minutes, hours, days to months and years; and can be both sources of pain and/or pleasure. Women also face negative social experiences in patriarchal societies, such as stigmatization, marginalization, subordination to male authority, violence and double burdens, only because of being women. It goes without saying that these experiences stand in contrast with those of the 'privileged man'. Hence reading the Qur'an using 'women's eyeglasses' conveys a completely different picture, one that is more in line with our expectations of gender justice. I use this 'eyeglasses' metaphor in my teaching and activism, to guide grassroots women, men and even children in incorporating women's experiences as lenses in their interactions with the Qur'anic text and its teachings.

What would it look like to apply lenses that are grounded in lived realities to the Qur'anic teachings on marriage? In its trajectory towards real justice for women, or *ḥaqīqī* justice, the Qur'an notes the 'starting point' perspective on marriage, which was shaped by the social norms and practices of the society in which it was revealed. In this 'hard' patriarchal social system, the institution of marriage solely served male interests. Wives were considered objects that fulfil their husbands' interests, especially their sexual satisfaction. Women's experiences and well-being were completely disregarded, which often resulted in daily experiences of violence and humiliation within the household. The Qur'an attempted to rectify these injustices with a 'step-by-step' approach: first, it established 'intermediate' mechanisms of protection and care within the patriarchal system (women need to be protected and maintained by their husbands, and husbands are requested to act with goodness and care). This is reflected in the concepts of *qiwāma* and *wilāya* (male authority and guardianship) that anchor classical rulings around family relations and still serve as the foundation of most contemporary family laws. Second, it provided an ultimate objective in the form of an ethical framework for marriage as a partnership of equals, in which both spouses' human dignity and equal responsibility are enhanced. It is our duty to move towards real justice for all by eliminating *qiwāma* and implementing equality between spouses.

Analysing a set of Qur'anic verses can help to illustrate how this Qur'anic ethical framework for marriage interacts with women's lived experiences (see also the chapter by Abou-Bakr, Lamrabet and Al-Sharmani in this volume).

This can be manifested in five pillars of marriage – spouses as partners in marriage (*zawj*); spouses protecting each other (*libās*); marriage as a solemn bond (*mīthāq ghalīẓ*); spouses treating each other with kindness (*bil ma'rūf*); and spouses solving problems through consultation (*tashāwur*) and mutual consent (*tarāḍī*).[7]

The first verse in the five pillars establishes the moral foundation of marriage and ties the ontological equality of all humans in creation to the equality of spouses in marriage:

> Another of His signs is that He created spouses from among yourselves for you to live with in tranquillity: He ordained love and kindness between you. There truly are signs in this for those who reflect. (verse 30:21)

The objective of marriage is not the husband's sexual satisfaction, but to find mutual 'tranquillity' (*sakīna*) for both 'partners' (*zawjayn*). God has not created a relationship of authority and submission between the spouses, but one shaped by 'love and compassion' (*mawadda wa raḥma*). *Mawadda* is love which benefits those who love. However, *mawadda* alone is not sufficient in a relationship because it remains self-centred. *Raḥma* is love which benefits the loved ones (see Abou-Taleb in this volume). *Raḥma* combined with *mawadda* in marriage ensures that both partners are contributing to one another's peace of soul and mind. Reading this verse through women's experiences allows us to stand against domestic abuse and discrimination. If our experience of marriage is not one that finds tranquillity nor one that is driven by love and compassion but is rather one of discrimination, domination and violence, then this is a sign that this relationship is against the Qur'anic teachings.

A second verse that is connected to the first emphasizes spouses caring for one another in a reciprocal and tender way: 'They are [close] as garments to you, as you are to them' (verse 2:187). The Qur'an uses a strong metaphorical description of spousal interdependence – they are both clothing (*libās*) for each other – to imply behaviour such as protecting each other's vulnerabilities, caring for each other's needs, and acting with tenderness in intimate and sexual relationships. Reading this in light of women's contemporary experiences

[7] In the Indonesian context, the concept of five pillars takes on extra significance because the structure mirrors the Pancasila, the five principles on which state governance rests.

within Muslim marriages, we can clearly see the gap between male-centred and often abusive spousal intimate relationships and the Qur᾿anic call for ethics of care and reciprocity. A marital relationship in which the wife is clothing (*libās*) for her husband, attending to his emotional and physical needs, but without reciprocity and *libās* from him, is a relationship that goes against the Qur᾿anic ethical teachings.

A third verse highlights the mutual responsibility of both partners in nurturing the marital bond: 'How could you take it when this is unjust and a blatant sin? How could you take it when you have lain with each other and they have taken a solemn bond from you?' (verse 4:21). The Qur᾿an here defines marriage as a 'solemn bond' (*mīthāq ghalīẓ*), one that involves two parties with equal and shared responsibility to maintain and nurture this 'solemn' bond. This verse pinpoints an important aspect of marriage, which is the emotional and physical investment of both partners 'while you have gone in unto each other'. This investment is not to be taken lightly and cannot be dismissed without taking into account the implications for both parties. Reading this through women's lived experiences, it is difficult to understand how discriminatory practices in Muslim contexts such as unilateral divorce (*ṭalāq*) are justified on religious grounds. How can a woman be divorced unilaterally, when she is playing an equal role in the 'solemn bond'? How can a man marry a second wife and abandon his first wife without emotional and financial support, when 'they have gone in unto each other' and he has taken a 'solemn pledge' in front of God?

The fourth verse addresses situations of marital conflicts or hardships in which both spouses are called to act with decency, dignity and kindness (*bil ma῾rūf*): 'Live with them in accordance with what is fair and kind: if you dislike them, it may well be that you dislike something in which God has put much good' (verse 4:19). This verse shows the Qur᾿an's awareness of the complexity of marital lived realities. The term '*bil ma῾rūf* means something that is good according to the social norms and provisions of Allah. During difficult times, the spouses need to hold on to their best ethical behaviour. Like in the verses above, this verse provides Muslim women with ethical concepts such as '*bil ma῾rūf* to make sense of their lived realities and guide them in the ways they shape and navigate their marital relations. A marriage that is not based on decent, kind and good behaviour, in times of joy as much as in times of hardship, does not fulfil the Qur᾿anic teachings.

The final example is a verse that sheds light on the importance of mutual consent (*tarāḍī*) and consultation (*tashāwur*) in marriage:

> … If, by mutual consent and consultation, the couple wish to wean [the child], they will not be blamed, nor will there be any blame if you wish to engage a wet nurse, provided you pay as agreed in a fair manner. Be mindful of God, knowing that He sees everything you do. (verse 2:233)

The Qur᾽an speaks again to both spouses on equal footing whose consent and desires are of equal worth, with neither privileged over the other. Reciprocity or mutuality is at the heart of the marital bond. In order to honour the 'solemn bond', to be 'clothing for one another', to find 'tranquillity' and 'love and compassion', the spouses need to communicate (*tashāwur*) and seek mutual consent (*tarāḍī*). Bringing this back to women's lived experiences, this verse gives an example of what a healthy marital relationship should look like. A marriage in which the wife has no decision-making powers and her perspectives and opinions are disregarded goes against Qur᾽anic teachings.

One result of reading the Qur᾽an in this way is that it demonstrates the ways in which the revelation humanizes women and wives, bringing them from a patriarchal system into a true Islamic system. Within a patriarchal system, men are seen as subjects, women as objects; women belong to men and are men's servants; men are the rulers over women on earth; men are primary and women secondary; men are more valuable than women; men are active and women are passive. But in a system where the moral foundation and ultimate mission of the Qur᾽an are fulfilled, both men and women – all human beings – are full subjects, who belong to Allah and not to other humans. They are Allah's servants and vicegerents (*khalīfa*) on earth, are primary as the vicegerent but secondary as the servants of Allah, are valuable based on their piousness, and are equally active in manifesting goodness and enjoying the benefits. Similarly, in a true system of Islam, marriage is not structured to benefit only husbands, but is based on the pillars mentioned above. The objective of marriage is not the husband's sexual pleasure, but is both spouses' peace of soul; relations are not based on power and ownership, but on mercy and love; husbands are not the owners of wives, but both are partners and clothing for one another; marriage is not a contract of ownership, but a solemn bond; husbands cannot do whatever they wish to wives, but both must respect and treat each other with kindness; husbands are not the sole decision makers, but both spouses consult and ensure mutual consent.

Centring women's experiences in reading the Qur᾽anic text opens the space for understanding relationships based on both parties' perspectives. Building on the work of Nasr Abu Zayd and amina wadud, I seek a way out of the patriarchal societal and linguistic boundaries of the sacred text. This opening is at the heart of the Qur'anic message itself: its ethical trajectory towards blessings for the universe and justice for all, including women. Through an analysis of a set of verses on parental and marital relations, I highlighted the disconnect between how the Qur'an is sensitive to the hardships and pains experienced by women and how they are discriminated against in their lived realities in contemporary Muslim contexts. Reading the Qur'an through the lenses of women's experiences, in light of its ethical framework, provides us with strong faith-based arguments to stand against patriarchal abuse and discrimination. This is the foundation upon which the religious scholars of KUPI (the Kongres Ulama Perempuan Indonesia/Congress of Indonesian Women Ulama) are bringing women back to the centre of producing religious knowledge that enhances the full humanity of all people, including women, to fulfil the Qur'an's ultimate mission.

3. WOMEN AS PRODUCERS OF RELIGIOUS KNOWLEDGE: THE INDONESIAN EXAMPLE

The patriarchal footprint is not only embedded in our political, legal, cultural and social systems, it also plays a critical role in our systems of knowledge production. The production of religious knowledge in Muslim contexts has not been spared from these patriarchal biases. The domination of male-centred narratives and the resulting invisibility and exclusion of women's experiences led to the production of discriminatory religious interpretations, norms and practices. These dominant religious discourses stand against the Qur'anic ethical trajectory towards justice. This disconnect between the aspirations in the Qur'an and the injustices of our lived realities is what led many Indonesian women and men to try to create mechanisms that bring our experiences back to the heart of religious knowledge production.

Despite years of activism on the ground and an increasing number of female religious scholars and preachers, Indonesian religious institutions and spaces remain dominated by men. This, coupled with the rise of extremist religious groups who promote misogynistic and anti-human rights discourses across Indonesia, has led Indonesian religious reformist scholars and women's rights groups to mobilize and launch the KUPI initiative. Three institutions were behind the design of this congress: Rahima,[8] a centre for information and education on women's sexual and reproductive health from an Islamic perspective,

[8] Rahima website: https://swararahima.com/

which works with female and male grassroots religious leaders; Alimat,[9] a network of organizations advocating for the reform of family laws and norms from an Islamic perspective; and Fahmina,[10] a centre of learning on Islam and gender issues that works with activists, religious leaders and policymakers.

The women and men involved in KUPI gathered for the first time in April 2017 at a female-led Islamic boarding school (Pondok Pesantren Kebon Jambu Al-Islamiy) in Cirebon, West Java, Indonesia. KUPI is the culmination of several years of knowledge production, capacity building and mobilization efforts in which the three founding organizations trained grassroots female and male religious leaders to raise awareness about gender discrimination and provide alternative religious discourses that are more in line with the Qur'anic principles of equality and justice.

Although the initiative is led by women, KUPI includes and addresses both women and men. In fact, the term '*perempuan*' (lit. 'woman') in '*ulama perempuan*' is not used to refer to the gender of the ʿulamaʾ but to a 'gender-justice sensitive perspective'. The KUPI official report sheds light on the importance of this term:

> In terms of language '*Ulama Perempuan*' is a compound word. The word 'ulama' is mentioned throughout the Qur'an and a number of Hadith texts. Linguistically, the word 'ulama' is the plural of the word 'alim' meaning a knowledgeable or learned person. The term is inclusive and is not limited to specific disciplines or particular genders. Socially, the term 'ulama' often refers to religious leaders who have an advanced understanding of Islamic roots and conduct themselves nobly providing guidance to people in their daily lives ...
>
> The word '*perempuan*' means 'woman' in Indonesian language...
>
> The two meanings above ['*ulama*' and '*perempuan*'] are used to differentiate between the terms female ulama [*perempuan ulama*] and women ulama [*ulama perempuan*]. The first term, 'female ulama', refers to women who have the characteristics of ulama, encompassing both women who possess gender perspective and those who do not. Meanwhile, the

[9] Alimat was born out of the 2009 Musawah Global Meeting and played a major role in Musawah's Knowledge Building Initiative on *Qiwamah* and *Wilayah* (2011–16) by conducting the pilot study for the Global Life Stories Project in 2011–12.

[10] Fahmina website: https://fahmina.or.id/

> term women ulama refers to all ulama, female or male, who possess and incorporate gender perspective in their actions. As a result, women ulama [*ulama perempuan*], refers to those who in their work, intellectually and practically integrate gender perspective with the sources and roots of Islam to respond to the realities of life to create and maintain a just and civil humanity. (KUPI, 2017, pp. 15–17)

In this chapter, I will use the Indonesian term '*ulama perempuan*' to mean religious scholars who are committed to gender justice, whether male or female.

KUPI participants can be categorized into two groups. The first is the *ulama perempuan*: academic scholars (rectors, deans, lecturers and university researchers); *pesantren* representatives (owners, caregivers, leaders and educators of Indonesian Islamic boarding schools); grassroots religious leaders and preachers; and faith-based activist groups. The second category comprises the 'friends' of the *ulama perempuan*: women survivors of violence; women's rights activists; experts; practitioners; representations of state institutions; and government officials. Among these 'friends' of *ulama perempuan* are male leaders of major Islamic organizations in Indonesia, such as Nahdlatul Ulama, Muhammadiyah and Majelis Ulama Indonesia.

The 2017 meeting of Congress was a huge success, with hundreds of Indonesian participants and more than thirty foreign guests from seven countries. This first KUPI gathering had three general objectives. The first was to shed light on the critical role played by women scholars in the history of Islamic civilization, and Indonesia in particular. The second was to place women at the centre of the production of religious knowledge in Indonesia. The third was to centre women's experiences as an authoritative source of knowledge in the process of producing religious norms and interpretations. This objective is particularly relevant to this chapter and to the development of my methodology of reading the Qur'an through women's experiences. KUPI's call is thus not limited to the inclusion of women in religious spaces, but to making women's experiences a 'methodological lens' and an integral part of mainstream religious knowledge and discourse. That is why the concept of '*ulama perempuan*' as explained earlier is crucial and goes beyond the gender of the scholar, but focuses on their perspective and sensitivity to the different gendered locations.

The idea of producing Islamic knowledge that furthers women's *ḥaqīqī* justice comes in response to the gender-biased Islamic knowledge that is typical throughout the world and has increased alongside the rise of fundamentalist

Muslim groups in Indonesia. Many people, including religious communities and religious leaders, are not conscious of women as full humans. In other words, they still believe that some gender-biased injustices within Islam are not offensive to the religion. Meanwhile, most decision-making positions in family, society, state and religious institutions are still dominated by males who often are not conscious of women's full humanity. Women are still considered as the consumers or objects of fatwas, rather than the producers. When this occurs, the idea of working for humans' benefit or best interests (*maṣlaḥa*) is incomplete, because it does not fully include women's humanity.

The 2017 KUPI meeting thus produced three religious opinions (fatwas) that take into account the perspective of Indonesian women's lived experiences. The three fatwas focused on sexual violence, child marriage and environmental destruction. This was the first time in Indonesia – and some would say in any Muslim-majority context – that women claimed the right and authority to produce religious opinions from the perspective of gender justice. Furthermore, these religious opinions were the result of a participatory process that included all participants in the Congress and used a multi-pronged framework, with the Qur'an, Hadith, opinions of religious scholars and the state constitution as primary sources,[11] informed by today's lived realities.

For the purpose of this chapter, I would like to draw attention to KUPI's fatwa on child marriage (see KUPI, 2017, pp. 89–108). Religious arguments are often used as obstacles for raising the legal minimum age of marriage in Muslim contexts. Patriarchal interpretations of the Qur'an and Hadith have led Muslim jurists (*fuqahā'*) to define the minimum age of marriage in ways that discriminate against girls and allow them to be married at a younger age than boys. Child marriage has also sometimes been justified as a way to control children's sexuality and prevent them from *zinā* (sexual intercourse outside marriage). These juristic opinions have had a significant impact in shaping marriage laws and practices in Indonesia with a complete disregard for women and girls' well-being (*maṣlaḥa*). That is why KUPI brought women into the conversation to centre girls' and boys' experiences in the way we read, interpret and derive rulings from the Islamic textual sources.

The fatwa calls for preventing all forms of marriage that would inhibit a person to realize the goals of *sakīna*, *mawadda* and *raḥma*, including child marriage. It begins with a description of the lived realities of child marriages in

---

[11] KUPI was inspired by Musawah's four-pronged approach towards knowledge production and adapted it to the Indonesian context and fatwa-making process (Musawah, 2009).

Indonesia, building on socio-economic data as well as on the participants' lived experiences (KUPI, 2017). Indeed, unlike the classical *fuqahā'*, many of the *ulama perempuan* in KUPI have themselves experienced early marriage and thus have an intimate knowledge of its harmful consequences. If the Qur'anic ethical trajectory is to achieve justice and ensure the well-being of all, including our children, then the practice of early marriage needs to be condemned and abolished. Child marriage negatively impacts the well-being and growth of children in many ways, and disproportionately harms girls more than boys. Child brides are more vulnerable to power imbalances and marital abuse, including sexual violence. Most of them must drop out of school or are unable to secure or hold on to good jobs. Child mothers are more likely to suffer health complications and have higher rates of maternal mortality. These are all examples of bodily and social experiences of women and girls that need to be addressed to achieve *ḥaqīqī* justice for women. While both girls and boys can be married as children, child marriage disproportionately harms girls because they may experience the painful processes of pregnancy, childbirth, puerperium (*nifās*) and breastfeeding. But since the *maṣlaḥa* of marriage in Islam is for both the husband and wife, child marriage must be prohibited even if the bodily danger is only for girls.

The fatwa also names state laws and constitutional principles that obligate the state to protect children from harmful practices and ensure children's rights – including that they must be free from violence and exploitation and have equal access to education and to grow in a healthy environment (KUPI, 2017, p. 92).

The rest of the fatwa focuses on Islamic textual sources – Qur'an, Hadith, opinions of 'ulama' and legal maxims (*qawā'id al-fiqhiyya*) – which KUPI analyses in light of women's harmful experiences of child marriage, alongside articles from the Indonesian Constitution. In terms of the Qur'anic arguments used to condemn this practice, the fatwa invokes seven verses and outlines their implications (KUPI, 2017, pp. 94–5):

- 30:21,[12] which shows that the physical and mental violence faced by child brides goes against the Qur'anic moral foundation of marriage as a place of tranquillity, compassion and love.

[12] 30:21: 'Another of God's signs is that God created spouses from among yourselves for you to live with in tranquillity: God ordained love and kindness between you. There truly are signs in this for those who reflect.'

- 4:9,[13] which raises awareness about the well-being of future generations and the imperative to stand up for those who are vulnerable and whose welfare is compromised, such as child brides.
- 3:110,[14] which is a call for action to no longer remain silent in the face of the harmful consequences of child marriage for girls and boys.
- 2:195,[15] such that reforming marriage laws and norms and protecting the best interests of children is an integral part of what the Qur'an calls 'doing good' and preventing 'self-destruction' related to the damaging consequences of child marriage (child and maternal mortality, violence, economic precariousness, etc.).
- 4:58,[16] which calls decision makers to act with justice and be accountable related to the violation of girls' human rights and well-being.
- 16:90,[17] which calls us to stand for justice (*'adl*) and act with goodness (*iḥsān*) and is a warning against the 'immorality, cruelty and oppression' that is at the heart of child marriage experiences.
- 58:11,[18] a verse used to highlight the importance of children's education, which is usually curtailed by early marriage.

The KUPI fatwa on child marriage ends with a series of recommendations for State actors, religious and community leaders, non-governmental organizations, parents, families and children (KUPI, 2017, pp. 103–5).

This fatwa was used as a reference in the recent amendment (2019) of Indonesia's Marriage Act No. 1 (1974), which raised the minimum age of marriage with formal, administrative parental permission for girls from 16 to

[13] 4:9: 'Let those who would fear for the future of their own helpless children, if they were to die, show the same concern [for orphans]; let them be mindful of God and speak out for justice.'

[14] 3:110: '[Believers], you are the best community singled out for people: you order what is right, forbid what is wrong, and believe in God ...'

[15] 2:195: 'Spend in God's cause: do not contribute to your destruction with your own hands, but do good (*aḥsinu*), for God loves those who do good (*muḥsinīn*).'

[16] 4:58: 'God commands you [people] to return things entrusted to you to their rightful owners, and, if you judge between people, to do so with justice: God's instructions to you are excellent, for He hears and sees everything.'

[17] 16:90: 'God commands justice (*'adl*), doing good (*iḥsān*), and generosity towards relatives and God forbids what is shameful, blameworthy, and oppressive. God teaches you, so that you may take heed.'

[18] 58:11: '... God will raise up, by many degrees, those of you who believe and those who have been given knowledge: He is fully aware of what you do.'

19 (it was already 19 for boys) and increased the minimum age of marriage for both women and men without formal, administrative parental permission to 21. The fatwa on sexual violence was referred to by the Indonesian parliament in drafting the Law on Eliminating Sexual Violence. In addition, KUPI's perspective on gender issues from a faith-based and holistic approach has been integrated into the Indonesian national module of training for marital officers.

In this process, the logic behind fatwa-making changes. In the traditional paradigm, the pattern in any women's issue – whether it relates to women being able to bike, preach or be a president – is: 1) if the activity absolutely can cause *fitna* to men, it is *haram* (prohibited); 2) if it may cause *fitna*, it is *makrūh* (should be avoided); 3) if it is guaranteed it will not cause *fitna* to men, it is allowed. The legal status for women's issues is determined by how the issue impacts men. The process that KUPI uses to approach fatwa-making flips the pattern: 1) if it is absolutely harmful for women, it is *haram*; 2) if it may cause harm to women, it is *makrūh*; 3) if it absolutely will not cause harm to women, it is *halal*.

KUPI and its fatwa deliberations have shown that it is possible to assert women's agency in the production of religious knowledge; and that it is necessary to include their lived experiences in the definition of collective well-being (*maṣlaḥa*).

CONCLUSION

This chapter proposes a methodology for approaching the Qurʾan that centres women's agency and the experiences of women and other marginalized groups in striving to uphold the Qurʾanic ethical trajectory towards bringing goodness or blessings to the universe and ensuring *ḥaqīqī* justice – or real, actual justice that takes experiences into account – for all, including for women.

The Qurʾan can be seen as a system that consists of an ultimate mission of bringing goodness to the universe, a moral foundation that rests on core concepts of *tawḥīd*, justice, *maṣlaḥa* and noble attitudes, and a method through which our lived realities are brought closer to the ultimate mission and foundation. The Qurʾan's ethical trajectory can be mapped through three types of verses representing the starting point in society, an intermediary stage and the final objective of reforming gender injustices in order to ensure the egalitarian moral foundation. Unfortunately, patriarchal interests have meant that women and their experiences, needs and well-being have been excluded from mainstream Qur᾽anic interpretations. Women's full humanity has not been recognized.

But the Qur᾽an itself recognizes women's experiences and locations, and offers the possibility for engaging, interacting and reading the text through gender-sensitive lenses. I have shown through a series of verses how the Qur᾽an is sensitive to the hardships and pains experienced by women, and thus that women's experiences must be recognized.

The implications of this can be seen in the Indonesian KUPI initiative's process of gender-sensitive ῾ulama᾽, both women and men, creating religious knowledge using women's lived experiences alongside Qur᾽anic ethics, Hadith, opinions of ῾ulama᾽ and the Indonesian constitution and state laws.

The Qur᾽an's ethical trajectory towards justice cannot remain frozen in the starting point or at the intermediary stages. We should strive towards reaching the ultimate mission of the Qur᾽an, which is to bring goodness and blessings to the universe, including to women as full humans.

In doing so, we need to raise awareness about the different locations of all human beings to counter the dominant patriarchal interpretations of the Qur᾽an. Reading the Qur᾽an in context implies adopting different lenses while always seeking to expand and include the experiences of those who are at the margins of society.

This chapter, and my engagement in KUPI, is a contribution to this process of reclaiming and reconciling the sacred text with our lived experiences. The methodology I propose builds on the work of reformist and feminist Muslim scholars. The disconnect 'between ethics and law' in Muslim family relations has come at a heavy price for women. Our duty now is to move forward towards *ḥaqīqī* justice for spouses, centring women's lived experiences to guide us in reshaping Muslim norms on gender and family relations from *qiwāma* and *wilāya* to reciprocity and mutual care.

REFERENCES

Abdul Kodir, Faqihuddin. 2019. *Qirā᾽ah Mubādalah: Tafsir Progresif untuk Keadilan Gender dalam Islam*. Yogyakarta: IRCISOD.

Abū Zayd, Naṣr Ḥāmid. 1999. *Dawā᾽ir al-Khawf: Qirā᾽a fī Khiṭāb al-Mar᾽a* (*Circles of Fear: Analysis of the Discourse about Women*). Beirut and Casablanca.

Al-Bazzār, Hāfiz Abu Bakr Ahmed. n.d. *Musnad al-Bazzār*. Al-Maktaba al-Shāmila. https://shamela.ws/index.php/book/12981

Belenky, Mary Field, Blythe McVicker Clinchy, Nancy Rule Goldberger and Jill Mattuck Tarule. 1986. *Women's Ways of Knowing: The Development of Self, Voice, and Mind.* New York: Basic Books.

al-Bukhārī, Muḥammad b. Ismāʿīl. 2000. *Ṣaḥīḥ al-Bukhārī.* Cairo: Jamʾiyyah al-Maknaz al-Islamy.

Kongres Ulama Perempuan Indonesia (KUPI). 2017. *Results of the Religious Consultation Congress of Indonesian Women Ulama.* Official Documents on Process and Outcome. Jakarta/Cirebon, Indonesia: Kongres Ulama Perempuan Indonesia.

Musawah. 2009. 'Musawah Framework for Action'. Petaling Jaya, Malaysia: Sisters in Islam.

Rahman, Fazlur. 1982. *Islam and Modernity: Transformation of an Intellectual Tradition.* Chicago: Chicago University Press.

Shaikh, Saʿdiyya. 2007. 'A Tafsir of Praxis: Gender, Marital Violence, and Resistance in a South African Muslim Community'. In *Violence Against Women in Contemporary World Religions: Roots and Cures,* edited by Daniel C. Maguire and Saʿdiyya Shaikh. Cleveland, OH: Pilgrim Press.

Al-Ṭabarī, Abu Jaʿfar Muḥammad ibn Jarīr. 1971. *Tafsīr al-Ṭabarī: Jāmiʿ al-Bayān ʿan Taʾwīl al-Qurʾān.* Beirut.

Taha, Mahmoud Muhammad. 1987. *The Second Message of Islam.* Syracuse: Syracuse University Press.

Wadud, Amina. 1999. *Qurʾan and Woman: Rereading the Sacred Text from a Woman's Perspective.* Oxford: Oxford University Press.

Wadud, Amina. 2009. 'Islam Beyond Patriarchy Through Gender Inclusive Qur'anic Analysis'. In *Wanted: Equality and Justice in the Muslim Family,* edited by Zainah Anwar. Petaling Jaya: Sisters in Islam.

iḥsān: A Mandate for Beauty and Goodness in Family Relations

Amira Abou-Taleb

This chapter investigates the Qurʾanic mandate for *iḥsān* in family dynamics and explores its relation to society. The Arabic root *ḥ.s.n*, of which *iḥsān* is a derivative, combines the meanings of beauty and goodness and fuses them together; it occurs 194 times in the Qurʾan.[1] I examine how the Qurʾan mandates *iḥsān* at difficult times in family relationships, such as during divorce and when parents are older and frail. The Qurʾan also mandates *iḥsān* towards those without families and towards disadvantaged members in society. These are all circumstances of increased vulnerability that can lead to transgression or exploitation. Such challenging situations, combined with systemic injustices, make the choice of putting forth beauty and goodness extremely difficult, albeit most needed. As *iḥsān* stands at the opposite end of transgression, I posit that the Qurʾan makes justice (*ʿadl*) a prerequisite for *iḥsān*. Thus, the Qurʾan's call to *iḥsān* propels believers

[1] The trilateral root is pronounced *ḥasun*; in the literature it is usually referred to as *ḥusn*, which will be used here for ease of pronunciation. I use the term *ḥusn* when I refer to the holistic concept within the Qurʾan, and I use the term *iḥsān* to refer to the act of manifesting *ḥusn*. The derivative '*iḥsān*' is a transitive form which indicates the presence of an object upon which beauty and goodness are manifested. Derivatives of *ḥusn* are intentionally not capitalized; I chose to deviate from the rules of standard English grammar in an attempt to remain closer to the connotations of humility inherent in the concept.

towards an ethical ascent that does not stop at justice but aims towards higher moral grounds.

The implications of this for gender are immense. Gender inequalities are the most widespread form of injustice today. Such inequalities not only discriminate against women, but have an adverse effect on men, as studies show how men also suffer from the ills of patriarchy (Plank, 2021). Patriarchal discourse and hierarchical gender ideologies reverberate between the private space of the home and societal systems around the world at large, and legal systems that are in place in many Muslim communities today uphold laws that reinforce male domination.[2] Such laws, for instance, give men the unilateral right to divorce, lack shared property injunctions to secure the livelihood of divorcees, and do not recognize mothers as legal guardians of their children. The disconnect between the Qurʾanic ethics of *iḥsān* and the ugliness of the lived realities inside Muslim families today (see, for example, Al-Sharmani, 2017) is too vast to fathom. Therefore, amending Muslim family laws in a manner that ensures gender justice is a pivotal step towards reclaiming the ethics of *iḥsān*, just as reclaiming *iḥsān* can help facilitate the law reform process.

Change, however, cannot be limited to the legal sphere; multidimensional reform work is necessary to rectify gender inequality across the board. Apart from society, the Qurʾan holds individual believers responsible for implementing its ethical worldview (*weltanschauung*). Living up to the Qurʾanic ethics of *iḥsān* mandates a significant rise in a believer's moral bar. Consequently, the intentional manifestation of *iḥsān* at the individual level is deemed necessary to prompt a much-needed paradigm shift that can effect a change of attitudes at the societal level – a change that turns the complacent attitude towards the ugliness of injustice into an active pursuit of the beauty and goodness of *iḥsān*.

In this chapter, I situate this study within the relevant scholarship and present a textual analysis that highlights how the Qurʾan makes *ḥusn* integral to creation itself and examines the divine mandate of *ʿadl* and *iḥsān*. My aim is to show the centrality of *ḥusn*/*iḥsān* to the Qurʾanic worldview. Next, I investigate *iḥsān* within the theme of family through a focus on couplehood and parent–offspring relations. I also undertake an analytical reading of the interpretations of these verses in the exegetical works of al-Ṭabarī (d. 310 AH/923 CE), al-Zamakhsharī (d. 538 AH/1144 CE) and al-Rāzī (d. 606

[2] For details of Muslim family laws from forty-seven countries, see Musawah's compilation of individual country reports at www.musawah.org/mapping-muslim-family-laws and Mir-Hosseini et al. (2013).

AH/1210 CE).[3] I investigate these seminal exegetical works because they are part of a canon of Islamic textual tradition that has had strong impact on current Muslim thought.[4] I conclude with reflections on the significance of *iḥsān* in today's Muslim communities.

This chapter is informed by a larger doctoral project that investigates *ḥusn* as an integral component of the Qur᾿anic *weltanschauung*.[5] In the doctoral dissertation, I adopt a holistic intra-textual close reading of the root *ḥ.s.n.* and methodically examine all its patterns throughout the Qur᾿an. I begin with a linguistic analysis to highlight how the meaning encapsulates and connects beauty and goodness. I then proceed to show how *ḥusn* is central to the world-view of the Qur᾿an and its ethical message. For this chapter I focus on the integral role *ḥusn* plays in creation and demonstrate how the Qur᾿an commands *iḥsān* to empower familial relationships that exhume beauty and goodness into society. In doing so, I adopt a multidisciplinary approach, drawing on studies from the fields of social and natural sciences.

1. STUDYING *ḤUSN* – BEAUTY AND GOODNESS

Most Arabic words consist of a root (*jidhr*) that acts as the repository of the meaning and derived patterns (*bunyān*) that allow for various word forms. The trilateral root *ḥ.s.n.* has no direct translation in English. Ibn Manẓūr (2005), Lane (1863) and Wehr (1994) describe it using a plethora of meanings that denote both beauty and goodness.[6] All derivatives of this root, such as *iḥsān, aḥsan, ḥusnā, ḥasan* and *muḥsinīn,* have the dual meanings of beauty and good-

---

[3] I use M. A. S. Abdel Haleem and M. Asad for verse translation, with some modifications, and my own translation for exegetical works.

[4] The exegetical works used are canonical: al-Ṭabarī's *Jāmiʿ al-Bayān ʿan Taʾwīl al-Qurʾān*, which is known for its reliance on narration (*tafsīr bi-l-maʾthūr*) and is also recognized as the initiator of the classical period of *tafsīr*; al-Zamakhsharī's *al-Khashāf*, an example from a renowned Muʿtazili thinker; and Fakhr al-Dīn al-Rāzī's *al-Tafsīr al-Kabīr*, which demonstrates his rational approach and harmonizing reason. See Ullah (2015) and Ma'Ṣūmī (1967, p. 366). To learn more about the concept of the 'canon' in the Muslim interpretive tradition see Reda and Amin (2020).

[5] The larger doctoral project is at the Faculty of Theology at the University of Helsinki, Finland.

[6] Ibn Manẓur in *Lisān al-ʿArab* (2005, vol. 13, p. 114) defines it as the opposite of both ugliness (*qubḥ*) and bad (*sayiʾ*). In one example it states that the term *ḥusnā* in 92:6 (*wa ṣaddaq bil ḥusnā*) signifies heaven itself. Hans Wehr (1994, p. 208) translates the meanings of *ḥusn* into English as 'to be handsome, beautiful, lovely, nice, fine, good, to be expedient, advisable, suitable, proper, fitting, to be in a proper state, be in a desirable condition'.

ness embedded within them. Derivatives such as *iḥsān* and *muḥsin* make the verb transitive, that is, having one or more objects. In this chapter I argue that *iḥsān* is an overarching Qurʾanic mandate; one that is integral to its ethical worldview.

While contemplating ethics (*akhlāq*) is part of a long-standing Islamic textual tradition, the holistic, systemic and methodological study of Qurʾanic ethics is predominantly a product of contemporary academic efforts.[7] My work is informed by many studies that include, but are not limited to, the twentieth century pioneering examination of the ethical principles in the Qurʾan by Muhammad A. Draz (2014); Fazlur Rahman's (1980; 1999) focus on morals as a platform for reform; and Toshihiko Izutsu's (2002) linguistic analysis of ethico-religious concepts in the Qurʾan. These efforts were followed in more recent scholarship of Khaled Abou El Fadl (2001; 2006; 2014), who consistently highlights the discord between contemporary legal manifestations and Qurʾanic ethics; Ramon Harvey's (2018) examination of social justice in the Qurʾan and his call for a dire need to synthesize modernity with Qurʾanic ethics (see also Moosa, 2020); Reinhardt (2002) and Al-Khaṭīb's (2017) focus on the study of Qurʾanic concepts; and Muqtedar Khan's (2019) work on political philosophy in which he presents *iḥsān* as the ultimate key to ensuring good governance. While all works on Qurʾanic ethics promote justice (*ʿadl*), some focus specifically on issues of gender (see, for example, chapters by Reda and Abou-Bakr, Lamrabet and Al-Sharmani in this volume; Wadud, 1999; 2006; Barlas, 2002; Ali, 2006). Mariam Al-Attar (2017 and in this volume) also explores Islamic ethical theory and its application to the question of gender.

Theologically, the concepts of beauty and goodness have historically been intertwined. This is because ultimate beauty and ultimate goodness are combined as a sense of completeness (*kamāl*) that traces its origin to God (Burckhardt, 1987). Beauty is more than a tangible aesthetic signifier but one that transcends physicality and can be perceived beyond sensory perception. In its internal capacity, beauty is understood to incorporate goodness as well. Al-Ghazālī (d. 505 AH/1111 CE) argued that external beauty is perceived by the 'eye of the head' and represented by the five senses, while internal beauty is privy to the 'eye of the heart'; the internal element is deeper and requires the discernment of both the heart and the mind (al-Ghazālī, 1998, vol. 4, pp. 357, 362–4). Neurologically, the human brain associates beauty with balance and

---

[7] I attribute the steadily increasing interest in Qurʾanic ethical inquiries to the increased concern for human rights and women's rights, as well as to the rise of post-modern study disciplines such as decolonial studies, liberation theology and identity politics, to name a few.

harmony, this is why nature brings pleasure to both the senses and the soul (Jacobsen et al., 2006). Professor of aesthetics Elaine Scarry (2013) links beauty with fairness by pointing that both rely on symmetry. She argues that the appreciation of beauty pushes one towards ethical justice and can, thus, help remedy social inequality.[8] On the psychological front, some view justice as a necessary prelude to seeking beauty. Psychiatrist Yehia Gaafar (2013) argues that experiencing injustice impedes a person's ability to sense beauty; when a violated person regains a sense of lost justice, they are much more apt to spread beauty in their surroundings. This correlation places *iḥsān*, understood as a call for internal and external beauty in the Qurʾan, in direct opposition to all forms of transgression.[9]

The Qurʾanic discourse draws heavily on both aesthetic and moral beauty. However, in my view, beauty as a value is severely underrated in the modern Muslim world. Most contemporary studies on beauty in the Islamic context are limited to the field of art. A key marker of traditional Islamic art lies in the way in which beauty and excellence are embedded in daily objects such as doors, plates, carpets, and lanterns; the objects themselves become the art (Keshani, 2008). This pursuit of beauty and goodness (goodness in the form of precision) pays homage to the divine by fusing the worldly (mundane objects) with the profound (beauty in craftsmanship). The sense of awe becomes part of the routine daily experiences. This explains why there is no ugliness in Islamic art (Erzen, 2011). The Qurʾan demands the same level of internalization of *ḥusn* in human relationships, a call that commands believers to integrate the beauty and goodness of *iḥsān* in everyday life. According to al-Ghazālī, God is the only true *muḥsin* (doer of *iḥsān*) and the real cause behind every act of human *iḥsān*. He posits that human beings are attracted to *iḥsān* by instinct (*fiṭra*).[10] In al-Ghazālī's view (1998, vol. 4, pp. 357, 362–4), a person who manifests *ḥusn* is in reality delivering a message from God.[11]

A study of traditional Islamic sources reveals that *iḥsān* has mostly been understood as kindness and forgiveness in human interactions and diligence

---

[8] She refers to John Rawls' definition of fairness as 'symmetry of everyone's relation to one another' (Scarry, 2013, p. 93).

[9] A recent study identified the concept of beauty in the Qurʾan as being mostly associated with virtue, the divine, nature, order and proportion (see Fahm, 2020).

[10] For a quick introduction to the concept of *fiṭra* see Kahteran (2006).

[11] It should also be noted that within the same seminal work (1998, vol. 3, p. 60), al-Ghazālī puts forward a construction of gender relations within marriage that calls for justice and *iḥsān* but perceives women as predominantly ill-mannered and feeble-minded. Such presentation divulges the prevalent patriarchal views of his time.

in observing God's rituals (Al-Khaṭīb, 2017, p. 100). In his linguistic study, Izutsu (2002, pp. 221–5) states that *iḥsān* applies to two classes of goodness: profound piety towards God and loving deeds towards others. I believe that making a distinction between piety towards God and loving deeds towards others is problematic as it instils a disconnect between the religious and the worldly spheres. The Qurʾan centralizes *iḥsān* as a divine command that promotes beauty and goodness in society; by enacting *iḥsān* in social relationships, one is answering a religious call. Manifesting *iḥsān* thus bridges the constructed gap between religion and the worldly by serving society through a spiritually motivated moral call.

In-depth examinations of *iḥsān* are more prevalent in the Sufi tradition (see, for example, Murata and Chittick, 1994). Across the different areas of study, most works that engage *iḥsān* draw their understanding from the very prominent hadith in which Gabriel asks the Prophet to define Islam, *imān* and *iḥsān*. The Prophet describes *iḥsān* by stating: 'It is that you should serve Allah as though you could see Him, for though you cannot see Him yet He sees you' (al-Nawawī, n.d., no. 2).[12] In this hadith, *iḥsān* represents the pinnacle of faith.[13] Despite this paramount role of *iḥsān* in the prophetic tradition, I was unable to find a systemic and comprehensive analysis of the concept in the Qurʾan.

Fazlur Rahman (1999, p. 9) critiqued traditional Muslim thinkers for not making the Qurʾan the primary source of ethics in Islam. This gap can be due to the atomistic, verse by verse, traditional exegetical approach which prevents a holistic view of Qurʾanic ethics. Al-Khaṭīb (2019) calls for a methodical approach to the Qurʾan; one that analyses the discourse by examining the various concepts within. He points to how the exegetes were concerned with the single direct meaning of the terms as they encountered them but did not elevate the meaning to the conceptual level. The analysis in this chapter supports this view and highlights the importance of understanding concepts to gain greater access to the overall meaning of the text.

Concepts represent comprehensive meanings through the use of abstract ideas. They allow us to mentally organize the world around us and act as the 'cornerstones of human cognition' (Avarguès-Weber and Giurfa, 2015, p. 3). Limiting the interpretation of the verses to the term-level, without examining the terms together as concepts, prevents the holistic understanding of

[12] This is the second hadith in the highly revered collection of forty hadiths by al-Nawawī and is also present in the canonical *Saḥīḥ* collections of both al-Bukhārī and Muslim.

[13] Another popular hadith in the *Saḥīḥ Muslim* collection (no. 91a) states that 'God is beautiful and loves beauty'.

the Qurʾanic ethical objectives. This study speaks to this concern by analysing elements of the Qurʾanic gender discourse through the conceptual lens of *iḥsān* in family relationships.[14] I begin by demonstrating how the Qurʾan makes *ḥusn* integral to creation itself and then examine the intricate relationship between *iḥsān* and justice (*ʿadl*).

1.1 Creation and *ḥusn* in the Qur'an

The concept of *ḥusn* is integral to creation itself. The Qurʾan regularly links sensory beauty with spiritual beauty to prompt good moral action. Many verses evoke visual and auditory aesthetics as they call upon the receiver to contemplate the beauty and goodness of the natural world. The verses usually end with a call to act in accordance with this beauty and goodness.[15] Verses 23:14; 32:7; 39:23; 40:64; 64:3 and 95:4 are examples in which *ḥusn* is associated with the divine act of creation of both universe and human being. In these verses, the derivative *aḥsan* appears as a noun at times and as a verb in others. For example, in 23:14 *aḥsan* is a noun that describes God as the 'best', most beautiful and most good of creators:

> then We made that drop into a clinging form, and We made that form into a lump of flesh, and We made that lump into bones, and We clothed those bones with flesh, and later We made him into other forms – glory be to God, ***aḥsan*** (most beautiful and most good) of creators! (verse 23:14)

The Qurʾan also presents creation as an act of *iḥsān* that stems from God, who is the ultimate beauty and goodness. This is not surprising, as the Qurʾan refers to God's collective attributes as the *ḥusnā* names of God (*asmāʾ Allah al-ḥusnā*).[16] Furthermore, in verses 32:7; 40:64 and 64:3, the term *aḥsan* is presented as an action verb denoting the act of creation itself. The verses reflect how it is through an act of beauty and goodness that God willed creation into being:

---

[14] See Abou-Bakr, Lamrabet and Al-Sharmani in this volume for a holistic analysis of the Qurʾanic discourse on marriage.

[15] For further details on Qurʾanic aesthetics, see Kermani (2014).

[16] Verse 95:4 also employs *aḥsan* as a noun, but in this case it marks human creation as one of *ḥusn* as well. The verse says: 'We create man in ***aḥsan*** state'.

> Who ***aḥsan*** [all his creation]. He first created man from clay. (verse 32:7)

> It is God who has given you the earth for a dwelling place and the heavens for a canopy. He shaped you, [and then] ***aḥsan*** form, and provided you with good things. Such is God your Lord, so glory be to Him, the Lord of the Worlds. (verse 40:64)

> He created the heavens and earth for a true purpose; He formed you and ***aḥsan*** your forms: you will all return to Him. (verse 64:3)

Along with *ḥusn* marking Creator and creation, the Qur'an in 39:23 describes itself as bringing forth a message of *ḥusn*.[17] The beauty and goodness of *ḥusn* therefore emanates from God, who is the ultimate *ḥusn*, is infused into all of creation including human beings, and is communicated through the Qur'an in a message of *ḥusn* to all people. Khaled Abou El Fadl (2014) also emphasizes the centrality of this Qur'anic ethical concept. He argues that *iḥsān* is at the core of the Qur'anic message; anything short of pursuing *iḥsān* is missing the soul of the scripture. He notes, accordingly, that a sense of beauty is intuitive to all human beings. The believers are ordained to put forth beauty just as God put it on to them. In what follows, I examine several verses that show how believing human beings are ordered to manifest this *ḥusn* into their world. I argue that a holistic reading of all the relevant verses reveals a full cycle of *iḥsān*; *ḥusn* is embedded into all creation and *iḥsān* is expected from humans in return.

1.2 A Divine mandate

The Qur'an assigns the human being as a vicegerent (*khalīfa*) on earth and mandates the manifestation of *iḥsān* upon all believers.[18] Although the Qur'anic verses are laden with the call for *iḥsān*, verse 16:90 stands out due to its stern and direct tone in mandating both justice (*'adl*) and *iḥsān*:

---

[17] Verse 39:23: 'God has sent down ***aḥsan*** of all teachings: a Scripture that is consistent and draws comparisons; that causes the skins of those in awe of their Lord to shiver. Then their skins and their hearts soften at the mention of God: such is God's guidance. He guides with it whoever He will; no one can guide those God leaves to stray.'

[18] For examples of the concept of human vicegerency see verse 2:30 of the Qur'an.

> God commands ***'adl*** (justice) and ***iḥsān***, and generosity towards relatives, and forbids what is shameful, ill conduct, and oppression; God exhorts you so that you might perhaps be reminded. (verse 16:90)

Positioning *iḥsān* as a divine order immediately following justice shows how integral the meanings of beauty and goodness are to the Qur'anic moral worldview, and how they are tightly entangled with the concept of justice. The morphology of the words plays an important role as well; *'adl* and *iḥsān* are presented as verbal nouns in gerundial form. The distinctive feature of the gerund form is that it presents the concept in an absolute form without tying it to a temporal restriction nor limiting it to a specific object. This means that the Qur'an instils *'adl* and *iḥsān* as absolute ethical values that transcend time and place. The Qur'an therefore establishes upholding justice and manifesting the beauty and goodness of *iḥsān* as imperative obligations incumbent upon all believers at all times.

Apart from the formal command to manifest *iḥsān* in the verse above, the Qur'an also appeals to the believers' sense of logic and gratitude as it enjoins them to live a life that reciprocates the *ḥusn* that has been granted to them. In verse 28:77 the Qur'an calls upon believers to mirror the beauty and goodness they have received:

> Seek the life to come by means of what God has granted you, but do not neglect your rightful share in this world. ***aḥsin*** to others as God has ***aḥsān*** to you. Do not seek to spread corruption in the land, for God does not love those who do this. (verse 28:77)

This verse uses *ḥusn* in verb form twice, showing how God commands believers to put forth the *ḥusn* they have received.[19] The beauty and goodness of *ḥusn* are then juxtaposed by an opposite term – *fasād* – which means ruin, decay, corruption and degeneration.[20] The verse qualifies *fasād* by tying it to acts of corruption upon earth (*fi al-ard*), thereby bringing the human obligation of maintaining balance and justice to the realm of worldly interaction. By juxtaposing *ḥusn* and *fasād*, the Qur'an presents the manifestation of *ḥusn* as an act of nurturing and flourishing that results in prosperity; it therefore

---

[19] This reciprocal factor of *ḥusn* appears in various other verses in the Qur'an, see 10:26 and 39:10.

[20] The term *fasād* stems from the root *f.s.d* (Wehr, 1994, p. 834).

brings the world in harmony and alignment with the *iḥsān* intrinsic in creation. As a result, acts of transgression and injustice are the antithesis of *ḥusn*; they violate the harmonious natural order. As injustice disrupts the balance and integrity of creation, upholding justice therefore becomes a prerequisite upon which *ḥusn* is established. By reciprocating *ḥusn* upon earth, the believer fulfils an obligation towards God and brings the earthly dwelling closer to the divine.

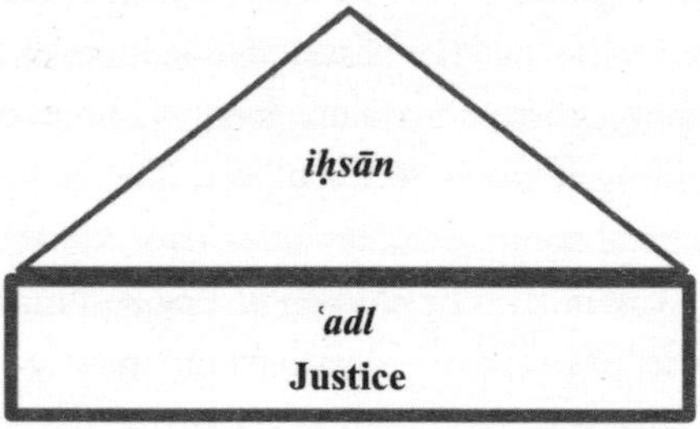

How does this Qurʾanic call for beauty and goodness relate to the lived realities of Muslim families? It is bewildering to juxtapose the moral mandate for *ʿadl* and *iḥsān* in the Qurʾan with statistics that report the Arab region as having the highest instances of gender-based domestic violence in the world (Sharafeldin, 2020). This alarming dichotomy makes the study of the ethics of *iḥsān* in the realm of Muslim marriage and family of particular significance.

2. CONCENTRIC CIRCLES OF SOCIETY

The Qurʾan layers interpersonal connections within society in concentric circles that begin with the innermost soul (*nafs*) and expand to include the partner (*zawj*), offspring, extended family, and continue to engulf further members of society. In this section I highlight the guiding premise upon which couplehood is presented in the Qurʾan. I then proceed to methodically examine verses that reflect familial relationships, guided by the concept *ḥusn*. The selected verses are viewed in conversation with one another as they collectively establish the Qurʾanic ethical worldview of manifesting *iḥsān* as a marker of relationships within families. These verses are part of a larger ethical mandate that incorporates Qurʾanic concepts such as *maʿrūf* (that which is commonly known to be good), *taqwā* (God-consciousness) and *birr* (decency and doing right by others), along with others examined by Abou-Bakr, Lamrabet and Al-Sharmani in this volume.

The Qurʾan addresses the single soul (*nafs*) as the starting point upon which the nucleus of couplehood is based. The soul and its mate (*zawj*) copulate and produce the next layer in the concentric circles, offspring.[21] This circle grows to include next of kin (*dhul-qurbā*) and goes on to encompass orphans and those who are vulnerable (*masākīn*). Guided by a call for *iḥsān*, these layers produce a ripple effect in which each resonates outward carrying the beauty and goodness of *iḥsān* to the next level. The layers of these concentric circles form networks that inevitably intertwine and create a broader community.

What is important to note is the fact that the Qurʾan commands the manifestation of *iḥsān* particularly in difficult situations, moments that can bring out the worst in a human being. In its call for *iḥsān*, the Qurʾan not only asks believers to refrain from the injustice of transgression, but commands that they recognize the 'other's' suffering and choose to act and speak in a manner that is beautiful and good. During strenuous times, across the layers of the concentric circles, the Qurʾan calls upon believers to be cognizant and respectful of vulnerability.

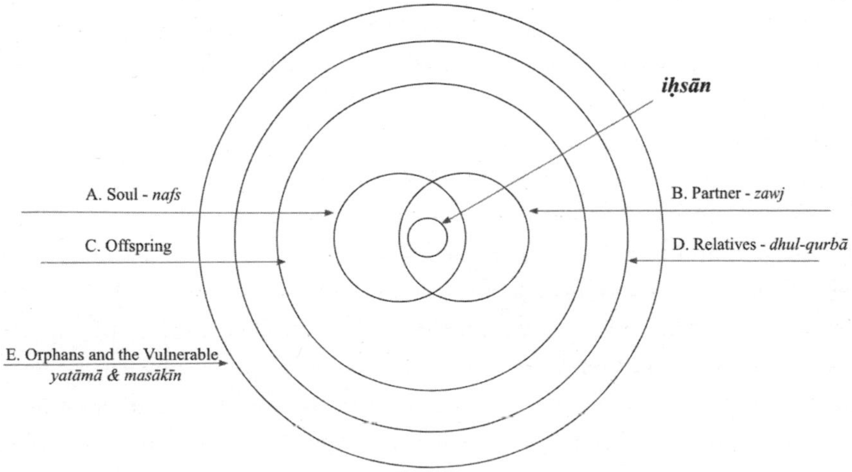

Concentric Circles of Society

[21] Verses 4:1; 7:189 and 39:6 are examples of verses that identify creation as coming from a single soul from which its mate is created.

In what follows, I investigate verses that reflect important family dynamics between couples and among parents and offspring, particularly in times of difficulty. I begin with couplehood and analyse how *iḥsān* is mandated in the strenuous time of divorce by looking at verses 2:229 and 4:128. I then turn to parent–offspring dynamics and examine the command for *iḥsān* in the parent's vulnerable old-age stage of life through an analysis of verses 17:23 and 46:15. I present my analysis of the relevant verses in conversation with the three studied exegetes: al-Ṭabarī, al-Zamakhsharī and al-Rāzī. The first exegete marks the beginning of the classical period of *tafsīr* and serves as a good example of tradition-based exegesis; the second is an exegete who belongs to the Muʿtazilite theological school; and the third presents the example of an exegete adopting a philosophical rational method in his exegetical work. My engagement with the three exegetes will show that while there are differences between their individual readings of the verses in question, they still constitute part of a larger discourse that has a shared outlook and perspective, particularly in relation to gender. This discourse notably lacks systematic and deep attention to the Qurʾan's ethical worldview and concepts and their role in informing the process of deriving rulings.

2.1 The family nucleus: *iḥsān* between couples

The Qurʾan presents couplehood as a nucleus of family that is grounded in reciprocal love and compassion. It establishes the union between couples upon two fundamental ethical concepts: the mutual exchange of love (*mawadda*) and compassion (*raḥma*). Verse 30:21 states that the objective of couplehood is to achieve a sense of tranquillity (*sakīna*).[22] A marriage of tranquillity, according to the Qurʾan, is therefore one based on reciprocal affection and empathy. The combination of affection and empathy as pillars of the relationship is not haphazard. The theory of compassionate love distinguishes between natural love and intentional 'other-centered love' (Fehr, Gordon and Sprecher, 2009, p. 3). When a person feels natural affection and love (*mawadda*) for their partner it is normal for them to derive

[22] Verse 30:21: 'Another of God's signs is that God created spouses from among yourselves for you to live with in tranquillity: God ordained love and kindness between you. There truly are signs in this for those who reflect.' Note that the root of the word *sakīna* is *s.k.n.* meaning 'calm' and 'stillness' (see Ibn Manẓur, 2005, vol. 13, p. 211).

joy from the beloved's happiness. Compassion (*raḥma*), however, implies a condition in which one has empathy for the 'other'. It conjures a sense of altruism associated with situations of need and vulnerability in which one makes an effort to alleviate the other's pain. Compassion (*raḥma*) thus cultivates human goodness (Gu et al., 2017). According to the Qur'an, God is the most compassionate (*al-Raḥmān al-Raḥīm*).[23] On various occasions the Qur'an links God's *raḥma* to human *iḥsān*. Verse 7:56 states that those who manifest *ḥusn* (*al-muḥsinin*) are themselves the closest to God's *raḥma*.

Mawadda
Raḥma
Instinctive & Spontaneous
Deliberate & Intentional

The Qur'an calls for a marriage in which the spouses not only rely on the natural romantic love that (ideally) exists between them, but also commit to building and nurturing a relationship of compassion and empathy which is particularly important at times of conflict.

In their interpretation of this important verse, neither al-Ṭabarī nor al-Zamakhsharī pay attention to the differences between *mawadda* and *raḥma*. Al-Rāzī (2003, 30:21), however, notes the difference. He states that the feeling of *mawadda* is one that is self-rewarding; it is an act that satisfies a need for the person in love (*hagat nafsihi*). On the other hand, he describes *raḥma* as the 'other's' need for a person (*ḥagat saḥibiḥi ilayḥ*). Al-Rāzī highlights the difference by giving an example of *mawadda* as being similar to a parent's natural love and care for their child. He illustrates *raḥma* by an example of a person in a battle who sees their enemy dying of thirst and decides to hand them water out of *raḥma*.

Although many marriages aspire for tranquillity (*sakīna*), not all achieve it. Verses 2:229 and 4:128 address difficult times in marriage, which can bring out the worst in the couple. It is particularly in such times that the Qur'an commands putting forth the beauty and goodness of *iḥsān*. When the tranquillity is disturbed beyond reconciliation, the couples may opt for divorce, a

[23] The concept of *raḥma* is prolific in the Qur'an in which the root *r.ḥ.m.* occurs over 500 times. The meaning of the root comes from the Arabic word for maternal womb (*raḥim*) as the mother is perceived to be the epitome of human compassion (see Ibn Manẓur, 2005, vol. 12, p. 232).

time that is often associated with distress. Manifesting *iḥsān* in this difficult time is an example of human *raḥma*.

> A divorce may be [revoked] twice, whereupon the marriage must either be resumed in what is known to be good (*ma'rūf*) or dissolved in ***iḥsān***. And it is not lawful for you to take back anything of what you have ever given to your wives unless both [partners] have cause to fear that they may not be able to keep within the bounds set by God: hence, if you have cause to fear that the two may not be able to keep within the bounds set by God, there shall be no sin upon either of them for what the wife may give up [to her husband] in order to free herself. These are the bounds set by God; do not, then, transgress them: for they who transgress the bounds set by God are the ones who commit injustice (verse 2:229; Asad translation)

Verse 2:229 calls upon the couple experiencing difficulty in the marriage to either remain together, abiding by what is commonly known to be good (*ma'rūf*), or to separate with the beauty and goodness of *iḥsān*.[24] Additionally, the second part of the verse addresses a situation where the continuation of marriage is neither desirable to the wife nor spiritually advisable to either. It affirms the right of the wife to release herself from the bond and redeem herself. The verse ends with a stern reminder that those who transgress against these boundaries of God (that is, of *ma'rūf* and *iḥsān*) are those who do injustice. In the *tafsīr* and *fiqh* tradition, verse 2:229 is designated as stipulating the number of valid revocable divorces initiated by the husband,[25] and the right of the wife to *khul'* divorce.[26]

[24] In 33:49 the Qur'an describes another divorce situation and mandates that the release be done in a beautiful manner (*saraḥan jamīlan*).

[25] With the third divorce pronouncement, the divorce becomes irrevocable and a new marital union may take place between the two only if the wife remarries another husband and that second marriage naturally ends in divorce or death of the husband.

[26] This is a divorce initiated by the wife, without having to prove fault-based grounds, in exchange for compensating the husband. Interestingly the exegetes and jurists stipulated that this divorce can only take place with the consent of the husband, although the verse does not support this interpretation nor does the incident that occasioned the revelation of this verse, which concerns one of the female companions who sought the help of Prophet Muhammad to free herself from her marriage. It is reported that Jamīla bint Sahl went to Prophet Muhammad and told him that she finds no fault with her husband but loathes

The ethical component of the verse is relatively sidelined. Several questions arise: What readings are possible if we foreground the key ethical concepts in the verse? How did the exegetes handle the concept of *iḥsān* in the verse? And what role did it play in the derivation of the aforementioned rulings?

Al-Ṭabarī (2009, 2:229) interprets the first part of 2:229 mainly as a postulate that places limits on the number of divorces allowed. He notes that in pre-Islamic times a husband could divorce and remarry his wife as many times as he wished, adding that this new decree liberates the wife from indefinite constraint and enables her to have control over her life. Regarding the mandate of 'release with *iḥsān*' (*tasrīḥ bi iḥsān*), he lists several tradition-based interpretations that translate the concept into concrete actions on the part of the husband: to release the wife in a manner that is just (*la yaẓlimuḥa shayy*ʾ*an*); to pay her full dues and refrain from harming or cursing her; to let the wife 'be' until the end of the waiting period (*ʿidda*), and then pay her any *mahr* that is due. Al-Zamakhsharī (2001, 2:229) follows suit by stating that *tasrīḥ bi iḥsān* means that the husband does not prolong the waiting period (*ʿidda*) with the deliberate intention of harming the wife. Al-Rāzī (2003, 2:229) also focuses his interpretation on addressing the limitations on the number of divorces. He states that *iḥsān* means that 'if he leaves her, he pays her financial dues and does not bad-mouth her nor cause people to be repulsed by her'.

The interpretations of three exegetes seem to affirm the dimension of justice that is integral to *iḥsān*. But their understanding of justice still remains shaped and constrained by their overall context-specific patriarchal construction of spousal relations. Thus, the husband's unequal power of divorce is not questioned. Moreover, key ethical concepts such as *iḥsān* are not foregrounded as the central message.[27]

Verse 4:128 presents another example of marital distress. In this case, the wife is harmed by the husband's alienation (*nushūz*). The Qurʾan, once again, mandates acting in *iḥsān*:

---

staying with him and wants to be freed from him. Muhammad instructed her to return the dower (an orchard) and told her she was freed from the marriage (see Tucker, 2008, p. 96; Al-Sharmani, 2017, p. 83).

[27] The connection between the release (*tasrīḥ*) and *iḥsān* is marked with the proposition '*bi*' indicating simultaneous action.

> If a wife fears high-handedness or alienation from her husband, neither of them will be blamed if they come to a peaceful settlement, for peace is best. Although human souls are prone to selfishness, if you ***taḥsinu*** [manifest *iḥsān*] and are mindful of God, He is well aware of all that you do (verse 4:128)

The verse speaks of a wife who is concerned about her husband's alienation (*nushūz*) and negligence (*iʿrād*) and recommends reconciliation (*sulḥ*). It warns against selfishness and emphasizes the importance of manifesting *iḥsān* and being God-conscious (*taqwā*). Al-Ṭabārī (2009, 4:128) interprets the verse as a call upon husbands to treat their wives with *iḥsān* 'even if you grow to hate their ugliness or behaviour'. He reads the verse as instructing husbands to be patient with the wives, pay their financial dues, and court them in a manner that is commonly known to be good (*maʿrūf*). Al-Zamakhsharī (2001, 4:128) understands the verse as asking husbands to put forth *iḥsān*, which entails maintaining the marital bond with their wives even if they [the husbands] have grown to hate them and in fact like/love (*ḥubb*) another. He adds that husbands should do so out of respect for the time they spent together (*muraʿāt ḥaq al-suḥba*). Al-Rāzī (2003, 4:128) simply states that the verse calls for *iḥsān* (repeats it as is without explaining) and avoiding injustice. He adds that this command may be addressing the husbands, or the couple, or those intervening to make amends.

Again, there is an understanding of *iḥsān* as being limited to some acts of justice and fairness on the part of the husband. The interpretations also tell us much about the gender dynamics of their time. It is a patriarchal system in which the husband's authority and privileges are taken for granted, and the verses are read as aiming not to change this system but rather temper its excesses. Thus, the husband is advised to be patient should he find his wife ugly and no longer desirable. He is advised not to abandon his financial obligations towards her because of interest in another wife. In other words, the exegetes read the verses as affirming benevolent patriarchy where the wife, though she is to be taken care of, remains the object and not the subject of the address. In these interpretations, the Qurʾanic concept *iḥsān* remains secondary and subsumed under this patriarchal system that is unquestioned. Additionally, gender bias has resulted in the exegetes' unequal understandings of the term *nushūz* in 4:128 above in comparison to the same term when it relates to the wife in 4:34. In the latter, *nushūz* has legal implications against the wife, while there are none in the case of the husband.

On the whole the examined exegetes adopt a practical approach that translates the verses into legal injunctions (*aḥkām*), mostly shaped by the norms of their contexts. In doing so, they pay much less attention to overarching moral values. In a recent work, Islamic studies scholar Johanna Pink (2018, p. 26) argues that pre-modern exegetes did not approach the Qurʾan from the perspective of deriving guidance, but focused their attention on explaining the text. I argue that such focus on the literal and practical explanation of the verses, in effect, blurs the significance of the Qurʾan as a book of moral guidance.

Although these interpretations may have mirrored the norms of their time, applying this understanding in today's context is highly problematic. The strong patriarchal undertones support a severely unbalanced power dynamic which, by today's standards, seems far removed from justice and twice removed from beauty and goodness. Verse 4:128 presents a difficult situation for the couple, one in which reconciliatory attempts have already been made to salvage the relationship. This is a time that usually fosters vulnerabilities, particularly for women who are financially dependent. The call for *iḥsān* reflects a Qurʾanic cognizance of the involved vulnerabilities. By mandating *iḥsān*, the Qurʾan instructs all the parties involved to be aware of the pain that may be present. It ensures that they do not lose sight of justice and goes further to implore them to act in a manner that prioritizes beauty and goodness.

Although the examples the exegetes provided reflect what they believed to be *iḥsān* according to the patriarchal standards of their day, in today's world the examples appear limiting and dangerously unfair. The Qurʾan commands *iḥsān* without constriction, and in doing so it allows the meanings of beauty and goodness to be ever-present in a continuously evolving manner, one that is in accordance with the evolution of humanity itself. The Qurʾanic mandate of *iḥsān* calls for the ongoing pursuit of beauty and goodness in a couple's relationship even when the union itself is being dissolved. Failing to unpack the meanings of beauty and goodness in *iḥsān* stifles this overarching moral aspiration. Limiting the implication of such a lofty pursuit to age old examples of another time and place should therefore only be read in such context, as examples of that particular time and place.

The Qurʾan establishes the initial union of couples as one that seeks the peace and tranquillity of *sakīna* and, in case of dissolution, ends with the beauty and goodness of *iḥsān*. The verses thus act as bookends that bracket the marital relationship, allowing it to live up to the values of love (*mawadda*) and compassion (*raḥma*), in all circumstances and across all stages. This guarantees that the couple remain grounded within a nurturing relationship regardless of their marital status and continues to serve them in their role as parents as well. Just as the Qurʾan mandates *iḥsān* in marriage, it extends the moral principle to the next level of family relationships, that between parents and offspring.

2.2 Immediate family: *iḥsān* in the parent–offspring relationship

The family is the nucleus around which the society is formed. The Qurʾan shows the desire to have children as one of life's sought-after pleasures, and it presents wealth and offspring as aspirational worldly claims.[28] Although not everyone has children, all offspring have parents. The Qurʾan highlights both sides of the parent–offspring relationship and promotes mutual intergenerational care. It emphasizes reciprocity whereby offspring care for their ageing parents, just as parents cared for them as they were growing. There is a difference however between the instinctive care most parents provide their children and the effort made by adult offspring to take care of older parents. Parental love for their offspring is generally instinctive and can often be described as 'unconditional selflessness'.[29] This falls into the category of self-rewarding love, mirroring the natural emotion of *mawadda* referred to earlier between loving couples. However, the case in which offspring care for their ageing parents mandates the empathy and compassion of *raḥma*; it entails a conscious and deliberate choice. Old age is often a time of increased frailty and physical limitation. It is also a time of internal vulnerability and 'emotions that prompt feelings of defencelessness' (Schröder-Butterfill and Marianti, 2006). Just as the Qurʾan mandated *iḥsān* during the difficult times

---

[28] Verse 18:46: 'Wealth and children are [but] adornment of the worldly life. But the enduring good deeds are better to your Lord for reward and better for [one's] hope.'

[29] This definition by biologist Jeremy Griffith is noted in Isaacs (2015, p. 241). It is important to note that not all parental relationships reflect this love in a healthy manner. For biological indicators of parental love, see Shinohara (2011).

in a couple's relationship, it implores the beauty and goodness of *iḥsān* at the challenging time of old age.

The emphasis placed on exercising *iḥsān* with parents cannot go unnoticed to anyone reading the Qur'an with any level of engagement. Verses 2:83; 4:36; 6:151;17:23; 29:8 and 46:15 explicitly mandate *iḥsān* towards parents. In five of these six verses this command comes directly after the command of *tawḥīd* (belief in the oneness of God). Only verse 29:8 does not adhere to this order, in fact, it implores believers to show *ḥusn* to parents even if they try to persuade them against *tawḥīd*.[30]

Verses 17:23; 46:15 and 2:83 serve as examples. The verses reflect the egalitarian ethics of the Qur'an by emphasizing that both parents are to be recipients of *iḥsān*. This mandate for *iḥsān* towards parents extends beyond a call to tend to their physical needs. It reflects the nuanced understanding the Qur'an shows for the psychological human needs as well. All three exegetes stress the importance of showing *iḥsān* to parents, but there is little attempt to engage with *iḥsān* at a deeper conceptual level. In most cases, the exegetes simply repeat the term *iḥsān* as it is in the interpretation, or use other derivatives of the same root *ḥ.s.n.* to describe it. The focus of the interpretations is mostly dedicated to philological considerations. As in marriage verses, the ethical dimensions of the verses are not significantly explored.

> Your Lord has commanded that you should worship none but Him, and to your parents ***iḥsāna***. If either or both of them reach old age with you, say no word that shows impatience with them, and do not be harsh with them, but speak to them respectfully. (verse 17:23)

Al-Ṭabārī (2009, 17:23) states that the Qur'an mandates *iḥsān* towards parents in 17:23 and calls for showing *iḥsān* (*tuḥsinu*) and *birr*. He does not elaborate upon the meaning of *iḥsān* but focuses instead on philology by listing different readings. He notes that the structure of the *iḥsān* command mirrors the syntactic order of 'to do good (*khayr*)' as opposed to 'to do that which is *khayr*'. This example might imply an inherent understanding of the goodness element embedded in *iḥsān*, although he does not explicitly state that. As for

[30] Verse 29:8: 'We have commanded people to *ḥusnā* to their parents, but do not obey them if they strive to make you serve, beside Me, anything of which you have no knowledge: you will all return to Me, and I shall inform you of what you have done.'

al-Zamakhsharī (2001, 17:23), he repeats the term *iḥsān* four times without explaining it. Al-Rāzī (2003, 17:23) exerts great effort in categorizing and listing the various possible meanings of the verse in general. With regards to *iḥsān*, he sees it as a Qurʾanic call for compassion (*shafaqa*) towards all people, adding that it begins with parents as they are the ones who have exerted the most effort in a person's life. He adds that the verse mandates the highest level of *iḥsān* towards parents and goes on to repeat the term *iḥsān* several times without unpacking its meaning. Referring to previous verse 17:19, which addresses heaven, al-Rāzī opines that showing *iḥsān* to parents is the highest form of striving towards heaven. Although the exegetes did address the importance of *iḥsān* towards parents, they did not attempt to dissect the meaning of the term itself. Furthermore, there is no emphasis on how the verse speaks to the concept of family in the Qurʾan, but this is typical of the traditional atomistic interpretive style.

By making it incumbent upon offspring to show *iḥsān* to both parents (*kilāhuma*), the verse emphasizes the important role both parents play in a person's life. The call for *iḥsān* is delineated by a set of actions which show that speaking to older parents with kindness, grace and generosity (*qawlan karīman*) is a consequence of *iḥsān*. This command may point to the increased mental frailty in old age which often causes forgetfulness. By mandating generosity in speaking, the Qurʾan draws attention to the vulnerability of this condition and suggests a move away from the logocentric speech of the mind towards one driven by pathos of the heart.[31] The Qurʾan thereby underscores the emotional component of *iḥsān* and highlights the importance of deep empathetic human connections. The command for *iḥsān* is therefore not limited to physical care but incorporates psychological and mental wellness as well. It brings to focus the meanings of beauty and goodness embedded in the root *ḥusn*.

The verse that follows the above command for *iḥsān* (17:24) summons the concept of *raḥma* by asking offspring to act in humility, out of mercy and compassion, to their parents. It also stresses the reciprocity of caring for parents just as parents cared for them.[32] The Qurʾan uses the gram-

---

[31] This insight is drawn from a conversation with Dr Yasmin Motawy, senior instructor in the Department of Rhetoric and Composition at the American University in Cairo, November 2020. For further information about Aristotle's ethos, pathos and logos see Fletcher (2015).

[32] Verse 17:24: 'And lower to them the wing of humility out of mercy and say, "My Lord, have mercy upon them as they brought me up [when I was] small".'

matical dual form to denote the act of upbringing (*kama rabayāni saghīran*) which indicates that the role of both parents is integral to the act of raising offspring. By confirming the dual responsibility of parenting, the Qur'an acknowledges the importance of both parents being present in the child's life. This is important to note, as fathers often view active parenting as being an exclusively maternal domain. It, subsequently, reflects the significant role each parent has in shaping a person's development. Such egalitarian parental ethics mirrors the egalitarian ethics established earlier in marriage. This should be read in connection to how the Qur'an constructs the relationship between divorced couples as one in which *iḥsān* persists even beyond the marriage itself. In doing so, the Qur'an establishes family, regardless of its configuration, as a location of reciprocated beauty and goodness at all times and under all conditions.

Another important call for *iḥsān* towards parents is in verse 46:15:

> We have commanded man ***iḥsān*** to his parents: his mother struggled to carry him and struggled to give birth to him – his bearing and weaning took a full thirty months. When he has grown to manhood and reached the age of forty he [may] say, 'Lord help me to be truly grateful for Your favours to me and to my parents; help me to do good work that pleases You; make my offspring good. I turn to You; I am one of those who devote themselves to You'.

The verse highlights the very special role mothers play in the early years and pays tribute to the tremendous effort a mother extends. Al-Ṭabarī (2009, 46:15) narrates two different readings for the derivative of *ḥusn* in the verse: in Medina and Basra it was read *ḥusnā* while in Kufa it was read *iḥsān*. He adds that both readings are acceptable because they deliver similar meanings. In doing so al-Ṭabarī confirms both elements of beauty and goodness as integral to the root and its mentioned derivatives.[33] Al-Ṭabarī goes on to state that the verse mandates *iḥsān* to both parents but highlights the role of the mother. This is due to the hardship she faces and mandates that she be treated with *birr*, and deserves dignity (*karāma*) and beautiful companionship (*jamīl al-suḥba*). He invests the bulk of the interpretation in explaining different readings of other terms and attempting to determine the age that marks adulthood. Al-Zamakhsharī (2001, 46:15) briefly repeats the various readings of

[33] It should be noted that in poetry the derivative *ḥusn* usually refers to beauty.

iḥsān mentioned by al-Ṭabarī but does not explore what is meant by them. He also spends some time addressing the age at which the mother should wean her child. As for al-Rāzī (2003, 46:15), he also lists the two readings but states that they are different in meaning. He posits that *iḥsān* is the opposite of harm (*isāʾa*) while *ḥusn* is the opposite of ugliness (*qubḥ*), and adds that the Qurʾan calls for both sentiments towards the parents. Al-Rāzī argues that the verse commands a person to show parents that which is '*ḥasan* to the point of *iḥsān*'. It is clear to see how the notions of both beauty and goodness are fused and embedded in his understanding.

The exegete's interpretation of *iḥsān* in the context of parents actively infuses the element of beauty. Al-Ṭabārī confirms the similarity in meanings of *ḥusn* and *iḥsān* and also uses the term beautiful (*jamīl*) to delineate how the mother should be accompanied. Al-Rāzī also explicitly states that beauty and goodness are integrated into the way one should treat parents. However, when the same exegetes explained the meaning of the same term *iḥsān* in the context of marriage, the component of beauty was not forwarded in their interpretation. According to the interpretations reviewed, *iḥsān* towards parents means acting in a beautiful manner while *iḥsān* in marriage is limited to the husband's fairness and not inflicting harm upon the wife. This inconsistency divulges the patriarchal lens through which the exegetes interpreted the verses. The distinctions in the way *iḥsān* is understood reflects the different ways relationships are perceived; parent–offspring relations are not like marriage. While parent-care can accommodate beauty as a tenet, the logic of benevolent patriarchy limits spousal relationships to a one-directional power dynamic in which a pious husband refrains from exploiting his wife. Such understanding is far removed from the Qurʾanic ethical decree which dictates manifesting the beauty and goodness of *iḥsān* in both marriage and with parents.

Abou El Fadl (2020) underscores the significance of the *iḥsān* command towards parents in 46:15. He argues that the preceding verse 46:13 unlocks the key to the entire sura and can be viewed as one of the most important verses in the entire Qurʾan.[34] Verse 46:13 states that *tawḥīd* and being on the 'straight path' (*istiqāma*) are the guarantees for earthly tranquillity and heavenly reward. The verses that follow explain what 'being on the straight path' entails and lists *iḥsān* towards parents as the first requirement. Accord-

[34] Verse 46:13: 'For those who say, "Our lord is God", and then follow the straight path there is no fear, nor shall they grieve.'

ing to Abou El Fadl this sura alerts believers to the critical role the family dynamic plays in laying the foundation of *istiqāma* and to finding earthly tranquillity. In his view, the institution of marriage is integral for a society to have a strong foundation. He posits that without family a person never feels truly grounded, as if trying to stand on quicksand. He points to the mercy and love that flow throughout verse 46:15. It shows how the relationship entails gratitude, with the mother putting forth love and sacrifice only to be rewarded with the same in the later stage of life. In his interpretation, Abou El Fadl states that the operative mandate for a healthy society is to treat parents beautifully.

It is important to take a closer look at 46:15 to appreciate the nuances within. The fact that the mother is singled out reflects the Qurʾanic emphasis on highlighting the instrumental role she plays. This is particularly significant when addressing a patriarchal society that downplays women's roles. Although the verse points to the mother's strife in rearing children, it still calls upon manifesting *iḥsān* towards both parents. The verse highlights the difficulty of the early childhood years yet does not limit the parental role to the early years. It shows how by age forty the adult offspring is able to appreciate the incredible role the parents played, and should be ready to reciprocate. The verse thus presents the full life cycle and juxtaposes the strength and pain endured by parents when children are young with their vulnerability and dependency in old age. The use of the prefix 'with' (*biʾ*) in 'bil-walidayn iḥsānan' mandates that parents be treated with *iḥsān*. This sentence structure reveals a power dynamic, one in which the offspring is the dominant party in control and is asked to offer *iḥsān* to the weaker parents. Care for elderly parents is not easy; it can be associated with a sense of burden and distress. Studies do, however, show that it also carries the potential for psychological and relational rewards (Marks, Lambert and Choi, 2002, p. 657; Miller, 2008, p. 19). Again, we note how the Qurʾan highlights emotional wellness as it mandates *iḥsān* at a difficult time of vulnerability. This reinforces the importance of intentionality, of choosing to act in *iḥsān* when it is easy to do otherwise. The alternating roles each generation plays in this verse presents an ongoing cycle of nurture and care. A cycle of beauty and goodness that begins with couples and extends through their offspring; a cycle that positions family as the infrastructure of a healthy and kind society.

While *iḥsān* towards parents is the main subject of the verses addressed in this section thus far, verse 2:83 establishes *iḥsān* as the core value that guides general social relationships. Verse 2:83 builds the concentric circles of society by creating layers which start with family then, gradually, extend to the community at large:

> Remember when We took a pledge from the Children of Israel: 'Worship none but God; show ***iḥsān*** to your parents and kinsfolk, to ***masākīn*** (orphans and the vulnerable); speak ***ḥusnā*** to all people; keep up the prayer and pay the prescribed alms'. Then all but a few of you turned away and paid no heed. (verse 2:83)

In this verse God speaks in the first person, listing the rules of a divine covenant (*mīthāq*) between God and believers. Following the initial command of worshipping the one and only God (*tawḥīd*), the covenant mandates *iḥsān*. This mandate of beauty and goodness begins with one's closest kin, parents, and proceeds to build concentric circles that expand outwards to engulf society. With regards to parents, al-Ṭabarī (2009, 2:83) states that *iḥsān* should be understood as doing that which is commonly known to be good (*ma'rūf*), to speak to them in a beautiful (*jamīl*) manner, to show them mercy (*raḥma*) and to pray for all this is good (*khayr*) for them. As for al-Zamakhsharī (2001, 2:83), he suffices by sharing different derivatives of *ḥusn* without offering an interpretation. Al-Rāzī (2003, 2:83) states that *iḥsān* mandates offspring to be a source of benefit to the parents and to avoid causing them any harm. It is again interesting to note the way in which al-Ṭabarī illustrates *iḥsān* in the case of elderly parents as opposed to the case of spouses in a turbulent marriage. In dealing with parents, he presents the concepts of beauty, mercy and goodness, but none of these sentiments are expressed in his illustrations of *iḥsān* in the case of divorce. These strikingly different approaches to the same Qur'anic decree lie at the crux of the gendered ideology that prevents an egalitarian view of marriage, an ideology that sets marriage as a hierarchical relationship and limits the profound potential of *iḥsān* as an overarching moral command.

By linking the private to the public, the Qur'an expands the circle of *iḥsān* to encompass the community at large. The verse above builds a ripple effect that extends *iḥsān* to encompass further members of society to include relatives and extended family (*dhul-qurbā*), orphans (*yatāmā*), and all those who are vulnerable/weak/poor (*masākīn*) and lack empowering family support.[35]

---

[35] The Qur'an does not make gender distinctions in the mandate of extending *iḥsān* to *dhul-qurbā*, *yatāmā* and *masākīn*.

This is particularly pertinent in today's world in which family structures are shifting, and thereby creating a need for familial-like care beyond the traditional family model. In societies where the vulnerable are often ostracized and shunned, the ethics of the Qurʾan demand that the faithful recognize situations of vulnerability and extend an arm of support. The Qurʾan envisions family as a repository of beauty and goodness, through a mandate of *iḥsān*, which grows to enshrine society. Conversely, when the ugliness of injustice is propagated at the intimate levels of marriage and family, it ripples out to reproduce layers of injustice that impact the entire society. Gender inequality is the most prevalent form of imbalance in the world at large. Reflecting upon the egalitarian family ethics forwarded in the Qurʾan can be a step towards transformative justice that affects the whole society. The concentric circles of *iḥsān* begin with a covenant of belief in God and a commitment to enact *iḥsān* in each layer of interaction that ripples out to the next; a system that holds a potentiality to ground the entire community in beauty and goodness.[36]

After mandating *iḥsān* to the different layers of concentric circles, verse 2:83 then adds a further layer of beauty and goodness by calling upon those entering into the covenant with God to speak *ḥusnā* (that which is beautiful and good) to all people (*al-nās*). The Qurʾan underscores the great impact a language of *ḥusn* can have on all relationships among all people. Such emphasis on the speech, once again, highlights the importance of psychological and emotional wellness and draws reference to the Qurʾan describing itself as a speech of utmost *ḥusn* in 39:23. The order of the verse ties belief in God with the manifestation of *ḥusn* into the world. The verse then reinforces this sentiment by imploring believers to uphold prayer and give alms (zakat) in a manner that further fuses the physical with the spiritual, making them fuel one another. It tells believers that true intimacy with God is not possible without a conscientious effort to make the beauty and goodness of *iḥsān* the marker by which one acts and speaks to the world and to God.

---

[36] Nevin Reda (2017) argues that *Surat al-Baqara* presents a concentrated version of the entire message of the Qurʾan. The emphasis verse 2:83 places on the value of *ḥusn* can thus be viewed as a model for human interaction at all times.

3. *IḤSĀN* AS A QUR'ANIC MANDATE: IMPLICATIONS FOR REFORM

Many contemporary Muslim family laws are disconnected from the needs and lived realities of families. They sustain gender hierarchy and different forms of legal discrimination against women.[37] Such legal systems reinforce outdated patriarchal ideologies that may have served the needs of centuries past yet fall short today. Prevalent modern Muslim norms also sustain patriarchal ideologies that have been embedded in the Islamic legal tradition. To address these challenges, multidimensional reform efforts are needed. The findings of this study point to several key elements that can inform these efforts.

This study suggests that the Qur'an's ethical concepts are not random or secondary to the construction of its central message and worldview. In fact, I argue that the moral concepts are the infrastructure upon which the Qur'an rests in order to deliver its message of guidance (*huda*). Among these concepts is *iḥsān*. Despite the 194 occurrences of the root in the Qur'an, its meanings have barely received attention in Islamic sciences at the conceptual level.[38] The Qur'an presents *ḥusn* as intrinsic to creation, which makes the appreciation of aesthetic and moral beauty part of the human *fiṭra*; human beings are attracted to the harmony present in internal and external beauty. Unfairness and injustice are forms of dehumanization that contradict the intrinsic sense of balance and harmony embedded into creation and into humanity.[39] Justice is thus the basis upon which *iḥsān* is built. The Qur'an commands *ʿadl* and *iḥsān* and places *iḥsān* at the opposite end of corruption (*fasād*) and transgression. Consequently, *iḥsān* is built upon a priori of *ʿadl*. To drive this point further, the Qur'an commands *iḥsān* at times of vulnerability, where unequal power dynamics can facilitate exploitation and transgression. Justice is hence the starting point from which the Qur'an pushes the moral bar higher towards

---

[37] For an ethically oriented interpretation of divorce verses, see Abou-Bakr and Al-Sharmani (2020).

[38] Not all the occurrences of the root in the Qur'an relate to or impact gender relations.

[39] An intrinsic human predisposition towards justice is supported by studies in cognitive behaviour in which young children appear to possess an innate concept of fairness; other studies reveal that children may even have a predisposition to altruism (see Wang et al., 2019; Li et al., 2016). A study by Warneken and Tomasello (2009) states that from a young age 'children have a biological predisposition to help others achieve their goals, to share resources with others and to inform others of things helpfully'.

the profound value of *iḥsān* where one chooses to do, and say, what is more beautiful.

The command for *iḥsān* makes each believer responsible for manifesting *ḥusn* in both actions and in speech. Each believing individual carries a responsibility towards promoting beauty and goodness in their surroundings. Hence *iḥsān*, as a key Qurʾanic ethical concept, can guide every individual in social relations such as marriage, parent–child relationships, etc., to exercise moral agency and spiritual growth by enacting goodness and beauty. This goodness and beauty necessitate a base of justice (equality of all human beings) to build upon it towards compassion, graciousness and kindness. Since the family is the nucleus that emanates values to the world, manifesting *iḥsān* begins at this deepest level of human connections and radiates outward to society. Religious studies scholar-activist Juliane Hammer has studied domestic violence in Muslim families. Her research highlights the many complacent bystanders consisting of surrounding family and community members who do not take an active stand against the abuse of which they are aware. Hammer refers to these groups as 'communities of silence' and argues that their attitude empowers abusers (Hammer, 2019, p. 94). Realizing the importance of standing up against transgression is, therefore, a primary step in the path towards *iḥsān*. The act of *iḥsān* requires sincere diligence in the desire to uphold the Qurʾanic values despite the discomfort of the situation. The intentionality of *iḥsān* is important to note. To show *iḥsān* amid the difficulty of divorce, towards ailing older parents, and to extend it beyond family mandates a deliberate and conscious effort.

'Giving Voice to Values' is a pedagogical theory created by Mary Gentile (2010, p. xiii) to facilitate turning values from thought into action. Her approach emphasizes the power of choice an individual has in standing up for what they believe to be right. The process starts by questioning set assumptions and reflecting upon how they have been enabled by society. The next step is preparing a set of responses to commonly heard rationalizations of questionable practices. Equipped with this ammunition, one rehearses an implementation plan that voices the desired values. The most important step is taking action by speaking up. According to Gentile, speaking up helps build 'moral muscle memory'. As the mind learns to internalize these values, acting upon them becomes second nature.

If this model is applied to uphold *iḥsān* in family relations, the first step would be to recognize the embedded unfairness in existing gender relations and the discrepancy between the ethics of *iḥsān* in the Qurʾan and the lived realities of many Muslim families. Families should begin by noting the double standard by which sons and daughters are treated in many households. The home should become an environment where egalitarian gender ethics are addressed, not suppressed. Living the ethics of *iḥsān* mandates speaking up against injustice in a manner that is both beautiful and good, one that reflects true compassion and stems from a place of love.[40]

In short, reclaiming and enacting the ethics of *iḥsān* is part and parcel of reform that needs to happen at the level of Muslim individuals and families. This Qurʾanic *iḥsān*-based approach to relationships stands in juxtaposition to the fear-based discourse propagated by the overly competitive modern materialistic world.[41] The former prioritizes the value of 'giving' over the benefit of 'taking', it veers society away from the mindset of scarcity towards an ideology of abundance. In doing so, this *iḥsān*-based approach establishes the *mawadda* and *raḥma* relationship spectrum as a model for all types of relationships across all interactions.[42] The Qurʾan calls for countering evil with the beauty and goodness of *iḥsān*. Verse 41:34 instructs believers to push away what is evil by putting forth what is *aḥsan* (more beautiful and good). The verse states that acting in such a manner can turn an enemy into an intimate friend.[43] Thus practising the ethics of *iḥsān* contributes to the well-being of individuals, facilitates the pursuit of marriage as a partnership of equals that supports spiritual growth, and nurtures families and larger communities as well.

Foregrounding the ethics of *iḥsān* is also an integral part of adopting a new and much needed approach towards Muslim legal tradition. Mohsen Kadivar, an Islamic studies scholar, argues in his chapter in this volume that the skewed emphasis within this tradition on legalities, rather than ethics, does not corroborate with the Prophet's role of being sent to reclaim ethics (*akhlāq*).

[40] Social activist and scholar bell hooks (2001) argues that 'love' must be understood as a verb and not a noun in order to help the world become a better place. The ingredients for this love verb are care, affection, recognition, respect, commitment, trust, as well as honest and open communication.

[41] When the possession of goods becomes the marker of value in a society, it prompts a culture of scarcity because material goods are finite. This helps promote feelings of rivalry and competition (see Boitano de Moras, Dutra and Schockman, 2017).

[42] The *iḥsān*-based approach can have great ecological implications when applied to dealing with the environment.

[43] Verse 41:34: 'And not equal are the *ḥasanā* and the bad. Repel [evil] by that [deed] which is *aḥsan*; and thereupon the one whom between you and him is enmity [will become] as though he was a devoted friend.'

This skewed emphasis may have been a natural product of the political and social circumstances of the early period when scholars focused on solving legal dilemmas that were necessary to manage the emerging Islamic empire. With the genealogical nature of *tafsīr* where each work builds on the predecessor, the focus on legalities became a marker of the genre itself. Kadivar also notes that less than 1 per cent of the verses in the Qurʾan address legal rulings, therefore jurists had to rely on extra-Qurʾanic resources to derive their rulings (*aḥkām*). By default, the patriarchal values of the time were the lens through which this process was construed.

As these early works form an important part of the scholarly canon, much of today's Muslim family laws are grounded upon these patriarchal interpretations. However, limiting our understanding of Qurʾanic ethical concepts, and in this case *iḥsān*, to the early interpretations shackles their timeless potential. Attempting to solve today's problems by searching for answers in the past assumes that humanity has not evolved across the centuries, a view that does not corroborate with developments in human rights generally, and particularly in women's rights. Intellectual and moral stagnation presents a disservice to the rich Islamic intellectual tradition and stands in contradistinction to the repeated Qurʾanic calls for reflection, pondering and discernment. Honouring this opulent scholarly tradition mandates following the precedent of engaging the intellect and the conscience, not blindly copying age-old solutions. Today's answers must be derived from engaging with the Qurʾanic text through a serious study of its ethical concepts and worldview. It means tapping into the unexplored richness of the text and its relevance and significance for present-day Muslims. More specifically for the purpose of legal reform efforts, the findings of this study suggest rethinking the relationship between Qurʾanic ethical concepts and the rulings that exegetes and jurists derived centuries ago. It is critically important on several fronts to understand how Qurʾanic ethical concepts can inform law-making in robust but also dynamic and context-specific ways.

To conclude, internalizing *iḥsān* as an overarching Qurʾanic moral concept can lead to transformative change in Muslim communities and beyond. Concepts are the 'glue that holds our mental lives together' (Murphy, 2002, p. 1). By choosing which concepts to emphasize, a society creates its own discourse. This study posits that the Qurʾanic ethical concept of *iḥsān* is integral to the glue that holds the moral conscience intact. Manifesting *iḥsān* completes the cycle which begins by God endowing *ḥusn* into all creation, and continues with the believer manifesting *iḥsān* across the multiple layers of concentric circles, starting with spousal relations.[44] By enacting *iḥsān*, Muslim individuals, families and societies can establish an egalitarian discourse that privileges justice, beauty and goodness in social relations with all people. This cycle of reciprocal *iḥsān* goes full circle to ultimately bring beauty and goodness to the person who set it forth. Verse 55:60 confirms this virtuous cycle when it asks: Can the reward of *iḥsān* be anything but *iḥsān*?

REFERENCES

Abou-Bakr, Omaima. 2015. 'The Interpretive Legacy of *Qiwamah* as an Exegetical Construct'. *Men in Charge? Rethinking Authority in Muslim Legal Tradition*, edited by Ziba Mir-Hosseini, Mulki Al-Sharmani and Jana Rumminger, pp. 44–64. London: Oneworld.

Abou-Bakr, Omaima and Mulki Al-Sharmani. 2020. 'Islamic Feminist Tafsīr and Qur'anic Ethics: Rereading Divorce Verses'. *Islamic Interpretive Tradition and Gender Justice: Processes of Canonization, Subversion, and Change*, edited by Nevin Reda and Yasmin Amin, pp. 23–66. Montreal: McGill-Queen's University Press.

Abou El Fadl, Khaled. 2001. *Speaking in God's Name: Islamic Law, Authority and Women*. Oxford: Oneworld.

Abou El Fadl, Khaled. 2006. *The Search for Beauty in Islam: A Conference of the Books*. Lanham, MD: The Rowman & Littlefield Publishing Group.

Abou El Fadl, Khaled. 2014. *Reasoning with God: Reclaiming Shari'ah in the Modern Age*. Maryland, London: Rowman & Littlefield.

Abou El Fadl, Khaled. 2020. *'Al-Aḥqaf' Qur'anic Hermeneutics Lecture Series*, 12 Sept. www.youtube.com/watch?v=6NMLIjCRMOk

Ali, Kecia. 2006. *Sexual Ethics and Islam: Feminist Reflections on Qur'an, Hadith, and Jurisprudence*. Oxford: Oneworld.

Al-Attar, Mariam. 2017. 'Meta-Ethics: A Quest for an Epistemological Basis of Morality in Classical Islamic Thought'. *Journal of Islamic Ethics* 1 (1–2): pp. 29–50.

Avarguès-Weber, Aurore and Martin Giurfa. 2015. 'Conceptual Learning by Miniature Brains'. *The Conceptual Mind: New Directions in the Study of Concepts*, edited by Eric Margolis and Stephen Laurence, pp. 3–27. Cambridge, MA: The MIT Press.

Barlas, Asma. 2002. *Believing Women in Islam: Unreading Patriarchal Interpretations of the Qur'an*. Austin: University of Texas Press.

Boitano de Moras, Aldo, Raúl Lagomarsino Dutra and H. E. Schockman. 2017. *Breaking the Zero-Sum Game: Transforming Societies through Inclusive Leadership*. Bingley, UK: Emerald Publishing.

Burckhardt, Titus. 1987. *Mirror of the Intellect: Essays on Traditional Science and Sacred Art*. Albany: State University Press of New York.

Draz, Muhammad A. 2014. *Dustūr al-Akhlāq fī al-Qur'ān*. Cairo: Dar al-Qulum.

---

[44] The concept of reciprocity is referred to earlier in verse 28:77.

Erzen, Jale Nejdet. 2011. 'Reading Mosques: Meaning and Architecture in Islam'. *The Journal of Aesthetics and Art Criticism* 69 (1): pp. 125–31.

Fahm, Abdulgafar Olawale. 2020. '"Everything has Beauty but Not Everyone Sees It": An Islamic Alternative to Assessing Beauty'. *Journal of Intercultural Communication Research* 49 (3): pp. 211–26.

Fehr, Beverley, Lynn Underwood Gordon and Susan Sprecher. 2009. *The Science of Compassionate Love: Theory, Research, and Applications*. Malden, MA: Wiley-Blackwell.

Fletcher, Jennifer. 2015. 'Analyzing and Integrating Ethos, Pathos, and Logos'. Chapter 6 in *Teaching Arguments: Rhetorical Comprehension, Critique, and Response*. Portland: Stenhouse Publishers.

Gaafar, Yahia. 2013. Television Interview (in Arabic). Cairo, Egypt: *CBC Broadcast*. 16 August.

Gentile, Mary. 2010. *Giving Voice to Values: How to Speak Your Mind when You Know What's Right*. New Haven: Yale University Press.

Al-Ghazālī, Abū Hamid. 1998. *Ihyā' 'Ulūm al-Dīn*. Cairo: Maktabat Masr.

Gu, Jenny, Kate Cavanagh, Ruth Baer and Clara Strauss. 2017. 'An Empirical Examination of the Factor Structure of Compassion'. *PLoS One* 12 (2): pp. 1–17.

Al-Ḥamalāwi, Ahmed b. Muhammed b. Ahmed. 1999. *Shadha al-'Urf fi Fann al-Sarf*, edited by Taha Abdel Raouf Sa'd and Sa'd Hassan 'Ali. Cairo: Al-Safa Publishing.

Hammer, Juliane. 2019. *Peaceful Families: American Muslim Efforts Against Domestic Violence*. Princeton University Press.

Harvey, Ramon. 2018. *The Qur'an and the Just Society*. Edinburgh: Edinburgh University Press.

hooks, bell. 2001. *All about Love: New Visions*. 1st edn. New York: Perennial.

Ibn Manẓūr. 2005. *Lisān al-'Arab*. Beirut: Dar Sadir.

Isaacs, David. 2015. 'Parental Love'. *Journal of Paediatrics and Child Health* 51 (3): pp. 241–2.

Izutsu, Toshihiko. 2002. *Ethico-Religious Concepts in the Qur'ān*. Montreal; Ithaca, NY: McGill-Queen's University Press.

Jacobsen, Thomas, Ricarda I. Schubotz, Lea Höfel and D. Yves v. Cramon. 2006. 'Brain Correlates of Aesthetic Judgment of Beauty'. *NeuroImage* 29 (1): pp. 276–85.

Kadivar, Mohsen. 2020. 'Rethinking *Fiqh* Rulings on Marriage through Structural *Ijtihad*'. Musawah Series of Knowledge Building Webinars: Reclaiming *'Adl* and *Ihsan* in Muslim Marriages: Between Ethics and Law. 11 August.

Kahteran, Nevad. 2006. '*Fitra*'. In *The Qur'an: An Encyclopedia*, edited by Oliver Leaman, pp. 210–13. London: Routledge.

Kermani, Navid. 2014. *God is Beautiful: The Aesthetic Experience of the Qur'an*. Malden, MA: Polity Press.

Keshani, Hussein. 2008. 'Art and Architecture'. In *The Islamic World*, edited by Andrew Rippin. London; New York: Routledge.

Khan, Muqtedar. 2019. *Islam and Good Governance: A Political Philosophy of Iḥsān*. Newark: Palgrave.

Al-Khaṭīb, Mutaz. 2017. '*Āyāt al-Akhlāq: Su'āl al-Akhlāq 'inda al-Mufassirīn*' ('Verses on Ethics: The Question of Ethics Among the Qur'an Exegetes'). *Journal of Islamic Ethics* 1 (1–2): pp. 83–121.

Al-Khaṭīb, Mutaz. 2019. 'Methodology of Approaching the Qur'an'. Istanbul, Turkey: Lecture at Fajr Academy. www.youtube.com/watch?v=zjmMKtXussw

Lane, Edward. 1863. *Arabic-English Lexicon*. London: Williams & Norgate.

Li, Jing, Wen Wang, Jing Yu and Liqi Zhu. 2016. 'Young Children's Development of Fairness Preference'. *Frontiers in Psychology* 7, art. 1274.

Marks, Nadine F., James David Lambert and Heejeong Choi. 2002. 'Transitions to Caregiving, Gender, and Psychological Well-Being: A Prospective U.S. National Study'. *Journal of Marriage and Family* 64 (3): pp. 657–67.

Martínez-Martí, María Luisa, María José Hernández-Lloreda, María Dolores Avia. 2016. 'Appreciation of Beauty and Excellence: Relationship with Personality, Prosociality and Well-Being'. *Journal of Happiness Studies* 17 (6): pp. 2613–34.

Ma'Ṣūmī, M. Ṣaghīr Ḥasan. 1967. 'Imam Fakhr Al-Din Al-Razī and His Critics'. *Islamic Studies* 6 (4): pp. 355–74.

Miller, Katherine I., Martha M. Shoemaker, Jennifer Willyard and Penny Addison. 2008. 'Providing Care for Elderly Parents: A Structurational Approach to Family Caregiver Identity'. *Journal of Family Communication* 8 (1): pp. 19–43.

Mir-Hosseini, Ziba, Kari Vogt, Lena Larsen and Christian Moe (eds). 2013. *Gender and Equality in Muslim Family Law: Justice and Ethics in the Islamic Legal Tradition*. London: I.B. Tauris.

Moosa, Ebrahim. 2020. 'Qur'anic Ethics'. *The Oxford Handbook of Qur'anic Studies*, edited by Muhammad Abdel Haleem and Mustafa Shah. Oxford: Oxford University Press.

Murata, Sachiko and William C. Chittick. 1994. *The Vision of Islam*. New York: Paragon House.

Murphy, Gregory L. 2002. *The Big Book of Concepts*. Cambridge, MA: MIT Press.

Al-Nawawī, Abū Zakariyyah Yaḥyā ibn Sharaf. n.d. *Imam Nawawī's Forty Hadith*.

Pink, Johanna. 2018. *Muslim Qur'anic Interpretation Today: Media, Genealogies and Interpretive Communities*. Bristol, CT: Equinox Publishing Ltd.

Plank, Liz. 2019. 'Why the Patriarchy is Killing Men'. *The Washington Post*, 13 September.

Rahman, Fazlur. 1980. *Major Themes of the Qur'an*. Minneapolis, MN: Bibliotheca Islamica.

Rahman, Fazlur. 1999. *Revival and Reform in Islam*. Oxford: Oneworld.

Al-Rāzī, Muhammad ibn 'Umar Fakhr al-Dīn. 2003. *Al-Tafsīr al-Kabīr/Mafatīḥ al-Ghayb*, edited by Emad Zaki Al-Baroudi. Cairo: Al-Maktaba al-Tawfikia.

Reda, Nevin. 2017. *The al-Baqara Crescendo: Understanding the Qur'an's Style, Narrative Structure, and Running Themes*. Montreal: McGill-Queen's University Press.

Reda, Nevin and Yasmin Amin (eds). 2020. *Islamic Interpretive Tradition and Gender Justice: Processes of Canonization, Subversion, and Change*. Montreal: McGill-Queen's University Press.

Reinhart, A. Kevin. 2002. 'Ethics and the Qur'ān'. In *Encyclopaedia of the Qur'ān*, edited by Jane Dammen McAuliffe, vol. 2, pp. 55–79. Leiden and Boston: Brill.

Scarry, Elaine. 2013. *On Beauty and Being Just*. Princeton University Press.

Schröder-Butterfill, Elisabeth and Ruly Marianti. 2006. 'A Framework for Understanding Old-Age Vulnerabilities'. *Aging and Society* 26 (1): pp. 9–35.

Selhub, Eva M. and Divina Infusino. 2009. *The Love Response: Your Prescription to Turn Off Fear, Anger, and Anxiety to Achieve Vibrant Health and Transform Your Life*. New York: Ballantine Books.

Sharafeldin, Marwa. 2020. '*Korona Tunādī bil al-Sahl al-Mumtani': Islāh Qawwanīn al-Usra fī al-'ālam al-'Arabī*' ('COVID-19 and the Need to Reform Discriminatory Family Laws in the MENA Region'). *Al-Shorouk*. 16 May.

Al-Sharmani, Mulki. 2017. *Gender Justice and Legal Reform in Egypt: Negotiating Muslim Family Law*. Cairo: The American University in Cairo Press.

Shinohara, Kazuyuki. 2011. 'Neural Correlates of Maternal Love, Paternal Love and Children's Love for their Parents'. *Neuroscience Research* 71, p. e12.

Al-Ṭabarī, Abu Jaʿfar Muḥammad ibn Jarīr. 2009. *Tafsīr al-Ṭabarī: Jāmiʿ al-Bayān ʿan Taʾwīl al-Qurʾān*, edited by Abd al-Hamid Madkour. 4th edn. Cairo: Dal al-Salam.

Taha, Muhammad. 2021. *Dhakr Sharqī Munqariḍ* (*Extinct Oriental Male*). Cairo: Al-Shorouk Publishing.

Tucker, Judith E. 2008. *Women, Family, and Gender in Islamic Law*. Cambridge, UK: Cambridge University Press.

Ullah, Kifayat. 2015. 'Al-Zamakhsharī'. In *Encyclopaedia of the Qurʾān*, edited by Jane Dammen McAuliffe. Online version. Georgetown University, Washington DC.

Wadud, Amina. 1999. *Qurʾan and Woman: Rereading the Text from a Woman's Perspective*. Oxford: Oxford University Press.

Wadud, Amina. 2006. *Inside the Gender Jihad: Women's Reform in Islam*. Oxford: Oneworld.

Wang, Yun, Dang Zheng, Jie Chen, Li-Lin Rao, Shu Li, Yuan Zhou. 2019. 'Born for Fairness: Evidence of Genetic Contribution to a Neural Basis of Fairness Intuition'. *Social Cognitive and Affective Neuroscience* 14 (5): pp. 539–48.

Warneken, Felix and Michael Tomasello. 2009. 'Varieties of Altruism in Children and Chimpanzees'. *Trends in Cognitive Sciences* 13 (9): pp. 397–402.

Wehr, Hans. 1994. *A Dictionary of Modern Written Arabic*, edited by J. Milton Cowan. 4th edn.

Welchman, Lynn. 2007. *Women and Muslim Family Laws in Arab States: A Comparative Overview of Textual Development and Advocacy*. Amsterdam: Amsterdam University Press.

Al-Zamakhsharī, Maḥmūd ibn ʿUmar. 2001. *Al-Kashshāf ʿan Ḥaqāʾiq Ghawāmid al-Tanzīl wa-ʿUyūn Al-Aqāwīl fī Wujūh al-Taʾwīl*. Beirut: Dār Ehia al-Tourāth al-ʿArābi.

LESSONS FROM THE PROPHET

Reclaiming Khadīja and Muhammad's Marriage as an Islamic Paradigm: Towards a New History of the Muslim Present

Shadaab Rahemtulla and Sara Ababneh

In this chapter, we examine the marriage of Prophet Muhammad and Khadīja bint Khuwaylid (d. circa 619 CE) to question hegemonic narratives on 'ideal' Muslim marriages.[1] These narratives portray Muhammad's marital life as relationships of power disparity (however compassionate and loving) with the Prophet marrying not only multiple wives, but also spouses who were significantly younger in age. Such portrayals have not been plucked out of the air; there is much truth to them. Over the course of his life, Muhammad had a total of thirteen wives and concubines, all of whom, with the exception of Khadīja, were junior to him (Stowasser, 2006). Perhaps the most (in)famous example is ʿĀʾisha bint Abū Bakr who, in one hadith report, stated that she was six years old when she was married to the Prophet, nine when the marriage was consummated.[2] To be sure, these marriages were not merely expressions of desire, but also about strengthening socio-political ties within the emergent Muslim polity: ʿĀʾisha, after all, was the daughter of the Companion Abū Bakr, Ḥafṣa the daughter of the Companion ʿUmar ibn al-Khattāb, and Umm Ḥabība the daughter of Abū Sufyān (Stowasser, 1994,

[1] An earlier version of this chapter was published in the *Journal of Feminist Studies in Religion* 37 (2) (Fall 2021), pp. 83–102. We are grateful to the journal editors for giving us permission to reprint it.

[2] Muhammad Ibn Saʿd, as cited in Spellberg (1994, p. 39).

p. 123), an enemy-turned-ally following the Conquest of Mecca (629–30). Given the centrality of the Sunna (prophetic precedence) in Islamic normative practice, the Prophet's marriages have indelibly shaped Muslim understandings of what constitute ideal marriages. Yet Muhammad also had a monogamous, twenty-five-year-long relationship with Khadīja, whose example paints a very different picture of Muhammadi marriage.

In this chapter, we ask what a Sunna based on this type of marriage would look like. Early biographical sources show that Khadīja was a powerful, respected businesswoman who had been in two previous marriages; that she was fifteen years senior to the Prophet (at the time of their marriage, she was forty years old and Muhammad twenty-five); and that she was Muhammad's employer, dispatching him to lead her trade caravan to Syria. The harmonious nature of their marriage is supported by the fact that, long after her death, we have hadith reports of Muhammad praising Khadīja's character, her conviction in his prophetic mission, and her unwavering support for the Muslim community. We even have a cluster of hadith reports in which ʿĀʾisha, often celebrated by (Sunni) Muslims as Muhammad's favourite wife, expresses her deep-seated jealousy of Khadīja. To quote ʿĀʾisha's own words: 'Never did I feel jealous of any woman as I was jealous of Khadīja'.[3]

But this chapter is not just about Khadīja; it is equally about Prophet Muhammad. Because gender is a *relational* category, Khadīja and Muhammad, as marital partners, necessarily act as foils of one another: to write about the former is, simultaneously, to make statements about the latter, and vice versa. By unearthing Khadīja's articulate and intelligent personality, we are trying, at the same time, to offer wider observations about Muhammad's *masculinity*: namely, that he was remarkably comfortable and secure within this (at least in terms of our current twenty-first-century sensibilities) non-hegemonic marital arrangement. At no point in their twenty-five-year relationship did he seem to feel threatened as a man. On the contrary, it appears that his manhood – our usage of the lowercase 'm' is more than just grammatical – bloomed over the course of their lives together. For twenty-first-century standards, the non-hegemonic character of this Muhammadi masculinity is the underlying theme that runs throughout the chapter, and a theme, we argue, that needs to be accented in liberationist engagements with the Sunna in order to reconceptualize Islamic marriage, in our own times, as an egalitarian partnership of equals.

[3] This hadith can be found in *Ṣaḥīḥ Muslim*, 1976, vol. 4, no. 5971; see also nos. 5972; 5973; 5974 and 5976.

This chapter first sets the stage for discussion by clarifying our methodology and unpacking our underlying conceptual framework. We then unpack two 'snapshots' of Khadīja's life: her marriage to the Prophet and her presence during the first Qur'anic revelations. Here, we draw on a number of *sīra* (biographical) sources, including Muḥammad ibn Isḥāq's (d. 767) biography of Muhammad, considered the first authoritative work on the Prophet's life; Muhammad ibn Sa'd's (d. 845) biographical dictionary of early Muslim women; Abu Ja'far al-Ṭabarī's (d. 923) historical compendium; and Isma'il ibn Kathīr's (d. 1373) biography of Muhammad. We conclude by clarifying the broader contribution of the chapter.

A HISTORY OF THE PRESENT

Let us first clarify our methodology. Drawing on the French post-structural philosopher Michel Foucault (1926–84), we are trying to write a (new) history of the present. Essentially, this method entails 'using history as a means of critical engagement with the present' (Garland, 2014, p. 367). A history of the present is based on a key premise: that history is an act of the present. Historical narratives often tell us more about *current* power relations than those of the past, functioning to justify a certain contemporary way of life and to legitimate certain practices. In doing so, post-Enlightenment histories present linear trajectories between current states, practices or social structures and those in the past. The most infamous examples are (western) world history narratives that go back to the Greeks and Romans. In terms of gender relations, choosing the Greeks and Romans as starting points paints a picture of patriarchy as being the normal, indeed natural, state of affairs. Similarly, realist International Relations theories draw on the Peloponnesian war (431–404 BCE) in order to justify a world order in which only the strongest survives (see Thucydides, 1972, including the introduction and notes by Finley). A critical part of history-writing is that certain historical moments/narratives are silenced and rendered invisible. The histories of matriarchal societies are left out of patriarchal world history narratives. Likewise, global orders in which nations and city-states lived peacefully together, and without imperial notions of expansion, are omitted in realist theories of the state.

Because our current reality is markedly unequal, shaped by hierarchical social relations and competing forces of power, certain discourses and practices (namely, those of the dominant social group) have become hegemonic, taking on an aura of neutrality. It is precisely this innocence that a history of the present seeks to deconstruct. Thus, the present reality is exposed as being not a natural order, let alone a divinely ordained one, but a social construction. By documenting the (often violent and coercive) historical trajectories of these discourses and practices – an act of archaeological recovery that Foucault calls 'genealogy' – a history of the present reveals the 'contingency' (Fuggle, Lanci and Tazzioli, 2016, p. 3) of these phenomena, and thus the contingency of the present as a whole. To quote Foucault, a history of the present 'disturbs what was previously thought immobile; it fragments what was thought unified; it shows the heterogeneity of what was imagined consistent with itself'.[4] It is important to point out that this is no mere academic exercise. By deconstructing the present vis-à-vis the past, the larger objective is to engage in 'transformative politics' (Fuggle, Lanci and Tazzioli, 2016, p. 3), to imagine the possibilities of reconstructing radically new presents which actually value alterity and difference. History, then, is a contested discursive site: while certain histories legitimize certain presents, other histories (of the present) question those hegemonic narratives, point to and excavate silences and, in so doing, unsettle the present social orders of inequality.

This raises a question in the Muslim context: what is our present? We argue that, in terms of gender relations, our present is marked by a glaring contradiction. On the one hand, Islamic marital paradigms – which we have inherited through historical narratives of the past – are deeply patriarchal; yet, on the other hand, our lived realities as Muslim couples and/or parents have drastically shifted. Irrespective of what Muslim patriarchs may claim in the public sphere regarding the 'proper' role of men as heads of the household, in practice men are no longer 'in charge' of their families as maintainers: today, women are also active in the workforce as co-providers, principal providers and even sole providers, such as the case of single working mothers. *This* is our present. Take the authors' own marital context: we are an academic couple, having met, now many moons ago, as doctoral students at Oxford. Having the same educational level naturally shaped the nature of our conversations, of how we related to each other: we engaged each other not simply as lovers, but also as colleagues, as thinkers and as activists committed to social justice and anti-colonial politics. In fact, it was this critical, intellectual connection that made us fall in love in the first place. In terms of age, Sara is three and

[4] Michel Foucault, as quoted in Garland (2014, p. 372). For the original quotation, see Rabinow (1984, p. 82).

a half years older than Shadaab: she was actually finishing her PhD when Shadaab began his. As a result, she also started her career earlier, working while Shadaab was doing his PhD. When we married, Shadaab, who is a Canadian Muslim of Indian descent, moved to Sara's country (Jordan) for nine years. So, our marriage was not patrilocal but a *matri*local one, in which the husband moves to the wife's home/country. Being a working couple also meant that when we had children, we divided childcare equally between us, thereby striving towards an egalitarian division of labour within the home. *This* is our present.

Our context is not exceptional; it is increasingly becoming a new norm. There is a manifest disjuncture between entrenched Muslim discourses of (hegemonic) masculinity and the fluid distribution of gender roles that have actually been unfolding on the ground, ones in which women are increasingly co-/bearing the burden of financial maintenance, among other roles, and yet without reaping, as a collective group, the social benefits of doing so.[5] And what we need to do now is to *recalibrate* our inherited, historical corpus of Islamic knowledge, and marital paradigms in particular, to reflect this new social reality. Silencing certain social realities is directly linked to silences in Islamic historical narratives. Said differently, accenting certain prophetic marital practices make current practices seem un/Islamic. By unearthing the example of Khadīja and her relationship to the Prophet, we want to re-examine a relationship, which despite not being silenced, has been strikingly absent when constructing normative narratives and histories of Islamic marriage. This is the history of the Muslim present which we seek to write.

A point of clarification is in order. In writing a new history of the Muslim present, we are not interested in apologetics, in superimposing our own modern subjectivities on to a premodern past. A history of the present should not be confused with 'presentism' – or, in lay terms, bad history-writing – which falls into the anachronistic trap of 'reading present-day social arrangements or cultural meanings back into history or claiming to discover phenomena in earlier times with the same significance and character they have today' (Garland, 2014, p. 367). Foucault himself sharply criticized historians who used contemporary terms and concepts to understand earlier societies (Roth, 1981, p. 36). In the context of this chapter, we want to clarify that we

[5] See Musawah (2016) for an overview of a qualitative social research project that documents the life stories of fifty-five Muslim women from nine countries between 2011 and 2013, teasing out the striking disparities between lived realities and 'Islamic' ideals.

are not trying to 'discover' egalitarianism – a manifestly modern notion – in the pre-modern Muslim past and thereby justifying egalitarianism in our own times. As feminists, we do not need to justify equality between women and men; as critical students of history, we are not claiming that Muhammad and Khadīja's relationship was egalitarian. It was not. As this chapter will demonstrate, Khadīja was, unequivocally, the more powerful partner in this vertical relationship and Muhammad was dependent on her in many ways. What we have in their example is a non-patriarchal, indeed acutely matriarchal, relation of power. And in writing a history of our present, we believe this remarkable (and admittedly unrepresentative) historical moment provides us with a critical prophetic resource, an alternative and yet authoritative archive – this is a marriage, after all, that lasted twenty-five years – with which to begin the project of reconstructing Muslim marriage, in our own times, as an egalitarian partnership of equals. Ours is a political intervention; we make no claim to objectivity. In sum, drawing on the marriage of Khadīja and Muhammad, we seek to reconstruct a different history of present Muslim marriages.

MASCULINITIES

Before examining this relationship in detail, let us unpack our conceptual framework: 'masculinities analysis'. Masculinity can be understood as what it means to be a man at a certain time and place. Masculinity is not a biological fact but, like femininity, is socially constructed. Just as the French feminist Simone de Beauvoir (d. 1986) famously stated that 'one is not born, but rather becomes, a woman' (de Beauvoir, 1989,[6] p. 267), so too is manhood a becoming, a product of socialization. Underlining the sheer diversity of men's experiences is key to masculinities studies. For 'gender does not confer privilege on *all* men', as categories like race and class intersect with masculinity in complex ways to create entrenched hierarchies among men (Dowd, 2010, p. 418, emphasis ours). Indeed, in contexts of war, violence is disproportionately inflicted on men's bodies (Dowd, 2010, p. 421), in particular the bodies of poor, young men who are sent off to die at the front. This is not to water down the sexist reality of patriarchy, to suggest that men do not collectively benefit, as a social group, at the expense of women. They certainly do. But the point is that there are critical gendered hierarchies *within* male circles: namely, there

[6] This book was originally published in 1949.

are 'hegemonic' masculinities, which represent a normative ideal of power, strength and control (despite being a minority, if not exceptional, experience), and 'subordinated' masculinities, which fall short of that constructed ideal (Connell and Messerschmidt, 2005, p. 832).

Drawing on the Italian Marxist Antonio Gramsci (d. 1937), we distinguish between 'hegemony' and 'direct domination'. Whereas direct domination entails violence and force, hegemony represents the successful mainstreaming of the worldview (the ideas, assumptions and lived experiences) of the ruling class within society as a whole. By buying into this worldview, by erroneously associating the ruling class' interests with their own interests, the working class gives their consent to the existing status quo.[7] Connecting this insight to gender, hegemonic masculinity is the ideal type of masculinity which is respected by society and which most men aspire to reach, but few actually do. Those who are regarded as hegemonic men benefit the most from the system. Furthermore, while hegemonic masculinities can, and often do, consolidate their privileged position by inflicting acts of brute violence on to subordinated masculinities (take, for instance, gang rape in a men's prison), what makes hegemonic masculinities hegemonic – as opposed to an act of direct domination – is that they have attained mass 'cultural consent' as the way of being a *real* man, even among men with subordinated masculinities (Connell and Messerschmidt, 2005, p. 846). It is important to clarify here that when we speak about hegemonic masculinity, we are describing the particular hegemonic masculinity of today, of our own times. Hegemonic masculinity also varies across space, but through a globalized empire of media and Hollywood movies we can nonetheless speak of a global hegemonic masculinity. A big part of this chapter is to point out the differences between our own understanding of masculinity and that of the time and space of the Prophet. Masculinity is not a frozen, timeless category, and just as masculinity changes with context, so too do constructions of the hegemonic, and by extension, the subordinate.

While most scholarship in the field of masculinities analysis tends to be descriptive, ethnographically documenting the lived experiences of men and teasing out the complexities and contradictions of malehood, (re)construction is also an integral part of the field: that is, conceptualizing and enacting a *feminist* masculinity. The place of masculinity has been contested within feminist circles, with some feminists arguing that masculinity is inherently patriarchal and thus ought to be categorically resisted, while others maintain

[7] For a useful though admittedly dated survey of Gramsci's theory, see Bates (1975).

that masculinity can, in fact, be reclaimed (Almassi, 2015). For the latter, then, masculinity is not essentially oppressive but a social practice that is shaped and thus can be reshaped. African American feminists have been particularly critical of 'woman-only' discourses within feminist circles (hooks, 2014, p. 68). bell hooks argues that simply dismissing men and masculinity outright reflects the privileged racial and class baggage of White feminists, who failed to see that

> patriarchy does not negate the existence of class and race privilege or exploitation, that all men do not benefit equally from sexism. They [White feminists] did not want to acknowledge that bourgeois white women, though often victimized by sexism, have more power and privilege, are less likely to be exploited, or oppressed, than poor, uneducated, non-white males. (2014, p. 69)

That being said, it is important to clarify that reconstructing a feminist masculinity is not simply about reclaiming a *subordinated* masculinity. The two are not necessarily the same. Going back to the concept of hegemony (as opposed to direct domination), subordinated masculinities can, and often do, still buy into the legitimacy and normative character of hegemonic masculinity, and thus can continue to benefit from patriarchy as a system. This type of subordinated masculinity is what the gender scholars R.W. Connell and James Messerschmidt call a 'complicit masculinity' (2005, p. 832). Instead, a feminist masculinity has a two-fold objective: to challenge the existing patriarchal construction of normative (read: hegemonic) masculinity and, in its place, to envisage alternative normative constructions which are committed to feminist values of gender equality and inclusion (Almassi, 2015). Men, therefore, have an important role to play in feminist struggles. Indeed, their active involvement is key to mainstreaming the struggle. However, men's role must be that of a genuine ally. In standing in solidarity with women, feminist men need to remain acutely aware of their own privileged, collective status as men (notwithstanding their own individual commitments to women's liberation), and channel their energies into confronting the sexism of fellow *men* (hooks, 2014, p. 83),[8] as opposed to speaking for women and their experiences.

---

[8] The Islamic scholar amina wadud has a similar position on progressive men's role in anti-patriarchal struggle. See Rahemtulla (2018, pp. 134–7).

Religion (or, rather, specific interpretations of religion) has been fundamental to propping up patriarchal masculinity. To quote the Islamic masculinities scholar Amanullah De Sondy (2011, p. 529):

> 'Be a man' might be a powerful general expression for the development of a young boy, but when one adds 'because this is the way that Allah wants you to be,' it becomes a particular way of creating a center point of gender and sexuality.

But religion can also become a powerful tool in its dismantlement, reformulating masculinity into an egalitarian practice. This is the wider objective that drives De Sondy's scholarship.[9] In terms of Qur'anic theology, he has argued that God is viewed as an 'overarching creating/maintaining force' that reduces all of creation – men and women – to equal submission, and this has lasting implications in terms of how gender roles are construed (2011, p. 530). To associate any segment of that creation (read: men) with the One God, as having a unique affinity to Him/Her/It, constitutes a form of idolatry (De Sondy, 2011, p. 530). De Sondy is especially interested in constructions of prophetic masculinities. And this is the larger contribution of our own chapter: to unearth the non-hegemonic character of the Prophet's first marriage to Khadīja, which lasted twenty-five years. The relationship between Khadīja and the Prophet, read against the grain of current understandings of masculinity and what it needs to entail, points us to very different forms of *Islamic* masculinities. It is this marriage that we turn to in the next section.

SNAPSHOT 1: MATRIMONY

In the biographical literature, we are basically given two 'snapshots' of Khadīja's life: 1) her marriage to Muhammad and 2) her presence during the first

---

[9] See, for example, De Sondy (2011; 2014). Note that Islamic masculinities, as a subject, remains acutely understudied. As the Moroccan scholar Lahoucine Ouzgane – a pioneering figure in the field – points out, scholarly attention on gender in the Middle East and North Africa has focused overwhelmingly on femininity and constructions of womanhood, failing to 'render Muslim men visible as gendered subjects' (Ouzgane, 2006, p. 1). See also Ouzgane (2011). As Ouzgane notes, the scholarship that does exist on masculinities studies has centred on questions of sexuality, in particular homosexuality in Islamic thought and homoerotic practices in Muslim social history. For the former, see Kugle (2010); for the latter, see El-Rouayheb (2009).

Qur'anic revelations. We actually have very little information about Khadīja (Razwy, 1990, p. 1; Stowasser, 1994, p. 185, fn 52). There is a silence in the early sources. We know that she was a successful and respected businesswoman, hiring men to trade her goods outside Mecca (Ibn Isḥāq, 1967, p. 82). According to one report found in Ibn Sa'd's biographical dictionary, Khadīja's 'caravan was equal to the general caravan of the [tribe of] Quraysh' (1995, p. 10, addition ours). As to how exactly she acquired such wealth, contemporary scholars have suggested that she inherited the commercial business from her father Khuwaylid ibn Asad and then, using her own entrepreneurial skills, expanded the business significantly (Ali, 2008; Razwy, 1990, pp. 6–8). Furthermore, it seems that Khadīja had been in two marriages prior to meeting the Prophet. Her first marriage was to Abu Hala ibn al-Nabbash of the tribe of Tamim, and together they had two sons: Hind and Hāla. Her second marriage was to 'Atiq ibn 'Abid of the tribe of Makhzūm, and with him she had a girl, also named Hind (Ibn Sa'd, 1995, p. 9). It is likely that the first marriage ended in divorce, while in the second marriage 'Atiq died, leaving Khadīja a widow (Watt, 2012). It is telling that, in the biographical sources, there is no stigma attached to the fact that Khadīja was a (widowed) divorcee, with children. Indeed, her *kunya* (title) throughout her life remained Umm Hind – the 'mother of Hind' – whom she bore with her first husband (Ibn Sa'd, 1995, p. 12). And it is important to add here that, among the Prophet's wives, Khadīja's marital background was not, by any means, exceptional. 'Ā'isha once boasted that she was the only virgin married to the Prophet (Spellberg, 1994, p. 39). This suggests that the rest of the Prophet's wives had had sexual relations with prior husbands (and in the case of Umm Salama and Umm Ḥabība, also had children with them) (Lings, 1983, p. 296), and this did not seem to have been a problem, a source of stigma, for the Prophet or the early Muslims. On the contrary, this was the norm; it was 'Ā'isha's virginity that was the exception.

The first snapshot that we have is of Khadīja's marriage to the Prophet. The two met through her business ventures. She had heard about Muhammad's honest character, and hired him to travel to Syria and trade her goods there. According to Ibn Isḥāq, this was a lucrative hiring decision, with Khadīja doubling her profits (1967, p. 82). Impressed by Muhammad's personality, Khadīja approached him and proposed marriage. In other words, not only was Khadīja Muhammad's employer and he her employee but, in the initiation of their marital relationship, Khadīja was the active player. She approached Muhammad; Muhammad did not approach her. The biographical sources even offer the wording of her proposal. To quote Ibn Isḥāq: 'O son of my uncle.[10] I like you because of our relationship and your high reputation among your people, your trustworthiness and good character and truthfulness' (1967, p. 82). Al-Ṭabārī adds that 'all the men of her tribe would have been eager to accept this proposal had it been made to them' (1988, p. 48).[11] Alongside underlining the respect that Khadīja commanded within Meccan circles, this statement suggests that, for classical scholars like al-Ṭabarī, there was nothing strange about the fact that a woman was the one proposing. Had it seemed odd, the biographers would certainly have commented on it. To be sure, Khadīja's proposal may not have been delivered directly. In Ibn Saʿd's account, Khadīja does not approach Muhammad herself but rather dispatches her close female friend Nafisa to propose on her behalf (Ibn Saʿd, 1995, p. 10). Moreover, following Khadīja's initial proposal, the Prophet's uncles approached Khadīja's father (or possibly her uncle), seeking her hand in marriage (Ibn Isḥāq, 1967, p. 83).[12] So while we have much to learn from Khadīja's initiation of the marriage, we still need to appreciate the wider patriarchal context in which she lived, and in which the formalities of her marriage were orchestrated.

In addition to being the initiator of the marriage, Khadīja was, and remained, the economic foundation of that union. Note that they had a *matri*-local relationship, not a patri-local one: that is, Muhammad moved into Khadīja's house and not vice versa (Lings, 1983, p. 37). This stands in sharp contrast to contemporary practices in Muslim societies (or, for that matter, in non-Muslim societies) in which patri-local marriage has become something of an unquestioned, hegemonic norm. Indeed, living inside the house provided and owned by the husband is often a basic foundation of *ṭāʿa* (a wife's 'obedience' to the husband) in the family laws of many Muslim-majority countries. Khadīja's wealth aside, it is essential to appreciate the economic difficulties and vulnerabilities which constantly plagued the Prophet's early life. In seventh-century Arabia, one had to be an adult, a mature person, in order to inherit, and because Muhammad's father (ʿAbdullah) and grandfather (ʿAbdul

---

[10] 'Son of my uncle' (*ibn ʿami*) is a term that refers to the husband, since the husband's father becomes, in a deferential manner, the uncle of the wife upon marriage.

[11] Al-Ṭabarī (1988, p. 48) also provides the wording of Khadīja's proposal, albeit slightly differently from Ibn Isḥāq: 'Cousin, your kinship to me, your standing among your people, your reliability, your character, and your truthfulness make you a good match.'

[12] Al-Ṭabarī (1988, p. 50) provides two reports: one in which the Prophet's uncles approach Khadīja's father Khuwaylid (which lines up with Ibn Isḥāq's account) and one in which they approach her uncle ʿAmr, the latter report claiming that Khuwaylid had already passed away.

Muṭalib) both died before he attained maturity, Muhammad did not inherit from either of them (Watt and McDonald, 1988, p. xxxi). As a result, financial want was a recurring demon in his life. In light of this reality, Qur'anic commentators have suggested that Muhammad's marriage to Khadīja, and the significant economic changes that it brought about for him, is alluded to in the Qur'an itself, specifically in verse 93:8 (Stowasser, 2003). The entire chapter – the Chapter of the Morning Brightness (*Surat al-Duḥā*) – reads:

> (1) By the morning brightness, (2) by the night when it is calm! (3) Your Lord has neither forsaken you [O Muhammad] nor is He displeased with you, (4) and the Hereafter shall be better for you than the world. (5) Soon your Lord will give you (that with which) you will be pleased. (6) Did He not find you an orphan, and shelter you? (7) Did He not find you astray, and guide you? (8) *Did He not find you needy, and enrich you?* (9) So, as for the orphan, do not oppress him; (10) and as for the beggar, do not chide him; (11) and as for your Lord's blessing, proclaim it.[13]

This gives us greater insight into the nature of their marital relationship. It is not the case that Muhammad simply 'moved up' economically as a result of his marriage to Khadīja; more profoundly than that, she gifted him with security and closure after a life of vulnerability. In their union, he was deeply dependent on her, but she was not dependent on him. And there is no evidence in the biographical sources suggesting that Muhammad and the first Muslims were ashamed of that reality or tried to conceal it in any way. On the contrary, premodern sources are frank about his poverty prior to marriage. For example, there is a legendary report that Muhammad, after receiving Khadīja's proposal, realized he did not have enough money to pay the dower (*mahr*), at which point Gabriel descended from the Heavens with valuable gems (Stowasser, 1994, p. 179, fn 38). Whether this actually occurred is, of course, irrelevant; the point is that there was no shame associated with Muhammad's inability to afford the dower.

As is well known, Khadīja was considerably older than the Prophet. The most common ages given are that, at the time of their marriage, she was forty years old and Muhammad twenty-five (Ibn Sa'd, 1995, p. 11). However, there are different numbers provided in the sources. Muhammad could also have been twenty-one or twenty-three (Watt, 2012). Al-Ṭabarī lists Khadīja's age

[13] Our emphasis. We have drawn on Qara'i (2004) for Qur'anic translations.

as twenty-eight (Kahn, 2010), while Ibn Kathīr includes a report stating that Khadīja could have been thirty-five or even twenty-five (1998, p. 191). Given that she would go on to mother six children with Muhammad, a number of contemporary scholars have concluded that the age of forty cannot be taken literally, and that she must have been younger.[14] Whatever her actual age may have been, what is clear is that Khadīja was the older partner, an established woman who 'had reached the full bloom of social maturity' (Ali, 2008). And what is most salient to our discussion is that Muhammad's masculinity was, significantly, not threatened by Khadīja's seniority. Note the *silences* of the narratives, what they do *not* say: at no point do the biographers express surprise, let alone alarm, at their marked age difference. There was apparently nothing abnormal about their arrangement. This stands in contrast to contemporary marital cultures (Muslim or otherwise) in which the man is often the older and more established partner, which of course has lasting consequences in terms of the power dynamics of the marriage.

In addition to Khadīja's articulate personality, age and economic stature, there are other elements of her relationship to Muhammad that can be extrapolated upon to support an egalitarian (re)reading of Muslim marriage. First, as mentioned earlier, their twenty-five-year marriage was monogamous. ʿĀʾisha states, in a report found in *Ṣaḥīḥ Muslim*, that 'Allah's apostle did not marry any other woman till her [Khadīja's] death' (vol. 4, no. 5975). Given that polygynous relations were the norm in seventh-century Arabia, some scholars have suggested that Khadīja may well have specified, in her marriage contract with Muhammad, that she could be his only wife, at least while she was alive (Ahmed, 1992, p. 49). Second, it is remarkable that all of Muhammad's sons died in their childhood, and that he only had daughters who survived. Khadīja and Muhammad had six children together: two sons (Qasim and ʿAbdullah) and four daughters (Zaynab, Umm Kulthūm, Fatima and Ruqayya) (Watt, 2012).[15] It seems that ʿAbdullah died shortly after birth (Kahn, 2010), while there are conflicting accounts regarding Qasim's age at death: some reports state that he died in infancy, while others claim that he had 'attained an age when he could ride, even on light, swift camels' (Ibn Kathīr, 1998, p. 190). Furthermore, it is telling that, out of all of Muhammad's marriages, Khadīja was the *only* wife who bore him children

---

[14] Karen Armstrong, as cited in Khan (2010). See also Razwy (1990, p. 169).

[15] Watt notes that the titles *al-ṭāhir* ('the Pure') and *al-ṭayyib* ('the Good') refer to ʿAbdullah, and that it is even possible that the names Qasim and ʿAbdullah may have referred to the same child.

who survived (Lings, 1983, p. 296). Mariyya al-Qibtiyya ('Mary the Copt'), whom Muhammad would marry later in his life and well after Khadīja's death, would give birth to a child named Ibrahim but he, too, would die in infancy. This dimension of the Prophet's life is something that we, as Islamic feminists, need to reflect upon. What does it mean that one of the current pillars of patriarchy, of hegemonic masculinity – specifically, fathering sons – is strikingly absent in the Prophet's life?

Admittedly, these are circumstances that were completely outside the Prophet's control: being unable to father a son was obviously not a choice that the Prophet made. But this reality provides us with a critical biographical counter-narrative to challenge the patriarchal imaginaries of our own times, in which to be a real man is often directly connected to fathering sons. Indeed, these circumstances have wider theological implications, suggesting that God, in His/Her/Its infinite justice and wisdom, sought to ultimately unsettle the patriarchal. To quote the Qur'anic interpreter Asma Barlas (2002, p. 121), is it

> a mere coincidence that he loses his father, Abdullah, in his own infancy, and all his sons in theirs; that only his daughters survive, at a time and in a place when people view girls as a curse?

And yet, despite all these various elements of Khadīja and Muhammad's relationship (or, perhaps, precisely because of them) their story continues to be retold in patriarchal ways. Using a history of the present sheds light on how *current* patriarchal sensibilities necessitate certain historical narratives to justify current social practices. For example, Syed A. A. Razwy – a contemporary Muslim scholar – refutes accounts that Khadīja had been in two previous marriages, insisting that Muhammad was her first and only husband (1990, p. 170). For some reason, Razwy *needs* Khadīja to be a virgin in the narrative; her prior sexual experiences with two other men seem to pose a problem, an obstacle for his idealized conception of prophetic marriage, despite the fact that virginity, as we noted earlier, is the glaring exception in Muhammad's marriages. Recall that 'Ā'isha was the only virgin that the Prophet married (Spellberg, 1994, p. 39). Curiously, Razwy also erases Khadīja's initiative in proposing to Muhammad. Instead, he portrays her friend Nafisa as orchestrating the whole arrangement, and on her own initiative: in Razwy's account, Nafisa is the one who thinks of Muhammad as a suitable match for Khadīja and approaches him, without even telling her (Razwy, 1990, p. 28). As a result of this twist in the narrative, Khadīja comes off as a shy, passive personality.

Martin Lings – another contemporary Muslim scholar – seems to have trouble negotiating Muhammad's economic vulnerabilities. In his (otherwise comprehensive) biography of the Prophet, he fails to mention Muhammad's manifest inability to pay the dower (*mahr*). That silence in Lings' narrative speaks volumes; his Muhammad has to be a Muhammad who can pay. Lings simply states that the dower was '20 she-camels' (1983, p. 36), thereby giving the misleading impression that Muhammad paid it himself, and that this payment was not a source of great anxiety for the Prophet.[16] As we discussed earlier, Muhammad's poverty did not seem to unsettle pre-modern biographers. It is modern biographers who are unsettled by the thought of a man's economic vulnerability, let alone the Prophet's. Pre-modern biographers, in contrast, were at peace with the man who could not pay.

Another source of current historiographical discomfort seems to be triggered by the idea of Khadīja as a (married) working woman. Going back to Razwy's account, he portrays Khadīja as giving up her career following her marriage to Muhammad, basically becoming a good Muslim housewife:

> Once Khadīja was married, she appears to have lost interest in her mercantile ventures and in her commercial empire ... of course, she never lost her genius for organization, now instead of applying it to her business she applied it to the service of her husband ... From the very first day, she took charge of her new duty which was to make the life of her husband happy and pleasant. (Razwy, 1990, pp. 37–8)

This passage tells us more about Razwy's own twentieth-century (and thus middle-class, Victorian influenced) context and biases as to what the qualities of a pious Muslim woman should be than it does anything about Khadīja's life. We do not have any evidence to suggest Khadīja retreated from her business pursuits into the home. The sources on this phase of their marriage are silent (Kahn, 2010). On the contrary, it is likely that Khadīja continued to earn *throughout* their marriage, for what else explains – as the Islamic scholars Leila Ahmed (1992, p. 42) and Kecia Ali (2008) have observed – Muhammad's

---

[16] It is worthwhile noting that, unlike Lings, Razwy acknowledges that Muhammad could not pay the dower himself, stating that his uncle Abū Ṭālib paid the amount of 400 gold pieces (1990, pp. 32–3).

ability to spend extended periods of time away from work to meditate in the Cave of Hira, where he would receive the first Qur᾽anic revelations? It is to this episode in the Prophet's life that we now turn.

SNAPSHOT 2: THE FIRST MUSLIM(A)

The second 'snapshot' of Khadīja emerges during Muhammad's election as prophet.[17] As noted above, Muhammad would spend long intervals meditating in the Cave of Hira. It was here, at the age of forty, that he encountered Gabriel, who informed him that he had been chosen as a Messenger of God (Ibn Isḥāq, 1967, p. 106), revealing the first Qur᾽anic verses (96:1–5).[18] Muhammad is intensely shaken by this encounter, worried that he has become possessed by a jinn or demon. He runs away, at which point Gabriel announces to him, again: 'O Muhammad, thou art the messenger of God, and I am Gabriel.' Muhammad then runs back home to Khadīja, crying out: 'Cover me! Cover me!' (*zammilinī, zammilinī*) (Lings, 1983, p. 45). She envelops his shivering body in a blanket and consoles him.

This is a well-known narrative. But what is less known is the biographical sources' discussion of suicide, specifically, in the accounts of al-Ṭabarī (1988) and Ibn Kathīr (1998). Here is a passage from al-Ṭabarī, narrating Muhammad's train of thought, in the first person, immediately after the revelation:

> There was not one of God's creation more hateful to me than a poet or a madman; I could not bear to look at either of them. I said to myself, 'Your humble servant is either a poet or a madman, but Quraysh shall never say this of me. I shall take myself to a mountain crag, hurl myself down from it, kill myself, and find relief in that way.' (1988, p. 71)

It was at this point, on the verge of taking his own life, that Gabriel speaks out and reassures Muhammad that he is indeed a Messenger. Furthermore, according to both al-Ṭabarī and Ibn Kathīr, the Prophet's suicidal thoughts were not an exceptional moment, but a *phase* that persisted throughout the

[17] Curiously, this second snapshot – appearing in key texts such as Ibn Isḥāq (1967), al-Ṭabarī (1988) and Ibn Kathīr (1998) – is entirely absent in Ibn Sa῾d's (1995) account.

[18] The wording of this passage is as follows: 'Read! In the name of your Lord who created, created humankind from a clot of blood. Read! Your Lord is the most generous, who taught by the pen, taught humankind that which it did not know.'

early revelatory period. Whenever there was a delay in revelation, the Prophet would sink into deep-seated depression and reconsider throwing himself off a cliff (Ibn Kathīr, 1998, p. 280; al-Ṭabarī, 1988, p. 76). Whatever Muhammad may have actually felt at the time, this narrative offers a very different type of prophetic masculinity: one shaped by profound feelings of anxiety, fear and insecurity. After all, what would people think of Muhammad? Surely, they would see him as a man possessed, or a poet, at best. Note that al-Ṭabarī and Ibn Kathīr do not seem to have any problem with the Prophet's dire mental state. That is, in their accounts they do not feel the need to gloss over or cover up Muhammad's thoughts and feelings. He is no less of a man because he cannot cope (quite understandably) with the idea that he is a prophet, and cannot bear all the difficulties that will now await him as prophet. While this suicide narrative is controversial and contested, what is clear is that the Prophet was greatly unsettled by the revelations, and to such a degree that his insecurities were directly addressed by the Qur'an itself. At various points, God reassures the Prophet that he is neither a soothsayer (*kahin*) nor a madman (*majnūn*) (52:29; 68:2). There are also numerous verses addressed to the unbelievers, clarifying that Muhammad is not a madman (*majnūn*), a poet (*sha'ir*) or a soothsayer (*kahin*) (7:184; 21:5; 23:70; 34:46; 36:69; 37:36; 52:30; 68:6; 69:41; 81:22).

As is well known, Khadīja played a seminal role in consoling Muhammad when he received the first revelations. She recognized the veracity of his prophetic calling immediately. Ibn Isḥāq narrates that Khadīja, on hearing what the Prophet had experienced in the Cave of Hira, stated: 'Rejoice, O son of my uncle and be of good heart! Verily, by Him in whose hand is Khadīja's soul, I have hoped that thou wilt be the prophet of this people' (Ibn Isḥāq, 1967, p. 107). Similar narratives can be found in the biographies of al-Ṭabarī (1988, pp. 68, 71–2) and Ibn Kathīr (1998, p. 279). After consoling the Prophet, Khadīja consulted her cousin Waraqa ibn Nawfal, who was a Christian and had studied the earlier scriptures, and he promptly confirmed Muhammad's prophecy (Ibn Isḥāq, 1967, p. 107; al-Ṭabarī, 1988, p. 68; Ibn Kathīr, 1998, p. 279). This episode could be read as problematic, for Khadīja acts here simply as a female messenger – a mechanical go-between – invoking the authority and knowledge of one man (her male cousin) to assuage the doubts of another (her husband). That is, she is not thinking and acting autonomously, as a woman. Indeed, in Lings' contemporary account, Khadīja repeats, verbatim, Waraqa's response to Muhammad (Lings, 1983, p. 45). But this is not the only role that the narratives offer us. During the early revelations, Khadīja also uses her own creative reasoning to reassure Muhammad that he is a genuine prophet. The following dialogue between Khadīja and Muhammad is taken from Ibn Isḥāq's account:

> 'O son of my uncle, are you able to tell me about your visitant, when he comes to you?' He replied that he could, and she asked him to tell her when he came. So when Gabriel came to him, as he was want, the apostle said to Khadīja, 'This is Gabriel who has just come to me'. 'Get up, O son of my uncle', she said, 'and sit by my left thigh'. The apostle did so, and she said, 'Can you see him?' 'Yes', he said. She said, 'Then turn around and sit on my right thigh'. He did so, and she said, 'Can you see him?' When he said that he could she asked him to move and sit in her lap. When he had done this she again asked if he could see him, and when he said yes, she disclosed her form and cast aside her veil while the apostle was sitting on her lap. Then she said, 'Can you see him?' And he replied, 'No'. She said, 'O son of my uncle, rejoice and be of good heart, by God he is an angel and not a satan'. (Ibn Isḥāq, p. 107)

In addition to Khadīja's sharp intelligence, this exchange captures the affection, the intimacy that existed between her and Muhammad, conveyed not simply through words but also physical contact and the proximity of their bodies. This dialogue can also be found in al-Ṭabarī and Ibn Kathīr, although in the latter's account there is a curious, patriarchal twist. While al-Ṭabarī (1988, p. 73) is clear that Khadīja is the one assuaging Muhammad's doubts (which is the intuitive, if not obvious, conclusion), Ibn Kathīr claims, on the authority of al-Bayhaqī, that Khadīja set up the entire exchange in order to assuage her *own* doubts about Muhammad's prophecy (1998, pp. 297–8). The implicit assumption is that Muhammad was (of course) convinced of his prophetic calling and did not require any sort of support or closure.

But Khadīja was not only a critical source of emotional support, but also economic support *throughout* the early history of Islam, until her death in 619. In (Sunni) Muslim memory, Abū Bakr is usually credited with this hallowed role, as he used his privileged class standing to assist the first Muslims, who were largely poor and economically disenfranchised. But Khadīja, too, played a key part in this regard, providing food, shelter and financial aid, especially when the Quraysh boycotted Muslim labour in an attempt to stifle Muhammad's monotheistic message (Razwy, 1990, pp. 130–1). Razwy makes a perceptive observation. Due to persecution by the Quraysh elite, two groups of Muslims fled to Abyssinia (in approximately 613 and 615, though the exact years are uncertain), seeking the protection of its Christian king – the Negus (*al-Najāshi*) – who was known for his justice and tolerance. Razwy writes:

> ... the refugees in these two groups were too poor to bear the expenses of travel to Abyssinia. Who equipped their caravans and paid their expenses so they were able to travel? The historians have not answered this question. But it is most probable that Khadīja equipped the caravans and financed the emigration. (1990, p. 138)

We have also not fully appreciated the level of sacrifice that Khadīja underwent for Islam: she did not simply *use* her wealth for the service of the faith; she *lost* it. Leila Ahmed points out that we do not have any records of Muhammad or his daughters inheriting from Khadīja after her death, concluding that Khadīja may well have lost all her wealth during the Meccan persecution (Ahmed, 1992, p. 48). And class standing cannot be reduced to the monetary, the fiscal alone. Social capital (commanding respect, being valued and considered 'important', having access to certain circles and spaces) is a core component of class privilege, and this is also something that Khadīja sacrificed on the altar of her faith, going from a comfortable life of honour and grace to being 'viewed as deluded by all but a handful of friends' (Kahn, 2010). This could not have been easy, to say the least. Indeed, it is plausible that the Meccan boycott, in addition to strangling Khadīja economically and socially, may have strangled her fatally, undermining her physical health and well-being at an advanced age (Razwy, 1990, p. 122; Kahn, 2010). Note, after all, that Khadīja (along with Muhammad's beloved uncle Abū Ṭālib) died at the end of the Meccan Boycott in 619, which is why that year is referred to as the 'Year of Sorrow' (*'ām al-ḥuzn*).

CONCLUSIONS: RECLAIMING KHADĪJA AS PARADIGM

Before closing, two points of clarification are in order. First, in this chapter, we do not mean to imply that Khadīja has been erased in Muslim memory. She is very much present. Yet despite her presence, despite every Muslim child learning about her, this somehow has not led Muslims to question and rethink what they regard as Sunna. Curiously, her twenty-five-year-long relationship to the Prophet did not become a marital model that Muslims across time and place sought to replicate: the example of Khadīja has not become paradigmatic. She is remembered in a *particular* way and, as far as gender justice and equality are concerned, a particularly inconsequential way. She is universally honoured, by all Muslims, as being the first Muslim, the first person to believe in Muhammad's prophecy, followed by Ali, the Prophet's adopted son Zayd, and Abū Bakr (Lings, 1983, p. 47). In the biographical tradition, we even have a miraculous report claiming that, before meeting Muhammad, Khadīja was participating in a pagan celebration in Mecca, when one of the idols began to speak, foretelling the coming of a prophet by the name of Ahmad (Stowasser, 2006). The other women present began to throw stones at the idol, but not Khadīja: she was struck by its words, listening to them attentively (Stowasser, 2006). This episode is significant not because of its veracity, of course, but because it captures the sheer depth of Khadīja's faith for Muslims, entering her heart before even encountering the Prophet. Furthermore, we have numerous texts sanctifying Khadīja's privileged status as a believer. In the Hadith collections of both *Ṣaḥīḥ Bukhārī* and *Ṣaḥīḥ Muslim*, we have reports in which Khadīja is promised a palace in Paradise.[19] Indeed, there are traditions in the *tafsīr* (Qur'anic exegetical) and *qiṣaṣ al-anbiyā'* ('Stories of the Prophets') literature in which Khadīja is praised as being one of the four best women of the world, alongside Fatima, her daughter; Mary, mother of Jesus; and Asiya, the wife of Pharaoh (Stowasser, 2003).

Second, we do not pretend to be the first to draw on Khadīja in a feminist, egalitarian way. Khadīja has become a central reference point for Muslim feminists, who maintain that her monogamous union with the Prophet should be treated as the marital norm, his later polygynous relationships the marital exceptions (Ali, 2008). Her professional achievements have been equally important. The writer Sufiya Ahmed, in an article rather anachronistically titled 'The First Feminist', passionately discusses the leadership qualities and entrepreneurial skills of Khadīja, and how she became a role model for Ahmed in her own struggles as a woman in an unjust, patriarchal world (2019, p. 30). To quote Ahmed's words:

> For me Khadīja was the first feminist and she inspired me to become one. She taught me to stand up for women's rights, for girls' rights, and to challenge inequality and misogyny. (2019, pp. 43–4)

---

[19] For *Ṣaḥīḥ Bukhārī*, see 'The Book of the Merits of the Ansar', nos. 3563, 3564, 3566 and 3567; 'The Book of Marriage', no. 4886; 'The Book of Good Manners', no. 5617; and 'The Book of Tawhid', nos. 7003 and 7015. For *Ṣaḥīḥ Muslim*, see nos. 5967, 5968, 5970 and 5971.

But we *are* trying to draw on Khadīja in a critical and unapologetic manner.[20] In this chapter, we have not tried to 'prove' that Khadīja and Muhammad were nascent feminists who upheld egalitarianism. This is not what writing a history of the present is about. At the beginning of this chapter we acknowledged, explicitly and unapologetically, the Prophet's numerous polygynous relationships and the acute power disparities (however loving) that existed within them. Instead, we have undertaken a feminist rereading of our inherited historical memory of the Prophet's life, focusing on his (non-egalitarian) relationship to Khadīja in the light of the hegemonic masculinities of our times. The argument that we are making is that the prophetic legacy, the historical memory that we have with us in our hands today, actually has conflicting tendencies, possibilities and horizons within it, comprising patriarchal and non-patriarchal elements, and because of centuries of male dominance the patriarchal elements have been discursively centred, acquiring the paradigmatic strength of normativity. We, in the spirit of social justice, have challenged that memory by privileging the non-patriarchal elements over the patriarchal ones. To put it another way: we are trying to 'balance out' a legacy of Islamic marital discourse and practice that continues to weigh in on the side of men, despite the radically different gendered context in which we now live. This is a central part of our chapter's contribution: to demonstrate, through a close textual documentation and analysis of these two snapshots of Khadīja and Muhammad's marriage, that there is ample historical material out there to make a compelling case, in our own present, for a feminist Sunna, for an egalitarian rethinking of Muslim marriage and, by extension, for an egalitarian Muslim masculinity.

Let us conclude on a grounded note, focusing on a brief example to highlight the concrete, legal ramifications of such a feminist rereading of the Sunna. *Kafā'a* literally means compatibility, but in personal status law or Muslim family law – which in our national context would be the Jordanian Personal Status Law – *kafā'a* refers to financial compatibility between spouses. This concept is taken from Islamic jurisprudence (*fiqh*) and goes back to the Ottoman Family Rights Law of 1917. Article 45 of this law stipulates that a husband has to be a woman's *kuf'* both monetarily and professionally. Monetary *kafā'a* is defined as the husband's ability to pay a woman's dower and her maintenance in a manner that she is accustomed to in her paternal home. Professional *kafā'a* means that 'the business of the husband or the profession

[20] For a critique of such apologetics in modern Muslim literature, see Ali (2015).

that he chose [has to be] similar in honor to that of the guardians of the wife' (Ottoman Family Rights Law, 1917, art. 47). In other words, the concept of *kafā'a* presumes that the husband is the principal (if not exclusive) breadwinner and it ensures that a woman does not get married to someone considered to be of a lower socio-economic background to her father.[21] According to article 22b of the Jordanian Personal Status Law (2010), a Jordanian woman's guardian – read: father – can actually dissolve a marriage conducted without his approval *if* the husband is not of the same, or higher, financial status than the bride's family.

This patriarchal (and classist) understanding of *kafā'a* in Islamic jurisprudence is squarely at odds, as this chapter has shown, with twenty-five years of prophetic matrimony. *Kafā'a*, as understood today, is the diametric opposite of the economic Sunna of the Prophet in his marriage to Khadīja. Indeed, if the Personal Status Law had been applied to Muhammad and Khadīja they would not even have been able to get married, had Khadīja's father objected on the grounds of financial and professional incompatibility. Centring their marital union in Islamic thought is critical, therefore, in not simply reforming aspects of Islamic jurisprudence, but in radically transforming its core assumptions in the spirit of gender justice. This is what it means to reclaim Khadīja and Muhammad's marriage as an Islamic paradigm.

REFERENCES

Ababneh, Sara. Forthcoming. 'Around We Go: A Brief Historical Overview of the Jordanian Personal Status Law'. In *Family Law and Gender in the Modern Middle East and North Africa*, edited by Adrien Wing and Hisham Kassim. Cambridge, UK: Cambridge University Press.

Ahmed, Leila. 1992. *Women and Gender in Islam*. New Haven: Yale University Press.

Ahmed, Sufiya. 2019. 'The First Feminist. In *It's Not About the Burqa: Muslim Women on Faith, Feminism, Sexuality, and Race*, edited by Mariam Khan. London: Picador.

Ali, Kecia. 2008. 'Khadijah'. *The Oxford Encyclopaedia of Women in World History*, edited by Bonnie G. Smith. Oxford: Oxford University Press.

Ali, Kecia. 2015. 'Muhammad and Khadija'. *Critical Muslim* 14 (1): pp. 53–63.

Almassi, Ben. 2015. 'Feminist Reclamations of Normative Masculinity: On Democratic Manhood, Feminist Masculinity, and Allyship Practices'. *Feminist Philosophy Quarterly* 1 (2): pp. 1–22.

[21] In later laws, age compatibility is added. See article 6 of the Jordan Law of Family Rights (1951). For a survey of Muslim family law in the Jordanian context, see Ababneh (forthcoming).

Barlas, Asma. 2002. *'Believing Women' in Islam: Unreading Patriarchal Interpretations of the Qur'an*. Austin: University of Texas Press.

Bates, Thomas R. 1975. 'Gramsci and the Theory of Hegemony'. *Journal of the History of Ideas* 36 (2): pp. 351–66.

Connell, R. W. and James W. Messerschmidt. 2005. 'Hegemonic Masculinity: Rethinking the Concept'. *Gender and Society* 19 (6): pp. 829–59.

De Beauvoir, Simone. 1989. *The Second Sex*. New York: Vintage Books.

De Sondy, Amanullah. 2011. 'Prophecy and Masculinities: The Case of the Qur'anic Joseph'. *Cross Currents* 61 (4): pp. 529–39.

De Sondy, Amanullah. 2014. *The Crisis of Islamic Masculinities*. London: Bloomsbury.

Dowd, Nancy E. 2010. 'Asking the Man Question: Masculinities Analysis and Feminist Theory'. *Harvard Journal of Law & Gender* 33 (2): pp. 415–30.

Fuggle, Sophie, Yari Lanci and Martina Tazzioli (eds). 2016. *Foucault and the History of Our Present*. New York: Palgrave Macmillan.

Garland, David. 2014. 'What is a "History of the Present?" On Foucault's Genealogies and Their Critical Preconditions'. *Punishment and Society* 16 (4): pp. 365–84.

hooks, bell. 2014. *Feminist Theory: From Margin to Center*. London: Routledge.

Ibn Ishāq, Muhammad. 1967. *The Life of Muhammad*, translated by A. Guillaume. Oxford: Oxford University Press.

Ibn Kathīr, Isma'il. 1998. *The Life of the Prophet Muhammad*, vols 1 & 2, translated by Trevor Le Gassick. Reading: Garnet Publishing.

Ibn Sa'd, Muhammad. 1995. *The Women of Medina*, translated by Aisha Bewley. London: Ta-Ha Publishers.

Jordan Law of Family Rights. 1951. Law No. 92 of 1951.

Jordan Personal Status Law. 2010. Law No. 36 of 2010. https://tinyurl.com/JordanPSL

Kahn, Tamam. 2010. *Untold: A History of the Wives of Prophet Muhammad*. Rhinebeck, NY: Monkfish Book Publishing Company (e-book).

Kugle, Scott. 2010. *Homosexuality in Islam: Critical Reflection on Gay, Lesbian, and Transgender Muslims*. London: Oneworld.

Lings, Martin. 1983. *Muhammad: His Life Based on the Earliest Sources*. Cambridge, UK: Islamic Texts Society.

Musawah. 2016. *Women's Stories, Women's Lives: Male Authority in Muslim Contexts*. Kuala Lumpur: Musawah.

Ottoman Law of Family Rights Law. 1917.

Ouzgane, Lahoucine (ed.). 2006. *Islamic Masculinities*. London: Zed Books.

Ouzgane, Lahoucine. 2011. '*The Rape Continuum:* Masculinities in the Works of Nawal El Saadawi and Tahar Ben Jelloun'. In *Men in African Film and Fiction*, edited by Lahoucine Ouzgane. Suffolk: Boydell and Brewer.

Qara'i, Ali Quli. 2004. *The Qur'an, with a Phrase-by-Phrase Translation*. London: Islamic College for Advanced Studies Press.

Rabinow, Paul (ed.). 1984. *The Foucault Reader: An Introduction to Foucault's Thought*. New York: Penguin Books.

Rahemtulla, Shadaab. 2018. *Qur'an of the Oppressed: Liberation Theology and Gender Justice in Islam*. Oxford: Oxford University Press.

Rahemtulla, Shadaab and Sara Ababneh. 2021. 'Reclaiming Khadija's and Muhammad's Marriage as an Islamic Paradigm: Toward a New History of the Muslim Present.' *Journal of Feminist Studies in Religion* 37 (2): pp. 83–102.

Razwy, Syed A. A. 1990. *Khadīja-tul-Kubra (The Wife of the Prophet Muhammad): A Short Story of Her Life*. Elmhurst, NY: Tahrike Tarsile Qurʾan.

Roth, Michael. 1981. 'Foucault's "History of the Present"'. *History and Theory* 20 (1): pp. 32–46.

El-Rouayheb, Khaled. 2009. *Before Homosexuality in the Arab-Islamic World, 1500–1800*. Chicago: University of Chicago Press.

Ṣaḥīḥ Bukhārī. n.d. http://sahihalbukhari.com/sps/sbk/

Ṣaḥīḥ Muslim. 1976. Edited by Muhammad Ashraf and translated by Abdul Hamid Siddiqui, vol. 4. Lahore: Hafeez Press.

Spellberg, Denise A. 1994. *Politics, Gender, and the Islamic Past: The Legacy of 'A'isha bint Abi Bakr*. New York: Columbia University Press.

Stowasser, Barbara F. 1994. *Women in the Qurʾan, Traditions, and Interpretation*. Oxford: Oxford University Press.

Stowasser, Barbara F. 2003. 'Khadija'. In *Encyclopaedia of the Qurʾān*, vol. 3, edited by Jane D. McAuliffe. Leiden: Brill.

Stowasser, Barbara F. 2006. 'Wives of the Prophet'. In *Encyclopaedia of the Qurʾān*, vol. 5, edited by Jane D. McAuliffe. Leiden: Brill.

Al-Ṭabarī, Abu Jaʿfar. 1988. *The History of al-Ṭabarī*, vol. 6, translated and annotated by W. Montgomery Watt and M. V. McDonald. Albany: State University of New York Press.

Thucydides. 1972. *History of the Peloponnesian War*, translated by Rex Warner with an introduction and notes by M. I. Finley. Oxford: Penguin.

Watt, W. Montgomery, and M. V. McDonald. 1988. 'Translators' Foreword'. In *The History of al-Ṭabarī*, vol. 6, written by Abu Jaʿfar al-Ṭabarī and translated and annotated by W. Montgomery Watt and M. V. McDonald. Albany: State University of New York Press.

Watt, W. Montgomery. 2012. 'Khadija'. In *Encyclopaedia of Islam*. 2nd edn. Leiden: Brill Online.

'Your Wife Enjoys Rights Over You' or Does She? Marriage in the Hadith

Yasmin Amin

'Whoever has married has completed half of his religion; therefore, let him be God-conscious regarding the other half' (al-Hindī, 2004, 3:49),[1] said Prophet Muhammad, declaring marriage a religious duty. There is no celibacy in Islam; marriage is strongly advocated both as a moral safeguard and a social necessity. The important qualification in this hadith (prophetic tradition) is the Prophet's reminder for both spouses to be God-conscious, reiterating the Qur'anic themes of *'adl* (justice) and *iḥsān* (kindness).

In her book, *Marriage and Slavery in Early Islam* (2010), Kecia Ali shows structural and functional similarities between marriage and slavery in the legal heritage sources. She analyses a variety of third/ninth-century legal texts demonstrating that jurists made comparisons between wives and slaves and between marriage and commercial transactions, which might not have been as offensive in their time as it is today. Ali shows that marriage as an institution was regarded as a legal outlet for sexual needs, with the dower (*mahr*) paid by the husband considered as legitimizing sexual intercourse with his wife, thereby justifying his dominion over her. The jurists also created a list of gender-differentiated

[1] The hadith-reports will be referenced according to the collection, the *juz'* (section), page and number of the report.

obligations for the spouses. For example, the husband's obligation to provide material support for his wife, called maintenance, obliged her to be sexually available to him at any time or place he chooses. Juristic discussions on the wife's right to sexual enjoyment were essentially limited to time allocations which husbands must uphold in cases of polygynous marriage (Ali, 2010).

Yet the Qur᾽an paints a completely different picture from the one created and promoted by the jurists: one of spousal affection and close relations. Verse 2:187 likens a spouse to a *libās* (garment, covering) for the other. It is a fact that garments are not only used for beautification, but also to cover any defects and protect from various conditions such as heat or cold. Additionally, the concept of *satr* (lit. hiding or covering) is also invoked, urging the spouses to cover each other's flaws or shortcomings (Ṣadr-ʿĀmilī, 2005, 1:495). Verse 4:4 calls the dower a free gift, not a price to pay. Verse 25:74 shows wives and offspring to be the comfort of the eyes, and finally verse 30:21 mentions companionship as *suknā* (synergy, comfort, protection) and speaks of love and compassion between the spouses.

The question is not really which image to follow, for jurists were human and could have made mistakes, departing from the divine ideal. Classical jurists were essentially all male and therefore applied an androcentric interpretation of the divine words, coding their interpretations into rules and regulations with limited concern for gender justice or equity. The real question is therefore how to correct the distorted image created by the jurists and how to come closer to the Qur᾽anic spirit and ideal. This chapter will attempt to offer an answer by looking at the excellent role model, the epitome of good manners, Prophet Muhammad, who was exemplified in verse 33:21 for Muslims to follow. How did the Prophet live his married life? How was he portrayed in the Hadith corpus as a husband? What did he say about marriage? How did he convey his understanding of marriage, while remaining God conscious? Can his marriage model be revived to improve the lived realities of contemporary Muslim women?

1. FEMINIST VIEWS OF HADITH

Since the early days of Islam, Hadith literature was used as a lens through which to interpret and understand the Qur᾽an. Muslim feminists have repeatedly highlighted that almost every aspect of the Hadith literature is problematic and controversial (Hassan, 1999, p. 248). They have listed numerous hadith-reports as untrustworthy, disputed particular narrators and questioned the authenticity of reports, calling for their re-evaluation in more egalitarian ways. Many have argued that women lost in the Hadith what they gained through the Qur'an. Ignaz Goldziher suggested that contradictions are so rampant in the Hadith that one's starting assumption has to be that any hadith-report does not go back to the Prophet, but rather reflects the interests of later Muslims (Melchert, 2020, p. 3).

Scepticism towards Hadith goes back to the time of the *tabi'ūn*,[2] whose critics claimed that certain hadith-reports were forged and should be disregarded by the jurists. Hadith sciences with their rigorous methodologies were developed by Muslim scholars partly to counter such claims and sift through the vastly increased corpus. Those who forged hadith-reports probably never thought how these reports contradicted the Qur'an, as they were forged to serve a political, social or ideological purpose. While the Qur'an provides ideals and values, society could not always rise to that level and instead dragged Islam down to its level. Hassan argues that although valid grounds exist for using Hadith with scepticism and caution, Fazlur Rahman correctly states that 'if the Hadith literature as a whole is cast away, the basis for the historicity of the Qur'an is removed with one stroke' (Hassan, 1999, p. 249, quoting Rahman, 1968, p. 73). Furthermore, verse 59:7 enjoins Muslims to accept whatever the Prophet gives them and to refrain from whatever he forbids, which includes his sayings and Sunna.[3] Additionally, working from within the tradition means not to discard problematic hadith-reports, but to find ways to deal with the problematic nature.

Feminists have been averse to using hadith-reports with regard to women's issues, choosing instead to quote relevant Qur'anic verses wherever possible. Azza Karam argues that Islamic/Muslim feminism will be rejected by the rest of society if it does not justify itself within Islam, working within the tradition, and concludes that failing such justification would be self-defeating (1998, p. 11).

Many feminists and reformists have highlighted the numerous androcentric and misogynistic hadith-reports and their role in constructing gender bias and non-egalitarian readings in the Islamic interpretative tradition. Fatima Mernissi, for example, used the same methodology and criteria of the classical

---

[2] The *tabi'ūn* are the generation after the Prophet's companions, also called the followers.

[3] Hadith scholars have also interpreted verses 53:3–4; 75:18–19; 24:54 and 4:64 to enjoin Muslims to follow hadith-reports.

Hadith scholars to contest the reliability of some transmitters, notably Abū Bakra and Abū Hurayra (Mernissi, 1991, pp. 49–81). Mernissi implicitly calls for a decanonization of *Ṣaḥīḥ al-Bukhārī*, considered the most authentic Sunni Hadith collection, to enable contemporary Muslims to develop a more critical attitude towards what is deemed as the 'authentic Hadith'. She asks: 'What conclusion must one draw from this? That even the authentic Hadith must be vigilantly examined with a magnifying glass? That is our right, Mālik ibn Anas tells us. Al-Bukhārī, like all the *fuqahā'* (jurists), began his work of collecting reports by asking for Allah's help and acknowledging that only He is infallible' (1991, p. 76).

Khaled Abou El Fadl, in contrast and like this chapter, values the preservation and study of Hadith as it can be mined for its historical, theological, ethical and moral insights. He argues that this process should be achieved through an 'epistemological arsenal that is available to us today – not through the epistemological tools that existed more than ten centuries ago' (2014, p. 318). He argues, like Goldziher, that due to the nature of Hadith, 'it is virtually impossible to attribute any specific report to a particular person in history, whether the Prophet or any of the early Muslim generations' (2014, p. 316). He writes that hadith-reports might retain kernels of truth going back to the Prophet, though they are more indicative of the memory of early Muslim generations and the contesting ideological currents that were prevalent at the time (2014, pp. 316–7).

Sa'diyya Shaikh (2012) critically evaluates hadith-reports, especially the implicit androcentric and patriarchal gender ideologies rooted in the Hadith found in *Ṣaḥīḥ al-Bukhārī*. She begins her feminist approach by drawing on a '"hermeneutics of suspicion" that critically analyses patriarchal biases in the texts' and attempts to destabilize the canonized interpretations of 'truth' (p. 26). She exposes discriminatory structures and values entrenched within these texts, to identify 'how such androcentric constructions compromised and sometimes even sabotaged the egalitarian ethical call of Islam'. She continues with a 'hermeneutics of reconstruction' to reveal alternative egalitarian gender accounts in the texts by extracting 'underlying images of women from predominantly male-centred records, with the goal of both redressing the broader silences and marginalization of women's lives and retrieving powerful empowering images of women' (p. 27). Moreover, this reconstruction identifies inconsistencies within the texts.

Faqihuddin Abdul Kodir (2013), similar to this chapter, defends the use of Hadith, arguing that ignoring or rejecting Hadith prevents feminist scholarship from locating an Islamically-grounded model of gender equality. He argues that a close historical reading of the Hadith permits a positive reading of the reports' intent and purpose (pp. 170–8). He states that such readings can provide different interpretations, allowing for gender-just meanings (p. 176).

Nimat Barazangi (2004; 2017), in contrast, focuses mainly on egalitarian and feminist interpretations of the Qur'an. She argues that Muslim women have a distinct role in rethinking Hadith to develop new theological readings, as they were excluded from the production of Hadith collections, though not from its transmission, especially in the formative period (Barazangi, 2004, p. 22). Barazangi reminds contemporary Muslims to recognize that Hadith should not supersede the Qur'anic text, despite the connection between the divine ideal and its most excellent practitioner, Muhammad, and that interpretations and practices should neither be rigid nor literal (2004, p. 28). In her second book, *Woman's Identity and Rethinking the Hadith* (2017), Barazangi confirms the necessity to modify the understanding of Islam from dogmatic religious law to a moral rational worldview. She calls for returning Hadith to its position as the second textual source after the Qur'an, along with providing an ethical rereading of the Hadith through verifying and validating the *matn* (textual body) of the Hadith by means of the Qur'an (2017, p. 1). She also calls for discarding reports that contradict the Qur'an. She highlights the fact that the Prophet was an agent of change, challenging the knowledge and practices of his time, reminding contemporary Muslims to abandon the outmoded representations and/or interpretations that are unjust, replacing them with the egalitarian intentions of the Qur'an (2017, p. 55).

2. METHODOLOGY

One way of transcending feminists' aversion to the use of Hadith, as well as the limitations of its authenticity, is to ask new questions. Kecia Ali (2006, p. 51) asks these: 'What are the implications of the Prophet's action for the contemporary world? Is his precedent binding or is it to be understood as limited to the particular circumstances of his time and place?' Other questions to be asked include: What is the tone of the Prophet's statements and, most importantly, were these statements meant to be prescriptive or rather descriptive and why? If they are prescriptive, then they should have led to the imposition of a rule or should have become legally established in *fiqh* (jurisprudence).

If they are descriptive, the question still arises whether these reports should be followed, since verse 33:21 instructs Muslims to emulate the Prophet. Moreover, many hadith-reports have a 'symbolic function' within Muslim reasoning and therefore offer the choice to take their validity at face value, without delving into the authenticity issue.

Barbara Stowasser used this methodology in her chapter 'The Mothers of the Believers in the *Ḥadīth*' (1992), arguing that the very existence of such accounts in the canonized Hadith compendia shows that they were accepted by a segment of the Muslim community to preserve them in the cultural memory. Thus, they are a valuable source of information regardless of their authenticity. Such reports reflect the mindset of their time and the patriarchal values governing gender relations in general and marriage in particular.

This chapter uses Stowasser's methodology, adding to it by putting the different reports in conversation with one another and with the Qur'an, to tease out whether these reports indeed go back to the Prophet or whether they reflect later Muslims' interests who inserted them into the Prophet's mouth and into the collections. This chapter will neither attempt to evaluate Hadith through a rigorous *isnād-cum-matn* analysis developed by Harald Motzki (2013),[4] nor date any of the Hadith traditions. Ash Geissinger notes that academic studies of Hadith often overemphasize the question of its origins, while ignoring the lengthy and complex histories of their reception (2021, p. 102). Geissinger further highlights that even if one could determine that a given hadith circulated in mid-first/seventh-century Arabia, this does not necessarily mean that the person to whom it was attributed actually said it. Moreover, Geissinger reminds that hadith-reports are part of a textual archive shrouded in complex historical debates around its formation, organization and interpretation, which were affected by the context of their times, be they historical, ideological, intellectual, political or otherwise.

The hadith-reports will be divided into four groups, then examined in four separate sections. The first section will look at the Prophet's views and actions regarding the foundations of marriage; the second group will examine dower and maintenance; the third section looks at how the spouses relate to one another in terms of mutual care, kindness, trust and conflict resolution; and, finally, the last section will analyse intimate relations and 'bedroom etiquette'. Considering the number of women-demeaning hadith-reports, some of these will be put into conversation with the hadith-reports from the four sections

[4] See especially the section entitled 'Motzki's *Isnād-cum-Matn* Analysis' (pp. 210–14).

and with the Qur'an to determine whether their use can be defended or whether rulings based on them are binding. The chapter concludes by exploring an alternative construction of Muslim marriage, based on ethics of equal value, sharing and real partnership, reflecting on how the Hadith can contribute to egalitarian models of marriage that are explored in this book.

3. ETHICS OF MARRIAGE IN THE SUNNA

3.1 Foundations of marriage

The accounts of the Prophet as a husband and his sayings affirm the Qur'anic view of piety, *taqwā* (God-consciousness) and love as the foundation for an ethical Muslim marriage. This chapter started with the Prophet's statement that marriage is half of one's religion (al-Hindī, 2004, 3:49), emphasizing that both spouses must be God-conscious within this union and suggesting that marriage is an integral part of every believer's quest to live the religious ideals. Moreover, enacting *taqwā* implies that spousal relations are to be based on the Qur'an's central ethical principles captured in terms of *'adl* (justice), *iḥsān* (goodness) and *ma'rūf*,[5] themes of this book.

Some hadith-reports echo certain legal concerns regarding marriage as an outlet for sexual needs. Abū Hurayra narrated that the Prophet said: 'If someone comes to you who is pleasing to you in terms of his manners and religion, then allow him to marry, for if you do not, this will cause *fitna* (sedition) on earth and widespread corruption' (al-Hindī, 2004, 16:317, no. 44695). This report addresses a concern not explicitly discussed in *fiqh*, namely that prospective spouses should be pleasing to one another. While consent of both spouses underlies any marriage, the Prophet here adds the additional element of appeal and attraction, thereby echoing the love and mercy mentioned in the Qur'an (25:74 and 30:21). Another report tells of a man informing the Prophet: '"O Messenger of God, I got engaged to so-and-so". The Prophet asked: "Did you look at her?", which he denied. He urged him: "Go and look at her. For it will serve to bring you closer"' (al-Mizzī, 1983, 11:4, no. 15015; see also al-Hindī, 2004, 16:290, no. 44526; Ibn Māja, 1998, 1:599, no. 1864).

---

[5] *Ma'rūf* means that which is good, acknowledged and known to be right. It is used 38 times in the Qur'an. The translations fail to reflect the subtleties of the Arabic, which also ties it to enjoining what is right and forbidding what is wrong, being understood and making sense to the community, being acknowledged and accepted by the community as applicable to itself.

Ensuring the existence of an initial appeal and attraction helps to buttress the budding love between the spouses. Another report explicitly linking marriage to love was narrated by Ibn ʿAbbās. The Prophet said: 'We have not seen anything better for the *mutaḥābīn* (lit. those in love or loving one another) than marriage' (Ibn Māja, 1998, 1:593, no. 1847).

The importance of love is illustrated through Muhammad's own marriage to Khadīja, which extended even beyond her death. Sources report that ʿĀʾisha said: 'The Prophet was always glad about a visit from Khadīja's sister Hāla bint Khuwaylid. Hāla asked to visit the Prophet and he was comforted' (Muslim, n.d., 4:1889, no. 2437). Al-Nawawī adds: 'His comfort meant he was happy about her visit because she would remind him of Khadīja's days, showing the sanctity of marriage in life and after death; honouring the wife's family after death' (al-Nawawī, 2017, 15:202, no. 2437). ʿĀʾisha also said: 'When the Prophet slaughtered a sheep he would send meat to Khadīja's friends. I was jealous and said: "Khadīja! Khadīja! Khadīja!" The Prophet answered: "*ruziqtu ḥubbuhā*"' (lit. 'I was blessed with her love'). Likening her love to *rizq* (Godly sustenance, Divine bestowal, Godly provision, heavenly gifts and blessings, God's favour) is such an endearing way to speak of her. It emphasizes the Qurʾanic theme of love, mercy and compassion between spouses. The theme of Khadīja's love as *rizq* is repeated in the sources in many different reports, of which the shortest just mentions that the Prophet said: 'I was blessed with her love' (Muslim, n.d., 4:1888, no. 75; Ibn Ḥibbān, 1993, 15:467, no. 7006; al-Ḥumaydī, 2002, 4:111, no. 3223; Ibn ʿAsākir, 1986, 1:85). All sources place this statement to a time after Khadīja's death. As discussed in the chapter in this book devoted to his twenty-five-year long monogamous marriage to Khadīja, this marriage can be regarded as a revolutionary practice by any standards.[6] Not only was she older than him, previously married twice and with children, but it was the Prophet who accepted her proposal, after working for her (Ibn Hishām, 1990, 1:189). Noteworthy is also the precedent for how to behave after losing one's spouse and more so when married again, not only to another wife, but to several.

Yet love was not the only factor determining the choice of a spouse. Mujāhid narrated that the Prophet said: 'A woman is chosen for marriage based on four characteristics: her wealth, her beauty, her lineage and her religion.' ʿAbd al-Malik b. Ḥabīb added that: 'Oh son of Adam, hold on tightly onto the one with religion' (al-Ḥumaydī, 2002, 3:114, no. 2320). In a slight

[6] For further exploration of this idea, see Rahemtulla and Ababneh in this volume.

contradiction downplaying the element of beauty, the Prophet is reported to have said: 'Do not marry women for their beauty, perhaps their beauty might make them haughty, do not marry them for their money, perhaps their money will overwhelm you, but marry them for their religion; a black slave[7] mindful of her religion is better for you' (al-Hindī, 2004, 16:292, no. 44537). Notwithstanding modern concerns regarding slavery and racial justice, this report reiterates the mindfulness stated in the chapter's opening paragraph, drawing attention to the fact that beauty and wealth are fleeting, but that religion is a lasting concern all the way to the Hereafter.

To illustrate the importance of religion and faith within a marriage, the Prophet said: 'God will have mercy on the man who awakens at night to pray and then wakes his wife to pray. If she refuses, he then sprinkles some drops of water on her face to awaken her to pray. God will have mercy on the woman who awakens at night to pray then awakens her husband to pray. If he refuses, she sprinkles some drops of water on his face to awaken him to pray' (al-Nasāʾī, 2001, 3:205, no. 1610; Ibn Abī Shaybah, 1989, 2:72, no. 6607). Encouraging one another to pray or praying together would strengthen the bonds between the spouses due to the shared spiritual undertakings. Noticeable is the repeated recommendation for both spouses individually, without a gender preference, negating the legal marital hierarchy, emphasizing that both spouses achieve spiritual advancement/growth together through mutual encouragement and through remaining God-conscious.

Another report advises men to marry widows or divorcees with children. Muhammad is reported to have said: 'Marry the mothers of the children, for I will boast of them on the Day of Judgement' (al-Hindī, 2004, 16:290, no. 44522). Ibn Sirīn narrated that the Prophet said: 'Forsake the barren beauty and marry the black fertile woman,[8] for I will boast of you on Judgement Day' (al-Hindī, 2004, 16:293, no. 44545). Children and progeny are important, as echoed in verse 25:74. Furthermore, the Qurʾan mentions caring for orphans twenty-three times. These reports encourage marrying women who have already had children, which stands opposed to both the legal as well as modern fixation on virginity as a preferred status.

[7] Though the words 'black slave woman' might offend modern sensibilities, the report shown here elevates the pious 'black slave woman' over beautiful, rich, noble women who neglect their religion.

[8] Considering that at that time in history, there were no medical tests or examinations to determine a woman or a man's fertility, the only indication of fertility was for men and women to already have children.

The Prophet himself married a number of women who were widowed or divorced, some of whom had children from previous marriages. The number of wives attributed to the Prophet varies within the sources (al-Qasṭallānī, 2017, 2:74). For some relationships several sources claim that a marriage took place, while others regard these women as *sara'ir* (slaves/concubines). Consensus is that the Prophet had thirteen wives and concubines, of whom nine survived him, though there is some dispute as to their identity (Stowasser, 2008). Agreed upon are Khadīja bint Khuwaylid, Sawda Bint Zamʿa, ʿĀʾisha Bint Abī Bakr, Zaynab bint Khūzayma, Ḥafṣa Bint ʿUmar Ibn al-Khaṭṭāb, Hind bint Abī Ummayya (Umm Salama), Zaynab Bint Jaḥsh, Juwayriyya Bint al-Ḥarith, Ṣafiyya Bint Ḥuyayy, Ramla Bint Abī Sufyān (Umm Ḥabība), Maymūna Bint al-Ḥārith, Māriya Bint Shamʿūn, also known as Mariyya al-Qibtiyya, and Rayḥāna Bint Yazīd. Fāṭima bint Shurayḥ is also mentioned as the reason for the revelation of verse 33:50.

Authors discussed the Prophet's marriages for centuries, some claiming that all his marriages had the political aspect of strengthening friendly relationships based on Arab customs (Watt, 1956, p. 287). Others attributed a divine reason for each marriage: Muhammad's marriage to Khadīja established the precedent of a woman initiating a marriage. Khadīja and Sawda were both older than him, indicating the irrelevance of such age-difference. Marriages to Ḥafṣa and ʿĀʾisha occurred to honour their fathers, his most loyal companions. His marriage to Zaynab bint Jaḥsh abolished adoption, while his marriage to Juwayriyya freed her people. He married Umm Salama for her wisdom, and Ramla bint Abū Sufyān to honour her for being a believer in spite of her father, one of Muhammad's ardent enemies. The marriages to Ṣafiyya, Rayḥāna and Māriya showed the permissibility of marrying Jewish and Christian women. The marriage to Maymūna set another precedent: that marriage immediately after ʿ*umrah* was permitted (ʿAbdu, 1999). Only two of his wives, ʿĀʾisha and Māriya, were said to have been virgins, with all others being divorcees and/or widows.

Despite theorizations about the Prophet's marriages being politically or socially motivated, the element of appeal and choice remains. Three of Muhammad's wives brought children to the marriage and Muhammad raised them lovingly as his own (see al-Maqrīzī, 1999, 6:295).[9] The Prophet said:

---

[9] Khadīja brought Hind b. Abī Hāla and his sister Hāla to the marriage. She later had Zaynab, Ruqayya, Umm Kulthūm and Fāṭima. Umm Salama's children were Salama, Zaynab, ʿAmr and Durra/Birra. Ḥabība, the daughter of Ramla bint Abi Sufyān and Ubayd Allah b. Jaḥsh, also grew up in the Prophet's household.

'Spending time with one's children is dearer to God Almighty than *i ʿtikāf*[10] in my mosque' (al-Āmidī, 1994, p. 205).

Love and mercy, as mentioned in both the Qur'an and the Prophet's advice to his community, were also practised by the Prophet, who was known for showing *rifq* (gentleness, kindness) to his wives, which is essential in any human relationship. The Prophet told his community: 'The best of you is the best man for his family, and I am the best one for my family' (Ibn Māja, 1998, 1:636, no. 1977; al-Tirmidhī, 1975, 5:709, no. 3895; Ibn Ḥibbān, 1993, 9:484, no. 4177; al-Bayhaqī, 1994, 7:770, no. 15699).

3.2 Dower and spousal maintenance

Though the Prophet encouraged marriage, he also knew it involved expenses. ʿAbd Allah narrated: 'The Prophet said: "Whoever can afford the *bā'a* (expenses of marriage) should marry, it helps in averting one's gaze and is a protection for the private parts. Whoever cannot afford it should fast; fasting is a shield"' (al-Bukhārī, 2001, 3:26 no. 1905; Muslim, n.d., 2:1018, no. 1400). Marriage expenses are most notably the dower and maintenance.

Considering that half of the Muslim community were immigrants who left everything behind to settle in Medina, the Prophet advised to keep the dower within reasonable, affordable limits. Sahl b. Saʿd narrated that when a man wanted to marry a woman without giving her dower the Prophet asked him: '"What have you memorized of the Qur'an?" The man listed the chapters he knew. The Prophet said: "That is her dower, what you know of the Qur'an"' (al-Bukhārī, 2001, 6:192, no. 5030; al-Tirmidhī, 1975, 3:413, no. 1114).

Solving the financial problems of this man was a specific case, yet that did not mean that women were encouraged to waive their dower universally. Additionally, this woman's dower was for him to teach her the chapters he memorized as a bridal gift, as in another version, the Prophet said: 'I have married her to you on condition that you teach the chapters to her and if God *yarzuqak* (blesses you) then compensate her' (al-Bayhaqī, 1994, 14:511, no. 14515; Ibn Ḥajar al-ʿAsqalānī, 1959, 9:209). This meant the bridal gift was non-negotiable, but could be paid in kind rather than in material value. The Prophet said: 'Do not raise women's dower prohibitively.' ʿUmar added: 'If it

[10] *I ʿtikāf* means leaving worldly activities and confining oneself in a mosque for prayers, worship and contemplation.

were an honour in this world, or out of piety in the Hereafter, the Prophet would have done so himself. He did not accept more than twelve ounces [of silver] for any of his daughters nor pay more to any of his wives' (Ibn Ḥanbal, 1995, 1:419, no. 340). ʿĀʾisha confirms this saying: 'He paid us twelve ounces and a half each' (al-Ḥākim al-Naysābūrī, 1990, 4:23, no. 6772; Abū Dāwūd, 2009, 3:444, no. 2106; al-Dārimī, 2000, 2:714, no. 2223), which amounts to five hundred dirhams. The same amount is stated in several sources (al-Bayhaqī, 1994, 14:487, no. 14468).

Yet, as with the example of the man paying in kind, the Prophet also did that. Anas b. Mālik narrated that Ṣafiyya's dower was her freedom, as the Prophet manumitted and married her (Ibn Abī Shaybah, 1989, 7:290, no. 36174). The same is said of Juwayriyya. Her stated dower was her people's freedom (Ibn Ḥajar al-ʿAsqalānī, 1959, 9:130).

The Prophet also acted as a marriage broker, offering Muslim men and women to one another in marriage. ʿUqba b. ʿĀmir narrated:

> The Prophet asked a man if he would welcome being married to so-and-so. He affirmed. He then asked the woman who also agreed. The Prophet performed the marriage. The man, however, did not pay her a dower, though he owned a share in Khaybar.[11] Many years later when he felt he was dying, he said: 'The Prophet married me to so-and-so and I did not pay her dower, nor did I give her any gift. I hereby ask you to witness that I am giving her my share in Khaybar as her dower.' (Abū Dāwūd, 2009, 2:238, no. 2117)

This emphasizes that the dower is one of the wives' rights, considered a debt owed to her if it remains unpaid. The Prophet is reported to have said: 'Whoever promised a woman a dower and God knows that he does not want to pay it to her, he deceived her and God. He permitted himself the use of her vagina with falsehood. When he meets God Almighty on Judgement Day, he will be meeting him as a *zāni* (fornicator, adulterer)' (al-Bayhaqī, 1994, 14:508, no. 14509). The emphasis is on the deceit, not on sexual relations in exchange for dower as described in *fiqh*, as the husband is called an adulterer for deceiving his wife by engaging in a legal sexual relationship based on deceit. The Prophet is also reported to have said: 'The most deserving of conditions

[11] Khaybar is an oasis north of Medina that was inhabited by Jewish tribes who grew date palms and engaged in commerce and craftsmanship, accumulating considerable wealth.

to be kept are those you stipulated in a marriage' (al-Bukhārī, 2001, 3:190 no. 2721; Muslim, n.d., 2:1035, no. 1418). Surprisingly, this report states that conditions can and were negotiated for marriage, which is ignored, even discouraged, in modern times.

While the Prophet encouraged marriage in general, there are certain types of marriages practised in *jāhiliyya* that he explicitly discouraged. These types are demeaning to women and objectify them as some form of merchandise, like the *fiqhī* view. The *shaghār* marriage is explicitly mentioned. Mālik explained that *shaghār* is when one man marries his daughter to another, provided that the other man marries his daughter to him, without any dower being paid. Mālik adds that the Prophet made his dislike and prohibition known (al-Dārimī, 2000, 3:1395 no. 2226; al-Bukhārī, 2001, 7:12, no. 5112), reinforcing that dower is a woman's right and needs to be paid to her.

Yet dower is not the only expense in a marriage. The sources narrate an episode with the Prophet's wives that ended with the revelation of verses 33:28–29, giving them the choice between 'the life of this world and its glitter' and 'God, his Prophet, and the Hereafter'. Hadith-reports present a conflicting story about an incident, leading to the Prophet's seclusion from all his wives for a month. There is no consensus in the Hadith literature about the reasons. They range between some kind of insubordination by some, talking back, material demands like clothes and luxurious articles that the Prophet was unable to fulfil, which would entail expenses and can be regarded as maintenance since they involve clothing, and ʿĀʾisha's and Ḥafṣa's jealousy of Mariyya. Whatever the reason, all accounts agree about the result, namely the Prophet secluding himself for a month in the mosque, and a fear in the community that he would divorce them all (al-Ṭabarī, 2000, 8:182–5).

Stating rights leads to avoidance of conflict and the Prophet did that when asked by a man: '"O Prophet! What are our wives' rights?" He replied: "To feed her when you eat, clothe her when you acquire clothes, not to strike her face, not to *tuqabbiḥ* (insult, curse) and not to separate from her except inside your home"' (Ibn Ḥanbal, 1995, 33:226, no. 20022; Abū Dāwūd, 2009, 2:244, no. 2142; al-Bayhaqī, 1994, 7:497, no. 14779). Feeding and clothing are considered an obligation for the husband and are part of the *nafaqa* (maintenance) allocated to women in *fiqh*, albeit in return for sexual availability. Yet the Prophet did not make maintenance conditional on anything. He is quoted as saying: 'The best Dīnār a man can spend, is the Dīnār he spends on his family' (al-Bayhaqī, 1994, 7:770, no. 15698; al-Hindī, 2004, 6:236, no. 1814;

Muslim, n.d., 2:69, no. 994). In various Hadith commentaries the word 'family' includes the wife and children, as well as slaves and servants.

Returning to the Qur'anic theme of love and mercy, and encouraging men to cultivate both in their marital life, the Prophet asserts that if a man gives his wife a drink of water, he will be rewarded, and if he puts a morsel of food in his wife's mouth it is considered *ṣadaqa* (alms, charity) (Ibn Ḥanbal, 1995, 28:386, no. 17155). Al-Bukhārī collected a report saying that when a man spends on his family, he is rewarded for it as having performed charity (al-Bukhārī, 2001, 1:20, no. 55). This again stands opposed to the legal concept of *nafaqa* being given in return for a service, be it domestic work or sexual, as these reports show that men are rewarded for spending on their wives and children regardless of any return.

Rights give rise to responsibilities, and not only financial ones. ʿAbd Allah b. ʿUmar narrated that the Prophet said: 'Everyone is a shepherd and is responsible for his flock, the Imam is a shepherd and is responsible for his flock, the man is a shepherd in his family and is responsible for his flock, and a woman is a shepherd in her husband's house and is responsible for her flock, and the servant is a shepherd for his master's money and is responsible for his flock' (Mālik Ibn Anas, n.d., 2:182, no. 2121; Ibn Ḥanbal, 1995, 8:83, no. 4495; al-Bukhārī, 2001, 2:5, no. 893; Muslim, n.d., 3:1459, no. 20). Making the wife responsible for her family in her home stands in direct opposition to the hierarchical view espoused by the jurists; more so that she shares this responsibility with her husband, with both being responsible for their flock.

3.3 Mutual care, kindness, trust and conflict resolution

This section deals with some of the ethical values that could be the cornerstones of spousal relations as illustrated by Prophet Muhammad's teachings and own conduct, including how to deal with complex situations in marriage and resolve conflicts. Marriage should be celebrated, as apparent from a report narrated by Anas b. Mālik that ʿAbd al-Raḥmān b. ʿAwf married an Anṣārī woman. 'The Prophet asked him: "How much did you pay her in dower?" He replied: "A weight of a date pip of gold."' The Prophet approved and asked him to make a *walīma* (wedding feast) even with only one ewe (al-Bukhārī, 2001, 7:21, no. 5153). ʿĀʾisha also narrated that the Prophet said: 'Announce marriages, in the mosques, and beat with tambourines' (al-Hindī, 2004, 16:291, no. 44535; Ibn Ḥanbal, 1995, 24:189, no. 15451; Ibn Māja, 1998,

1:611, no. 1895 and 26:53, no. 16130). A marriage announcement is one of the pillars of a valid marriage called *ishhār* (Qabalān, 1999, p. 64).

Not only were marriages to be celebrated, but joy should continue within a marriage. The Prophet advised playfulness and fun with one's family. He is reported to have said: 'Everything other than remembering God, is merely *lahw* (amusement, aimless waste of time, diversion, games and other pastime activities) or *sahw* (omission, carelessness, forgetfulness, inattention), except for four: A man walking purposefully, disciplining his horse, playfulness with his family, and teaching/learning how to swim' (al-Nasāʾī, 2001, 8:177, no. 8891).

Marriage is also about entertainment and having fun together. ʿĀʾisha said:

> The Abyssinians went to the mosque to perform. The Prophet asked me: 'O Ḥumayrāʾ,[12] would you like to go watch them?' I affirmed. He stood at the door and I leaned my chin on his shoulder touching his cheek (al-Bukhārī, 1989, 7:33, no. 5211; Muslim, n.d., 4:1894, no. 2445) ... He asked: 'Have you had enough?' I replied: 'Do not rush, O Prophet, it is not that I like watching them, but I wanted women to know my place in your heart/affections. (al-Nasāʾī, 2001, 8:181, no. 8902; Ibn Ḥanbal, 1995, 40:339, no. 24297)

Abū Bakr narrates that he visited the Prophet and found him resting with his robe covering his face, while two girls were beating a tambourine for ʿĀʾisha. He reprimanded her. The Prophet uncovered his face and said: 'Let them be, for these are the days of ʿĪd' (Ibn Hishām, 1990, 1:189; al-Bukhārī, 1989, 2:23, no. 987).

Sources also point out that the Prophet was observant and sensitive to any changes in his wives' moods. ʿĀʾisha narrated that the Prophet told her: '"It is not hidden from me when you are pleased and when you are angry with me." She asked: "How do you know that?" He replied: "If you are pleased with me you swear by the God of Muhammad and when you are angry you swear by the God of Ibrāhīm." She replied: "Yes, by God, I just avoid your name"' (Ibn Ḥanbal, 1995, 40:12, no. 24012; al-Bukhārī, 2001, 8:21, no. 6078; Muslim, n.d., 4:1890, no. 2439). Sources also recorded that when one of his wives

---

[12] *Ḥumayrāʾ* literally means little reddish one; it was one of the nicknames the Prophet gave ʿĀʾisha.

became angry, the Prophet used to place his hand on her shoulder and say: 'Oh God, forgive her all her sins and let her heart's anger evaporate and save her from temptations' (Ibn ʿAsākir, 1986, 1:85).

He used to have nicknames for his wives. For example, he said to ʿĀʾisha: 'Oh ʿĀʿish,[13] this is Jibrīl greeting you' (al-Bukhārī, 1989, 5:29, no. 3768). He also called her 'al-Ḥumayrāʾ' (little reddish one) because of her fair skin (Ibn Māja, 1998, 2:826, no. 2474 and al-Ṭabarānī, 1994, 22:400, no. 1000). They also exchanged gifts. For example, ʿĀʾisha made a black *burda* (cloak) for the Prophet (Abū Dāwūd, 2009, 4:54, no. 4074; al-Bayhaqī, 1994, 2:588, 4184). The Prophet sent some gifts to al-Najashi, Negus of Abyssinia: a garment and several ounces of musk. As the Negus had died, they were returned, so he gave each of his wives an ounce of musk and gave Umm Salama the rest of the musk and the garment (Ibn Ḥanbal, 1995, 45:247, no. 27276).

Happiness and joy are beautiful feelings. Beauty, as mentioned above, can be the basis for mutual attraction and appeal, which is why the Prophet advised husbands and wives to beautify themselves for one another. The Prophet saw a man with dishevelled hair, and told him: '*Iḥlaq* (cut, shave) it, for it increases your beauty/handsomeness' (Nābulusī, 2006, 1:79; al-Ḥurr al-ʿĀmilī, 2007, 1:416). Ibn Abbas said of himself: 'I *atazayyan* (adorn myself) for my wife just as I like her to adorn herself for me.' Then he recited verse 2:228 'and they have rights similar to those against them in a just manner' (al-Baghdādī, 1955, 1:226). Jaʿfar al-Ṣādiq narrated that the Prophet said: '*Tahaya*ʾ (prepare) for your wife as you like her to prepare for you' (al-Nuʿmān, 1995, 1:133; al-Ṭabarsī, 1987–8, 30:36). The Prophet also took care of his appearance and *tajammala* (beautified himself) for his family. While he was combing his hair, looking into a water container in her room, ʿĀʾisha said: '"Looking into the mirror and combing your hair, while you are God's Messenger and the best of his creations?" He replied: "God Almighty loves for his servants to prepare for their family and to beautify themselves"' (al-Majlisī, 2008, 16:249).

Beauty also translates to *rifq* (gentleness, kindness), essential in any human relationship. ʿĀʾisha reported that the Prophet said: '*Rifq* is not found anywhere unless *zānahu* (beautifies), and when it is removed it *shānahu* (disgraces) it' (Muslim, n.d., 4:2004, no. 1491). ʿĀʾisha also reported that the Prophet told her: 'O ʿĀʾisha, God is kind and loves kindness. He gives rewards for kindness that He does not give for violence. He gives what he does not give for anything else ... Whoever forbids kindness forbids *khayr*

[13] ʿĀʿish is a short form of ʿĀʾisha; it is an endearing change of her name to a nickname.

(goodness)' (Abū Dāwūd, 2009, 2:53, no. 701; Ibn Abī Shaybah, 1989, 5:209, no. 25303; Muslim, n.d., 4:2003, no. 2592). Therefore, it is not surprising to find the Prophet repeatedly enjoining kindness and gentleness in general and in a marriage in particular. He is reported to have said: 'The believers with the best of faith are those with the highest morals, best manners and kindest to their families' (Ibn Ḥanbal, 1995, 40:242, no. 24204; al-Tirmidhī, 1975, 5:9, no. 2612; Ibn Ḥibbān, 1993, 9:484).

Respect is also a recurrent theme in the reports, directed at both the spouses. Respect is best demonstrated by how the Prophet treated his wives in public for all to see. A case in point is Umm Salama. The Prophet followed her advice many times, most notably during the Treaty of Ḥudaybiyya (Sayyid al-Ahl, 1981, p. 24). Her reputation of being wise and her positive involvement in political affairs such as Ḥudaybiyya as well as the honorific given to her, *'Aym al-'Arab'*,[14] show how respected and revered she was (al-Suweidy, 2006, p. 66). Umm Salama joined the Prophet on his journey to perform the pilgrimage in 6 AH/627 CE, which failed and resulted in the Treaty of Ḥudaybiyya (Ibn Sa'd, 1990, 2:95; al-Ḥalabī, 1902, 3:9). The Prophet asked everyone repeatedly to cut their hair and slaughter their sacrifices, but nobody listened because they were angry, thinking the treaty unfair to the Muslims and disappointed not to be performing the pilgrimage. He complained to Umm Salama: 'Thrice have I commanded the people to slaughter their animals and shave their heads. But look how listless and indolent they are!' She comforted him and advised him to do his duty and perform his own rites in an open place for all to see (al-Bukhārī, 2001, 3:182). Realizing the sense of this advice, he followed it, picking a camel, bringing it out into the open, then slaughtering it, pronouncing: 'Allahu Akbar! Allahu Akbar!' The result was exactly as Umm Salama had predicted. It was reported that her wisdom was appreciated and acknowledged (Ibn Ḥajar al-'Asqalānī, 1959, 5:347).

The story about how Abū Sufyan and 'Abd Allah Ibn Umayya accepted Islam also shows that Umm Salama participated in the events of Mecca's conquest. Ibn Isḥāq reported that these two men met the Prophet, requesting the permission from Umm Salama, who asked on their behalf saying: 'Your paternal cousin and maternal cousin, who is also your in-law, are requesting to see you'. The Prophet refused saying that his paternal cousin dishonoured

[14] The word *'aym'* was used by the Arabs as a title for widows and unmarried women. When Umm Salama's husband, Abu Salama, died, the Muslim community bestowed the title *'Aym al-'Arab'* on her.

him, while his maternal cousin shamed and insulted him in Mecca. Umm Salama interceded on their behalf again, until the Prophet took pity on them. They renounced their old faith and joined the fold of Islam (al-Ḥalabī, 1902, 3:77).

Sources also preserved a *mashhūr* (famous) report attributed to the Prophet, advising his community to take *'ilm* (knowledge) of religion[15] from this little Ḥumayrā', thereby honouring 'Ā'isha in public. Even though this report has been classified as forged, it was preserved in the collections making it part of the community's collective memory (al-Ḥalabī, 1999, 4:300, no. 9834; al-Sakhāwī, 1985, p. 197; al-Suyūṭī, 1987, p. 79).

Another admirable behaviour next to respect is trust. Trust is essential between spouses, and privacy is also important. The Prophet discouraged breaking marital trust by revealing marital secrets. He is reported to have said: 'The most evil of people in the sight of God on Judgement Day is the man who is intimate with his wife, and then he divulges her secret' (al-Ḥumaydī, 2002, 2:404, no. 2365; Ibn Abī Shaybah, 1989, 4:39, no. 17559; Muslim, n.d., 2:1060, no. 1437 and Abū Dāwūd, 2009, 4:268, no. 4870). Yet trust is more than keeping secrets. The Prophet discouraged suspicions and doubts, especially regarding morals. Therefore, he never entered his wives' rooms suddenly without knocking on the door, especially after returning from a journey. A report is recorded in several collections where the Prophet prohibits entering one's home at night without knocking. Muslim adds in his *Ṣaḥīḥ* that this is especially important if the husband has been away for a long time (al-Bukhārī, 2001, 3:7, no. 1801; Ibn Ḥibbān, 1993, 6:430, no. 2715; Muslim, n.d., 3:1528, no. 715). This consideration is also to give the women time to look their best. Moreover, it allows husbands to be patient and trusting. Jealous husbands have been known throughout history to commit violent acts (Franzway et al., 2019, p. 93). The Prophet addressed jealousy and suspicion in one report where he is quoted as saying: 'There is a type of jealousy that God loves, and a type that God hates. The type of jealousy he loves is based on suspicions; the one he hates is jealousy without suspicions' (Ibn Māja, 1998, 1:643, no. 1996). This means that if the husband does not suspect his wife of specific wrongdoing, he should trust her implicitly and therefore not be jealous. Wives can also be jealous, especially in a polyandrous marriage, where there is no equality. The Prophet addressed this saying: 'Whoever has two wives and has a preference for one over the other, come Judgement Day, his scale will be slanted and not

[15] Different versions mention half of the religion or a big part of the religion.

balanced' (al-Fāsī, 2003, 3:1236; al-Mundhirī, 1960, 4:129). Therefore, equality and fairness are paramount.

Jealousy is a recurrent theme in the reports about the Prophet's marriages. However, it is the Prophet's way of dealing with the fights that is interesting, for he neither enjoyed nor encouraged fights over his attention, but comforted the hurt or laughed off pranks with them all. For instance, it was narrated that Ṣafiyya went on a journey with the Prophet. He saw her crying and went to console her. She complained that she was given a slow camel. The Prophet later discovered that Zaynab was behind that choice of mount and avoided visiting Zaynab in her quarters for a while, but then forgave her (al-Nasāʾī, 2001, 8:261, no. 9117). Another incident reports that Ṣafiyya had a falling out with Ḥafṣa who belittled her, saying: 'A Jew's daughter!' Ṣafiyya started to cry. The Prophet asked her what she was crying about. She told him to which he replied: 'You are the daughter of a Prophet, niece of a Prophet, and married to a Prophet, so why is she boasting to you?' (Ibn Rahwayh, 1991, 4:261; Ibn Ḥibbān, 1993, 16:193, no. 7211).

Other incidents were reported in the sources as anecdotes, especially food fights. In one report ʿĀʾisha said: 'I brought the Prophet some *khazīra*[16] that I had cooked for him and said to Sawda, with the Prophet sitting in between: "Eat!" She refused. I said: "Eat or I will smear it on your face!" She still refused. I took some from the bowl and smeared it on her face. The Prophet laughed and then took some and put it on her hand saying: "Smear it on her face" and he laughed ...' (al-Nasāʾī, 2001, 8:162, no. 8868; al-Ḥumaydī, 2002, 9:456). Another food fight is described when the Prophet was with some of his wives and another wife sent a bowl of food over. ʿĀʾisha struck the servant's hand and the bowl fell and broke in two. The Prophet put the two halves together, rescuing the food into them, saying: 'Your mother is jealous.' He waited until someone brought another bowl from ʿĀʾisha's room and gave it to the owner of the broken one (Ibn Abī Shaybah, 1989, 7:301, no. 36282; Ibn Ḥanbal, 1995, 19:84, no. 12027; al-Bukhārī, 2001, 7:36, no. 5225).

Ḥafṣa narrated that al-Shifā bint ʿAbd Allah used to chant *ruqyat al-namla*, an incantation against sores. The Prophet asked al-Shifā to teach it to Ḥafṣa, however he did not mean the incantation, but the *jāhiliyya* wedding song bearing the same name. Its lyrics say: 'The bride wears shoes with soles, puts henna on her hands, kohl on her eyes and does everything except disobey her man.' This was an allusion to Ḥafṣa and her disobeying

[16] A dish made from boiled fatty meat, salt and flour.

Muhammad (Ibn Abī Shaybah, 1989, 5:43, no. 23540; Ibn Ḥanbal, 1995, 44:45, no. 26450; al-Nasāʾī, 1997, 7:75, no. 7501). He wanted to reprimand her for revealing his secret, yet opted to use this method rather than openly chastizing her.[17]

In these last reports, laughter and jokes are used to take the edge off the situation. ʿĀʾisha is reprimanded for her jealousy and the resulting broken bowl through a joke, as is Ḥafṣa, packaging the reprimand with laughter so as not to hurt their feelings. Faults can be pointed out and corrected through laughter, thereby contributing to the moral health of the individual and by extension the community (Laude, 2005, p. 120). An individual is invited to laugh at the transgression as it has not caused serious damage to the prevailing norms in ethical, religious, social, aesthetic or sensitive terms (Winkler, 1998, p. 1166). Moreover, laughter signals that harmony can be restored without much effort, which is essential in a polygynous marriage.

The ideal marriage according to the Prophet's example and his sayings is – much like the Qurʾan – based on love, mutual care, kindness and trust, as well as companionship and joy. Marriage is a shared responsibility built on mutual respect; conflicts are resolved with magnanimity and wives are not controlled but trusted. The shared responsibility is also translated to sharing household duties, which are not only for women, as Muhammad helped his wives with the housework. ʿĀʾisha was asked what the Prophet did at home. She replied: 'He does as *ahlihi* (family, wives) do' (Ibn Ḥanbal, 1995, 40:274, no. 24226; al-Bukhārī, 1989, 8:14, no. 6039). In another report she said:

---

[17] The classical commentators, exegetes and traditionists provide two opinions for the occasion of the revelation of verse 66:1: 'O Prophet! Why do you prohibit yourself from what Allah has made lawful to you, seeking to please your wives?'

In one version, the Prophet prohibits himself from being intimate with Mariyya al-Qibtiyya. The sources say that Ḥafṣa became upset when the Prophet was intimate with Mariyya on the day allocated to Ḥafṣa, after she had asked permission to go visit her father ʿUmar b. al-Khaṭṭāb and possibly spending the night there, as she had received news that he was gravely ill. He was well and Ḥafṣa returned and found Mariyya with the Prophet in her house. She became very upset and according to the sources reprimanded the Prophet, saying: 'O Messenger of Allah, in my house and on my bed?' The Prophet reassured Ḥafṣa and promised not to touch Mariyya again if she did not divulge this secret and kept it to herself. However, Ḥafṣa revealed the secret to ʿĀʾisha, who told other wives, aggravating the situation further. This is one of the reasons stated for the Prophet leaving his wives and moving to the mosque for a month. For details, see al-Nasāʾī (2001, 36:21, no. 3959) and al-Ṭabarī (2000, 13:147).

In the second version ʿĀʾisha and Ḥafṣa were upset that the Prophet was spending more time with his wife Zaynab on account of a honey drink she would serve him, so they secretly agreed to pretend to be offended by its odour. The Prophet did not want to offend his wives, so he swore an oath and prohibited himself from ever drinking it again.

'He was like other men, sewed his own garment, milked his ewe, and served himself' (Ibn Ḥajar al-Haythamī, 1998, 1:494, no. 327). There are several versions of this report with different household duties being performed by the Prophet. In one, ʿĀʾisha replied: 'He was a human being who deloused his garment and milked his sheep' (al-Bukhārī, 1989, 1:279, no. 541; Ibn Ḥibbān, 1993, 12:489, no. 5675). Interestingly Ibn Ḥanbal preserves a report quoting ʿĀʾisha saying: 'The Prophet used to mend his robe and repair his soles. He did what all men did in their homes' (Ibn Ḥanbal, 1995, 43:289, no. 26239), pointing to the fact that other men were active in the household as well and did not leave all chores to their wives.

Not living up to one's responsibilities leads to conflicts and discord within a marriage. The Prophet reminded his community to eliminate discord by reducing problematic discourse and fault-finding. He is reported to have advised: 'A believer should not *yafrak* (find faults with) a female believer, for if he dislikes one of her characteristics, he would find another one pleasant/appealing' (Ibn Ḥanbal, 1995, 14:99, no. 8363; al-Nawawī, 2017, 10:58, no. 1469). The Prophet urged his community to sort out differences amicably and encouraged communal participation to solve marital discord. He is reported as saying: 'One of the best forms of intercession is to intercede between two partners in a marriage' (Ibn Māja, 1998,1:635, no. 1975). When intercession failed to save a marriage and it came to divorce, the Prophet still encouraged the survival of the marriage through reconciliation.

3.4 Sexual intimacy

The next section will look at what the Prophet said about intimate relations and what his wives reported about the Prophet's 'bedroom etiquette', and most importantly how dower and maintenance are not tied to sexual availability. Sex is considered *fitrah* (human nature), however, in Islam its fulfilment is restricted within the legal institution of marriage. Islam recognizes the purpose of intercourse as not only for procreation, but also for pleasure. In *fiqh*, however, men's sexual desire is privileged and encouraged, while women's desire is feared and regulated; marriage in general is tied in the legal compendia to a focus on sexual relations, with maintenance conditioned on the wife's sexual availability at all times.

Islam does not promote celibacy, which is clearly shown in the following report:

> Three men came to the Prophet's wives asking about how the Prophet worshipped. When they were told they said: 'How can we compare ourselves to the Prophet; he was forgiven all his prior and future sins'. One man said: 'I pray all night'. The other said: 'I perpetually fast and do not break the fast'. The third one said: 'I stay away from women, I will never marry'. The Prophet came in and said: 'Are you the ones who said such and such? By God, I fear for you. I am the most God fearing, yet I fast and break my fast, pray and sleep, and marry women. He who does not like my Sunna is not of my community.' (al-Bukhārī, 2001, 7:2, no. 5063)

Setting an example for his community, the Prophet encouraged its members to marry and enjoy intimacy.

Pleasure or sexual gratification was never meant to be for men only. ʿĀʾisha said:

> ʿUthmān b. Mazʿūn's wife used to beautify herself, put on perfume, and then she left him and came to see me. I asked: 'Is he there or is he absent?' She replied: 'Being there is the same as being absent'. The Prophet entered the room and heard her story. He went to ʿUthmān and asked him: 'ʿUthmān, do you believe in what we believe in?' He replied: 'Yes, O Prophet of God'. The Prophet said: 'Then take us as an example, do like we do, care for your wife and give her what is due to her, fulfilling her rights'. The next day ʿUthmān's wife went to ʿĀʾisha and said: 'What happens to other women [that is, having sexual intercourse] happened to us'. (Ibn Ḥanbal, 1995, 41:273, no. 24753; Ibn Ḥajar al-ʿAsqalānī, 1994, 17:588, no. 22851)

In another report, ʿUthmān b. Maẓʿūn told the Prophet: '"O Messenger of Allah! I feel shy, for my wife sees my nakedness (*awra*)". The Prophet replied: "Why should that be when Allah has made you garments for one another?" He replied: "I hate this". The Prophet said: "My wives see mine and I see theirs"' (al-Haythamī, 1994, 4:294, no. 7561).

ʿUthmān was not the only man whose behaviour was corrected by the Prophet. ʿAbd Allah b. ʿAmr fasted every day and worshipped the entire night reciting the daily Qurʾanic revelation in *tahajjud*.[18] When he got married

[18] *Tahajjud* is a supererogatory prayer which is recommended, but not compulsory and is prayed after the obligatory nightly prayer and before the obligatory morning prayer at dawn.

his father asked his wife how he was treating her. She said: 'An excellent man, who has not slept in my bed nor removed my veil since I came to him!' ʿAmr went to ask the Prophet for advice. The Prophet called ʿAbd Allah and told him: 'Do not do this. Fast and break your fast, pray and sleep, because your body has a right over you, your eyes have a right over you, and your wife has a right over you' (al-Bukhārī, 2001, 6:196, no. 5052; al-Nasāʾī, 2001, 4:209, no. 2389). The fact that a wife has sexual rights has been emphasized and encouraged. Men were told that to fulfil a wife's right would be rewarded. Abū Dharr narrated: 'The Prophet said: "Intercourse is a *ṣadaqa* (charity)". He was asked: "O Prophet, will one of us fulfil his desire and be rewarded for it?" He said: "If it was performed by unlawful means it would be punished for being sinful, therefore if it is performed lawfully, it will be rewarded"' (Muslim, n.d., 2:697, no. 1006; al-Bayhaqī, 1994, 4:316, no. 7823).

The Prophet reiterated in many reports that women have needs just like men (Ibn Hubayra, 1996, 5:318, no. 1742). However, these needs were to be fulfilled in a loving playful manner and be mutually fulfilling. ʿAbd Allah al-Anṣārī was advised to be playful and allow his wife to be playful in return (al-Bukhārī, 2001, 7:66, no. 5367; Ibn Ḥibbān, 1993, 16:87, no. 7138; al-Bayhaqī, 1994, 7:129, no. 13471). Wives were advised not to repress their passion as the Prophet is reported to have said: 'The best wife is the one who engages with her husband and takes off the shield of modesty' (al-Majlisī, 2008, 100:239).

Before engaging in intercourse, mutual desire should be awakened if it was not present. The Prophet advised men, saying: '"None of you should fall on their wives as cattle do, but let there be a messenger between you first". He was asked: "What messenger?" He replied: "Kisses and [sweet] talk"' (al-Ghazālī, 1984, 2:74). In a different report with the same conclusion Anas narrated that the Prophet said: 'Three things are of ill manners: a man befriending a man without knowing his name and *kunya* (teknonym); a man preparing food for his brother who does not come; and a man having intercourse with his wife without *mudāʿaba* (foreplay) or sending a messenger of playfulness and kisses, for a man should not fall on his wife like a beast' (al-Albānī, 1979, 13:179, no. 6075).

Awakening desire with foreplay is also the topic of the following report attributed to the Prophet: '"Do not fall on your wife, unless she feels the same lust like you, so that you do not precede her [in climaxing] and leave her with emptiness". He was asked: "How so?" He replied: "You kiss her, touch her, and whisper to her, and when you see that she has come to feel the same, then be intimate with her"'. The commentary adds that if a man fulfils his desires before his wife, he would be loath to continue (Ibn Qayyim al-Jawziyya, n.d., 7:300). Anas narrated that the Prophet said: 'If a man has intercourse with his wife, then he should give her pleasure (literally charity), then if he fulfils his needs, he should not rush her until she has also been satisfied.' The commentary adds that leaving her unsatisfied would harm her and prevent her from fulfilling her desire (Ibn Qayyim al-Jawziyya, n.d., 7:300). Though *fiqh* regulates women's sexuality and hardly acknowledges women's needs, Ibn Qudāmā, the Ḥanbalī jurist, quotes the Prophet as saying: 'Do not begin intercourse until your wife feels the desire you feel, lest you fulfil your desires before she does' (Ibn Qudāma, 1997, 8:136). The undesirability of haste is emphasized in a report attributed to the Prophet in which he said: 'If someone wants to be intimate with his wife, he should not rush her, for women have needs' (al-Ḥurr al-ʿĀmilī, 2007, 20:118, no. 25184).

None of the Prophet's wives narrated any intimate details, yet they narrated some reports about 'bedroom etiquette', especially during menstruation. Not only were foreplay and playfulness recommended, but also being intimately close and enjoying one another, without intercourse.

Anas reported that when a Jewish woman menstruated, she would be forbidden from eating with her family or keeping their company at home. The companions asked the Prophet about that and verse 2:222 was revealed. The Prophet said: 'They can engage in everything except sexual intercourse' (Ibn Ḥanbal, 1995, 19:356, no. 12354; al-Dārimī, 2000, 1:700, no. 1093; al-Tirmidhī, 1975, 5:214, no. 2977; Abū Dāwūd, 2009, 1:67, no. 258). Maymūna, the Prophet's wife, said: 'If the Prophet wanted to approach one of his wives intimately while she was menstruating, he would ask her to wear a loincloth' (Ibn Ḥanbal, 1995, 44:427, no. 26855; al-Bukhārī, 2001, 1:68, no. 303; Muslim, n.d., 1:243, no. 295). ʿĀʾisha narrated the same (Ibn Ḥanbal, 1995, 40:325, no. 24280). Umm Salama narrated a more detailed report saying that she was sleeping next to the Prophet when she felt her menstruation start. She got up and took her precautions. The Prophet asked her whether her menses started, which she affirmed. He lifted the bedspread and invited her back to bed. She added that he used to kiss her while he was fasting (al-Bukhārī, 2001, 1:71, no. 322). ʿĀʾisha reports the same (Ibn Ḥanbal, 1995, 41:325, no. 24824).

Unlike in *fiqh* manuals, where intercourse is presented as the main issue, intimacy is also found in sharing loving gestures and caresses. ʿĀʾisha narrated that when she was menstruating, the Prophet used to approach her intimately without engaging in intercourse and making sure beforehand that she was wearing an *izār* (loincloth) (Ibn Ḥanbal, 1995, 40:495, no. 24436;

al-Dārimī, 2000, 1:695, no. 1078; Abū Dāwūd, 2009, 1:55, no. 213). ʿĀʾisha also reported that when she was menstruating, the Prophet used to bring her a bowl to drink from, then he would take it and put his lips on the same place she had her lips on prior. She added that when they ate, she would take a bite off the roast and hand it to him and he would put his mouth on the same place to take a bite (Ibn Ḥanbal, 1995, 40:384, no. 24328; al-Dārimī, 2000, 1:704, no. 1101; Muslim, n.d., 1:245, no. 300). Though *fiqh* reduces marriage to intercourse, the Prophet's example shows that intercourse was not the main aim. For the Prophet and his wives, tenderness, caresses and intimate closeness were equally important.

While foreplay is essential, the aftermath was also mentioned. ʿĀʾisha narrated that she used to perform her *ghusl* (purity wash) with the Prophet from the same vessel/container (Ibn Ḥanbal, 1995, 43:125, no. 25981; al-Bukhārī, 2001, 1:59, no. 250). The same report was narrated naming other wives of the Prophet (Ibn Ḥanbal, 1995, 38:404, no. 572; al-Dārimī, 2000, 1:579, no. 776), for example Maymūna (al-Bukhārī, 2001, 1:60, no. 253), and Umm Salama (al-Bukhārī, 2001, 1:71, no. 322). ʿĀʾisha also narrated that she used to perform her *wuḍūʾ* (ablutions) with the Prophet from the same container (Ibn Māja, 1998, 1:131, no. 368). Washing together prolonged the intimate closeness.

None of the reports that explicitly mention sexual intercourse, foreplay or aftermath name the dower as a price to pay in return. Neither is maintenance mentioned in connection to sexual intimacy. The only criteria mentioned are mutual desire and satisfaction, as well as creating a close bond.

As demonstrated, the Prophet addressed a myriad of topics, starting from enjoining and recommending marriage as his Sunna, to advice about choice of spouse, not being excessive in dower, being kind and gentle, avoiding jealousy and suspicion, sharing responsibilities in the home and more. The Prophet extended suitability of spouses to young, old, divorced, widowed, Christian, Jewish, free and enslaved women, without mentioning any preferences except their *taqwā*. Significantly, he mentioned the wife's right to maintenance without returns or obligations, to good treatment and companionship, preserving religion and spirituality, preparing one's self using adornments, helping her to maintain herself and not revealing intimate or marital secrets. He repeatedly enjoined kindness and gentleness and set the example by practising what he preached, emphasizing that women have emotions, thoughts, desires, needs and should be treated accordingly. Most importantly, he treated his wives lovingly and respectfully, paying attention to their feelings and moods, preserving religion and spirituality, preparing himself for them, helping at home with household chores and respecting them in private and in public. The Prophet not only discouraged but forbade celibacy, pointing out that fulfilling one's desire within the legal outlet of marriage would result in rewards. He advised men to satisfy their wives and not seek their own gratification and urged wives to forget modesty with their husbands, recommending foreplay and closeness after the act or during menstruation when intercourse was prohibited. Nowhere did the Prophet mention dower and maintenance in return for any services, be they in the home or of a sexual nature. All this compares to the Qur᾿anic marriage ideal and contrasts drastically with the *fiqhī* one, which ignores women's emotional and sexual needs, focusing only on men's wishes. In addition, the *fiqhī* commercial aspect of marriage, reducing it to an exchange of dower and maintenance for sexual availability, is completely overturned in the Prophet's words and practices.

4. TACKLING DISCRIMINATORY HADITH-REPORTS

As mentioned above, reports were indeed uttered by the Prophet, while others were put into his mouth to reflect the interests of later Muslims. Therefore, the various reports should be compared and contrasted. As for marriage in general, as demonstrated, the Prophet practised what he preached. Interestingly, some of the reports above recommend men achieving spiritual advancement and growth through being ethical, kind, loving and fair husbands, reversing the traditional *fiqhī* view that it is the wife's deference and obedience that are her ticket to paradise. Most importantly, Muhammad mentioned the wife's right to maintenance and companionship without any strings attached, and urged not to reveal intimate or marital secrets, reiterating the Qur᾿anic concept of *satr* (covering failings). Moreover, fairness between wives was another topic the Prophet pressed on his community both through preaching and practising it by treating his wives equally. When it came to intimacy in marriage, the Prophet also preached and practised the same, in accordance with the Qur᾿an. He also restricted intimacy to marriage, but he did not limit it to only male fulfilment.

Yet, there are numerous reports that limit women's agency even in their own homes and perpetuate the myth of a marital hierarchy. The most famous among them is the one claiming that the Prophet said: 'If I were to command anyone to prostrate before another, I would command women to prostrate before their husbands, because of the special right given to husbands by Allah over them' (al-ʿAynī, 1980, 1:203; al-Mubārakfūrī, 2014, 4:271, no. 1159). In a blatant contradiction to the Qurʾanic verse 4:32 promising rewards to men and women based on their deeds, another report places the husband between his wife and God by claiming that the Prophet said: 'By the One in whose hand Muhammad's soul is, no woman can fulfil her duty towards Allah until she fulfils her duty towards her husband' (Ibn Māja, 1998, 1:595, no. 1853; Ibn Ḥibbān, 1993, 9:479, no. 4171).

Furthermore, many reports ascribed to the Prophet and contrary to his own practice and sense of justice tell women that they must obey their husbands even if these husbands are wrong or unjust (al-Hindī, 2004, 16:339). A logical flaw is apparent in a report ascribed to the Prophet saying: 'If a man orders his wife to move from a red mountain to a black mountain and [again] from a black mountain to a red mountain it is incumbent upon her to obey' (Ibn Māja, 1998, 1:595, no. 1852). This exaggerated obligation for women to obey such a ridiculous, tiring and useless request serves to show that obedience in all other matters is compulsory on wives.

Moreover, many reports condemn women's sexuality and limit their sexual participation to pleasing their husbands whenever and wherever he wishes. Most famously a report claiming that the Prophet said: 'God created ten parts of *shahwa* (desire), and then made nine parts in women and one part in men. Had God not given them *ḥayāʾ* (bashfulness) in proportion to their appetite, every man would have nine women clinging to him' (Ibn Ḥabīb, 1992, 153). In a different version the Prophet allegedly said: 'Desire was made into ten parts, of which nine parts were made in women, and one in men; had it not been for the modesty that was imposed on women with regard to their desires, every man would have nine *mughtalimāt* (nymphomaniacs)' (al-Ṭabarānī, 1995, 1:178, no. 567; al-Ḥumaydī, 2002, 5:81, no. 3775). This hadith is classified as *aḥād* (solitary). Additionally, there is a logical flaw in the narrative, for if women were indeed given nine parts of desire, they would require nine men to fulfil it and nine men would be crowding over one woman. Therefore, one can only conclude that the discussion of sex in the legal sources is based mostly on men's sexual fantasies, whereas women's opinions and voices are completely absent from the discussion.

Such narratives are found in abundance and in various versions, such as one claiming that the Prophet said: 'If a man calls his wife to his bed and she refuses, and he goes to bed angry, the angels will curse her until she awakens in the morning' (al-Bukhārī, 2001, 4:116, no. 3237; Muslim, n.d., 2:1060, no. 1436). This report comes in numerous variants that all urge the wife to comply immediately. In one version, she has to obey even if she is on the back of a camel (Abū Dāwūd, 2009, 3:457, no. 2063; Ibn Ḥanbal, 1995, 39:456, no. 17; al-Bayhaqī, 1994, 7:477, no. 14713). Interestingly, Ibn Ḥanbal supplies a classification that this report has a *muḍṭarib* (irreconcilable uncertainty) *isnād*. The second variant urges the wife to comply even if she is in front of an oven (Ibn Abī Shaybah, 1989, 3:558, no. 17135; Ibn Ḥanbal, 1995, 39:456, no. 17; al-Tirmidhī, 1975, 3:457, no. 1160; al-Nasāʾī, 2001, 8:187, no. 8922). Ibn Ḥanbal again classifies this as *ḍaʿīf* (weak) because of Muhammad b. Jābir, an untrustworthy narrator in the *isnād*. Al-Tirmidhi classified the same report as *ḥasan gharīb*.[19]

The *muḥaddithūn* (Hadith scholars) themselves recognized that these reports did not mirror the Prophet's behaviour and his adherence to the Qurʾan, as ʿĀʾisha reported that: 'His manner was the Qurʾan' (Ibn Ḥanbal, 1995, 42:183, no. 25302; al-Bukhārī, 1989, 1:160, no. 308; and al-Qasṭallānī, 2017, 2:102). According to Hadith scholars the authenticity of these traditions ranges from *ḍaʿīf* (weak) to *hasan gharīb* (good yet strange). Interestingly, all of them are *āḥād* reports (singular transmissions) that do not reach the level of *tawātur* (several transmissions). There is no question that these traditions have serious theological, moral and social consequences (Abou El Fadl, 2001, p. 212). In addition to a very important fact, they tarnish the Prophet by portraying him as someone who not only says everything and its opposite, but also contradicts the Qurʾan and God's will.

Hallaq (2009, pp. 16–22) explains that the four sources of Islamic law are the Qurʾan, the Prophet's Sunna, *ijmāʿ* (consensus) and *qiyās* (analogical reasoning). As mentioned above, the Qurʾan paints a different image of marriage and the Sunna reinforces that same Qurʾanic image, both in the words and deeds of the Prophet, one of love, mercy and compassion rather than a contractual transaction requiring a payment in exchange for a service. What remains are the women-demeaning hadiths that go both against the Qurʾanic spirit, as well as the Prophet's example, pointing to forgeries or a faulty *qiyās*. This can be corrected by revisiting the basis of *fiqh* rulings by re-examining the Qurʾan and the Prophet's example. Most importantly, the

[19] *Ḥasan gharib* can be translated as 'good yet strange'. *Ḥasan* (good) is used to describe a report whose authenticity is not as well-established as that of *ṣaḥīḥ*. *Ghārib* is a report conveyed by only one narrator or having an addition in the text that differs from other narrations of multiple narrators, or it is narrated through various chains of transmitters but having within one of its chains an addition in the *isnād*.

ijmāʿ (consensus) is controversial and is more of a myth perpetuated by male scholars and theologians. In fact, there is no real consensus, as there is no *ijmāʿ* on the definition of *ijmāʿ* itself, on whose it is (whether the entire community or only its clerics), on the competence of the constituent members, on the period covered, on the scope of its subject matter, on the source of its authority, on whether matters of creed and dogma fall within its scope, on whether it must be on the basis of positive expression or can be based on the silence of some, and finally, once a so-called consensus is reached, on whether it can be modified in the future based on new evidence (Farooq, 2011, p. 160). Yet, when male privilege was at stake, male legal scholars and jurists protected their own interests by ignoring the divine text and the Prophet's example, basing their rulings on their own 'consensus'.

Furthermore, the reports presented in the above sections speak of love, justice, kindness and beauty in all its different applications. However, as Ayubi (2019) points out, marital ethics in classical sources have little to do with love. Ayubi examines the work of ethicists al-Ghazālī (d. 505 AH/1111 CE), al-Ṭūsī (d. 597 AH/1274 CE), and al-Dawānī (d. 907 AH/1502 CE), noting that in the sections on marriage the definitions and explanations of what love for a wife means are conspicuously omitted. These ethicists 'imagine the household as a macrocosm of the ethically ordered *nafs*, rather than a shared home built on a male–female love partnership' (Ayubi, 2019, p. 115). In their view, according to Ayubi, the husband applies discipline and ethical principles to rule over his wife and the rest of the household for the purpose of his greater good. Moreover, in the eyes of these ethicists ideally a wife will bear a man his children, take care of his home and property, and serve as his deputy to allow him to pursue his own goals. However, Ayubi emphasizes that 'even as the ethicists take care to define the ideal wife, their discussions on this subject demonstrate their conflicted views on the nature of women and how best to deal with them' (2019, p. 124). Noteworthy is that all three ethicists were also jurists, with conflicted views between ethics and *fiqh*. Al-Ṭūsī was a Jaʿfarī jurist, while both al-Ghazālī and al-Dawānī were Shāfiʿī jurists.

A particular genre can differ quite significantly from another in how the subject matter, here marriage, is treated and to what end. Even as different genres discuss the same subjects, sometimes using similar materials, the end result may be different. According to Muhammad Qasim Zaman, this is 'a realization that has been slow in coming to many areas of Islamic studies. Without such recognition, however, interpreting the meaning and significance of particular texts, their relationship to works of the same or other genres, and judgments about their place in Islamic historiography or intellectual history ... may often prove to be quite misleading' (1996, p. 2).

CONCLUSION

This chapter attempted to put different prophetic reports in conversation with one another and extended that process to comparing the images emanating from different genres (Qur'an and Sunna). The aim is to reveal the image of marriage as intended by the Qur'an and as found in Hadith – an image based on ethics, justice, love and mercy. The chapter showed how the Prophet was portrayed in the Hadith corpus as a loving, understanding husband. It also conveyed how the Prophet viewed marriage through the advice he gave his community as well as his own behaviour.

In contradiction to the hadith-reports discussed above, legal manuals not only tied maintenance to sexual availability and compliance, but also limited maintenance to material values of food, drink, clothing and housing, thereby completely ignoring spiritual, religious, ethical, intellectual, aesthetic and emotional values, as advised and practised by Muhammad. Jurists limited their discussions of fairness between co-wives to the husband's overnight stay, also ignoring all other values, despite the Prophet mentioning jealousy and trust issues. The imbalance between husband's and wife's rights is noticeable in *fiqh*, contrary to the Prophetic example.

It is clear from the reports discussed that *fiqhī* manuals departed greatly from the example of the Prophet, and it was these rulings that guided the development of contemporary family laws. The conversations between the different reports and genres show the historical progression of the gradual discrepancies between the letter and the spirit of the law. Additionally, they show that the Hadith literature was manipulated with cultural accretions resulting in modifications. However, it is possible to use traditional – along with new – methodologies to better align laws and practices with the Prophet's example.

The prophetic marriage model can be revived to improve the lived realities of contemporary Muslim women through emulating Muhammad's behaviour and following his advice given in the reports. The prophetic advice was prescriptive and should have been incorporated into the regulations and rules of *fiqh*. There are two tools that allow this, namely *istiḥsān* and *istiṣlāḥ*. *Istiḥsān* (juristic discretion) linguistically means to seek the good, aiming at the best.

It is a legal principle whereby laws are established based on guidelines and injunctions from the Qur'an and the Hadith. It is simply the expression of the idea that equity and justice as defined by God must determine both the formulation and interpretation of laws (Pereira, 2002, p. 79). Additionally, *istiṣlāḥ* (consideration of benefit) means to seek what is correct and wholesome in a way that public and individual good must be the criterion for the development of the law. It holds that the Qur'an and Hadith lay down the framework of the law (Pereira, 2002). *Istiḥsān* and *istiṣlāḥ* were derived from Qur'anic verses 39:18[20] and 39:55[21] and were used in jurisprudence to justify many extensive departures from the literal meaning of the Qur'an, yet they were never invoked to improve the juristic idea of marriage to a more equitable and just one for women.

Discourses on Muslim woman are never monolithic; they are varied and contradictory, depending on the power structures involved in the process (Zayzafoon, 2005, p. 190). Khaled Abou El Fadl argues 'the consensus of one generation does not bind another, and an immoral unanimity is immoral all the same' (2006, p. 116). Therefore, we need a new *qiyās* using the same traditional, as well as new, methodologies, asking new questions and using old and new analytical tools to revisit the subject. An overhaul of *fiqh* is much needed to generate a new discourse, possibly and hopefully leading to a new consensus that reclaims *'adl* and *iḥsān* in Muslim marriages.

REFERENCES

'Abdu, Muhammad. 1999. *Ḥikmat Ta'addud Zawjāt al-Nabī*. Cairo: Dār al-Ḥaramayn.

Abdul Kodir, Faqihuddin. 2013. 'Gender Equality and the Hadith of the Prophet Muhammad: Reinterpreting the Concepts of Mahram and Qiwama'. In *Gender Equality and Muslim Family Law: Justice and Ethics in Islamic Legal Tradition*, edited by Ziba Mir-Hosseini, Kari Vogt, Lena Larsen and Christian Moe, pp. 169–89. London: I.B. Tauris.

Abou El Fadl, Khaled. 2001. *Speaking in God's Name: Islamic Law, Authority and Women*. Oxford: Oneworld.

Abou El Fadl, Khaled. 2006. *The Search for Beauty in Islam: A Conference of the Books*. Lanham, MD: Rowman & Littlefield.

[20] Verse 39:18: 'Those who listen to the word, then follow the best of it; those are they whom Allah has guided, and those it is who are the men of understanding.'

[21] Verse 39:55: 'And follow the best that has been revealed to you from your Lord before there comes to you the punishment all of a sudden while you do not even perceive.'

Abou El Fadl, Khaled. 2014. *Reasoning with God: Reclaiming Shari'ah in the Modern Age.* Lanham, MD: Rowman & Littlefield.

Abū Dāwūd, Sulaymān b. al-Ashʿath al-Sijistānī. 2009. *Sunan Abī Dāwūd.* Beirut: al-Maktaba al-ʿAṣriyya.

Al-Albānī, Muḥammad Nāṣir al-Dīn. 1979. *Silsilat al-Aḥādīth al-Ḍaʿīfah wa-al-Mawḍūʿah wa-Atharuhā al-Sayyiʾfī al-Ummah.* Damascus: Tawzīʿ al-Maktab al-Islāmī.

Ali, Kecia. 2006. *Sexual Ethics and Islam: Feminist Reflections on Qurʾan, Hadith, and Jurisprudence.* Oxford: Oneworld Publications.

Ali, Kecia. 2010. *Marriage and Slavery in Early Islam.* Cambridge, MA: Harvard University Press.

Al-Āmidī, ʿAbd al-Wāḥid b. Muhammad. 1994. *Mukhtaṣar Jawāhir al-Kalām fī al-Ḥikam wa-al-Aḥkām: Muʿjam Mufahras lil-Ḥikam al-Nabawīyah.* Beirut: Markaz al-Dirāsāt wa-al-Buḥūth al-ʿIlmīyah.

Amin, Yasmin. 2020. 'Conclusion'. In *Islamic Interpretive Tradition and Gender Justice, Processes of Canonization, Subversion, and Change,* edited by Nevin Reda and Yasmin Amin, pp. 365–75. Montreal: McGill-Queen's University Press.

Al-ʿAynī, Abū Muhammad Maḥmūd b. Aḥmad Badr al-Dīn. 1980. *ʿUmdat al-Qāriʾ Sharḥ Ṣaḥīḥ al-Bukhārī.* Beirut: Dār Iḥyāʾ al-Turāth al-ʿArabī.

Ayubi, Zahra. 2019. *Gendered Morality: Classical Islamic Ethics of the Self, Family, and Society.* New York: Columbia University Press.

Al-Baghdādī, ʿAlī b. Muhammad Khāzin. 1955. *Lubāb al-Taʾwīl fī Maʿānī al-Tanzīl.* Cairo: Maktabat wa-Maṭbaʿat Muṣṭafá al-Bābī al-Ḥalabī wa-Awlāduh.

Barazangi, Nimat. 2004. *Woman's Identity and the Qurʾan: A New Reading.* Gainesville, FL: University Press of Florida.

Barazangi, Nimat. 2017. *Woman's Identity and Rethinking the Hadith.* London: Routledge.

Al-Bayhaqī, Aḥmad b. al-Ḥusayn. 1994. *Al-Sunan al-Kubra,* edited by Muḥammad ʿAbd al-Qādir ʿAṭā. Beirut: Dār al-Kutub al-ʿIlmiyya.

Al-Bukhārī, Muhammad b. Ismāʿīl. 1989. *Al-Adab al-Mufrad,* edited by Muhammad Fuʾād ʿAbd al-Bāqī. Beirut: Dār al-Bashāʾir al-Islāmiyya.

Al-Bukhārī, Muhammad b. Ismāʿīl. 2001. *Al-Jāmiʿ al-Musnad al-Ṣaḥīḥ* (also known as *Ṣaḥīḥ al-Bukhārī*). 9 vols. Beirut: Dār Ṭawq al-Najāh.

Al-Dārimī, ʿAbd Allah ʿAbd al-Raḥmān b. Bihrām. 2000. *Musnad al-Dārimī,* edited by Ḥusayn Salīm al-Dārinī. Riyadh: Dār al-Mughnī.

Farooq, Mohammad Omar. 2011. *Toward Our Reformation: From Legalism to Value-Oriented Islamic Law and Jurisprudence.* Washington D.C.: International Institute of Islamic Thought.

Al-Fāsī, ʿAlī ibn Muḥammad Ibn al-Qaṭṭān. 2003. *Al-Iqnāʿ fī Masāʾil al-Ijmāʿ,* edited by Fārūq Ḥamāda. Damascus: Dār al-Qalam.

Franzway, Suzanne, Nicole Moulding, Sarah Wendt, Carole Zufferey and Donna Chung. 2019. *The Sexual Politics of Gendered Violence and Women's Citizenship.* Bristol, UK; Chicago, IL: Policy Press.

Geissinger, Ash. 2021. 'Applying Gender and Queer Theory to Pre-modern Sources'. In *The Routledge Handbook of Islam and Gender,* edited by Justine Howe, pp. 101–15. London; New York: Routledge, Taylor & Francis Group.

Al-Ghazālī, Abū Ḥāmid Muhammad. 1984. *Iḥyāʾ ʿUlūm al-Dīn.* 4 vols. Beirut: Dār al-Maʿrifa.

Al-Ḥākim al-Naysābūrī, Muḥammad b. ʿAbd Allāh. 1990. *Al-Mustadrak ʿalā al-Ṣaḥīḥayn*. Beirut: Dār al-Kutub al-ʿIlmiyya.

Al-Ḥalabī, ʿAlī b. Burhān al-Dīn. 1902. *ʾInsān al-ʿUyūn fī Sīrat al-Amīn al-Maʾmūn* (also known as *al-Sīrā al-Ḥalabīyya*). 4 vols. Beirut: al-Maktab al-Islāmī.

Al-Ḥalabī, ʿAlī Ḥasan ʿAlī. 1999. *Mawsūʿat al-Aḥādīth wa al-Athār al-Ḍaʿīfa wa al-Mawḍūʿa*. Riyadh: Maktabat al-Maʿārif li-l-Nashr wa-l Tawzīʿ.

Hallaq, Wael B. 2009. *An Introduction to Islamic Law*. Cambridge: Cambridge University Press.

Hassan, Riffat. 1999. 'Feminism in Islam.' In *Feminism and World Religions*, edited by Arvind Sharma and Katherine K. Young, pp. 248–78. Albany, N.Y.: State University of New York Press.

Al-Haythamī, Nūr al-Dīn ʿAlī b. Abī Bakr. 1994. *Majmaʿ al-Zawāʾid wa-Manbaʿ al-Fawāʾid*. 10 vols. Cairo: Maktabat al-Qudsī.

Al-Hindī, ʿAlāʾ al-Dīn ʿAlī al-Muttaqī b. Ḥusām al-Dīn. 2004. *Kanz al-ʿUmmāl fī Sunan al-Aqwāl wa al-Afʿāl*, edited by Maḥmūd ʿUmar Dumiyātī. Beirut: Dār al-Kutub al-ʿIlmiyah.

Al-Ḥumaydī, Muhammad b. Fattūḥ al-Azdī. 2002. *Al-Jamʿ bayn al-Ṣaḥīḥayn al-Bukhārī wa Muslim*, edited by ʿAlī Ḥusayn al-Bawāb. Beirut: Dār Ibn Ḥazm.

Al-Ḥurr al-ʿĀmilī, Muhammad b. al-Ḥasan b. ʿAlī b. al-Ḥusayn. 2007. *Wasāʾil al-Shīʿa ilā Taḥṣīl Masāʾil al-Sharīʿā*. 9 vols. Beirut: Muʾassasat al-Aʿlamī li-al-Maṭbūʿāt.

Ibn Abī Ḥātim, ʿAbd al-Raḥmān b. Muḥammad. 2009. *ʿIlal al-Ḥadīth*. Cairo: Maktabat al-Khānjī.

Ibn Abī Shaybah, Abū Bakr ʿAbd Allāh b. Muhammad. 1989. *Muṣannaf Ibn Abī Shaybah fī al-Aḥādīth wa-al-Āthār*, edited by Saʿīd Laḥḥām and Muhammad ʿAbd al-Salām Shāhīn. Beirut: Dār al-Fikr.

Ibn Anas, Mālik. n.d. *Al-Muwaṭṭaʾ*. Cairo: Dar Iḥyāʾ al-Kutub al-ʿArabiya.

Ibn ʿAsākir, Abd al-Raḥman b. Muhammad b. al-Ḥasan b. Manṣūr. 1986. *Kitāb al-Arbaʿīn fī Manāqib Ummahāt al-Muʾminīn*. Damascus: Dār al-Fikr.

Ibn Ḥabīb, ʿAbd al-Malik. 1992. *Kitāb Adab al-Nisāʾ al-Mawsūm bi-Kitāb al-Ghāyah wa al-Nihāyah*, edited by ʿAbd al-Majīd Turkī. Beirut: Dār al-Gharb al-Islāmī.

Ibn Ḥajar al-ʿAsqalānī, Aḥmad b. ʿAlī. 1959. *Fatḥ al-Bārī bi-Sharḥ Ṣaḥīḥ al-Bukhārī*. Beirut: Dār al-Fikr.

Ibn Ḥajar al-ʿAsqalānī, Aḥmad b. ʿAlī. 1994. *Itḥāf al-Mahara bi-l-Fawāʾid al-Mubtakara min Aṭrāf al-ʿAshara*. Edited by Zuhyar b. Nāṣir al-Nāṣir. 19 vols. Medina: Majmaʿ al-Malik Fahd li-Ṭibaʿat al-Muṣḥaf al-Sharīf.

Ibn Ḥajar al-Haythamī, Aḥmad b. Muḥammad. 1998. *Ashraf al-Wasāʾil ilā Fahm al-Shamāʾil*. Beirut: Dār al-Kutub al-ʿIlmīyah.

Ibn Ḥanbal, Aḥmad. 1995. *Musnad al-Imām Aḥmad b. Ḥanbal*, edited by Aḥmad Muhammad Shākir. 8 vols. Cairo: Dār al-Ḥadīth.

Ibn Ḥibbān, Muḥammad. 1993. *Ṣaḥīḥ Ibn Ḥibbān*, edited by Shuʿayb Arnāʾūṭ. Beirut: Muʾassasat al-Risālah.

Ibn Hishām, ʿAbd al-Malak. 1990. *Al-Sīra al-Nabawiyya*, edited by Ṭaha ʿAbd al-Raʾūf Saʿd. 2 vols. Beirut: Dār al-Jīl.

Ibn Hubayra, Yaḥyā b. Muḥammad al-Shaybānī. 1996. *Al-Ifṣāḥ ʿan Maʿānī al-Ṣiḥāḥ*. Riyadh: Dār al-Waṭan.

Ibn Māja, Muhammad al-Qazwīnī. 1998. *Sunan Ibn Māja*. Cairo: Dar Iḥyā' al-Kutub al-'Arabiyya.

Ibn Qayyim al-Jawziyya, Abū 'Abd Allah Muhammad b. Abū Bakr b. Ayūb. n.d. *Zād al-Ma'ād fī Hady Khayr al-'Ibād*. Beirut: Dār al-Kutub al-'Ilmiyya.

Ibn Qudāmā, Muwaffaq al-Dīn 'Abd Allāh b. Aḥmad. 1997. *Al-Mughnī*. 10 vols. Riyadh: Dār 'Ālam al-Kutub.

Ibn Rahwayh, Isḥāq b. Ibrāhīm. 1991. *Musnad Isḥāq b. Rahwayh*, edited by 'Abd al-Ghafūr al-Balūshī. 5 vols. Medina: Maktabat al-Imān.

Ibn Sa'd, Muhammad. 1990. *Al-Ṭabaqāt al-Kubrā*, edited by Muhammad 'Abd al-Qādir 'Aṭā. 8 vols. Beirut: Dār al-Kutub al-'Ilmiyya.

Kamali, Mohammad Hashim. 2012. *Shari'ah Law: An Introduction*. Oxford: Oneworld Publications.

Karam, Azza. 1998. *Women, Islamists and the State: Contemporary Feminisms in Egypt*. London: MacMillan Press.

Laude, Patrick. 2005. *Divine Play, Sacred Laughter, and Spiritual Understanding*. New York: Palgrave Macmillan.

Al-Majlisī, Muḥammad Bāqir b. Muḥammad Taqī. 2008. *Biḥār al-Anwār al-Jāmi'ah li-Durar Akhbār al-A'immah al-Aṭhār*, edited by Maḥmūd Duryāb Najafī and Jalāl al-Dīn 'Alī Ṣaghīr. Beirut: Mu'assasat al-A'lamī lil-maṭbū'āt.

Al-Maqrīzī, Taqiyy al-Dīn. 1999. *Imtā' al-Asmā' Bimā li-l-Nabiy min al-Aḥwāl wa-l-Amwāl wa-l-Ḥafada wa-l-Mitā'*, edited by Muhammad 'Abd al-Ḥamīd al-Namīsī. 15 vols. Beirut: Dār al-Kutub al-'Ilmiyya.

Melchert, Christopher. 2020. 'Introduction'. In *Modern Hadith Studies: Continuing Debates and New Approaches*, edited by Belal Abo-Alabbas, Michael Dann and Christopher Melchert, pp. 1–8. Edinburgh: Edinburgh University Press.

Mernissi, Fatima. 1991. *The Veil and the Male Elite: A Feminist Interpretation of Women's Rights in Islam*. Cambridge, MA: Perseus Books.

Al-Mizzī, Jamāl al-Dīn Yūsuf. 1983. *Tuḥfat al-Ashrāf bi-Ma'rifat al-Aṭrāf*. Bombay: al-Dār al-Qayyima.

Motzki, Harald, with Nicolet Boekhoff-van der Voort and Sean W. Anthony. 2013. *Analysing Muslim Traditions: Studies in Legal, Exegetical and Maghāzī Ḥadīth*. Leiden: Brill.

Al-Mubārakfūrī, Muhammad 'Abd al-Raḥmān b. 'Abd al-Raḥīm. 2014. *Tuḥfat al-Aḥwadhī bi Sharḥ Jāmi' al-Tirmidhī*, edited by Khālid 'Abd al-Ghanī Maḥfuẓ. Beirut: Dār al-Kutub al-'Ilmīyah.

Al-Mundhirī, 'Abd al-'Aẓīm b. 'Abd al-Qawī. 1960. *Al-Targhīb wa-al-Tarhīb min al-Ḥadīth al-Sharīf*. Cairo: al-Maktabah al-Tijārīyah al-Kubrā.

Muslim, Ibn al-Ḥajjāj al-Qushayrī al-Naysābūrī. n.d. *Al-Musnad al-Ṣaḥīḥ bi Naql al-'Adl 'an al-'Adl ila Rasūl Allah* (also known as *Ṣaḥīḥ Muslim*), edited by Muhammad Fu'ād 'Abd al-Bāqī. Beirut: Dar Iḥyā' al-Turāth al-'Arabī.

Nābulusī, 'Afīf. 2006. *Fiqh Ahl al-Bayt: Mabānī al-Fatāwā al-Wāḍiḥah*. Beirut: Dār al-Hādī lil-Ṭibā'ah wa-al-Nashr wa-al-Tawzī'.

Al-Nasā'ī, Aḥmad b. Shu'ayb. 1997. *Mukhtaṣar Sunan al-Nasā'ī*, edited by Muṣṭafā Dīb Bughā. Damascus: al-Yamāmah lil-Ṭibā'ah wa-al-Nashr wa-al-Tawzī'.

Al-Nasā'ī, Aḥmad b. Shu'ayb. 2001. *Al-Sunnan al-Kubra*, edited by Ḥasan Muḥamad 'Abd al-Mun'im Shalabī. 12 vols. Beirut: Mu'asassat al-Risāla.

Al-Nawawī, Abū Zakariyyā Muḥyī al-Dīn b. Sharaf. 2017. *Ṣaḥīḥ Muslim bi-Sharḥ al-Nawawī*. Beirut: Dār al-Kutub al-ʿIlmiyah.

Al-Nuʿmān, Abū Ḥanīfa b. Muhammad. 1995. *Taʾwīl al-Saʿāim*, edited by ʿĀrif Tāmir. Beirut: Dār al-Aḍwāʾ.

Pereira, Faustina. 2002. *The Fractured Scales: The Search for a Uniform Personal Code*. Calcutta: Stree.

Qabalān, Hishām. 1999. *Al-Zawāj fi-l-Islām wa Ashkāl al-Zawāj al-Mustaḥdath*. Beirut: Muʾassasat al-Riḥāb al-Ḥaditha.

Al-Qasṭallānī, Aḥmad b. Muḥammad. 2017. *Al-Mawāhib al Laduniyya bi al-Minaḥ al-Muḥammadīyah*, edited by Ṭāhā 'Abd al-Ra'ūf Sa'd. Cairo: al-Maktabah al-Azharīyah lil-Turāth.

Rahman, Fazlur. 1968. *Islam*. Garden City, NY: Doubleday and Company.

Ṣadr, Muḥammad Ṣādiq. 2002. *Falsafat wa-Akhlāqiyat al-Zawāj*, edited by Muḥsin Mūsawī. Beirut: Dār al-Maḥajjah al-Bayḍā'.

Ṣadr-'Āmilī, Sayyid Abbas. 2005. *An Enlightening Commentary into the Light of the Holy Qur'an*. Edited by Kamal Faghih Imani. Translated by Celeste Smith. Isfahan: Amīr-ul-Muʾminīn ʿAlī (a.s.) Library.

Al-Sakhāwī, Muḥammad b. ʿAbd al-Raḥmān. 1985. *Al-Maqāṣid al-Ḥasana fī Bayān Kathīr min al-Aḥādīth al-Mushtahira ʿala al-Alsina*. Beirut: Dār al-Kitāb al-ʿArabī.

Sayyid al-Ahl, ʿAbd al-ʿAzīz. 1981. *Ṭabaqāt al-Nisāʾ al-Muḥaddithāt: min al-Tabaqā al-ʿŪlā ila al-ṭabaqā al-sadisā*. Cairo: Maṭabiʿ al-Ahrām al-Tijārīya.

Shāhīn, ʿAbd al-Ṣabūr. 1991. *Mawsūʿat Ummahāt al-Muʾminin: Dirāsah fī Siyarihunna wa-Marwīyātihunn*. Cairo: al-Zahrāʾ lil-Iʿlām al-ʿArabī.

Shaikh, Saʿdiyya. 2012. *Sufi Narratives of Intimacy: Ibn ʿArabi, Gender and Sexuality*. Chapel Hill, NC: University of North Carolina Press.

Stowasser, Barbara. 1992. 'The Mothers of the Believers in the *Ḥadīth*'. *The Muslim World* 82 (1–2): pp. 1–36.

Stowasser, Barbara Freyer. 2008. 'Wives of the Prophet'. *Encyclopaedia of the Qurʾān*, edited by Jane Dammen McAuliffe. Online version. Georgetown University, Washington DC: Brill.

Al-Suweidy, Amal. 2006. *Fiqh al-Ṣaḥābiyāt*. Beirut: Dār Ibn Ḥazm.

Al-Suyūṭī, Jalāl al-Dīn Abū al-Faḍl ʿAbd al-Raḥmān. 1987. *Al-Durrar al-Muntathira fī al-Aḥādīth al-Mushtahira*. Cairo: Dār al-Iʿtiṣām.

Al-Ṭabarānī, Sulaymān b. Aḥmad. 1994. *Al-Muʿjam al-Kabīr*. 25 vols. Cairo: Maktabat Ibn Taymiyya.

Al-Ṭabarānī, Sulaymān b. Aḥmad. 1995. *Al-Muʿjam al-Awsaṭ*. 10 vols. Cairo: Dār al-Ḥaramayn.

Al-Ṭabarī, Abū Jaʿfar Muḥammad b. Jarīr b. Yazīd. 2000. *Jāmiʿ al-Bayān ʿan Taʾwīl āy al-Qurʾān* (also known as *Tafsīr al-Ṭabarī*), edited by Aḥmad Shākir. 24 vols. Beirut: Muʾassat al-Risāla.

Al-Ṭabarī, Muḥibb al-Dīn Aḥmad b. ʿAbd Allāh. 1970. *Al-Samṭ al-Thamīn fī Manāqib Ummahāt al-Muʾminīn*. Aleppo: Maktabat al-Turāth al-Islāmī.

Al-Ṭabarsī, Ḥusayn Taqī al-Nūrī. 1987–8. *Mustadrak al-Wasāʾil wa-Mustanbaṭ al-Masāʾil*. Beirut: Muʾassasat Āl al-Bayt li-Iḥyāʾ al-Turāth.

Al-Tirmidhī, Muhammad b. ʿĪsā. 1975. *Sunan al-Tirmidhī*, edited by Aḥmad Muhammad Shākir. 15 vols. Cairo: Maktabat wa Maṭbaʿat al-Bābī al-Ḥalabī.

Watt, William Montgomery. 1956. *Muhammad at Medina*. Oxford: Clarendon Press.

Winkler, Markus. 1998. 'Komik, das Komische: 'Zur Vorgeschichte des neuzeitlichen Begriffs'. In *Historisches Wörterbuch der Rhetorik*, edited by Gert Ueding, vol. 4, pp. 1166–8. Tübingen: Max Niemeyer.

Zaman, Muhammad Qasim. 1996. 'Maghazi and the Muhaddithun: Reconsidering the Treatment of "Historical" Materials in Early Collections of Hadith'. *International Journal of Middle East Studies* 28 (1): pp. 1–18.

Zayzafoon, Lamia Ben Youssef. 2005. *The Production of the Muslim Woman: Negotiating Text, History, and Ideology*. Lanham, MD: Lexington Books.

Qirā'a Mubādala: Reciprocal Reading of Hadith on Marital Relationships

Faqihuddin Abdul Kodir

One of the challenges in developing a theology of gender justice in Islam relates to the process of interpreting Hadith. There are two main stances regarding Hadith on women's issues. The first approach considers Hadith as a primary source of Islamic teachings, using it to justify male superiority and domination over women. The second approach challenges the validity of the Hadith tradition and disregards it in the project of developing a theology of gender justice. Both views are problematic. The first distances Muslims from the global call for gender equality and human rights. The latter discards one of the main sources respected by Muslims and leaves believing advocates of gender justice without an authority of shared tradition that they can invoke within their communities.

In this chapter, I propose a new methodology to approach Hadith literature, which I call a 'reciprocal reading' (*Qirā'a Mubādala*). This approach aims to fill the gaps outlined above through a process of reinterpreting hadiths on gender issues, especially within the family, so men and women are treated as subjects who are addressed equally by the meanings contained in the texts. I argue that hadiths that traditionally have been interpreted only for men or only for women should be reinterpreted to uncover their substantial meanings and direct those meanings equally to all. This approach suggests that the hadiths on marital relations revolve around a reciprocal relationship between the marrying couple who both love, care for and serve each other, as well as together take responsibility to do what is best for the family.

This methodology is grounded in several basic premises in Islamic teachings. First, *tawḥīd* (the oneness of God) is a fundamental Qurʾanic principle that affirms that all people, regardless of gender, are created by God to share the mandate of serving as *khalīfa* (vicegerents) on earth. As such, the relationship between individuals should be that of synergy, partnership and cooperation and not hierarchy, dichotomy or domination. Second, Islamic teachings address all people without distinction. These teachings are grounded in the Qurʾanic ethics of human dignity and principle of well-being. In addition, Islamic texts continue to be open to interpretation by present and future generations so they remain relevant and meaningful, while at the same time serving as a source of teachings on noble morals (*akhlāq karima*).

The methodology of reciprocal reading is inspired by the hermeneutical work of ʿAbd al-Ḥalīm Muḥammad Abū Shuqqa (1924–95), as represented in *Taḥrīr al-Marʾa fī ʿAṣr al-Risāla* (*The Liberation of Women at the Time of the Prophecy*) (1990). He compiles thousands of hadiths about women's rights in Islam and reinterprets them using the principle of what he calls equality (*musawa*) in Islam.

The chapter consists of four sections. I begin with a brief review of the main scholarly approaches towards the question of gender in Hadith, then introduce Abū Shuqqa's interpretive approach of equality (*musawa*). In the second section, I explain the proposed methodology of reciprocal reading ('*Qirāʾa Mubādala*'), its rationale, and its foundations in the Qurʾan and the traditional Islamic legal theory (*uṣūl al-fiqh*). The third section expounds on the methodology and its implementation. I start by applying it to selected hadiths related to marital relations, then reflect on the ways in which the reciprocal reading builds on but also departs from Abū Shuqqa's methodology. The fourth and final section discusses the Indonesian context where I work as scholar activist, and explains why and how this methodology is useful in engaging with different actors around gender inequality and presenting the case for egalitarian Muslim marital relationships without jettisoning or discrediting the Hadith tradition. I also note the limits of this methodology and areas for further work and development.

1. READING HADITH FOR GENDER

According to traditional Islamic legal theory, the Qur'an and Sunna are the two primary sources of Islamic rulings. The Qur'an is the words of Allah (*swt*) as revealed to the Prophet Muhammad (pbuh), while Sunna consists of traditions and practices of the Prophet. Hadiths are narratives that record what the Prophet said and did. During the formalization of the juristic schools, the Sunna became Hadith-centred, with hadiths increasingly playing a bigger role in law-making (see El Shamsy (2013) and Nevin Reda's chapter in this volume). Many issues of Islamic theology, law and popular religious traditions are derived from the Hadith tradition, rather than from the Qur'an.

1.1 Overview of approaches

Although there have been many contemporary efforts to reinterpret the Qur'an to advocate for gender equality, there have been few gender-based studies on Hadith texts. This is despite the fact that Islamic teachings on gender relations are much more often drawn from Hadith than Qur'anic verses. Indeed, at the grassroots level, Muslims live with Hadith – and with the traditional misogynistic interpretations – and many believe these texts and their interpretations are the real words of the Prophet.

The first specific collection of hadiths on women, which almost completely established the traditional interpretation about the nature, role and fate of women in Islam, was the book *Aḥkām al-Nisā* (*Rulings on Women*) by 'Abd al Rahmān Ibn al-Jawzī (d. 597 AH/1201 CE).[1] Later, new collections similar to this work emerged. They include *Ḥusn al-Uswa fī mā Thabata 'an Allāh wa Rasūlihī fī al-Niswa* (*Good Example on What is Stated by God and His Messenger on Women*) by Muḥammad Ṣiddīq Ḥasan Khān al-Qannūjī (d. 1307 AH/1890 CE) and *Sharḥ 'Uqūd al-Lujjayn fī Bayān Ḥuqūq al-Zawjayn* (*Joining Two Oceans; Interpretation of Rights of Spouses*) by Muḥammad b. 'Umar al-Nawawī al-Bantānī (d. 1314 AH/1897 CE). Similar contemporary collections of hadiths circulate widely in the Muslim world today, such as works of

[1] There is a new publication of *Kitāb 'Ishrat al-Nisā* by Aḥmad b. Shu'ayb al-Nasā'ī (d. 303 AH/915 CE), which is a collection of hadiths on women's issues. I do not include it as a specific collection since it is originally a chapter of the book *Sunan al-Nasā'ī* by the same author.

Muḥammad ʿAlī al-Hāshimī (2013), Muḥammad Farīja (1996), and Sādiq ibn Muḥammad al-Hādī (2009).

These collections convey misogynistic interpretations of the hadiths. The authors, using a literal approach to Hadith, claim, for example, that women are deficient in intellect and religion; a woman's testimony is worth half that of a man; God created women from the crooked ribs of men; women are a source of temptation for men; and women most likely will be inhabitants of Hell in the Hereafter. Based on these interpretations, women are restricted from going out of the home and forbidden from travelling unless accompanied by close relatives. Furthermore, women are expected to act as obedient wives and servants of their family. Thus, their prayers should take place at home rather than in mosques. In these texts, men are women's leaders and people led by women will never achieve prosperity. These Hadith-based ideas are visible in many works of contemporary clerics, such as the works of Ibn Bāz (1988, 1994, 1995) and al-ʿUthaymīn (1989, 1998, 1999), the most referenced clerics for contemporary Salafi Muslims around the world. Moreover, the Saudi cleric al-Najdī (1999, vol. 16, pp. 39–45) endorses inequality between men and women in Islam based upon hadiths related to the deficiency of female intellect and religion.

This misogynistic tendency has led some to refute the authority of Hadith, especially in the project of gender equality in Islam. Fatima Mernissi (1991), the Moroccan feminist scholar, undertook a comprehensive critical reading of hadiths. Grounding her theory in a historical criticism approach, Mernissi argues that all hadiths demeaning women are traditions of misogyny falsely attributed to the Prophet and accordingly are not authoritative sources for Islamic teachings. Riffat Hassan (1991) and Asghar Ali Engineer (2001) also hold that hadiths generally are a source of patriarchal Islam and are not authoritative for constructing a notion of egalitarian Islam. This approach towards Hadith is also present in the works of Syed Mohammed Ali (2004) and Ibn Qarnās (2011).

Another response is to accept the Hadith literature but circumvent some of the seemingly harsh literal meanings of the texts. Those who prefer this approach attempt to find an ethical message in each hadith that enables friendlier interpretations for women. This argument is present noticeably in the works of scholars such as Ghāda al-Khurasānī (1979), Fāṭima ʿUmar Nāṣif (1989), Muḥammad al-Ghazālī (1989), Kaukab Siddique (1990), Yūsuf al-Qaraḍāwī (1991), Hiba Raʾūf Izzat (1995), and Mohja Kahf (2000). These initiatives are generally partial and limited. In contrast, Abū Shuqqa offers a holistic effort in his 1990 collection and reinterpretation of thousands of hadiths on women's issues, *Taḥrīr al-Marʾa fī ʿAṣr al-Risāla* (*The Liberation of Women at the Time of the Prophecy*), which presents a reading that favours women's rights and advocates gender equality.

I find all the mainstream approaches – misogynism, rejection of Hadith and partial readings – problematic and limiting. I am a Muslim scholar activist from Indonesia, where many Muslim communities firmly believe in both Hadith and gender equality within Islam. Given this perspective, I believe it is necessary to engage in the project of gender equality in a way that accepts the authority of Hadith but allows for reinterpretation. I therefore propose a methodology that engages with and builds on Abū Shuqqa's hadith-based egalitarian interpretative method, as it provides a path for reinterpretation towards gender equality and further development.

1.2 Abū Shuqqa and hermeneutics of equality

ʿAbd al-Ḥalīm Muḥammad Abū Shuqqa (1924–95) wrote his six volume *Taḥrīr al-Marʾa fī ʿAṣr al-Risāla* (*The Liberation of Women at the Time of the Prophecy*) to liberate women from conservative interpretations and move towards equality (*musawa*) in gender relations.[2] The main elements of his interpretation are evident in four themes: women's full humanity; a non-segregated society as an ideal Muslim community; the active agency of women in public activities; and mutuality and reciprocity in all matters related to the spousal relationship, including sexual intimacy. Although Abū Shuqqa opines that women's place is primarily at home, he argues that women should have equal rights to education, economics, social relations and politics. In order to ensure wider opportunities for women to enjoy their rights in public, men are encouraged to take part in domestic work. Men and the entire society are also obliged to ensure conditions through which women can participate in the public sphere.

Although Abū Shuqqa still agrees with the mainstream juristic rulings on marriage, the nature and tone of his presentation is different. Cognizant of the potential abuse of a husband's authority within the traditional juristic concept of marriage, he emphasizes the purposive principle of the rules,

---

[2] This section is derived from my 2017 article, 'Seeds of Gender Equality within Islam: Abū Shuqqa's Approach to Hadith on Women's Liberation'.

which in turn eclipses male authority. He argues further that it is vital to foreground the principle of partnership when re-establishing new interpretations on marriage. In this process, the notion of 'spouses each helping the other' is the most obvious moral injunction that shapes marital relationships. In his interpretation, this principle emerges in every stage of the marital relationship, from the proposal of marriage until dissolution through death or repudiation. In general, Abū Shuqqa does not engage with the root causes of unequal gender relations. However, he sheds misconceptions about women that are prevalent among many Muslims. His work provides the basis for reciprocal relationships between the sexes.

Abū Shuqqa's interpretative approach to Hadith begins with his acknowledgement of male biases within prevalent traditional interpretations. He thereby seeks strategies of centring women, particularly by mainstreaming the notions of partnership, mutuality and reciprocity. He also acknowledges that empirical research on women is very important to produce contemporary interpretations of hadiths on gender issues. He demonstrates his initiative for centring women in the entire interpretative approach of the *Taḥrīr* by including the experiences of the female Companions of the Prophet as religious authority and a source of Islamic teachings on gender relations. These experiences, according to Abū Shuqqa, represent the original prophetic guidance on gender relations. He names these experiences 'practical and applied Hadith' (*al-aḥādīth al-ʿamaliya al-taṭbīqiyya*) on relationships between men and women in diverse aspects of life. He also attributes prophetic guidance (*hady al-nabī*) to the deeds of ʿĀʾisha, Umm Ḥarām and Zaynab bint Jaḥsh.[3] Indeed, he alludes to the idea that there are Sunna of the Prophet and of the early women of Islam. He reorganizes his collection of the hadiths into new themes and chapter headings in which women are visible, knowledgeable, demonstrate noble morals and are shown as active participants in domestic and public activities.

A significant element of his method is to include women as subjects in the process of reading hadiths, which can be referred to as 'hermeneutics of equality'. This is important because Arabic is a gendered language in which stories are mostly structured using a masculine expression. This method has two important features. It raises awareness about the discriminating context

[3] ʿĀʾisha and Zaynab bint Jaḥsh were wives of the Prophet and Umm Ḥarām was a member of the tribe of al-Khazraj, al-Ansâr, Medina. She was the sister of Umm Salim, the aunt of Anas ibn Mālik, and the wife of ʿUbâdah Ibn as-Sâmit.

of the text, and then shifts towards an egalitarian understanding. Having established this, the method then counters traditional hermeneutics that puts the onus only on women to be responsible for everything regarded as religious deviation. He aims to balance the meaning by centring women in the stories of the text. He proposes an interpretive approach that re-examines and limits the application of hadiths on gender issues that contradict established principles (*mukhtalaf wa mushkil al-aḥādīth*). Based on the principles of human dignity, autonomy and responsibility of women, Abū Shuqqa reinterprets the problematic hadiths by limiting the scope of meaning only to certain contexts, privileging the metaphorical meaning, and focusing on the main message that ethically binds Muslims and affirms inclusivity and partnership.

The bulk of Abū Shuqqa's thesis is the possibility of rereading Hadith texts to establish a theological base for gender equality from within an Islamic perspective. This initiative occurs within the context of contemporary struggles of Muslims for gender equality. It concerns interpretative attempts to perceive Hadith positively as a source of Islamic teachings for meaningful lives and just relations between women and men. While Abū Shuqqa's interpretation of egalitarian gender relations is debatable, his methodological approach to Hadith deserves ample appreciation because it lays the foundation for further efforts to unearth Islamic bases of mutuality and reciprocity in gender relations. Building on his approach, I propose a method that ensures that women become central subjects in the entire process of interpretation and their experiences become authoritative bases of reading. My aim is to guarantee application of the fundamental concept of equality within a partnership, as introduced by Abū Shuqqa, in the entire process of reading Hadith and in its results.

2. RECIPROCAL READING (*QIRĀ ʾA MUBĀDALA*): METHODOLOGY

The basis of the methodology of *Qirā ʾa Mubādala* (reciprocal reading) is to adopt interpretive lenses that unearth principles which can lead to equal cooperative relationships between men and women in all spaces, both within the family and in society.

Therefore, the main premise of the *Qirāʾa Mubādala* method is to ensure that men and women are equal subjects in the texts. The textual tradition requires both men and women to work to achieve what is beneficial (*jalb al-maṣlaḥa*) and prevent what is harmful (*dar' al-mafsada*). For any text that is literally addressed to men, this principal meaning must be found so it can also be used to address women. Similarly, the principal meaning of any text that is literally addressed to women must be found so it can also be used to address men. Gender equality is the main requirement for creating ideal gender relations of reciprocity, partnership and cooperation.

2.1 The Qur'anic basis for *Qirā'a Mubādala*

Qirā'a Mubādala, or reciprocal reading, is grounded in two key Qur'anic principles: the principle of *tawḥīd* and the Qur'anic affirmation of reciprocal relationships between men and women. In what follows, I will expound on each.

The concept of *mubādala* has strong roots in the most fundamental teaching of the Qur'an – *tawḥīd*, or the belief in the oneness of Allah (*swt*). The Qur'anic sentence '*lā ilāha illallāh*' ('There is no God but God'), which is recited often, is a declaration about the oneness of Allah as the only Essence that deserves to be worshipped and obeyed absolutely. Declaring *tawḥīd* means declaring two things: first, recognition of the oneness of Allah, and second, affirmation of the equality of all human beings before God. There is no God other than Allah, which means there is no intermediary between God and God's vicegerents, and there is no one who can become a god for others. No man nor woman can become a god or servant for one another because both men and women are equal servants of Allah.

In this matter, the Muslim theologian amina wadud affirms that *tawḥīd* is the theological basis for equality between men and women. This equality becomes the foundation for reciprocal relationships between men and women (see Wadud, 1999; 2006; 2009; 2015). According to wadud, taking part in a patriarchal social system that makes men superior and women subordinate is engaging in an act of *shirk* (recognizing another god other than Allah) and *istikbār* (arrogance), which is contradictory to the concept of *tawḥīd*. *Tawḥīd* ensures a direct relationship between each woman and God, without any man as an intermediary. Since humans are meant to have vertical relations only with God, the relations between men and women need to be horizontal, with both parties equal. As such, what needs to be built among and between humans – regardless of gender – is cooperation and reciprocity, not superiority and domination.

According to wadud, patriarchy is not only about men's domination over women, but is also about centring men's existence, thinking, knowing and acting. In a patriarchal system, women's worth is inferior to that of men. The opposite condition – where only the existence of women is centred – is also contradictory to *tawḥīd*. Shifting to a *tawḥīd* perspective requires changing from patriarchy into reciprocity, domination into cooperation, hegemony into equality and competition into collaboration. This, according to wadud, is the basic value of the fundamental relation between men and women, in both domestic and public spheres. Consequently, opportunities for women should open widely for their equal participation in the public sphere. Their contributions in both public and private spheres should also be recognized. Unlike patriarchy, which sets a hegemonic social system between men and women, *tawḥīd* mandates a reciprocal, equal, collaborative and cooperative social system.

This *tawḥīdic* horizontal social system will allow the principle of justice to be achieved. According to the Indonesian Qurʾanic scholar Nur Rofiah (2019, pp. 30–2), in the context of gender relations, *tawḥīd* provides a fundamental view about equality and justice in the status, position, roles and value of men and women. First, men and women are spiritually created from the same essence (*min nafsin wāḥida*), and physically through the same process. Second, in Islam, men are not the primary creatures and women the secondary. Both are equally primary creatures who are capable of implementing and undertaking the role of vicegerent on the earth, and both can become equally secondary before Allah when they become the servants of God. Third, women do not dedicate their life to the benefit of men, but both men and women are equally required to dedicate their life to the benefit of all God's creatures. Fourth, women need not absolutely obey men, but both must equally obey Allah for the benefit of all. Fifth, the quality of human beings is not determined by their biological sex, but by their *taqwā* (God-consciousness) and the deeds they do to benefit human beings and the universe.

The equality of all humans and the importance of reciprocal relationships between them is another important Qurʾanic principle that informs the reciprocal reading. The literature around the circumstances of revelation in verses 3:195 and 33:35, for example, explicitly refers to women's concerns that the Qur'an did not appreciate their contributions, especially their public roles such as participation in migration (hijra) and defending the community (jihad). Verse 2:218 talks about belief (*imān*), hijra and jihad. However, it does not explicitly mention women and therefore most people at the time (and now) understood these verses as addressing men only. In contrast, verse 3:195 explicitly mentions women (*unthā*) and men (*dhakar*) in its discussion of belief, hijra, jihad, war and martyrdom.[4]

Verse 9:71 also supports the main idea of *mubādala* in gender relations. This verse affirms that men and women are to be '*awliya*' (guardians)' of each other. Being a guardian means being the protector, supporter, the person in charge and the leader. Thus, the Qur'an calls on men and women to support and help each other in all life aspects, worship and social works. They are both called to promote kindness and prevent harm, pray, pay alms and be obedient to Allah and the Prophet. In verse 3:195, they are both called on to fulfil the duty of hijra and jihad. Both men's and women's beliefs are accepted and recognized by Allah. Their good deeds are counted without any discrimination, and they are both rewarded exponentially and promised heaven (verses 9:71; 3:195; 4:124; 16:97; 40:40; 48:5; 57:12). Conversely, they will equally be held accountable for their bad deeds (verse 40:40). Whoever steals or commits adultery, whether man or woman, will be punished without any discrimination (verses 5:39; 24:2–3). All humans, regardless of gender, must obey God's command and the Prophet Muhammad (verse 33:36). Neither men nor women can become the object of slander or be hurt (verses 33:58; 85:10). They both are requested to lower their gaze and to protect their chastity (verse 24:31). If they make mistakes, both men and women are advised to repent, apologize and return to the way of Allah (verses 33:73; 47:19; 71:28).

There are other Qur'anic verses which also clearly affirm reciprocity and cooperation in the relations between men and women in the family domain. For example, verse 2:187 regards husbands and wives as garments to one

[4] See al-Shawkānī (1991, juz 1, p. 461 and juz 4, p. 325). This story can be found in most major books of Qur'anic exegesis when they explain the causes of revelation of verse 33:35, while the main books of Hadith which tell these stories are *Sunan al-Tirmidhī*, 2000, nos. 3295, 3517; and *Musnad Aḥmad ibn Ḥanbal*, 2000, nos. 27218, 27246.35. The numbering of hadiths in this article refers to the books of Hadith (*Ṣaḥīḥ al-Bukhārī*, *Ṣaḥīḥ Muslim*, *Sunan al-Tirmidhī*, *Sunan Abī Dāwūd*, *Sunan Ibn Māja*, *Sunan al-Nasā'ī*, *Muwaṭṭa' Mālik*, and *Musnad Aḥmad ibn Ḥanbal*) published by Jam'iyyah al-Maknaz al-Islamy (Cairo, 2000). Translations are taken from Sunnah.com, with some minor modifications made for clarity.

another; verse 2:233 asks parents not to hurt each other but to be happy and to consult with each other; verse 2:232 calls on husbands and wives to be content with each other; and verse 4:21 emphasizes the beauty of sexual intimacy between husband and wife. These verses also affirm the reciprocal relationship between men and women.

In all the above verses, the Qurʾan clearly mentions men and women in its messages. In the Arabic language, which differentiates between men and women and uses a masculine structure, to include women explicitly was something new. This new approach that was initiated by the Qurʾan – mentioning both sexes explicitly – can be categorized as a *tashrīh* (explanatory) approach. There are many verses which mention both sexes explicitly. This can become the basis for a textual argument for gender equality. It also highlights the importance of affirming both sexes in all processes of interpreting Islamic sources, especially if the neutral texts are being used to negate the presence of women.

2.2 Reciprocal reading and *uṣūl al-fiqh*

The *Qirāʾa Mubādala* method is designed to address several methodological problems of interpreting hadiths. One such problem is partial reading, in which only a sentence or a phrase from the text is used as the normative basis of an interpretation without considering broader principles of Islamic teachings such as mercy, noble character, or the objectives of the Shariʿa (*maqāṣid al-shariʿa*). Worse than that, as pointed out by Abū Shuqqa, many weak and even false or inauthentic hadiths have been used as references. According to Abū Shuqqa, many of these false hadith-created norms related to women violate precedents from earlier Muslim generations that are written in Hadith books. The method of *Qirāʾa Mubādala* has the potential to integrate partial texts with the main principles of Islam. Such a holistic integration in reading texts can be found in the tradition of Islamic classical interpretation, especially in *uṣūl al-fiqh* (principles of Islamic jurisprudence).

The term *uṣūl al-fiqh* literally means the foundations of understanding. This discipline deals with how to extract laws from their sources, especially the Qurʾan and Hadith, and how to apply these on the level of reality. In its long history, this science offers many methods of how to extract meaning from limited source texts to include things in an ever-expanding and infinite reality. This begins from the simplest method known as reasoning by analogy (*qiyās*) to a fairly complex theory of the five objectives of the law (*maqāṣid al-shariʿa al-khamsa*), taking into account the hierarchy of human needs.

Uṣūl al-fiqh also has a fairly complex theory about how a word or a sentence has meaning within the Arabic language, and if and how it can include new meanings. One concept that is relevant here is whether a word for male (*mudhakar*) also includes female (*muʾannath*). This relates to the concept of *taghlīb*, in which three types of meanings are usually discussed.[5]

The first type concerns words such as '*an-nās*', '*al-ins*' and '*al-bashar*', which all refer to 'human beings'. All of these words are regarded as gender neutral, thus include both men and women. The second type concerns words such as the Arabic word '*man*', which is a pronoun that means 'someone'. Even though this is in the masculine form in its sentence structure, it includes both men and women. The third type is words used only for men, unless there is another indication that diverts the meaning, such as '*rajul*' or '*rijāl*', which mean 'a man or men', or the words '*al-muʾmin*' or '*al-muʾminūn*', which means 'believing man' or 'believing men'. Similarly, some words are specific to women, such as '*imraʾa*' or '*nisāʾ*', which mean 'a woman or women', and '*al-muʾmina*' or '*al-muʾmināt*', which mean 'a believing woman' or 'believing women'.[6]

The second type of words, such as the Arabic word '*man*' in verse 2:112 about someone who surrenders to Allah, are understood by many scholars to be gender neutral. However, the Arabic word '*man*' in verse 2:30, about someone who is chosen to be the vicegerent of Allah, is understood to be only for the Prophet Adam, who is male, as someone in charge of and a preserver of the earth. This means that Eve or other human beings are not included. If we are consistent with the rule, '*man*' in verse 2:30 should also mean every human being, both men and women, become responsible for the mandate from Allah to make this earth prosperous.

---

[5] The concept of *taghlīb* related to gender means that within the linguistic structure the male form of a word takes precedence over the female form. Therefore, a masculine noun can include and refer to both male and female.

[6] It is true that there are also other ʿulamaʾ who have different opinions, namely that the Arabic word '*man*' is intended only for men, and women cannot be automatically included except when there is an indication that allows women to be included in that word. See this discussion in al-Zarkashi (2000, pp. 231–2).

For the third type, many ʿulamaʾ regard masculine words such as '*rajul*' or '*al-muʾminun*' to include women. Imam Ibn Hazm (d. 456 AH/1064 CE), for example, firmly stated that when the plural masculine form has an additional letter '*waw*' and '*nūn*' in the adjective, it becomes neutral and includes men and women. One such example is '*al-muʾminūn*', which means believers. If there is no indication to specify men, then this word is for both men and women. The argumentation is that Islamic texts as representations of Islamic teachings revealed from Allah to the Prophet Muhammad are basically directed to both sexes, not to one sex excluding the other (see Ibn Hazm, 2005, p. 369).

Ibn al-ʿArabi (d. 543 AH/1148 CE), in interpreting verse 24:30, also argues that '*al-muʾminūn*' includes both men and women. The additional word '*al-muʾmināt*' after *al-muʾminūn* is an affirmation to ensure readers do not forget women as subjects. It was this affirmation which was demanded by women in the Prophet Muhammad's era and was responded to positively with various verses explicitly mentioning women (see Ibn al-'Arabi, 1988, juz 3, p. 379).

Similarly, the word '*rajul*' in various hadith texts is male, but its meaning is also directed to women (al-Munāwī, 1937, juz 4, p. 220). Ibn Ḥajar al-ʿAsqalānī, for instance, states: 'Mentioning men in Hadith texts does not exclude women, women are included with men in the content of the text' (1993, vol. 2, p. 147). This was expressed when he explained a Hadith text about seven people who will be protected by Allah later in the day of resurrection (*Ṣaḥīḥ al-Bukhārī*, 2000, vol. 1, no. 663). The text literally uses masculine words for these seven people, such as '*shāb*' ('young men') and '*rajul*' ('adult men'). In Ibn Ḥajar al-ʿAsqalānī's perspective, these seven people who will be protected by Allah are any people, male or female, who have become just leaders, spent their young age worshipping God, love the mosque, love others because of Allah, are not easily tempted by lust because of fear of Allah, always give charity secretly and often cry when remembering God in quiet moments alone (Ibn Ḥajar al-ʿAsqalānī, 1993, vol. 2, p. 147).

The above explanations provide strong inspiration for the idea that source texts in Islam must be understood reciprocally (*mubādala*), such that women cannot be excluded from texts that are structurally masculine. The basic argument for this is that Islam and its basic texts are for all people, men and women. Similarly, even though earlier ʿulamaʾ do not discuss this, this principle should also apply to texts directed to women.

3. RECIPROCAL READING (*QIRĀʾA MUBĀDALA*): APPLICATION

With the *Qirāʾa Mubādala* method, all people are addressed and are equal subjects of the conversation in all texts. Therefore, this method assumes that the underlying message of any text – whether general, addressed to men only or women only – is applicable to all people. This assumption is based on three basic premises: 1) that Islam is for all humanity, so its texts should address everyone regardless of sex; 2) that the Qurʾanic principle of human relations is cooperation and reciprocity, not hegemony and power; and 3) that Islamic texts are open for reinterpretation to allow the previous two premises to be reflected in every interpretative effort.

Using these three basic premises, the *Qirāʾa Mubādala* method of interpretation finds that the main idea of each text is always compatible with the universal principles of Islam and applicable for all. The principle that Islam must be compatible and suitable with human needs of all times and all spaces must also mean that Islam fulfils the needs of both men and women, not just one or the other. Similarly, the 'objectives of the *Shariʿa*' (*maqāṣid al-shariʿa*) must be interpreted in light of this ontological equality between all human beings.

This leads us to the division of Islamic texts into three groups: texts which contain fundamental values (*al-mabādiʾ*); texts which contain thematic principles (*al-qawāʿid*); and texts which contain teachings and norms that can be implemented (*al-juzʾiyyāt*). The method of *Qirāʾa Mubādala* mostly works in the third type of texts (*al-juzʾiyyāt*), with the main goal to find meanings suitable with the other types (*al-qawāʿid* and *al-mabādiʾ*).

The interpretive process starts with the fundamental values of Islamic teachings (*al-mabādiʾ*), such as greeting anybody without exception, the virtue of piety, the reward/punishment for one's deeds, justice and blessing for all without any discrimination, respecting human dignity. Other examples of these general teachings are being kind to others, being grateful, helping each other and working together. These teachings are applicable to all people, regardless of gender.

Thematic principles of Islamic teachings (*al-qawāʿid*) are related to main issues such as economics, politics and marriage. For example, the thematic principles related to spousal relationships are drawn from verses that identify key pillars of marriage, such as marriage as a solemn covenant (verse 4:21); reciprocity between the couple (verses 2:187; 30:21); mutual agreement and consent (verse 2:233); treating each other well (verse 4:19); consulting each other (verse 2:233) (see the chapter by Nur Rofiah in this volume for more on these pillars). These teachings should inform the formulation of laws, agreements, contracts, conduct in marriage and household issues. These are thematic principles (*al-qawāʿid*), and not fundamental values (*al-mabādi'*), because they are thematically related to the issue of marriage and the household. However, these also demonstrate implementation of the fundamental values, namely *tawḥīd*, justice, cooperation and welfare.

The texts, teachings and laws on 'relations between men and women' can be categorized as specific and contextual implementation of the above principles. Roles for men (husbands) and women (wives) in domestic or public spaces are categorized as specific, contextual teachings (*al-juz'iyyāt*), and must be compatible with both *al-mabādi'* and *al-qawāʿid*. Social and marital issues in which either men or women are mentioned are usually categorized as *al-juz'iyyāt* issues that can be reinterpreted in order to be compatible with the principles of *al-mabādi'* and *al-qawāʿid*. This would include issues such as women's political leadership, the value of women's testimony and spousal rights and duties.

On this level, the *Qirā'a Mubādala* method of interpretation ensures the compatibility of *al-juz'iyyāt* texts with the main thematic principles (*al-qawāʿid*) and fundamental values (*al-mabādi'*). The *Qirā'a Mubādala* method approaches Islamic teachings holistically. It is premised on the notion that Islamic teachings are solid, coherent and related to each other (verse 4:82). Technically, texts on the principles should become an umbrella for holistically unearthing specific meanings in other texts. Therefore, before interpreting a text using the *Qirā'a Mubādala* method, we first need to identify the nature of the texts: whether they are categorized as *al-mabādi'*, *al-qawāʿid* or *al-juz'iyyāt*. Partial texts cannot directly be re-interpreted through the *Qirā'a Mubādala* method if the 'meaning' compatible with the thematic principle and fundamental values is not yet found.

There are three steps to this method when applied to gender relations. The first is to ensure that the texts which are to be interpreted address relations between men and women, either in the family or in the larger society. The second step is to ensure that the texts mention both men and women, for example one as the subject and the other as the object, or explicitly mention one of the two genders and implicitly refer to the other. The texts which explicitly suggest a reciprocal relationship already do not need to be read using the *Qirā'a Mubādala* method. These texts can actually become the basis for interpreting the implicit *mubādala* texts. The third step is to pay attention to whether the texts contain a main message that is based on fundamental values or thematic principles (*al-mabādi'* or *al-qawā'id*) or related to specific conduct (*al-juz'iyyāt*). The message of the texts about principles (that is, gaining benefits and avoiding harm) can be directly applied to the parties who are not mentioned. For texts on specific conduct, however, the message must be developed into a more general one first – such as what can be done to promote benefits or avoid harm – and then can be applied to both parties.

3.1 Reciprocal reading of selected hadiths on marriage

According to the process of reciprocal reading, the starting point is identifying hadiths that establish the guiding principles for all human relations. These principles call on all people to treat one another with integrity, not to oppress one another and not to humiliate or hurt one another. The following hadiths are good examples of these principles:

> Abū Hurayra reported Allah's Messenger (pbuh) said: 'Do not envy one another, do not hate one another, do not argue, do not enter into a transaction when the others have entered into that transaction; be fellow-brothers (to others) and servants of Allah. A Muslim is the brother of a Muslim. He neither oppresses him nor humiliates him nor looks down upon him. The *taqwā* is here, [and while saying so] he pointed towards his chest thrice. It is a serious evil for a Muslim that he should look down upon his brother Muslim. All things of a Muslim are inviolable for his brother in faith: his blood, his wealth and his honour.' (*Ṣaḥīḥ Muslim*, 2000, vol. 2, no. 6706)

> Yahya related to me from Malik from Amr ibn Yahya al-Mazini from his father that the Messenger of Allah, may Allah bless him and grant him peace, said, 'There is no injury nor return of injury.' (*Muwaṭṭa' Mālik*, 2000, no. 1432)

The above hadiths assert relationships of justice in which everyone commits not to inflict harm or oppression on others, and to treat them with compassion and care. Other foundational hadiths also call people to love each other, help each other and to be virtuous:

> Masruq narrated: 'We were sitting with ʿAbdullah bin ʿAmr who was narrating to us (Hadith). He said, "Allah's Messenger (pbuh) was neither immoral nor purposefully doing immoral things. And he used to say, 'The best among you are the best in character.'"' (*Ṣaḥīḥ al-Bukhārī*, 2000, vol. 3, no. 6104)

> Abū Hurayra narrated: 'Allah's Messenger (pbuh) kissed Al-Hasan bin ʿAli while Al-Aqraʾ bin Habis at-Tamim was sitting beside him. Al-Aqraʾ said, "I have ten children and I have never kissed any one of them". Allah's Messenger (pbuh) cast a look at him and said, "Whoever is not merciful to others will not be treated mercifully."' (*Ṣaḥīḥ al-Bukhārī*, 2000, vol. 3, no. 6063)

> An-Nawwas bin Samʾan narrated, 'I asked the Messenger of Allah (pbuh) about virtue and sin and he replied, "The essence of virtue is (manifested in) good morals, whereas sinful conduct is that which turns in your heart (making you feel uncomfortable) and you dislike that it would be disclosed to other people."' (*Ṣaḥīḥ Muslim*, 2000, vol. 2, no. 6680)

In the first hadith above, good character is affirmed as the core of human excellence and is also what Prophet Muhammad embodies as a role model. The second hadith underscores the importance of compassion within the family. The third affirms the importance of embracing good ethical values and constant self-reflection and moral accountability. These hadiths are numerous and must be understood to apply not only to relationships among men or women, but also between men and women both in society and within households. Therefore, these values and principles must also be the foundation for interpreting the hadiths that specifically address men as husbands or women as wives.

Accordingly, prophetic reports that are addressed linguistically to women only or men only are also to be read as applying to both since their underlying ethical teachings are meant for men and women equally. For example, there are a number of hadiths that state that 'women' who do not fulfil their husband's sexual needs will be cursed by the angels or 'women' who ask for divorce without any strong reason will be prohibited from entering paradise.

> Abū Hurayra narrated: 'The Prophet (pbuh) said: "When a man calls his wife to come to his bed (for marital relations), and she refuses to come, and he spends the night in anger, the angels curse her till the morning."' (*Ṣaḥīḥ al-Bukhārī*, 2000, vol. 3, no. 5248)

> Thawban narrated: 'The Prophet (pbuh) said: "If any woman asks her husband for divorce without some strong reason, Paradise will be forbidden to her."' (*Sunan Abī Dāwūd*, 2000, vol. 2, no. 2226)

These texts discuss the spousal relationship but only mention women as the subject in the texts – women are requested to show kindness to their husband or risk going to hell. In principle, it is impossible for Islam to instruct or threaten individuals just because they are women. Therefore, we need to find a meaning which is applicable for both men and women. We can refer back to the Qur'anic verses and hadiths that outline Islamic principles (*al-mabādi'*) that apply to men and women equally. Both are expected to be believers, to do kindness, to be grateful, to serve others and to maintain the unity of the household. Similarly, the five pillars of the marital relationship (*al-qawā'id*) derived from the Qur'an apply to both husbands and wives: both men and women are partners and a pair, and both must strongly protect the marriage ties, treat each other well, consult with each other, and try to make each other happy and comfortable. Therefore, the teachings of the above texts, based on the *mubādala* approach, apply to either spouse, whether man or woman. Husbands are also obligated to be grateful for the kindness of their wives, to fulfil the sexual needs of their wives, and not to divorce their wives without any justifiable reason, if they do not want to risk going to hell.

Similarly, the hadiths which are usually understood to target men – such as directives to treat their wives well and always be kind – are also ethically applicable and directed at women to act in the same ways towards their husbands.

> Abū Hurayra reported: 'Messenger of Allah (pbuh) said, "The believers who show the most perfect faith are those who have the best behaviour,

> and the best of you are those who are the best to their wives.'" (*Sunan al-Tirmidh*, 2000, vol. 2, no. 1195)

> Abū Hurayra reported: 'Allah's Apostle (pbuh) said, "He who believes in Allah and the Hereafter, if he witnesses any matter he should talk in good terms about it or keep quiet. Act kindly towards women, for woman is created from a rib, and the most crooked part of the rib is its top. If you attempt to straighten it, you will break it, and if you leave it, its crookedness will remain there. So act kindly towards women."' (*Ṣaḥīḥ Muslim*, 2000, vol. 1, no. 3720)

Good treatment, noble character, being kind and being responsible are the fundamental norms (*al-mabādiʾ*) that guide the marriage relationship (*al-qawāʿid*). Men or husbands are more commonly mentioned in certain hadiths such as the above because socially they had more authority in various societies in this world, including in Arabia. The Prophet Muhmmad also stated in his final speech that a husband's authority should be used for the benefit of women and not arbitrarily, violently and cruelly.

> Sulaiman bin Amr bin Ahwas said: 'My father told me that he was present at the Farewell Pilgrimage with the Messenger of Allah. He praised and glorified Allah, and reminded and exhorted (the people). Then he said: "I enjoin good treatment of women, for they are prisoners with you, and you have no right to treat them otherwise, unless they commit clear indecency."' (*Sunan Ibn Māja*, 2000, no. 1924)

Thus, two persons who are united in marriage are equally expected to have noble morals, be responsible, and to always treat each other well, without any exception.

If we refer back to the hadith about the creation of women from a crooked rib, we find that this text is misunderstood. It is also often combined with another hadith.

> Abū Hurayra reported: 'Allah's Messenger (pbuh) said, "Act kindly towards woman, for woman is created from a rib, and the most crooked part of the rib is its top. If you attempt to straighten it, you will break it, and if you leave it, its crookedness will remain there. So act kindly towards women."' (*Ṣaḥīḥ al-Bukhārī*, 2000, vol. 2, no. 649)

> Abū Hurayra reported: 'Allah's Messenger (pbuh) said, "The woman is like a rib; if you try to straighten her, she will break. So if you want to get benefit from her, do so while she still has some crookedness."' (*Ṣaḥīḥ al-Bukhārī*, 2000, vol. 3, no. 5239)

When the husband finds his wife temperamental, emotional and hard, then she may be seen as a bent rib. If these negative characteristics are not 'straightened', then she will continue 'to bend', or be temperamental and hard. If he forces the bent rib to straighten, it can break. Broken here, according to the Prophet himself, means divorce. The Prophet asked the husband, in such a wife's condition, to continue to treat her well and be gentle, to be with her, to help her stop being temperamental and to prevent divorce.

By applying *Qirā'a Mubādala*, the same advice can be addressed to women who find their husbands temperamental, emotional and harsh. If the husband is in this condition, he is like a bent rib. He may continue to bend, or he may break if he is forced to be straightened. Therefore, his wife must also treat him well, be gentle and to be with him. This would help her husband stop being temperamental, and thus the break-up of the marriage will be avoided. This is because a core teaching from the prophetic tradition to husbands and wives is to advise each other and encourage each other to goodness. This is affirmed by a hadith that teaches mutual kindness by explicitly addressing men about their wives and also explicitly addressing women about their husbands.

> Abū Hurayra narrated: 'The Messenger of Allah (pbuh) said: "May Allah have mercy on a man who gets up at night and prays, then he wakes his wife and she prays, and if she refuses he sprinkles water in her face. And may Allah have mercy on a woman who gets up at night and prays, then she wakes her husband and prays, and if he refuses she sprinkles water in his face."' (*Sunan Abī Dāwūd*, 2000, vol. 1, no. 1308)

An example of a hadith that specifically addresses women is the one that promises women paradise should they die when their husbands are pleased with them.

> Umm Salama narrated: 'God's Messenger said, "Any woman who dies when her husband is pleased with her will enter paradise."' (*Sunan al-Tirmidhī*, 2000, vol. 1, no. 1194)

This hadith, so far, has only been interpreted to encourage women to always seek to please their husbands and follow their wishes so that they can enter paradise. This understanding is of course not reciprocal and can even be misguided if it is practised in absolute terms. If we use the *Qirā ʾa Mubādala* method, however, the substance of this hadith is about doing a deed that helps us enter paradise, in this case ensuring our partner's pleasure in us. This pleasure, of course, occurs because we have done good things for our partner. In other words, the text is about a married couple who live in a reciprocal relationship in which they complement, strengthen and cooperate with each other, so that each feels happy with the other. This relationship can enable the spouse, whether husband or wife, to live happily in this world and facilitates their salvation in the hereafter.

This has been a brief exploration of how the *Qirā ʾa Mubādala* method can be applied to selected hadiths. It should be noted that the method also has limitations. This method can only be applied to texts that are relational between men and women. Texts about faith, worship or news cannot be the object of this method. In some cases, this method can also be used in a misguided way, such as to support the practice of female circumcision using a reciprocal understanding of the practice of male circumcision. This understanding of *mubādala* is incorrect, because *Qirā ʾa Mubādala* must find a principled meaning and not a technical one. Circumcision is technical; the principle is health and pleasure. For women, of course, health and pleasure can be achieved without being circumcised, and research shows that it can be harmful to women's health. Despite such limitations, the potential of *Qirā ʾa Mubādala* is that it highlights the fundamentals and principles and allows us to engage with the Hadith tradition in a holistic manner.

3.2 Comparative analysis of Abū Shuqqa and *Qirā'a Mubādala*

As already explained, *Qirā ʾa Mubādala* is inspired by and therefore also engages in dialogue with Abū Shuqqa's interpretative methodology. Abū Shuqqa never used the term *mubādala*. He used the term *musawa* several times, not in relation to his methodology of interpretation, but regarding the value of equality between men and women. When talking about the roles of husband and wife, Abū Shuqqa also used the term *mutamāthila*, which can be interpreted as 'similar to each other', and the term *mutabādila*, which can be interpreted as 'interchangeable with each other'. These two terms also do not directly talk about his methodology of interpretation. However, in the practice of interpreting both Qurʾanic verses and hadith texts, Abū Shuqqa applied a method which could be referred to as '*Qirāʾa Mubādala*'. For example, the term '*ṭāba lakum*' in verse 4:3, which is literally translated into 'good for you men', is interpreted to be 'good for all of you family members, male and female, mother, father and children'. Therefore polygamy, in his opinion, can only be permitted if it is also good for all family members (Abū Shuqqa, 1990, juz 5, p. 291). This also applies to the hadith that says the beauty of the world is a pious wife and the one about the Prophet Muhammad's advice for men to marry women who can help them prepare well for the afterlife.

> Abdallah b. ʿAmr reported: 'God's Messenger said, "The whole world is to be enjoyed, but the best thing in the world is a good woman."' (*Ṣaḥīḥ Muslim*, 2000, vol. 1, no. 3716)

> Thawban said: 'When the verse concerning silver and gold was revealed, they said: "What kind of wealth should we acquire?" Umar said: "I will tell you about that". So he rode on his camel and caught up with the Prophet, and I followed him. He said: "O Messenger of Allah what kind of wealth should we acquire?" He said: "Let one of you acquire a thankful heart, a tongue that remembers Allah and a believing wife who will help him with regard to the Hereafter."' (*Sunan Ibn Māja*, 2000, no. 1929)

The first hadith is interpreted by Abū Shuqqa to apply to both men and women. Therefore, the best thing in the world for a wife is a good husband, just as a good wife is the best thing in the world for a husband. Similarly, the second hadith also applies to women in addition to men, and accordingly means that women are equally encouraged to marry pious husbands to help them in the spiritual journey towards the afterlife (Abū Shuqqa, 1990, juz 5, pp. 13–14).

Abū Shuqqa also discusses the question of authority (*qiwāma*) and obedience (*ṭāʿa*) in marriage. He refers to verse 4:34 and several hadiths in relation to this subject matter, such as the following:

> Abdullah bin ʿUmar narrated: 'The Prophet (pbuh) said, "Every one of you is a guardian and every one of you is responsible (for their wards). A ruler is a guardian and is responsible (for his subjects); a man is a

guardian of his family and responsible (for them); a wife is a guardian of her husband's house and she is responsible (for it), a slave is a guardian of his master's property and is responsible (for that). Beware! All of you are guardians and are responsible (for your wards).'" (*Ṣaḥīḥ al-Bukhārī*, 2000, vol. 3, no. 5243)

Abu Umamah narrated: 'The Prophet used to say: "Nothing is of more benefit to the believer after *taqwā* of Allah than a righteous wife whom, if he commands her she obeys him, if he looks at her he is pleased, if he takes an oath concerning her she fulfils it, and when he is away from her she is sincere towards him with regard to herself and his wealth."' (*Sunan Ibn Māja*, 2000, no. 1930)

Although Abū Shuqqa argues that these textual sources call for a relationship of cooperation and mutual help between the spouses, his interpretation maintains a gendered and hierarchical construction of spousal roles. He argues that husbands are obligated to assume responsible leadership that is beneficial to women and all family members. Similarly, wives are obligated to obey their husbands, but it is obedience that serves the common benefit of the family. When a man's leadership is irresponsible or even evil, the woman has the right to remind him and does not have to obey him. Abū Shuqqa in this case does not really apply a *mubādala* reading; the husband has a claim to *qiwāma*, and *ṭā'a* is the obligation of the wife. However, by applying the *Qirā'a Mubādala* method, I argue, in contrast, that husbands and wives can either or both equally assume responsible leadership and/or cooperative deference to this leadership depending on which aspect of their lives is the focus, their respective abilities at that time of their lives, and the circumstances and needs of their family. The overall aim is to strive together towards the benefit of the couple and all family members according to their respective abilities.

Lastly, it is important to build on Abū Shuqqa's model of collecting valid Hadith texts in one book and rearranging them in themes that better reflect the values of equality (*musawa*) and the principle of reciprocal relationships (*mutabādila*). We can do the same and better with special collections of Hadith about family law and ethics that emphasize reciprocity and cooperation between spouses and family members. Recent experiences of women in diverse family forms can be a reflective reference in compiling thematic collections of hadiths. This contrasts with the classical books, such as *Ṣaḥīḥ al-Bukhārī*, in which the hadiths about marriage are arranged in a way that explicitly addresses only men as the subject of marriage and places women as their objects. We can also title this new collection of hadith in more neutral way. Unlike Abū Shuqqa's title 'Liberating Women', we can call it 'Collection of Hadith on Ethics in Family Law'.[7] As with Abū Shuqqa's work, this collection also needs to include the fundamental Qur᾿anic verses to strengthen its perspective and substance. The hadiths that outline guiding principles for human relationships (including gender) must also be put at the beginning as a foundation. Hadith texts that literally lack a reciprocal meaning must be given a short interpretation in this collection to direct readers towards a more reciprocal meaning or provide the social context in which the text was produced to highlight its spirit and apply it to our present context.

4. *QIRĀ᾿A MUBĀDALA* IN THE INDONESIAN CONTEXT

In this final section, I shed light on the Indonesian context where I am located as a scholar activist and how this context has motivated my work on the *Qirā᾿a Mubādala* methodology. *Qirā᾿a Mubādala* was developed from and together with the women's empowerment movement in Indonesia,[8] especially among the Nahdlatul Ulama Islamic *pesantren* (boarding schools). This movement was synergized with various other Islamic organizations, Islamic college academics, women's religious gatherings, study circles, women empowerment activists and certain government institutions. This movement began in the early 1990s and has thus far culminated in the Kongres Ulama Perempuan Indonesia (Indonesian Congress of Women Ulama, 'KUPI'), which convened from 24–27 April 2017 at a traditional Islamic boarding school that is led by a woman scholar.[9] More specifically, this method was developed from and

---

[7] Inspired by Abū Shuqqa, I created a collection of hadiths which place fundamental texts as the foundation for partial texts on women's issues (see Abdul Kodir, 2019a).

[8] I have been part of this women's empowerment movement since late 1999, through *Forum Kajian Kitab Kuning* (FK3) institutions, Rahima, Fahmina and Alimat, and became one of the core committee members in Kongres Ulama Perempuan Indonesia (KUPI, Congress of Indonesian Women Ulama) in 2017. The *Qirā᾿a Mubādala* method, along with the '*Keadilan Hakiki*' (*haqiqi* justice/real justice) approach, as described in Nur Rofiah's contribution to this volume, was officially launched in this Congress and was discussed intensively by key figures in August 2018 before finally being published as Abdul Kodir (2019b). To date, more than 5,000 copies have been printed and sold. All explanations of the *Qirā᾿a Mubādala* method in this chapter are explained in more detail and with more examples in the book.

[9] For more on KUPI, see Nur Rofiah's contribution to this volume.

for Muslim communities who believe in certain traditions, certain references or certain books, and simultaneously have faith in just gender relations that must be practised in everyday life. I conceptualized the methodology, but this knowledge would not have been possible without the involvement of all of these actors and influences.

The *Forum Kajian Kitab Kuning* (FK3), a study circle of Islamic boarding schools led by Nyai Hj. Sinta Nuriyah Wahid and KH Husein Muhammad, for example, criticized weak and fake hadith in the book *Syarh Uqud al-Lujjayn*, a boarding school reference book on marital relationships. In addition, the FK3 offered a reinterpretation of the book by using the *mubādala* perspective for those Islamic boarding schools still using the book. This method, which I subsequently named *Qirā 'a Mubādala*, enables people who believe in and still refer to this book to give new meanings that are more balanced and just. It also allows them to emphasize the importance of reciprocity and cooperation in the spousal relationship.[10] The *mubādala* method was also used in an online study of the book *Iḥyā ' 'Ulūm al-Dīn* by Imam Ghazālī (d. 555 AH/1111 CE) conducted by the Indonesian scholar Ulil Abshar Abdallah, during which the group read an authoritative text that literally addresses only men in a way that includes women as subjects.

Another relevant factor is my involvement in various trainings and seminars with judges of religious affairs and employees of the Office of Religious Affairs in Indonesia. In incorporating the *mubādala* method into these events, I invite them to apply the method to the primary Islamic law reference they know: the 1991 Indonesian *Kompilasi Hukum Islam* (Compilation of Islamic Law, 'KHI'). It is not helpful to simply criticize the KHI, which is the only authoritative reference they employ, when no alternative is available and reforms of Islamic law still face political obstacles. Instead, the judges and religious affairs employees produce more gender-just legal interpretations during the seminars and trainings by referring to the articles and verses from the KHI that have the most obvious ethical messages, and then reinterpreting the other articles and verses in a way that is compatible with these ethical meanings.[11]

---

[10] Learning from FK3, I wrote and published a book for typical Islamic boarding schools that could be used as an alternative reference (Abdul Kodir, 2012).

[11] The Ministry of Religious Affairs of the Republic of Indonesia has published a guidebook for organizing pre-marital courses that places more emphasis on relationships that are based on the principles of reciprocity, cooperation and justice. Since the end of 2015, the Ministry has also taught the contents of this book to more than 1,500 Ministry heads, extension workers and lower-level employees who come in direct contact with community services.

In reflecting on my activism experiences, the *Qirāʾa Mubādala* method will make it easier for scholars and activists to refer to the most basic principles guiding human relations in Islam without having to jettison Islamic texts. These principles include doing good for each other, helping each other, supporting and complementing each other. The partial meanings of specific hadiths are referred back to the main hadiths and the foundational verses of the Qurʾan for ethical and moral guidance. Therefore, we are no longer trapped in the methodology of explaining the Qurʾan with hadith (*bayān al-Qurʾan bi al-ḥadīth*), which often results in a more partial hadith text being considered as the only final and binding explanation of the Qurʾan. On the contrary, the fundamental meaning of these partial hadiths must be found in a way that is compatible with the main message of the Qurʾan. This main meaning, and not the partial meaning in the literal text, should be final and binding.

CONCLUSION

The methodology of *Qirāʾa Mubādala* can contribute to building knowledge that shows how Hadith can inspire just relationships, especially in the context of reforming Muslim family laws towards gender justice. In the spirit of *Qirāʾa Mubādala* on Hadith, all research endeavours should be directed to find ethical meanings about reciprocity and cooperation within spousal relationships. This initiative will keep us from lengthy research and endless debate about the weaknesses or validity of a hadith text. We can immediately accept all traditions, especially those which classical scholars determined to be authentic hadiths. Our efforts can then be mobilized to rearrange the series and collection of hadiths in a way that better reflects the Prophet's mission, as described in verse 21:107 as '*wa mā arsalnāka illa raḥmatan lil ʿalāmīn*' ('We have not sent you, [O Muhammad], except as a mercy to the worlds'). Then we can develop constructive meanings with reference to these ideas.

Notably, the *Qirāʾa Mubādala* method allows for a holistic approach towards our textual tradition that foregrounds key fundamental values and thematic principles. While the process of developing *Qirāʾa Mubādala* is still in an early stage, it could be further conceptualized and expanded to reinterpret a variety of religious, legal and cultural texts or even to understand and analyse social realities. For now, the *Qirāʾa Mubādala* method can be used to engage with the Hadith tradition as a source of ethical principles for gender equality and justice. *Wallahu aʿlam* (Allah knows best).

REFERENCES

Abdul Kodir, Faqihuddin. 2012. *Manbaʿ al-Saʿādah: fī Usus Ḥusn al-Muʿāsharah wa-Ahammīyat al-Taʿāwun wa-l-Mushārakah fī al-Ḥayāh al-Zawjīyah (Sources of Happiness on the Principles of Mutual Goodness in Marriage Relations)*. n.p.

Abdul Kodir, Faqihuddin. 2017. 'Seeds of Gender Equality within Islam: Abū Shuqqa's Approach to Hadith on Women's Liberation'. In *Interfaith Dialogues in Indonesia and Beyond: Ten Years of ICRS Studies (2007–2017)*, edited by Leonard Chrysostoms Epafras, pp. 151–62. Geneva: Globalethics.net.

Abdul Kodir, Faqihuddin. 2019a. *60 Hadith Sahih Khusus untuk Hak-hak Perempuan dalam Islam Dilengkapi Penafsiranya*. Yogyakarta: Divapress.

Abdul Kodir, Faqihuddin. 2019b. *Qirā'ah Mubādalah: Tafsir Progresif untuk Keadilan Gender dalam Islam*. Yogyakarta: IRCISOD.

Abū Dāwūd, Sulaymān b. al-Ashʿath al-Sijistānī. 2000. *Sunan Abī Dāwūd*. Cairo: Jamʾiyyah al-Maknaz al-Islamy.

Abū Shuqqa, ʿAbd al-Ḥalīm Muḥammad. 1990. *Taḥrīr al-Marʾa fī ʿAṣr al-Risāla; Dirāsa an al-Marʿa Jāmiʿa li-Nuṣūṣ al-Qurʾān al-karīm wa Ṣaḥīḥayn al-Bukhārī wa Muslim (The Liberation of Women at the Time of the Prophecy)*. 4 vols. Kuwait City: Dār al-Qalam.

Ali, Syed Mohammed. 2004. *The Position of Women in Islam: A Progressive View*. Albany: SUNY Press.

Al-Bukhārī, Muḥammad b. Ismāʿīl. 2000. *Ṣaḥīḥ al-Bukhārī*. Cairo: Jamʾiyyah al-Maknaz al-Islamy.

Engineer, Asghar Ali. 2001. 'Islam, Women, and Gender Justice'. In *What Men Owe to Women*, edited by John C. Raines and Daniel C. Maguire. New York: State University of New York Press.

Farīja, Muḥammad. 1996. *Huqūq al-Marʾa Al-Muslima fī al-Qurʾān wa al-Sunna*. Beirut; Damascus: al-Maktab al-Islāmī.

Al-Ghazālī, Muḥammad. 1989. *Al-Sunna al-Nabawiya Bayn Ahl al-Fiqh wa Ahl al-Ḥadīth*. Beirut: Dār al-Shurūq.

Al-Hādī, Sādiq ibn Muḥammad. 2009. *Al-Marʾa fī al-Sunna al-Nabawiya al-Muṭahara*. Alluka. www.alukah.net/publications_competitions/0/6525/

Al-Hāshimī, Muḥammad ʿAlī. 2013. *Shakhṣiyya al-Marʾa Al-Muslima kamā Yaṣūghuhā al-Islām fī al-Kitāb wa al-Sunna*. Cairo: Dār al-Salām.

Hassan, Riffat. 1991. 'Muslim Women and Post-Patriarchal Islam'. In *After Patriarchy: Feminist Transformation of the World Religions*, edited by Paula M. Cooey, William R. Eakin and Jay B. McDaniel. New York: Orbis Books.

Ibn Anas, Mālik. 2000. *Muwaṭṭaʾ Mālik*. Cairo: Jamʾiyyah al-Maknaz al-Islamy.

Ibn al-ʿArabi, Abū Bakr. 1988. *Aḥkām al-Qurʾān*, edited by Ali Muhammad al-Bajawi. Beirut: Dar al-Jil.

Ibn Bāz, ʿAbd al-ʿAzīz ibn ʿAbd Allāh. 1988. *Khaṭar Mushāraka al-Marʿa li al-Rajul fī Maydān ʿAmalih*. Cairo: Maktabat al-Sunna li al-Tawzīʿ.

Ibn Bāz, ʿAbd al-ʿAzīz ibn ʿAbd Allāh. 1994. *Fatāwā al-Nisā*. Medina; Cairo: Dār Ibn Rajab; Dār al-Ṭibāʿah.

Ibn Bāz, ʿAbd al-ʿAzīz ibn ʿAbd Allāh. 1995. *Fatāwā al-ʿUlamā li al-Nisā*. Cairo: Maṭbaʿat al-Sunna.

Ibn Ḥajar al-ʿAsqalānī, Aḥmad b. ʿAlī. 1993. *Fatḥ al-Bārī fi-Sharḥ Ṣaḥīḥ al-Bukhārī*. Beirut: Dar al-Fikr.

Ibn Ḥanbal, Aḥmad. 2000. *Musnad Aḥmad ibn Ḥanbal*. Cairo: Jamʾiyyah al-Maknaz al-Islamy.

Ibn Hazm, ʿAlī ibn Aḥmad. 2005. *Al-Iḥkām fi Uṣūl al-Aḥkām*, edited by Mahmud Hamid Uthman. Cairo: Dar al-Hadith.

Ibn Qarnās. 2011. *Al-Ḥadīth wa-l-Qurʾān*. Baghdad: Manshūrāt al-Jamal.

Ibn Māja, Muḥammad al-Qazwīnī. 2000. *Sunan Ibn Māja*. Cairo: Jamʾiyyah al-Maknaz al-Islamy.

Kahf, Mohja. 2000. 'Braiding the Stories: Women's Eloquence in the Early Islamic Era'. In *Windows of Faith: Muslim Women Scholar-Activists in North America*, edited by Gisela Webb, pp. 147–71. New York: Syracuse University Press.

Al-Khurasānī, Ghāda. 1979. *Al-Islām wa Taḥrīr al-Marʾa: Awwal Mawsuʾa ʿan al-Marʾa al-ʿArabiyya ʿabr al-ʿUṣūr*. Beirut: Dār al-Siyāsa.

Mernissi, Fatima. 1991. *The Veil and the Male Elite: A Feminist Interpretation of Women's Rights in Islam*. Reading, MA: Addison-Wesley.

Al-Munāwī, ʿAbd al-Raʾūf ibn Tāj al-ʿĀrifin. 1937. *Fayḍ al-Qadīr: Sharh al-Jāmʿi al-Sahīh*. Cairo: al-Maktabah at-Tijariyah al-Kubra.

Muslim, Ibn al-Ḥajjāj al-Qushayrī al-Naysābūrī. 2000. *Ṣaḥīḥ Muslim*. Cairo: Jamʾiyyah al-Maknaz al-Islamy.

Al-Najdī, Abd al-Raḥmān ibn Muḥammad. 1999. *Al-Durar al-Saniyya fī al-Ajwiba al-Najdiya; Majmūʾat Rasāʾil wa Masāʾil ʿUlamā Najd al-ʿAlām min ʿAṣr al-Shaykh Muḥammad ibn Abd al-Wahʾhāb ilā ʿAṣrinā Hādhā*. 16 vols. n.p.

Al-Nasāʾī, Aḥmad b. Shuʿayb. 2000. *Sunan al-Nasāʾī*. Cairo: Jamʾiyyah al-Maknaz al-Islamy.

Nāṣif, Fāṭima ʿUmar. 1989. *Huqūq al-Marʾa wa Wajibatuhā fī Ḍawʾ al-Kitāb wa-l-Sunna*. Doctoral thesis at Umm al-Qura University-Mecca.

Nur Rofiah. 2019. 'Prolog: Qirā'ah Mubadalah Sebagai Syarat Tafsir Agama Adil Gender'. In *Qirā'ah Mubadalah: Tafsir Progresif untuk Keadilan Gender dalam Islam*, by Faqihuddin Abdul Kodir. Yogyakarta: IRCISOD.

Al-Qaraḍāwī, Yūsuf. 1991. *Kayfa Nataʿāmal Maʿa al-Sunna al-Nabawiyya: Maʿālim wa Ḍawābiṭ*. Riyadh: Maktaba al-Mu'ayyad.

Raʾūf Izzat, Hiba. 1995. *Al-Marʾa wa-l-ʿAmal al-Siyāsī: Ruʾya Islāmiya* (*Woman and Political Work: An Islamic Perspective*). Herndon, VA: International Institute of Islamic Thought.

El Shamsy, Ahmed. 2013. *The Canonization of Islamic Law: A Social and Intellectual History*. Cambridge: Cambridge University Press.

Al-Shawkānī, Muhammad bin Ali. 1991. *Fatḥ al-Qadīr*. Beirut: Dar al-Khayr.

Siddique, Kaukab. 1990. *Liberation of Women Through Islam*. Kingsville, MD: American Society for Education and Religion.

Al-Tirmidhī, Muḥammad b. ʿĪsā. 2000. *Sunan al-Tirmidhī*. Cairo: Jamʾiyyah al-Maknaz al-Islamy.

Al-ʿUthaymīn, Muḥammad ibn Ṣāliḥ. 1989. *Fatāwā wa Rasāʾil al-Uthaymīn*. Cairo: Maktabat al-Turāth al-Islāmī.

Al-ʿUthaymīn, Muḥammad ibn Ṣāliḥ. 1996. *Al-Zawāj*. al-Sunbulawayn: Maktabah ʾIbād al-Raḥmān.

Al-ʿUthaymīn, Muḥammad ibn Ṣāliḥ. 1998. *Al-Fatāwā al-Nisāʾiya*. Cairo: Maktabah al-ʾIlm.

Wadud, Amina. 1999. *Qur'an and Woman: Rereading the Sacred Text from a Woman's Perspective*. New York: Oxford University Press.

Wadud, Amina. 2006. *Inside the Gender Jihad: Women's Reform in Islam*. Oxford: Oneworld.

Wadud, Amina. 2009. 'Islam Beyond Patriarchy'. In *Wanted: Equality and Justice in the Muslim Family*, edited by Zainah Anwar, pp. 95–112. Petaling Jaya, Malaysia: Sisters in Islam.

Wadud, Amina. 2015. 'The Ethics of *Tawhid* over the Ethics of *Qiwamah*'. In *Men in Charge? Rethinking Authority in Muslim Legal Tradition*, edited by Ziba Mir-Hosseini, Mulki Al-Sharmani and Jana Rumminger, pp. 256–74. London: Oneworld.

Al-Zarkashi, Badruddin. 2000. *Al-Bahr al-Muhīt fi Uṣūl al-Fiqh*, edited by Muhammad Muhammad Tamir. Beirut: Dar al-Kutub al-Ilmiyah.

ISLAMIC LEGAL THEORY AND ETHICS

Rethinking Muslim Marriage Rulings through Structural *Ijtihād*

Mohsen Kadivar

Since the early twentieth century it has increasingly become apparent that Muslim jurists' understandings of what constitutes 'Islamic law' are no longer in line with the demands of the lived realities of Muslims. What were accepted as religious rulings have been contested by modern standards of justice and the notions of rationality. By the second part of the twentieth century, *fiqh* rulings pertaining to almost the entire area of human and social interactions (*muʿāmalāt*) had been thrown into question.

In this chapter, I revisit some juristic (*fiqh*) rulings on marriage that have become problematic and unacceptable in light of contemporary standards of justice and social realities. Muslim scholars have approached these rulings from their own perspectives, which encompass at least four characteristics: denomination (for instance, Sunni or Shiʿa), legal school, theological school and a specific methodological approach. My analysis is from the standpoint of a reformist Shiʿi Usūli[1] jurist (*faqīh*) advocating 'structural *ijtihād*', which entails revising the principles and foundations of *fiqh* (*al-ijtihād fi al-uṣūl wa al-mabānī*). By the term *uṣūl*, I refer to juristic methodology (*uṣūl al-fiqh*) including linguistics (*mabāhith al-alfaẓ*); by *mabāni*, I refer to the principles

[1] The Usūli (rationalists) are the majority school of Shiʿa jurisprudence which, in contrast to the minority Akhbari (textualists), hold reason (*ʿaql*) as a source for the derivation of law.

of other areas of Islamic sciences, notably theology (*kalām*), ethics (*akhlāq*), Qur'anic exegesis (*tafsīr*) and the science of Hadith (*ʿilm al-hadīth*), as well as revisiting epistemological, cosmological, physiological, sociological and anthropological premises of Islamic sciences. I contend that the task of the *faqīh* is to ascertain that the laws defended in the name of Islam are just and ethical and that, to do so, we need to revisit the principles and foundations underpinning the traditional juristic methodology (*uṣūl al-fiqh*).

This chapter is in the genre of *al-fiqh al-istidlāli* (argumentative jurisprudence)[2] and consists of two main parts. In the first part, I outline contemporary approaches to rulings in classical *fiqh*, and then set out the key premises and requirements of structural *ijtihād*. In the second part, I apply structural *ijtihād* in four areas of marriage law where the classical *fiqhi* rulings have been increasingly contested since the early twentieth century: marriage of minors; rights and duties in marriage; unequal rights of spouses to divorce; and men's right to polygamy. I argue that, for rulings in these four areas to remain valid as Shariʿa rulings, and thus applicable as 'Islamic law', they should meet the four criteria: justice, ethics, reasonability and effectiveness according to the standards of the time.

1. STRUCTURAL *IJTIHĀD* AND ITS REQUIREMENTS

Ijtihād, which literally means 'effort/exertion', has been the source of dynamism within Islamic legal tradition for many centuries. It denotes the process of reaching judgements on points of law, referred to as Shariʿa rulings (*aḥkām al-shariʿa*), via *uṣūl al-fiqh* (principles of jurisprudence). These rulings encompass commandments, prohibitions, precepts and laws that jurists interpret to be mandated within Islam.

Broadly speaking, Muslim theologians and jurists (Sunni and Shiʿa) can be divided into four categories: traditionalists, fundamentalists, semi-reformists and reformists.[3] Traditionalists, sometimes called conservatives,

[2] A genre of writings in which the jurist (*faqīh*) provides the reasoning (textual and rational) for his legal opinion (fatwa), i.e., textual proofs and rational arguments on which the ruling is based.

[3] I am aware that this categorization does not reflect the complexity and diversity of the situation but, as I hope will be clear later, it is merely to highlight the points of difference and convergence between traditional *ijtihād* and the structural *ijtihād* that I am advocating as a reformist Usūli jurist.

are those jurists who adhere to classical *fiqh* rulings and methodology; they constitute a strong majority in religious centres of learning. Fundamentalists are those who resort to violence to enforce a rigid interpretation of these classical rulings as 'state law'; in both Sunni and Shiʿi Islam, they constitute a much smaller group than traditionalists. Semi-reformists are those who seek to reform classical *fiqh* rulings without rethinking their traditional foundations. Although they constitute a small minority in the seminaries, they are in the majority in modern universities and among educated Muslims around the globe. Reformists are those jurists and scholars who advocate a holistic and comprehensive reform based on the core foundation and principles of Islamic thought and jurisprudence. In contrast to semi-reformists who concentrate on piecemeal reforms, reformists argue that it is not enough to simply reinterpret rulings within the traditional framework, that is, traditional *ijtihād*; what is required is rethinking the underpinnings of classical juristic methodology. They contend that meaningful reform in *fiqh* rulings is the fruit of two deep reforms: that of the juristic methodology (*uṣūl al-fiqh*) and that of its foundations (*mabāni*), which involves other areas of Islamic intellectual thought; in other words, structural *ijtihād*. It is only then that modern issues, such as the emergence of nation-states and the expansion of discourses of citizenship, human rights, gender equality and democracy, can be addressed from within an Islamic framework.

In what follows I outline the premises on which structural *ijtihād* rests, that is, the three salient features by which it differs in approach from traditional *ijtihād*. These are: 1) having a minimalist rather than maximalist expectation of religion (*al-tawaqquʿ min al-dīn*) as the source of norms and law, which leads to a minimalist *fiqh*; 2) considering human rationality to be a source of ethics; and 3) evaluating rulings (*aḥkām*) as either timeless or time-bound.

1.1 Expectations of religion

The boundaries of religion, or what we can expect of religion, is a subject in modern theology and philosophy of religion.[4] In pre-modern times, the realm

[4] To my knowledge, Abdolkarim Soroush, the well-known Iranian public intellectual, was the first to discuss the term 'expectations of religion' in Persian. He elaborated his ideas in two articles, 'Essentials and Accidentals in Religion' and 'Maximalist Religion, Minimalist Religion', both available in English in Soroush (2008, pp. 63–117). My approach differs from his on several major points.

of religion was much broader and covered many aspects of social life, such as the fields of medicine and law. For instance, today, so-called *ṭibb al-nabī* (prophetic medicine) or *al-ḥudūd wa al-taʿzīrāt* (penal rules) are no longer considered essentials of Islam, but instead are seen as practices of the past that are now part of medical and legal knowledge.

We need to ascertain what subjects and issues belong exclusively to divine knowledge (revelation, scripture and prophetic tradition) or at least where religion plays the key role. We must also recognize what subjects and issues cannot be answered by revelations, scripture and traditions of the Prophet, and thus are exclusively the realm of human reasoning. In other words, we need to define what religious essentials are and what our expectation of religion should be. This does not mean that religious discussions must be restricted to the essentials and expectations in the divine revelation, scripture and prophetic tradition. Non-essentials or the issues beyond these expectations can be discussed, but should be seen as secondary and accidental, at least in our time (if not from the beginning).

'Structural *ijtihād*' draws on and further develops the concept of 'expectations of religion'. I argue that keeping the expectation of religion in our minds can have deep effects and benefits in *uṣūl al-fiqh* and the process of *istinbāṭ* (inference); it prepares the ground and clarifies the premises for the deliberations of Shariʿa-based proofs (*adilla al-shariʿa*). For instance, in deriving Shariʿa rulings for many modern issues (*mustaḥdatha*), traditional jurists presume that the Lawmaker (that is, God) has intended there to be a ruling for every new issue. But the concept of 'expectations of religion' shows us this presumption is not self-evident and needs argumentation.

Within the framework of structural *ijtihād*, I argue that we should restrict our expectations of Islam to eight areas: 1) the meaning of life; 2) knowledge about God; 3) knowledge about the Hereafter (*al-akhira*); 4) knowledge about the unseen world (*al-ghayb*); 5) supporting and safeguarding morality and ethics (*al-akhlāq*); 6) acts of worship (*al-ʿibādāt*); 7) quasi-rituals (*shibh manāsik*), which means restrictions on eating, drinking and sexual relationships; and 8) a very few aspects of human interactions (*muʿāmalāt*), such as the prohibition of usury (*ribā*). The first four of these eight are the main fields of Islamic philosophy and theology, while the last four are major fields of practical Islamic teachings, or Islamic ethics and jurisprudence (Kadivar, 2017). As I shall explain later in the chapter, the application of structural *ijtihād* will lead to minimalist jurisprudence.

1.2 Human rationality as the source of ethics

Another important premise of structural *ijtihād* is that ethics and morality are derived through human reason, and not exclusively from revelation. According to Cydney Grannan (n.d.):

> Generally, the terms *ethics* and *morality* are used interchangeably, although a few different communities (academic, legal, or religious, for example) will occasionally make a distinction ... Both morality and ethics loosely have to do with distinguishing the difference between 'good and bad' or 'right and wrong'. Many people think of morality as something that's personal and normative, whereas ethics is the standards of 'good and bad' distinguished by a certain community or social setting ... Ultimately, the distinction between the two is as substantial as a line drawn in the sand.

In Islamic literature, the term for both ethics and morality is '*akhlāq*'. Islamic moral theology or Islamic ethics is a theological discipline concerned with identifying and elucidating the principles that determine the quality of human behaviour in the light of Islamic scripture and prophetic tradition.[5]

There are two main approaches to ethics and morality in Islam. The first approach was adopted by the Muʿtazilites, who once constituted the majority, and in contemporary times by reformist Usūli Shiʿas. For them, morality and ethics are absolutely rational, universal disciplines that have common ground in all traditions. The role of religion is to support morality and ethics with the guarantee of reward and punishment in the next world. In other words, ethical and moral principles are not among *al-aḥkām al-taʾsīsīya wa al-mawlawiyya*, that is, positive rulings that were created or founded by Islam, but are classified as *al-aḥkām al-imḍāʾiya wa al-irshādiyya*, that is, existing pre-Islamic rulings that Islam ratified. In ratified rulings, it is human reason – which is God's gift – that plays the primary role, and religion plays only a confirmatory role.

In the other approach, moral values are defined by divine revelation. This is the predominant approach of the major theological schools of Sunni Islam, such as Ashʿāira, Māturidiyya and Hanābila. According to this approach,

---

[5] For more information on Islamic ethics, see Denny (2005), Moosa (2005; 2018), Reinhart (2005), Sachedina (2005).

ethical values and moral norms as well as Shariʿa rulings are given by God – the Lawgiver – and Muslims discover them through scripture. The methodology for deriving ethical principles is not rational, but textual.

'Structural *ijtihād*' operates within the framework of the first approach, which is rational ethics. Of course, Muslim scholars may highlight some moral values and ethical rulings in some situations, and prefer others at a time of probable conflict between them. There is a fundamental question here: Do we have any moral and ethical principles exclusive to Islam that do not have parallels in other traditions? If the response is 'No', we must admit that moral and ethical rulings are not among those matters that are governed by divine revelation; they are neither *taʿabbudi* (devotional) nor *tawqifī* (beyond rational) rulings that we should obey without question.[6] In other words, the Qurʾan and the Sunna are not the primary sources for morality and ethics; they are necessary but secondary sources that play a great role in clarifying moral and ethical principles.

1.3 Timeless or time-bound?

The primary principle (*al-aṣl al-awali*) in traditional *uṣūl al-fiqh* is that all textual injunctions are timeless unless proved by definite evidence to be time-bound. The main function of religion is defined as delineation of the duties of humankind by 'the law' as found in Islam's textual sources (the Qurʾan and Sunna). The original Lawmaker is God or His Prophet. Deriving legal rulings from Islam's textual sources is the role of jurists (through *ijtihād*), and their products are Islamic rulings that cover rituals, civil law, financial law, criminal law, public law and international law – in other words, all aspects of law. There is no difference between these areas in the derivation of rulings. All of them are parts of *fiqh* and the jurist does not need any special knowledge or expertise for discussing each of them. One can derive rulings on each of these areas from scripture as long as one is an expert in *fiqh*.

By contrast, structural *ijtihād* starts from the premise that all legal rulings in the Qurʾan, Sunna and *fiqh* are time-bound unless we can find valid evidence/proof (*dalīl*) that they are timeless and permanent. This is an argument that is

---

[6] *Tawqifī* includes *taʿabbudi*. The difference between the two is that the latter requires the intent of closeness to God (*qasd al-qurba*). Both depend on the revelation or prophetic tradition, nothing else.

determined by our expectations of religion, and the *dalīl* (evidence/proof) for this primary principle is not based on textual but on rational sources – a position that is not tolerated by those who believe that religion is purely a matter of the text.

On the basis of the above, I argue that the very term 'Islamic law' needs to be problematized. Law in its essence is time-bound. There is a direct relationship between law and the situation of time and place. Values and virtues could be timeless and permanent, but it is difficult to accept the concept of timeless rulings and laws. This principle of the philosophy of law is unanimously accepted in modern legal systems. Of course, we can merge human-made law with our Islamic values and virtues and call it 'Islamic' regarding those values and virtues, but we cannot preserve the rulings of past centuries in the context of Arabia, especially in their traditional forms and patterns, and consider them sacred.

The Qur'an never called itself a 'Book of Law'; instead it is a 'Book of Light' or 'Book of Guidance'. Light or guidance can be found in divine ethical virtues or moral values, but it is meaningless to seek light or guidance in verses relating to penal codes or polygamy or slavery. How could the Qur'an be a book of law, when its legal verses are less than 1 per cent of the whole (if matters of *'ibādāt* are excluded)? There are about fifty legal verses in the Qur'an.[7] The content of these verses can be divided into two: permanent Islamic values, and temporal rulings fitted to the time of revelation and to Arabia. For example, verse 5:38 ('Cut off the hands of thieves, whether they are man or woman, as punishment for what they have done – a deterrent from God: God is almighty and wise') expresses a permanent value that theft is a sin and crime that should be punished by governments. But cutting off the hands of a thief, without any doubt, is a temporal ruling.

Prophet Muhammad did not introduce himself as Lawmaker, and did not identify his mission as completing a legal system. Instead, he said, 'I was sent to complete the noble morality.'[8] What we can find of legal terms in his spiritual legacy as prophetic tradition can be divided into two. First are his administrative rulings, coming from his role as ruler, not his prophethood.

[7] The jurists have differed on the number, the upper limit being 500 verses.

[8] *'Innamā Buithtu li utammima makarim al-akhlāq'* (*Sunan al-Bayhaqi al-Kubra*, no. 20571); *'Innamā Buithtu li utammima sālih al-akhlāq'* (al-Bukhāri, *al-Adab al-Mufrad*, no. 273; Ibn Sa'd, *al-Tabaqat al-Kubra*, 1:192; al-Hakim al-Nayshaburi, *al-Mustadrak*, no. 4221; *Musnad Amad ibn Hanbal*, no. 8939; Ibn 'Asakir, *Tarikh Dimashaq*, 6:276, no. 1). For more information, see al-Albani (1993, 1:112, no. 45).

There is no evidence that such rulings are permanent and timeless. Second are rulings that are due to his prophethood, which undoubtedly are our respected Sunna, prophetic tradition. There is no Shariʿa-based evidence or proof that his teachings on human interactions (*muʿāmalāt*) are intended as permanent and timeless rulings.

To elaborate, let us take for example the rulings on women's rights in the Qurʾan and Sunna. These rulings were directly relevant to the economic, political, social and cultural situation of early Islam. We can find patriarchal patterns of family and society reflected in these rulings. Men's domination and superiority over women were justified on the basis of men's greater physical power, a fact that could not be neglected at the time. The gender ideology and the position of women in the modern era are different from those of the pre-modern era. The rulings for these two eras could not be the same. Those who want to impose the rulings of the pre-modern era on to the modern era, without any meaningful change or with just a few minor revisions, and think this is the implementation of sacred Shariʿa or divine law, are completely mistaken. What they preserve is only the early customs of seventh-century Arabs, or abrogated Islamic rulings. What should be preserved are divine permanent values and timeless standards, nothing else.

In addition, the exegetes of the Qurʾan, the compilers and interpreters of Hadith, and the jurists were almost all male, and their masculinity influenced their understandings of religious texts, their compilations and interpretations. All of these legal texts were written from a male perspective. It is natural that most of these texts and their interpretations do not satisfy Muslim women in modern times, and are inconsistent with egalitarian legal values. At the time of the revelation, as I have demonstrated in my work, rulings were all, according to the standards of the time, more just, rational, moral and functional than other existing laws (Kadivar, 2021, pp. 273–304).[9]

Keeping these points in mind, I argue that if we do not find evidence or proof (*dalīl*) of the permanence of family rulings in Shariʿa, it means that they are time-bound. For a *fiqh* ruling to remain valid for our time, it should meet all four aforementioned criteria based on textual evidence or proof. Among these four criteria, the most important is justice, which acquires a particular significance in the area of women's rights and is where the Qurʾan puts the emphasis.

---

[9] This work was originally published in Persian in 2008.

2. APPLYING STRUCTURAL *IJTIHĀD* TO JURISPRUDENCE ON MUSLIM MARRIAGE

Before revisiting rulings on the family and marriage with different approaches and types of *ijtihād*, three preliminary notes are in order.

First, I have set forth my general standpoint on the question of gender equality in my earlier work, arguing that the Qurʾan and Sunna should be reread in light of the fundamental equality between men and women (Kadivar, 2013). Both reason and the revelation require that women be treated with justice and according to what is commonly accepted as good or right (*maʿrūf*). The gist of my argument there is as follows: in line with Aristotle, the classical jurists approached the issue of women's rights on the basis of a notion of justice that recognizes rights for individuals in proportion to their 'deserts'; since they saw women to be 'inherently lesser than men', they were entitled to lesser rights. Such a notion of justice, which I call deserts-based justice (*al-ʿadāla al-istiḥqāqiyya*), leads to proportional justice, which has become indefensible and unjustified in modern times. Contemporary rationality recognizes humans as rights-holders, and thus upholds fundamental equality and egalitarian justice. We need to revisit *fiqh* rulings on women's rights in light of a notion of justice that is based on equality (*al-ʿadāla al-musawatiyya*), including equality between men and women, which is more consistent with the Qurʾanic spirit and Islamic ethical standards.

Second, I believe that there are at least three Islamic ethical values at play in family affairs. The first is the requirement of chastity and modesty for both men and women. Second, one of the priorities in Islamic ethics is the institution of the family and the protection, safety and financial and spiritual needs of its members. Third is the respect for the individuality of the spouses; one aspect of both men's and women's lives is their role in the family, but this is not the only one.

Finally, I want us to return to the domain of minimal *fiqh* that, as I argued earlier, embraces rulings on rituals (*ʿibādāt*) and only a small part of those relating to social life (*muʿāmalāt*). *ʿIbādāt* (for example, prayer, fasting, hajj and zakat) are matters between the believer and God, and rulings relating to them do not constitute what is called 'law'. Those relating to *muʿāmalāt*, which are matters of social relationships (contracts, for example), can be called law as they are open to rational argument. But there is a third category of acts that are either required or prohibited, such as bans on drinking alcohol and eating pork, that can be referred to as *shibh manāsik* (quasi-ritual). They are neither fully devotional, like *ʿibādāt*, nor exclusively social and rational, like *muʿāmalāt*.

Sexual activity and relationships fall under this third category of ritual-like acts. Marriage is necessary for any type of sex; divorce is necessary for its termination; and a number of sexual acts are prohibited. Of course, marriage is more than sex. Marriage and its consequences and correlations constitute large portions of any book of *fiqh* or Islamic jurisprudence. Marriage as a contract is governed by the general principles of human contracts, but sexual relations are a different matter. We should not mix rulings relating to the former with the latter. So-called 'Shariʿa-based family law' is inconsistent in many respects with modern civil laws. This is exactly the focus of our subsequent discussion: four areas of rulings on marriage that have become particularly problematic in contemporary times.

2.1 The marriage of minors

According to the *ijtihād* of traditional jurists, the marriage of a minor girl is permissible, even before puberty. The renowned jurist Muhammad b. Ahmad b. Abi Sahl al-Sarakhsi (1009–1090 CE) built on the following textual evidence to support of the marriage of minors: a) the Prophet married ʿĀʾisha when she was six years old, and brought her to his house when she was nine; b) verse 65:4 mentions the waiting period (*ʿidda*) for minors: 'those who have not menstruated as yet' (al-Sarakhsi, 1989, vol. 4, p. 212). On the basis of such arguments, a variety of traditional jurists issued rulings over many centuries regarding the father's compulsory guardianship of, and ability to marry off, a minor daughter; the ability of the girl to annul the marriage; and the permissibility of having sexual relations with a minor (see, for example, al-Qaraḍāwī, 2017, pp. 88–93; al-Najafi, 2012, vol. 30, pp. 209, 783–4; Yazdi, 1999, vol. 5, pp. 509–10; Makarem Shirazi, 2011, vol. 1, pp. 36–7, 39). In sum, the majority position in traditional *fiqh* holds that: a) forced marriage of a minor girl by her guardian is permissible; b) she does not have the right to annul this marriage when she reaches puberty, except in the Hanafi school; c) all sexual pleasure with a minor wife (apart from penetration) is allowed; d) under Shiʿi *fiqh*, full sexual intercourse with a minor wife before she reaches puberty or the age of nine is absolutely prohibited, while

Sunni *fiqh* permits it with the agreement of her guardian if the minor wife has the physical capacity.[10]

As already discussed, in structural *ijtihād*, a Shariʿa ruling should be tested by four criteria: justice, ethics, reasonability and functionality in comparison with alternative solutions. If a ruling, even if supported by explicit textual sources (the Qurʾan and Hadith), is not confirmed by all four of these criteria, it means that this ruling is not a valid Shariʿa ruling.

According to structural *ijtihād* and the application of four necessary criteria, the marriage of underage girls is forbidden. It is not just, ethical, reasonable according to the values and standards of our time, and it is not functional because in most legal systems it is a crime.

In other words, it is necessary to take account of modern sciences such as the psychology of minors, the psychology of marriage, comparative family law, and so on, subject to the requirements of reasonability, justice and ethics. To enter a marriage is a major decision that can be made only by two adults, not the guardians of minors. These are self-evident axioms and do not need any textual source. On the contrary, any textual source that opposes these self-evident axioms should be abrogated or dismissed as temporal evidence that is no longer valid.

In sum, marriage of underage girls is an affront to contemporary notions of childhood and ethical and moral sensibilities, and is harmful to the girl. Therefore, it must be prohibited. This prohibition is the result of independent reasoning. Marriage is by definition a contract between two adults with the consent of both parties. This minimal condition is not available in the marriage of underage girls, especially before puberty. Textual evidence such as verse 65:4 should be interpreted in the context of referring to females who are not minors but do not menstruate for some reason. Likewise, the case of ʿĀʾisha and hadith evidence must be understood in context, including confirming accuracy of the reports; such evidence cannot be generalized. Rulings based on such evidence are restricted to their times.

Based on the above, structural *ijtihād* and the reformist approach hold the following:

---

[10] Yousef Sanei (1937–2020), the Iranian Shiʿite semi-reformist jurist, supported the right of a wife to cancel a marriage made by her guardian after puberty (n.d., vol. 2, p. 148). He determined thirteen years old as the age of puberty for girls (Sanei, 2006).

1. The minimum age of marriage – that is, the beginning of adulthood, which depends on local conditions and culture – is determined by the parliament of each country after consultation with a professional committee including gynaecologists, youth psychologists, sociologists, lawyers and theologians. It is not exclusively a religious issue, but a multidimensional one. We should keep in mind that puberty is only one criteria of adulthood; adulthood is more complicated than simple bodily or sexual puberty.
2. Any kind of sex with minors (even with their consent or the permission of their guardians) should be defined as a crime.[11] This criminality is greater before puberty.
3. This type of marriage cannot be treated as valid by permission of guardians or courts.
4. The marriage contracts of underage or minor girls are null and void.

2.2 Equal rights and duties in marriage

In all classical schools of Islamic jurisprudence (*fiqh*), all expenses of marital life or maintenance (*nafaqa*) are exclusively on the shoulders of the husband. Because of this, he is the head of the family. If the wife has any business and income, she can save her money and does not have any responsibility for the expenses of marital life. She is not responsible for housework and does not have any other duties, even taking care of babies or breastfeeding. She is entitled to demand wages from her husband for performing any of these services. The only duties of the wife are protecting her chastity, total obedience and availability for sex whenever her husband requests, which is termed *tamkīn* in traditional *fiqh*.

I confine the discussion to the views of Shiʿa jurists. In *Wasila al-Naja* (*The Instrument of Salvation*), the well-known book of fatwas, Abolhassan Esfahani (1860–1946), the Iranian Shiʿite authority in Najaf, states:

> *Nushūz* (discord and animosity) of the wife means the absence of the required obedience, including unavailability for having sex (*tamkīn*), not removing abhorrent conditions that are obstacles to his pleasure and enjoyment of her, relinquishing cleansing and beautifying herself if the husband requests; as well as leaving his home without his permission,

[11] The representatives of the citizens in the parliament decide about punishment.

> etc. Refusing to perform services such as cooking, washing the dishes, cleaning the house, sewing, etc., that do not affect availability for sex (*istimtā'*), does not count as *nushūz*. ...
>
> The maintenance (*nafaqa*) of the wife is the duty of her husband if the marriage is permanent (*dā'ima*), not temporal, and if the wife has been obedient to her husband in those issues that obedience is required by the wife. Therefore, for a disobedient wife (*nāshiza*), there is no maintenance ...
>
> If the wife has *shar'i* acceptable excuses, such as menstruation, *ihram* on hajj, or required fasting, or disease, or travel or leaving the house with the husband's permission, she is eligible for *nafaqa* even in the case of failure of *tamkīn*. (2013, pp. 478, 467–8, 478–9)

One can say that in marriage the spouses exchange *tamkīn* and *nafaqa*, that is, the wife's availability for sex and the husband's provision of maintenance. The contemporary Shi'a jurist Naser Makarem Shirazi (born 1924) has done further study of the subject, and confirmed that *nafaqa* is for marital life (*zawjiyya*), *tamkīn*, pregnancy and breastfeeding, and that there is a consensus among Muslim jurists that the husband's responsibility for *nafaqa* is one of the essentials of Islam (2011, vol. 3, pp. 428–9). After exploring all the verses of the Qur'an related to the subject, he stated that: 'We did not find any verse in the Qur'an that proves the requirement of *nafaqa* except in two periods: pregnancy and breastfeeding.'[12] This goes against the general consensus that *nafaqa* is a requirement throughout marital life. At the same time, according to Makarem Shirazi's study, the hadiths indicating that a husband must provide *nafaqa* for his wife are clear and undeniable (2011, vol. 3, p. 435). The consensus is that the necessary conditions for *nafaqa* are the permanence of the marriage and the wife's *tamkīn* (al-Najafi, 2012, vol. 32, pp. 524–5). Makarem Shirazi accepted the consensus on the former, but on the latter (*tamkīn*), after exploring all the evidence, he concluded that 'although some of this evidence is challengeable, it is possible to rely on the others' (2011, vol. 3, p. 440). It is clear that the argument regarding *tamkīn* is not strong.

---

[12] The verse supporting a *nafaqa* obligation during pregnancy and breastfeeding is 65:6: 'House the wives you are divorcing according to your means, wherever you house yourselves, and do not harass them so as to make their lives difficult. If they are pregnant, maintain them until they are delivered of their burdens; if they suckle your infants, pay them for it. Consult together in a good way – if you make difficulties for one another, another woman may suckle the child for the father.'

According to structural *ijtihād*, both spouses could be responsible for the expenses of marital life, not only the husband. Whether working inside or outside the home, both spouses may contribute to the costs and expenses of their marital life with their income and personal property. When both spouses share the expenses, it is not acceptable to require that the husband be the maintainer, and the wife be secondary and dependent. Each of the spouses may carry out care and housework; if the wife does this without wages, she is eligible for maintenance. The husband's duty to pay maintenance is restricted to the time of pregnancy and the first two years after childbirth, which is the requirement of substantive justice. There is no head of the family.

The position established by structural *ijtihād* requires reasonability, justice and egalitarian ethics. This position is much stronger than the argument of traditional *fiqh* that *nafaqa* is the exclusive duty of the husband. I have not yet found any reliable evidence to support this exclusive claim. The Qur'an explicitly supports only the requirement for the husband to pay the wife's *nafaqa* at the time of her pregnancy and breastfeeding. Second, the hadiths regarding *nafaqa* as the exclusive duty of the husband are reflections of specific situations and cannot be generalized. Third, egalitarian justice demands that spouses share their care and economic responsibilities in marriage in general in ways that work for the well-being of the family.

2.3 Equal rights to divorce

According to traditional *fiqh*, the dissolution of marriage takes three forms: *ṭalāq*, that is by the request of the husband; *khulʿ*, that is by the request of the wife; and *mubārat*, where both sides request separation. *Ṭalāq* is the husband's right and is defined as a unilateral act (*īqāʾ*). It requires neither the consent of the wife nor that she be informed. Although *khulʿ* takes place on the initiative of the wife (who must pay compensation, which is usually part or all of the dower), the husband's consent to divorce is required. His consent is also necessary for *mubārat*. In other words, in traditional *fiqh* no form of dissolution of marriage (*ṭalāq*, *khulʿ* or *mubārat*) can happen without the husband's consent; he is the only one who can end a marriage (Esfahani, 2013, pp. 523–9).

As is evident, women do not have an equal right to divorce: first, men have the absolute right to divorce under *talaq*, and can divorce their wives whenever they want, and for any reason. Women do not have any legal right to reject the divorce; it is a unilateral act (*īqāʾ*). Second, divorce initiated by women is possible, but depends on two conditions: payment of compensation to the husband, and his consent. This means that if the husband does not want to divorce his wife, the wife cannot separate except through the court and a long and complex procedure of proving the impossibility of reconciliation. This is the majority (*mashhūr*) position of the Shiʿi jurists (al-Najafi, 2012, vol. 34, pp. 5–164). As in the Shiʿa school, I did not find any Sunni jurist who supported *khul*ʿ without the agreement of the husband (Ibn Qudāmā, 1997, vol. 10, pp. 267–323; al-Zuhaili, 1985, vol. 7, pp. 480–508). In other words, the right ultimately rests with the man as well.

In his 2001 book on divorce, Yousef Sanei (1937–2020) followed the consensus of the distinguished Shiʿi jurists of the past,[13] but in 2007 he expressed a new idea with regard to *khul*ʿ: 'There is no choice for the husband except to accept his wife's request for divorce' (Sanei, 2007a). So, if his wife requests a divorce and is willing to pay the compensation, it is required (*wājib*) for the husband to implement the divorce. If the husband refuses, the court will implement it (Sanei, 2007b). This would be a big step forward.

According to structural *ijtihād*, divorce, like marriage, should be a consensual process. The termination of a marriage contract *always* needs the consent of both parties. The wife has the same right as the husband to divorce, as in marriage. Any discrimination in divorce cannot be justified or accepted. After one or both of the spouses officially requests a divorce, the court begins the process, decides on the financial settlement, and will eventually issue the official divorce certificate to terminate their marital life. At the time of divorce, the husband should provide compensation to the wife (for housework and care of the children), if he did not pay it before.

More clearly, neither spouse – especially the husband – has the right to terminate the marriage without the consent of the other. Second, the wife is not required to pay compensation to the husband in exchange for divorce. She has the same rights to divorce as her husband. Third, the final divorce formula (*inshaʾ sighat al-ṭalāq*) is implemented by a judge in court, after hearing from both sides and concluding that reconciliation is impossible, and that the divorce was not pronounced by the husband.

The argument of structural *ijtihād* for egalitarian divorce is the requirement of 'justice' that is supported by ethical values and rational proofs (*al-dalīl*

[13] For example, Abu al-Salāh al-Halabi, Taqi b. Najm al-Din (d. 1055) in *al-Kāfī*; Shaykh al-Tāʾifa al-Tūsi, Muhammad b. al-Hassan (995–1067) in *al-Nahaya fi Mujarrad al-Fiqh wa-l-Fatawa*; Sayyid Ibn Zuhra, Hamza b. Ali al-Halabi (1117–1189) in *Ghunya al-Nuzūʿ*; and Ibn Hamza al-Tūsi, Muhammad b. Ali (thirteenth century) in *al-Wasila*.

al-ʿaqli). The relevant Qurʾanic verses are not *naṣ* (clear or certain, without any other probable indication), so their apparent meanings could be interpreted as supporting egalitarian divorce. The authentic hadiths that do not support egalitarian divorce have lost their credibility because of their deep conflict with the criterion of contemporary notions of justice; in other words, they led to the rulings of past ages. The requirement of justice is much stronger than all textual evidence.

2.4 Polygyny

The primary form of marriage in Islam is monogamy. The Prophet's marriage with Khadīja, his beloved wife, was monogamous. Almost all Muslims in almost all countries today are monogamous, even in the few Muslim-majority countries where polygyny is legal. There is no doubt that a form of restricted polygyny *was* accepted in Islam. Was this restricted polygyny essential to Islam or was it one of the temporal rulings of Islam belonging to a specific situation? Here, I explore two positions in contemporary Islamic thought on this subject, one Sunni and the other Shiʿi. Both reflect traditional *ijtihād* and a traditional perspective: It is a man's right to have up to four wives simultaneously. The only condition for polygyny (that is not exclusive to female orphans) is justice, interpreted in this way: the husband must deal with his wives equally in their beds and in maintenance.

Yūsuf al-Qaraḍāwī (born 1926), a Sunni jurist, argues that polygyny is allowed clearly in the Qurʾan and the Sunna of the Prophet, and condemns its unconditional and permanent prohibition. According to him, the correct meaning of Qurʾanic verse 4:129 ('You will never be able to treat your wives with equal fairness, however much you may desire to do so …') is not the prohibition of polygyny. He argues that the verse indicates that human nature makes absolute justice in a husband's treatment of multiple wives impossible in matters of the heart and sexual desire. Therefore, the husband must try as much as he can to treat his wives with equal justice, and allowance is made for men's emotions and passions (al-Qaraḍāwī, 2017, pp. 269–72).

The 1967 Iranian 'Family Protection Law' (amended in 1973) allowed polygynous marriages with the first wife's official permission and a court judgement. This law was not only left intact after the revolution of 1979, but it was included as a stipulation (*sharṭ ḍimn al-ʿaqd*) in 'official marriage contracts'. In addition, this law enables the wife to become a representative of her husband in order to divorce herself on his behalf in specific situations, including polygyny.[14] This could not be inserted without the approval of Ayatollah Khomeini (1902–89), leader of the Islamic Republic of Iran. Yet neither he nor any other Shiʿi jurist (to my knowledge) published this important restriction on polygyny in their books of fatwa or their *al-fiqh al-istidlāli* books, where the textual proofs and rational arguments for rulings are elucidated. Therefore, we can say that Shiʿa jurists tolerate this ruling, even though they are reluctant to acknowledge it in their own work.

According to structural *ijtihād*, the primary form of marriage in Islam is between one woman and one man. Polygyny is a secondary form, for times of necessity (*ḍarūra*), provided that its practice does not entail injustice and harm to any of the parties involved. In other words, it is an exception for specific situations, with the strict permission of the court. After the court's permission, the necessary condition for polygyny is the first wife's official permission, without which a marriage with another wife is not only null, but also a crime.

CONCLUSION

Rulings on marriage and its consequences and correlations constitute a large portion of any *fiqh* book. Today, most of these rulings cannot be regarded as just, reasonable or moral, and are less functional than other laws. We must ask ourselves: Are these rulings Islamic? I argue that they *were* Islamic because they *were* reasonable, just, moral and more functional than other existing laws at one time; they were in line with the values and standards of the people at the time of revelation, and that is why people accepted them. But they can no longer be accepted today. And while well-intentioned, the patchwork twentieth-century efforts to reform these rulings, led by semi-reformists, do not go far enough to address today's needs and contexts.

Traditional jurisprudence does not fit the mentality of modern times. Traditional *ijtihād*, whether applied by traditionalist or semi-reformist jurists and scholars, embodies a patriarchal perspective on women in the family and society. It is based on deserts-based notions of justice (*al-ʿadāla al-istihqāqiyya*) and scriptural justification.

We need a new paradigm. This is what structural *ijtihād* aims to achieve. Its approach to marriage is based on egalitarian notions of justice (*al-ʿadāla*

[14] For more information, see Mir-Hosseini (2012).

al-musawatiyya), an approach that reflects the mentality of our times. It sets out the common ground of all arguments (*al-adilla*) for rulings on marriage: the requirements of reasonability, justice, ethics and better functionality according to the mentality of this time.

Shariʿa is the Islamic way of life, and encompasses the permanent standards, principles, ethical values and rites of Islam. We should not return to the past. We should bring our tradition to the mentality of today, preserving our principles and standards and rereading the rulings on Islamic marriage in this context.

REFERENCES

Al-Albani, Mukammad Nasir al-Din. 1993. *Silsilat al-Ahādith al-Sahīha*. Riyad: Maktaba al-Maʿarif lil-Nashr wa al-Tawziʿ.

Denny, Frederick Mathewson. 2005. 'Muslim Ethical Trajectories in the Contemporary Period'. In *The Blackwell Companion to Religious Ethics*, edited by William Schweiker, pp. 268–77. Malden, MA: Blackwell.

Esfahani, Abolhassan. 2013. *Wasila al-Naja*, with commentaries of Ruhollah Mousawi Khomeini. Tehran: Muʾassesa-ye Tanzim wa Nashr-e Āthār-e Emam Khomeini.

Grannan, Cydney. n.d. 'What's the Difference Between Morality and Ethics?' *Encyclopedia Britannica*. Online version.

Ibn Qudāmā, Abdullah ibn Ahmad. 1997. *Al-Mughnī*, edited by Abdullah b. Abdul-Muhsin al-Turkī and Abdul-Fattah Muhammad al-Hulw. Riyadh: Dār ʿĀlam al-Kutub.

Kadivar, Mohsen. 2009. 'Human Rights and Intellectual Islam'. In *New Directions in Islamic Thought: Exploring Reform and Muslim Tradition*, edited by Kari Vogt, Lena Larsen and Christian Moe, pp. 47–73. London: I.B. Tauris.

Kadivar, Mohsen. 2011. 'From Traditional Islam to Islam as an End in Itself'. *Die Welt des Islams* 51 (3): pp. 459–84.

Kadivar, Mohsen. 2013. 'Revisiting Women's Rights in Islam: "Egalitarian Justice" in Lieu of "Deserts-Based Justice"'. In *Gender and Equality in Muslim Family Law: Justice and Ethics in the Islamic Legal Tradition*, edited by Ziba Mir-Hosseini, Lena Larsen, Christian Moe, and Kari Vogt, pp. 213–34. London: I.B. Tauris.

Kadivar, Mohsen. 2015. '*Ijtihad* in *Usul al-Fiqh*: Reforming Islamic Thought through Structural *Ijtihad*'. *Iran Nameh* 30 (3): pp. xx–xxvii.

Kadivar, Mohsen. 2017. '*Intizar az Din va Nou-andishi-ye Dini*' ('Expectation of Religion and Reformist Thinking'), Part 1. https://kadivar.com/16093

Kadivar, Mohsen. 2021. *Human Rights and Reformist Islam*, translated by Niki Akhavan as part of the series *In Translation: Modern Muslim Thinkers*. Edinburgh: Edinburgh University Press in association with Aga Khan University Institute for the Study of Muslim Civilisations.

Makarem Shirazi, Naser. 2011. *Anwār al-Fiqaha fi Ahkām al-ʿItra al-Tāhira, Kitāb al-Nikāh*. Qom: Dār al-Nashr al-Imām Ali ibn Abi Tālib.

Mir-Hosseini, Ziba. 2012. 'The Politics of Divorce Laws in Iran: Ideology versus Practice'. In *Interpreting Divorce Laws in Islam*, edited by Rubya Mehdi, Werner Menski and Jørgen Nielsen, pp. 65–83. Copenhagen: DJØF Publishing.

Moosa, Ebrahim. 2005. 'Muslim Ethics?' In *The Blackwell Companion to Religious Ethics*, edited by William Schweiker, pp. 237–43. New Jersey: Blackwell.

Moosa, Ebrahim. 2018. 'Recovering the Ethical: Practices, Politics, Tradition'. In *The Shari'a: History, Ethics and Law*, edited by Amyn B. Sajoo, pp. 39–58. London: I.B. Tauris.

Al-Najafi, Mohammad Hasan. 2012. *Jawāhir al-Kalām fī Sharḥ Sharā'i' al-'Islām*, edited by Haydar al-Dabbagh. Qom: Mu'assisa al-Nashr al-Eslāmi.

Al-Qaraḍāwī, Yūsuf. 2017. *Fiqh al-Usra wa Qadāya al-Mar'a*. Turkey: al-Dar al-Shāmiyya.

Reinhart, A. Kevin. 2005. 'Origins of Islamic Ethics: Foundations and Constructions'. In *The Blackwell Companion to Religious Ethics*, edited by William Schweiker, pp. 244–53. Malden, MA: Blackwell.

Sachedina, Abdulaziz. 2005. 'Islamic Ethics: Differentiations'. In *The Blackwell Companion to Religious Ethics*, edited by William Schweiker, pp. 254–67. New Jersey: Blackwell.

Sajoo, Amyn B. (ed.). 2018. *The Shari'a: History, Ethics and Law*. London: I.B. Tauris.

Sanei, Yousef. 2006. *Bolugh-e Dokhtarān, Feqh wa Zendegi ('Fiqh and Life') series, no. 7*. Qom: Meutham Tammār.

Sanei, Yousef. 2007a. *Fiqh al-Thaqalain (al-Talāq)*. Transcribed by Diyā' al-Murtadawi. Tehran: Mu'assesa-ye Tanzim wa Nashr-e Āthār-e Emam Khomeini.

Sanei, Yousef. 2007b. *Wujūb-e Talaq-e Khul' bar Mard* (The Requirement of *Khul'* Divorce for the Husband), *Feqh wa Zendegi* ('Fiqh and Life') series, no. 8. Qom: Maytham Tammār.

Sanei, Yousef. n.d. *Majma' al-Masāil: Istiftāt*. Qom: Webbook.

Al-Sarakhsi, Muhammad b. Ahmad b. Abi Sahl. 1989. *Al-Mabsūt*. Beirut: Dār al-Ma'rifa.

Schweiker, William (ed.). 2005. *The Blackwell Companion to Religious Ethics*. New Jersey: Blackwell.

Soroush, Abdolkarim. 2008. *The Expansion of Prophetic Experience: Essays on Historicity, Contingency and Plurality in Religion*, translated by Nilou Mobassar, edited with an introduction by Forough Jahanbakhsh. Linden: Brill.

Yazdi, Mohammad Kazem Tabataba'i. 1999. *Al-'Urwa al-Wuthqā*, with commentaries of permanent jurists. Qom: Mu'assisa al-Nash al-Eslami.

Al-Zuhaili, Wahba. 1985. *Al-Fiqh al-Islāmi wa Adilitahu*. Damascus: Dār al-Fikr.

Reform of *Uṣūl al-Fiqh* and Marriage: A Spiritually Integrative Approach

Nevin Reda

> O you who believe, stand up for *qisṭ*[1] (social justice), as witnesses to God, even if it is against yourselves, your parents, and closest ones. Whether rich or poor, God can best take care of both. Do not follow your personal desires, so you can act with *ʿadl* (justice). If you distort things or turn away, God is experienced in what you do.
>
> Qurʾan 4:135[2]

When Muḥammad ibn Idrīs al-Shāfiʿī (d. 204 AH/820 CE) travelled from Iraq to Egypt, he introduced a new theory of *fiqh* (ethical-legal reasoning, jurisprudence) that increased the importance of the sacred texts in contradistinction to the living practice of the community, thus changing his jurisprudence to suit the new environment (El Shamsy, 2013, pp. 91–117). A student of Mālik ibn Anas (d. 179 AH/795 CE), he had no qualms respectfully critiquing the work of the great master and developing his own ethical-legal theory (*uṣūl al-fiqh*),[3] even at the basic foundational

[1] *Qisṭ* can also be translated as 'equity' and *ʿadl* as 'equality'. For more, see below.

[2] All translations from the Arabic are mine, unless otherwise stated.

[3] Wael Hallaq (2009, pp. 1–6) has pointed to the function of *fiqh* as both law and ethics in pre-modern Muslim societies; I translate *uṣūl al-fiqh* as ethical-legal theory to highlight both these dimensions.

level. His life story suggests a dynamic thinker who was not afraid to come up with new ideas and who was humble enough to change them when they no longer suited the context. He is not alone in the Islamic tradition; in fact, he and several others were so innovative and impactful that they triggered the development of whole schools of Islamic jurisprudence and have become their eponyms – the Ibāḍī, Zaydī, Jaʿfarī, Ḥanafī, Mālikī, Shāfiʿī, Ḥanbalī and Ẓāhirī schools – thereby contributing to the pluralistic and dialogic character of Islamic ethical-legal thinking.[4]

This chapter attempts to recapture some of the dynamism of these early thinkers, respectfully critiquing the methodologies of *uṣūl al-fiqh*, introducing a new theory that better fits the needs of our time, and applying it to the case of marriage and divorce. It consists of three parts, each devoted to one of these aims. Rather than locate itself in one school, it is in conversation with the tradition in its entirety, drawing on all of them, as it adds yet another methodology to a tradition that is rich in diversity. However, what makes this methodology different is its Islamic feminist, spiritually integrative lens and its concern for justice (*ʿadl* and *qisṭ*), since classical methodologies lack a distinct mechanism (for example, a principle/*aṣl*) that would suggest a concern for justice, including basic gender justice. This curious lack allows masculinist caprice to go unchecked in both the substantive and procedural aspects of Islamic ethical-legal deliberations and needs to be addressed at the methodological level. In the tradition of amina wadud (1992, pp. 1–10), this new theory is based on the assumption that men and women think differently, have different vantage points, and that women's perspectives are sorely needed to address gender-based and other injustices and to provide balance. Due to limitations of space, this chapter focuses on providing a basic framework for marriage and divorce and does not discuss many of the finer details, including child custody, inheritance, *kadd wa-saʿāya* (matrimonial wealth),[5] the calculation of alimony, adultery and same-sex relations among other things.

[4] The remaining six eponyms are ʿAbd Allāh ibn Ibāḍ (d. 86 AH/704 CE), Zayd in ʿAlī (122 AH/740 CE), Jaʿfar al-Sādiq (d. 148 AH/765 CE), Abū Ḥanīfa al-Nuʿmān (d. 150 AH/767 CE), Aḥmad ibn Ḥanbal (d. 241 AH/855 CE) and Dawūd al-Ẓāhirī (d. 270 AH/884 CE).

[5] This expression literally means 'toil and industry' and refers to a wife's share in the earnings of her husband, over and above what she needs to maintain her lifestyle. It is based on the case of Ḥabība bint Ruzayq, whose husband died, and for whom ʿUmar ibn al-Khaṭṭāb ruled that she receive half the matrimonial wealth, prior to distributing inheritance shares. This right is similar to contemporary divorce settlements in some countries; however, it could also be developed to apply in the husband's lifetime, while remaining married to the husband (see Kaʿwāsh, 2009).

1. METHODOLOGICAL CRITIQUE OF *UṢŪL AL-FIQH*

1.1 Contextual problems in *uṣūl al-fiqh*

Problems in *uṣūl al-fiqh* are of two kinds: contextual and source-related. Contextual problems have to do with the existing schools' failure to change their methodologies in ways that take into account the emergence of the modern state. Legal norms and structures in pre-modern times were very different from what they are today in most Muslim-majority countries, which have constitutions, courts of appeal, parliaments, a police force and other instruments for the production and implementation of law that were not present in pre-modern contexts. This failure to develop jurisprudence at the methodological and conceptual level has resulted in a complex and murky situation, where women are the ones who most often fall through the cracks.

For example, Article 2 of the Egyptian constitution affirms 'the values of Shariʿa as the main source of legislation', which allows pre-modern constructions of marriage and divorce a foothold in the legal system and their use as an instrument to harm women (Constitution of the Arab Republic of Egypt, 2014). This foothold can be noted in the phenomenon of unregistered, 'Shariʿa-compliant', *ʿurfi* (customary) marriages, which are not legally recognized when it comes to women's rights to sue for financial support and alimony. Prior to the reforms to Personal Status Law in the 2000s, women in such marriages could also not sue for divorce. Paradoxically, such marriages are suddenly 'recognized' in courts when it comes to punishing women for the crime of combining two 'husbands' (*al-jamʿ bayn zawjayn*), if they should fail to obtain a divorce from their unofficial 'husband' prior to officially marrying someone else.[6] On the one hand, such women could not sue for divorce and alimony and, on the other, if they tried to (re)marry, they could receive a punishment of up to two years in jail. They are thus effectively in limbo.

As one can see in this example, Shariʿa (more accurately: *fiqh*)[7] now functions as an ill-defined, parallel system of 'law' that confuses the definitions of marriage and divorce to the detriment of women. Two parallel, conflicting

---

[6] Prior to the reforms of Personal Status Law that occurred in the 2000s, women in unregistered or *ʿurfi* marriages could also not sue for divorce (Al-Sharmani, 2014, p. 33).

[7] Musawah and many Islamic feminists distinguish between Shariʿa and *fiqh*, defining *fiqh* as the human, fallible interpretation of Shariʿa.

definitions for marriage and divorce now exist: those of the state that require registration, and the medieval constructs that only require two witnesses. This leaves plenty of room for unregistered, legally invisible quasi marriages and divorces to thrive.[8] Despite the fact that such 'marriages' (and divorces) deny women their ability to sue for their God-given Qur'an-mandated rights in court, contemporary jurists pronounce them lawful. Unilateral divorce, polygyny and other expressions of inequality ensure that men are not disadvantaged in these parallel systems; they can just remarry and leave the first wife hanging indefinitely. Pre-modern constructions of marriage assumed that the presence of two witnesses is sufficient for a woman to be able to prove her marriage in court and thus sue for her rights; however, such witnesses could die, change their mind, or falsify their testimony.

Today, the norms have become more rigorous and require registration, but *fiqh* has remained rigid. Pre-modern constructions have been sacramentalized, and many contemporary jurists are either unwilling or unable to find solutions to the contextual problems within the parameters of their respective methodologies, allowing for the perpetuation of systemic and structural oppressions and for harm to befall women rather than change their definitions of marriage and divorce to include registration. These methodologies have embedded mechanisms within them that contribute to this rigidity and that have impeded the schools' ability to keep up with changing times. This phenomenon hints at the deep-rootedness of the problems in *uṣūl al-fiqh*. Accordingly, a new methodology of *uṣūl al-fiqh* is needed; it must rethink the underlying assumptions and principles of *fiqh* in ways that fill up these cracks and successfully transition between pre-modern and contemporary systems of law and governance.

1.2 Source-related problems in *uṣūl al-fiqh*

The second kind of problems in *uṣūl al-fiqh* are source-related, that is, they have to do with the foundational principles or sources for deriving laws. One should note that the word *aṣl* (singular of *uṣūl*) means 'principle', 'source', 'foundation' or even 'root' in the Arabic language. Four such main principles exist in classical constructions of *uṣūl al-fiqh*: Qur'an, Sunna, consensus (*ijmāʿ*) and reason, usually in the form of reasoning by analogy (*qiyās*). A number of minor

[8] For the abuse of North American women's rights, see al-ʿAlwānī (2012, pp. 221–3).

principles vary from school to school, including juristic preference (*istiḥsān*), consideration of common good (*istiṣlāḥ*), custom (*ʿurf*), blocking the means of harm (*sadd al-dharrāʾiʿ*) and presumption of continuity (*istiṣḥāb*). The following critique focuses on the four main principles.

1.2.1 *The Qurʾan*

There are two major problems with how early jurists used the Qurʾan as a source in the derivation of law: the first has to do with the marginalization of most Qurʾanic verses in the process of law-making and the second is concerned with how the verses were interpreted.

Most scholars assume that only about 350 verses have legal signification (*āyāt al-aḥkām*), which is about 5 per cent of the Qurʾan, while the remaining 95 per cent do not, thus discounting their implications in ethical-legal deliberations (Kamali, 2008, p. 19). Narratives, for example, are generally not considered to have legal signification. One such narrative is the story of Adam and Eve, which portrays marriage as a monogamous union of two: one man and one woman (as opposed to a polygynous union). Accordingly, scholars do not view monogamy as the ontological norm, but rather polygyny.

Moreover, the approximately 5 per cent of verses that make it into the corpus of *āyāt al-ahkām* (legal verses) are interpreted in ways that do not always account for changing contexts and how meanings are constructed over time. The diachronic aspect of the interpretive process can be noted in the historical development of the constructs *qiwāma* (male authority) and *wilāya* (male guardianship), which were the subject of an earlier Musawah project (see Abou-Bakr, 2015; see also Afsaruddin, 2020). In the domain of law-making, interpretation most often follows the *tafsīr bi-l-maʾthūr* (exegesis by transmission) method, which approaches Qurʾan interpretation in small bits, usually on a verse-by-verse basis, and limits the interpretation of these verses only to what certain early individuals came up with, as transmitted by later narrators.[9] This method of interpretation was generally hostile to language-based exegesis, claiming that only first and early second-generation exegetes had the authority to interpret the verses (*ahl al-taʾwīl*). As a result, much of *tafsīr* (exegesis) is characterized by atomism and sometimes even linguistic inaccuracy. Examples include the polygyny verse (verse 4:3), in which the word *yatāmā* is interpreted as fatherless, underage girls, although the word occurs

[9] For more, see Reda (2020).

only in the masculine plural in the same passage (and everywhere else in the Qurʾan) and even though the word is explained to include adult (widowed) women as well as children (verse 4:127).[10] This change in meaning functions as the first step to removing the primary condition for polygyny in the Qurʾan – social justice (*qisṭ*) to the families of deceased men that outweighs the inherent inequality of polygynous unions, whether between husband and wife or between co-wives (Reda, 2020). Another example is the word *nushūz* in verse 4:34, which was interpreted figuratively as 'arrogance' instead of literally as 'getting up and walking away' (see below), thereby allowing men to beat their wives while, at the same time, denying a woman the right to walk away from a marriage (see Reda, 2019a).

1.2.2 *The Sunna*

Hadiths (reports traced back to the Prophet Muhammad, pbuh) and *āthār* (reports traced back to one of the Companions of the Prophet or their immediate successors) form most of the primary textual basis for injustices against women. From a methodological perspective, the use of Hadith as a principle in the derivation of law is also problematic in two ways: the weight given to hadiths and their interpretations.

The relationship between hadiths and the Qurʾan has had its ambiguities in the history of Islamic thought, with early scholars disputing which of the two sources had the authority to overrule the other (Reda, 2013). Rationalists (*ahl al-raʾy*),[11] led by Abū Ḥanīfa (d. 150 AH/767 CE), maintained that the Qurʾan is more authoritative and that contradicting hadiths should be rejected, while Traditionalists (*ahl al-ḥadīth*) claimed that the Sunna is a judge over the Qurʾan and abrogates it (*al-sunna qāḍiya ʿalā al-Qurʾān wa-nāsikha lah*) (see al-Dārimī, 1978, nos. 586–90; al-Qaraḍāwī, 1991, p. 9).

After al-Shāfiʿī, the dispute settled in favour of a revised *ahl al-ḥadīth* position, asserting that hadiths explain an (otherwise) ambiguous Qurʾan, although one should note the continuation of hadiths' ability to abrogate the Qurʾan in Sunni thought (but not the Qurʾan's ability to abrogate hadiths).

---

[10] The application of *yatāmā* to widows is also attested in ancient Arabic poetry: *inna al-qubūr tankaḥ al-ayāmā: al-niswa al-arāmil al-yatāmā* (the graves have marital relations with the single ones: the widowed *yatāmā* women) (Ṭayfūr, 1908, p. 103). For more, see Reda (2020).

[11] 'Rationalists' can also be used to refer to the Muʿtazila, which is an important theological school in the history of Islam. Here, I use 'rationalist' to refer to the Ḥanafī and other legal schools, which are also known for their use of reason.

Jaʿfarī legal theory is a little clearer on this subject, since it has historically privileged the juridical authority of the Qurʾan over hadiths (*ḥākimiyyat al-Qurʾān*),[12] while Ibāḍīs have outright rejected the notion of hadiths abrogating the Qurʾan, although in practice this doesn't work as well (for example, *kafāʾa* below). As a result of this murky relationship, most scholars consider hadiths to be an independent source of law-making and tend to favour hadiths over and above the Qurʾan, although this phenomenon is clearer among Traditionalist schools (Shāfiʿī, Ḥanbalī, Mālikī) than Rationalist ones (Ḥanafī, Jaʿfarī, Zaydī). Examples are numerous; I highlight two below: the hadiths that support male guardianship of women and the worthiness/suitability (*kafāʾa*) hadiths.

Guardianship hadiths include Abū Hurayra's 'A woman cannot marry off another woman, nor a woman herself; only a prostitute marries herself off by herself [meaning, without a male guardian]'.[13] This hadith and others have been used to deny women the right to represent themselves in a marriage contract without a male guardian, which is to turn them into perpetual minors, at least in the Shāfiʿī, Mālikī and Ḥanbalī schools (but not in the Ḥanafī, Zaydī and Jaʿfarī schools). However, all four Sunni schools give the guardian the right to revoke a woman's marriage, if the guardian deems the bridegroom unworthy, thus actively preventing her from her marriage (*iʿḍāl*) (see also Noor and Lee, 2014). In classical *fiqh*, a guardian could even force a minor girl into an unwanted marriage (*walī mujbir*). Although underage marriage has now been abolished in most Muslim-majority countries, it is still practised as a lived reality in some parts of the Muslim world. As Ibn Rushd notes in *Bidāyat al-Mujtahid* (*The Distinguished Jurist's Primer*), this and similar hadiths contradict the text of verses in *Surat al-Baqara* (verses 2:230, 232),[14] as well as other hadiths (Ibn Rushd, 2004, vol. 3, pp. 36–43). In the Jaʿfarī school, Muḥammad al-Gharawī and Yāsir Māziḥ have pointed

[12] See also Zaynab al-ʿAlwānī's (2012) *ḥākimiyyat al-nuṣūṣ* (juridical authority of the texts).

[13] See al-Jazīrī, al-Gharawī and Māziḥ (1998, vol. 4, p. 75). One should note that al-Jazīrī left off the last clause of this hadith.

[14] Verse 2:230: 'Then, if he divorces her, she is no longer lawful for him until she marries another husband. Then, if he divorces her, there is no blame on either of them if they decide to get back together, provided that they can keep the limits set by God. And these are the limits set by God, which He makes clear for people who know.'

Verse 2:232: 'When you divorce women, and they reach the end of their waiting period, do not prevent them from marrying their husbands, if they have come to an agreement among themselves in a fair manner. This is the advice given to those among you who believe in God and the Last Day. This is more virtuous for you and purer and God knows and you do not.'

to verses 4:3 and 5:1[15] and hadiths to support a woman's entitlement to marry herself off without a *walī* (Ibn Rushd, 2004, vol. 4, p. 71). The notion that a woman who is of age and in full command of her faculties needs a male guardian in order to contract a legal marriage and cannot marry against his wishes embeds inequality and injustice into the marriage. Such a ruling has its basis in the problematic use of hadiths and their conceptualization as an independent principle in the derivation of law.

As Zanariah Noor and Nazirah Lee (2014) have shown, the hadiths requiring that a bridegroom be considered 'worthy' (*kufʾ*) of the bride are considered weak. Nevertheless, different *madhāhib* (schools of *fiqh*; singular: *madhhab*) have different requirements for *kafāʾa*, including lineage, religion, profession, freedom, religiosity and wealth (but not chastity) (al-Jazīrī, al-Gharawī and Māziḥ, 1998, vol. 4, pp. 84–90). Noor and Lee (2014) have provided an example of the 'lineage' category in Malaysia: when a woman who is deemed *sharīfa* (noble, descendant of the Prophet)[16] marries someone who is not, her male 'guardian' has the legal right to revoke her marriage. A male *sharīf*, however, has the right to marry a non-*sharīfa* without hindrance from his family. The Ibāḍī *madhhab* also insists on social *kafāʾa*, citing consensus (Noor and Lee, 2014).

The second problematic element is that interpretation of hadiths is notoriously difficult, since they are short, cryptic reports and do not generally give information on the surrounding circumstances, making them liable to numerous interpretations. Unlike the Qurʾan, of which different parts can be used to explain other parts and which is *mubīn* (clear, clarifies things) (verses 5:15; 12:1), one generally cannot use a hadith to interpret another hadith. It is not unusual to find contradictory hadiths (even reported by the same Companion).[17]

---

[15] Verse 4:3: 'If you fear that you will not do social justice to widows and orphans, then marry whoever is favourably disposed toward you from among the women: two, three or four at the same time; however, if you fear that you will not uphold equality, marry one woman or what your right hands possess. This will bring you closer to not committing grave injustice.' Verse 5:1: 'O you who believe, fulfil your contracts. Livestock animals have been made lawful for you, except for what is recited to you. You are forbidden to kill game while you are on pilgrimage – God rules however He wants.'

[16] *Sharīf*/*sharīfa* is a common term for descendants of the Prophet in the Arab world; in South Asia and Southeast Asia, the term *sayyid* (lord) is more common.

[17] For example, Abū Hurayra is known to have reported, 'There is no such thing as infection', and then later to have reported, 'Do not mingle the sick with the healthy', attributing both to the Prophet. When confronted with his earlier statement and pressed for an explanation, Abū Hurayra got angry and mumbled in Ethiopic. It seems even well known Traditionists, such as Abū Hurayra, forgot what they themselves had said, much less the Prophet, or got confused,

For example, how does one interpret the very problematic hadith, 'I have not left a *fitna* (trial) more harmful to men than women' (Ibn Ḥajar al-ʿAsqalānī, n.d., no. 4805)? What does the word *fitna* entail? Is it that women are sexual temptresses and therefore men must control their women's sexuality and keep them under lock and key, or is it that women are liable to be bullied or pushed into the background by men, and thus the community needs to guard women's rights extra carefully and ensure equality in its laws? These are two very different interpretations with very different repercussions for women. If one examines the Qurʾan, it mentions *fitna* and its derivatives sixty times: in connection with the two angels Hārūt and Mārūt (verse 2:102), targets of oppression (verse 10:85), visions (verse 17:60), God (verses 29:2–3), general testing of faith (verse 29:2), a she-camel (verse 54:27), wealth (verse 64:15), children (verse 64:15), number of angels (verse 74:31) and persons persecuting Muslims (verse 85:10), among other meanings, but never sexualized or in connection with women. Given the fact that the word *fitna* has numerous occurrences in the Qurʾan, none of which are in a sexual sense, the first interpretation is very problematic, despite its popularity among jurists. One has to wonder at their choice of interpretation, when the second meaning – targets of bullying and oppression – does occur and is well attested in the Qurʾan. Time-wise, the Qurʾan is closer to the Prophet Muhammad and is therefore a better reflection of his intended meaning than any extraneous notions that jurists should choose to impose upon the text; however, the Qurʾan does not seem to have been part of their interpretive methodology. Moreover, what should one do with contradictory hadiths, such as 'For every people there is a trial (*fitna*), and the trial of my people is money'; 'The only thing I fear for my people is misleading Imams (*al-aʾimma al-muḍillīn*)'; and 'What I fear most for my people is the deed of the people of Lot'?

Now which one did the Prophet fear most: women, money, misleading Imams, or the deed of the people of Lot? As one can see from this example, more effort needs to be put into interpretive methodologies and into re-historicizing hadiths. The chapters by Yasmin Amin, Faqihuddin Abdul Kodir and Shadaab Rahemtulla and Sara Ababneh in this volume are excellent steps in this direction.

1.2.3 *Consensus*

In the contemporary context, consensus serves to 'sacramentalize' medieval jurists' constructions, including those of marriage and divorce, under the

---

which creates dilemmas for Hadith scholars when attempting to harmonize between these conflicting reports. See, for example, al-Nawawī, n.d., hadith no. 2221.

pretext that it elevates a ruling or idea out of the realm of the uncertain (*ẓannī*) and into the realm of the certain (*qaṭʿī*) (see Hallaq, 1986a, p. 427).[18] In other words, it is used as a tool to solidify medieval injustices in *fiqh* and works against reform and/or development of the Islamic ethical-legal tradition. This is particularly apparent in the legal realm, where it serves to lend 'divine' justification to unjust laws and rulings. Without claims of consensus, such ideas would lose much of their authority, as well as the rationale for their legitimization and implementation. The importance of claims of consensus can be noted in the Ḥanbalī jurist Ibn Qudāmā's compendium *al-Mughnī*, in which he employs the principle to argue for the permissibility of forced child marriages of prepubescent girls and the continuation of such forced marriages in the present-day context (see Baugh, 2017, pp. 7–10, 230–7).[19] An example for consensus overruling the Qurʾan is the case of the primary condition for polygyny (above), which Abū Bakr ibn al-ʿArabī (n.d., vol. 1, p. 310) has declared 'dropped' (*sāqiṭ bil-ijmāʿ*) and al-Qurṭubī (2006, vol. 6, p. 26) considers to be 'unintelligible' (*laysa lahu mafhūm*), both citing consensus.[20] Consensus is probably the most authoritative and influential of the principles in practice and the one in most need of reformulation.

Contrary to common perceptions, consensus is a murky concept and almost impossible to determine, except for the rare cases when the rulings or ideas stem from the Qurʾan. Nevertheless, many scholars have written on consensus, including Mālik, al-Shāfiʿī (1938, pp. 471–6, 533–55), al-Qāḍī ʿAbd al-Jabbār (d. 415 AH/1025 CE) (al-Asadabādī, 1963, vol. 17, pp. 165–77, 212), Abū Muḥammad ʿAlī ibn Ḥazm (d. 456 AH/1063 CE) (Ibn Ḥazm and Ibn Taymiyya, 1357 AH), Abū Ḥāmid al-Ghazālī (d. 505 AH/1111 CE) (n.d., vol. 2, pp. 322–36), Taqī al-Dīn ibn Taymiyya (d. 728 AH/1327 CE) (Ibn Ḥazm and Ibn Taymiyya, 1357 AH), and al-Shahīd al-Thānī (d. 966 AH/1558 CE) (Hallaq, 2009, pp. 118–20), with very different and often opposing conceptualizations. Today, most would follow al-Ghazālī and Ibn Ḥazm's notion of the consensus of qualified scholars, which has historically excluded most Muslims, especially women, who

[18] One should note that accusations of 'closing the gate of *ijtihād* (legal reasoning)' are not accurate, since medieval discussions of this phenomenon centred on eschatological expectations of the death of scholars (see also Hallaq, 1986b; 1984). For the use of the principle of consensus to silence voices fighting for women's equality in no-fault divorce, equal weight given to testimony in court, and rights to inheritance, see Al-Sharmani (2013, pp. 81–2, 85–6, 95).

[19] For a discussion of primary sources on child marriage, see Amin (2020).

[20] For more, see Reda (2020).

generally did not have access to higher education except for the rare few.[21] The evidence used to establish the authoritativeness of this principle consists mainly of hadiths with single chains of transmission, often weak, such as 'My nation will never agree on an error' (al-Ghazālī, n.d., vol. 2, 301–2). But the text is quite specific, stating 'my nation' (*ummatī*) and not 'the scholars'. The practicalities of figuring out who agrees and who does not agree from among the Muslim community are insurmountable, for even in the impossible scenario of asking every single Muslim on the planet at any given time, what about the ones who are deceased and the ones yet to be born? Even if one should restrict consensus to scholars, the definition of who qualifies is murky, and the process by which their opinions are gathered is even more ill-defined. As scholars have pointed out in the past and in the present, anyone who claims to know the consensus of the scholars, much less the entire Muslim nation, cannot, in fact, do so.[22]

With regard to the Qur'an, one should note that restricting consensus to 'qualified' scholars is a very elitist notion and runs contrary to its egalitarian spirit. This scripture is quite clear on the subject of taking up a religious-legal authoritative elite (*arbāb*), likening it to a breach of monotheism and disassociating Muslims from this practice (verse 3:64). Indeed, this is the way of believers as explained in the Qur'an (verse 4:115),[23] so if one wants to remain faithful to the Qur'anic conceptualization of monotheism, a consensus of elite scholars seems out of the question.[24] Moreover, the only Qur'anic occurrences of *ijmā'* in the same root (*jidhr*) and form (*binya*)[25] depict consensus as a tool to marginalize and oppress minority voices or weak individuals who are standing up for the truth: in the case of Noah's people against Noah, Joseph's brothers when throwing him

---

[21] Al-Azhar, for example, was established in 971 CE but only opened its doors to a cohort of women in 1961, almost a thousand years later.

[22] Compare also Aḥmad ibn Ḥanbal's statement, 'Whosoever claims consensus is lying', in Ibn Qayyim al-Jawziyya (1423 AH, vol. 2, pp. 53–4). See al-Shāfi'ī, 1938, pp. 534–5. See also Ibn Taymiyya's critique of consensus in Ibn Ḥazm and Ibn Taymiyya (1357 AH). Ibn Taymiyya was critical of the possibility of consensus beyond the first two or three generations of Muslims and this may also have been Ibn Ḥanbal's position, although not as clearly expressed. For a modern perspective, see Baugh (2017).

[23] Both al-Ghazālī (n.d., vol. 2, pp. 299–300 and 300 note 2) and 'Abd al-Jabbār (1963, vol. 17, p. 203) consider verse 4:115 to be a proof-text for consensus; however, based on the assumption that 'the way of the believers' is exemplified in their own practice, not in how the Qur'an depicts the way of the believers.

[24] For more on the meaning of *arbāb* and the Qur'anic notion of monotheism, see Reda (2015).

[25] The Arabic word *ijmā'* is a Form IV (*ajma'a, yujmi'u, al-ijmā'*).

into the pit, and Pharaoh's magicians against Moses (verses 10:71; 12:15, 102; 20:61–64). All of these negative portrayals hint at how consensus is misused today and just how vital it is to reformulate this principle.

1.2.4 *Reason*

The Islamic ethical-legal tradition has developed several rationalist principles which find diverse expression in the *madhāhib*, including *istiḥsān* (juristic preference), *istiṣlāḥ* (consideration of common good), *istiṣḥāb* (presumption of continuity), *sadd al-dharāʾiʿ* (blocking the means of harm) and *ʿurf* (custom). In the classical works, *qiyās* (reasoning by analogy) is the most important one, but it was applied in a haphazard fashion that depended on personal inclinations and juristic preference. One can imagine a scenario in which *qiyās* is employed to ensure women have equality, for example, in divorce. However, despite *qiyās* (and historical and linguistic evidence to the contrary), classical jurists constructed divorce (*ṭalāq*) as a distinctly male prerogative, which they could exercise unilaterally without the wife's permission, sometimes even irrevocably in one sitting (see Ahmad, 2009).[26] Jurists have historically not paid sufficient attention to power dynamics when conducting *qiyās*, using it to appropriate rights for men that are exclusive to women in the Qurʾan (for example, slander (verse 24:4)), while not transferring what they consider to be exclusive male rights to women (for example, polygyny (verse 4:3)). Among all the existing schools of jurisprudence, the Ẓāhirī school is the most critical of *qiyās* and does not accept it unless a case can be made based on language (see Ibn Rushd, 2004, vol. 1, introduction; al-ʿAlwānī, 2012, p. 311), although for different reasons than the ones pointed out here (Ibn Rushd, 2004, vol. 1, introduction). The Jaʿfarī school takes a similar position, allowing a language-based cause (*al-ʿilla al-manṣūṣa*), but not purely inferential reasoning by analogy (see Hallaq, 2009, p. 121). The Ibāḍī school also does not allow *qiyās*.

It is noteworthy that none of the schools have developed a mechanism to ensure that *qiyās* is applied justly and not haphazardly or dependent on masculinist whim. Although justice is especially emphasized in Zaydī and Jaʿfarī theology, this concern has not translated into an independent methodological

[26] Most Sunnis and contemporary Ibāḍīs accept the validity of triple *ṭalāq*, but not Jaʿfarīs, early Ibāḍīs, Ḥanbalīs (Ibn Taymiyya and Ibn al-Qayyim), and Ẓāhirīs. Supporters of triple *ṭalāq* generally cite the example of ʿUmar (which Ibn Taymiyya argues was in very particular historical circumstances) and as a means to punish the husband (without consideration for the wife, who is often most hurt by triple *ṭalāq*). For more, see al-Azri (2011; 2012).

principle in these schools or any of the other schools of Islamic jurisprudence. The principle of *ʿurf* (custom) allows the perpetuation of injustices, whether those inherited from pre-Islamic times or those that have come up in the Islamic tradition. Accordingly, although the Islamic tradition has developed a rich repertoire of rationalist tools, justice is not in evidence at the methodological level.

In light of the above, all the four major principles in Islamic ethical-legal theory have problematic methodological assumptions or are applied in problematic ways, pointing to the need to revisit and conceptualize them in ways that fit the present-day context, in keeping with the dynamic nature of the tradition.

2. RECONSTRUCTING *UṢŪL AL-FIQH*: A SPIRITUALLY INTEGRATIVE METHODOLOGY

The ethical-legal theory that I propose below is composed of four principles: Qurʾan, Sunna, reason and consultation (*shūrā*). Each of these principles is similar in some ways to its historical antecedent, but is structured and conceptualized differently in order to overcome both the contextual and source-related problems. The proposed theory is Qurʾan-centric, giving more weight to the Qurʾan than to the other principles. The new consultation principle that replaces consensus attempts to solve not only the source-related problems of this particular principle, but also the contextual problems of *uṣūl al-fiqh*, forming a bridge between *fiqh* and contemporary law and ethics.

2.1 The Qur'an

The approach to the Qurʾan argued in this chapter differs from classical approaches in three ways: attention to linguistic accuracy, integration of an ethical and spiritual dimension, and reliance on the entire Qurʾan for ethical-legal signification. Several women exegetes have produced pioneering works in the area of Qurʾan exegesis, emphasizing the importance of the linguistic meaning of the text and approaching the Qurʾan as a whole, including ʿĀʾisha ʿAbd al-Raḥmān, amina wadud, Asma Barlas, Nimat Barazangi and Zainab al-Alwani. The methodology delineated in this chapter builds on these foundations, privileging the literal meanings of words as they appear in the Qurʾan at the time of the Prophet Muhammad (as opposed to later meanings) and approaching the Qur'an holistically. These features are well-known in modern exegesis and fall under the popular 'interpreting the Qur'an by means of the Qur'an' category (*tafsīr al-Qur'ān bil Qur'ān*).

Some scholars have also underlined the importance of ethics, including Lamrabet, Abou-Bakr and Al-Sharmani in this volume. My methodology also highlights ethics, however, with one major addition: it adds a spiritual dimension. In this new spiritually integrative methodology (*manhaj rūḥānī*), the Qur'an is conceptualized as an organized spiritual method for individuals and communities to grow from the animal self (literally, the self that commands to evil, *al-nafs al-ammāra bil sū'*) to the perfected self (*al-nafs al-kāmila*),[27] each sura functioning as a step in this process and building upon previous ones (Reda, 2019b; 2019a). Islamic moral psychology envisions various stages along the path of spiritual advancement, the first of which is for the self to grow from the animal self to the self-critical self (*al-nafs al-lawwāma*), thereby moving from the ego-centric, unbridled behaviours of the lowest self to the self-restraint, watchfulness and ethical behaviours of the next higher level. Uncovering the Qur'an's ethical norms and values is thus the first step along the path to spiritual advancement and an important part of this new hermeneutic. The use of a spiritually integrative methodology allows one to connect ethics to the broader Qur'anic worldview, but also to respond to the rising interest in spirituality in many parts of the world.

Another effect of utilizing a spiritually integrative approach has to do with how the Qur'an in its entirety is viewed as having ethical-legal signification. Today, in the emerging field of Islamic spiritual care and psychotherapy,[28] scholars and practitioners recognize that there are different methods of communi-

[27] Since *al-nafs al-kāmila* does not appear in the Qur'an, it is also possible to replace it with *al-nafs al-muṭma'inna* (the reassured, tranquil, peaceful, secure self), which can also be supported by the Qur'an's organization. *Al-nafs al-kāmila* derives from Muḥyī al-Dīn ibn 'Arabī's (d. 638 AH/1240 CE) notion of the perfected human being (*al-insān al-kāmil*).

[28] Canada is probably unique in using the term 'spiritual' in spiritual care and counselling for what is better known as 'pastoral' care and counselling or chaplaincy. The Canadian Association for Spiritual Care changed its terminology to become more inclusive – formerly it was known as the 'Canadian Association for Pastoral Practice and Education'. This new nomenclature also reflects the emergence of this profession, as well as psycho-spiritual therapy (spiritually integrative psychotherapy), which is regulated by the College of Registered Psychotherapists of Ontario. In the Muslim world, this profession also seems to be gaining ground, as can be noted in the phenomenon of *murshidāt* in Morocco – the term *irshād dīnī* is the closest Arabic term for chaplaincy and spiritual/pastoral care and counselling, although it is not an exact match.

cation that can also affect behavioural change beyond direct commands and prohibitions. A counsellor may use narrative therapy, ask questions, or utilize theological reflection, empowering and assisting their client to find solutions to everyday problems in their journey of healing and growth. These different therapeutic methods have their counterparts in the Qurʾan, which all form part of the sacred book's distinct style of communication. Accordingly, all these different techniques can have ethical-legal ramifications and the entire Qurʾan needs to be taken into consideration.

2.2 The Sunna

In the Qurʾan, the Prophet is portrayed as an exemplar for Muslims (verse 33:21). Like many classical methodologies, the role of Hadith literature is envisioned here using the notion of *uswa ḥasana* (exemplar). However, I distinguish between *uswa* and *rabb* (Rabbi, religious-legal authority), which the Qurʾan categorically forbids (verses 3:64, 79–80). An exemplar or role model, who one may voluntarily imitate, differs from a religious-legal authority, whose word is law and functions as an independent source of law. Like Aḥmad ibn Ḥanbal, I make a distinction between the educational role of preaching and the ethical-legal function of law-making.[29] However, while Ibn Ḥanbal required firm *isnāds* for law-making but not preaching, I do not consider most of the legal hadiths to be firm enough for independent law-making. Unlike the Qurʾan, hadiths are not witnessed, that is, no two witnesses testified to having heard the Prophet say each hadith prior to its inclusion in the canonical books of hadiths (the Prophet had prohibited recording them). The Islamic tradition clearly distinguishes between *shahāda* (testimony, witnessing) and *riwāya* (narration) of hadiths, and since narration is not accepted as firm evidence when adjudicating disputes, neither should it be in the laws that get applied in the adjudication of disputes. *Mutawātir* (frequently attested) hadiths that have two or more reliable narrators at every stage of the transmission process are rare and maybe even non-existent (Brown, 2009, pp. 104–6). Accordingly, hadiths

[29] 'If we narrate from the Messenger of God, God's peace and blessings be upon him, concerning permitted and prohibited things (*al-ḥalāl wa al-ḥarām*), traditions and rulings, then we are strict with chains of transmission; but if we narrate from the Prophet, God's peace and blessings be upon him, concerning virtuous deeds and what does not impose a ruling or remove it, then we are easy-going with chains of transmission.' For this well-known saying of Imām Aḥmad, as well as similar sayings by others, see al-Baghdādī (2012, p. 124).

cannot be utilized as a stand-alone principle in law. Hadiths, though, can be used in conjunction with other ethical-legal tools, for example, the Qurʾan, reason, or as historical sources, as long as the hadiths or their interpretations do not conflict with the Qurʾan and its ethical framework. One should note that, although the Qurʾan is the best attestation of the Prophet's example, hadiths can also be a very valuable resource when approached thoughtfully, critically and constructively (see, for example, Barazangi, 2015; Reda, 2004).

2.3 Reason (*ʿaql*)

This methodology incorporates the rich tools of reason that the various *madhāhib* have crafted over the centuries with the addition of a new principle: consideration of justice or, in Arabic, *istiʿdāl* (seeking justice).[30] From the classical tradition, one should note two tools that are of particular importance today: the theory of *maqāṣid* (objectives of the law), which is utilized in contemporary jurisprudence of Muslim minorities, and the legal maxims (*qawāʿid fiqhiyya kulliyya*), a genre that resembles early codification attempts.[31] Both have their roots in the Qurʾan – *maqāṣid* depends on identifying the benefits of Qurʾanic legislation and the maxims attempt to formulate rules based on the legislation.

Consideration of justice, too, stems from the Qurʾan and its nuanced treatments and terminology. The Qurʾan commands justice, utilizing two different words for justice: *ʿadl* (equality, justice) and *qisṭ* (equity, social justice, transformational equality). Both are verbal nouns (*maṣdar*), equivalent to the English infinitive or gerund, and so denote action. They have very different meanings, as Ramon Harvey has vividly demonstrated in *The Qurʾan and the Just Society* (2019). He translates *ʿadl* as 'personal ethics', along the lines of a person's internalized moral compass, and *qisṭ* as 'societal justice' (2019, pp. 20–1).

[30] Like *istiḥsān*, *istiṣḥāb* and *istiṣlāḥ*, the new term *istiʿdāl* is a Form X (*istafʿala*, *yastafʿilu*, *al-istifʿāl*), a verbal noun that denotes lending something or someone the action or quality that the Form I implies. It means ensuring that the ruling and/or ethical judgement has the qualities of *ʿadl* and *qisṭ*.

[31] The most important work in the *maqāṣid* and *fiqh al-aqalliyāt* (*fiqh* of minorities) genre in the area of marriage is al-ʿAlwānī (2012). For a constructive critique of their practicality and the addition of an overarching ethos to the *maqāṣid* to make them more manageable, see Reda (2018). For more on legal maxims, see Kamali (2008, pp. 141–61). In connection with marriage, the most important work in the genre of legal maxims is probably that of Muḥammad ibn ʿAbd Allāh ibn ʿĀbid al-Ṣawwāṭ (2001), whose work is based on that of Ibn Taymiyya.

I have chosen 'social justice', 'equity' and 'transformational equality' for *qisṭ* because they make more sense in my particular context from a translation theory perspective. 'Social justice' has more common ground in the target language and culture (English); Musawah uses the term 'transformative equality' to describe equality that is embedded in the Qur'anic notion of justice (Musawah, 2017). 'Equity' is perhaps the best translation for *qisṭ*; however, it has historically been misused to perpetuate injustices against women, which is why I'm not using it here until its positive meaning is better established. Building on my own work and the valuable work of Harvey (2019) and Musawah (2017), I define *ʿadl* as justice and/or equality. It is a notion that begins with formal equality and that can go deeper – formal equality means treating people identically, irrespective of their backgrounds, situations, or personal characteristics (see Musawah, 2017). Harvey (2019, p. 20) points out its root meaning from *ʿidl*, half the burden on the beast of burden's back, which is used to counterbalance the other half. The Arabic word for justice thus also means equality and has nuances of a continuous weighing of burdens. Equality (*ʿadl*) can be at the superficial level or deeply ingrained; it can be just or unjust, for example, in the case of a tyrant who oppresses everyone equally. *ʿAdl* is a concept that is continuously in motion, growing as individuals and communities learn to consider systemic and other injustices and thus affecting more profound manifestations of equality. A third Qur'an-inspired word, *taṭfīf* (cheating, discrimination), is also important for this new principle. It is a hapax legomenon, occurring only as a masculine plural active participle (*muṭaffifīn*, sura 83), and denotes those who fall below the minimum baseline of formal equality. Accordingly, *ʿadl* can have different manifestations, depending on an individual or community's growth; however, it must never fall below the minimal baseline of formal equality. Otherwise, it falls into the blameworthy *taṭfīf* category, without even a pretence of justice.

Qisṭ is the mechanism by which *ʿadl* grows and matures. It denotes taking into account social inequalities, systemic and structural oppressions, and power imbalances and adjusting behaviours accordingly, by allocating more resources and rights to the vulnerable in order to achieve equality in society. It is therefore a more in-depth and comprehensive form of justice that is tempered with the divine quality of compassion (*raḥma*).[32] Consideration of justice is thus a

[32] Elsewhere (2018, p. 16), I translate *raḥma* as loving-kindness, since in the Arabic language this word has two components: the love/tenderness/feelings component and the kindness/generosity/giving component.

process that starts with *ʿadl* and can be adjusted and trumped by *qisṭ*, when the vulnerabilities of individuals and social groups so dictate. The requirement for men to give the bride-gift to women is just such an expression of *qisṭ*, as well as maintenance and divorce settlements. In my reading of the Qurʾan, the *qisṭ* imperative is never used to privilege the powerful and disempower the vulnerable or to promote systemic or other oppressions. In fact, those who seek to privilege themselves and deny others equal treatment are described by a special word: the above-mentioned *muṭaffifīn* (cheaters, discriminators). A whole sura (83) is devoted to warning people off such behaviours.

Istiʿdāl (seeking justice) in the domain of ethical-legal theory is a process that starts with discerning the minimum baseline of formal equality and other deeper norms of justice that have gained widespread acceptance. It is followed by *istiqsāṭ* (seeking social justice, equity), which means examining the context, looking for vulnerabilities and power imbalances, and making adjustments accordingly. At a superficial level, *qisṭ* and *ʿadl* (in the sense of equality) are in tension with one another, *qisṭ* necessarily incorporating inequalities to achieve a higher, more deeply rooted, systemic, structural and/or interpersonal equality. Affirmative action (a policy of favouring individuals from groups that have suffered discrimination in education and jobs), for example, is a contemporary expression of *qisṭ*. There are also numerous Qurʾanic examples of *qisṭ* in the area of marriage relations and otherwise. Veering away from the minimal expectation of formal equality (or established norms of *qisṭ*) in order to disempower the vulnerable is an expression of *taṭfīf*; when performed on the basis of gender, it becomes gender discrimination (*taṭfīf jinsī*).

Consideration of justice is thus the very careful, context-specific weighing of both *ʿadl* and *qisṭ* and determining the best possible outcome, given the existing vulnerabilities. As a principle, justice can be applied on its own or in conjunction with other principles, such as *qiyās*. It is also a measure of success of a process of ethical reasoning; a ruling that falls into the realm of *taṭfīf* can thus be deemed a failure, with success dependent on the appropriateness of the ruling to the context and the existing vulnerabilities. This new principle emphasizes justice in *uṣūl al-fiqh*, which, so far, did not have a stand-alone principle to ensure this important value in processes of ethical-legal reasoning.[33]

[33] One should note that in some modern renditions of the theory of *maqāṣid*, justice can be included. The classical five *maqāṣid al-sharīʿa* are the protection and preservation of the religion, life, intellect, lineage and wealth. For a brief overview of some of the expansions that have occurred in the theory of *maqāṣid*, see Kamali (2009, pp. 27–8).

This lack is a serious shortcoming in Islamic ethical-legal theory and, given the aspirations for justice at various social and political levels in the Muslim world today, it needs to be addressed. Otherwise, the inherent injustices in *fiqh* will continue to diminish this discipline and it will continue to fail the aspirations of present-day Muslims and even repel them. Due to the importance of justice as a value in the Qurʾan, *istiʿdāl* needs to encompass the rational principles and take precedence over them. From the various avenues that require justice today, marriage takes primary position, since this relationship is the first and foremost human relationship from an ontological and spiritual perspective, as I indicate below. It is a place where partners grow and where children are reared and acquire values. Without equality in marriage, there can be no equality in society. Due to the importance of marriage for people's spiritual growth, marriage is a good location to start applying this new principle.

2.4 Consultation (*shūrā*)

The principle of *shūrā* is similar to its predecessor *ijmāʿ* in its incorporation of a collective, deliberative element into the process of ethical reasoning and law-making, however, with two major differences: replacing the problematic term *ijmāʿ* with one that is positively depicted in the Qurʾan and making the process of opinion-gathering more feasible. *Shūrā* also has the potential to justify law, which is something that consensus implicitly attempts to do. However, consensus is restricted to elite scholars of the past while *shūrā* allows for reimagining who else gets to have a voice. In the Qurʾan, *shūrā* occurs as a behavioural norm for believers (verse 42:38), in the example of the Prophet (verse 3:159), and even in weaning a child (verse 2:233).[34] In the context of

[34] Verse 42:38: 'The ones who responded to their Lord and established prayer and their affairs are conducted through mutual consultation among them.'

Verse 3:159: 'It was out of God's loving kindness that you were gentle with them. If you were harsh with a hard heart, they would have dispersed from around you, so pardon them and seek forgiveness for them. Consult with them in affairs. When you have decided on a course of action, put your trust in God: God loves those who put their trust in Him.'

Verse 2:233: 'The ones who give birth suckle their children for two whole years for whoever wants to complete the suckling. The ones to whom a child is born are responsible for their provision and clothing in a fair manner. No one is required to do more than they are able. No mother shall be harmed on account of her child, nor father on account of his. Heirs carry the same responsibility. If both parents have consulted together and agree to wean the child, they will not be blamed, nor will you be blamed if you have someone else suckle the child as long as

governance, it is presented as a very egalitarian, 'democratic' process and a characteristic of a responsible leader (verses 27:29–44; 42:38; 3:159) (see also Reda, 2013). Women are clearly depicted in *shūrā* processes, for example, at the governance level in the story of the Queen of Sheba (verses 27:29–44) and in family situations in the weaning of a child.

Shūrā is also an elastic concept: it can be applied to small or large groups, each of which can be clearly defined. Accordingly, if consultation is conducted at the level of the state, citizens of an entire country can participate through their democratically elected representatives. In such instances, when *shūrā* is conducted in parliaments and other vehicles of public consultation and law-making, *shūrā* can turn ideas into law. If consultation is conducted at the level of a *madhhab* or smaller group, it becomes the ethical reasoning and judgement of that particular school or group. Ideas that start out in the realm of ethics, as the ethical-legal reasoning of particular groups, can migrate into the realm of law if they pass through appropriate consultative channels. The scale and processes of *shūrā* distinguish between which *fiqh* rulings become law and which need to remain in the realm of ethical deliberation. *Fiqh* functions differently in these two domains: *fiqh* that remains in the realm of ethical deliberation, if revivified, can serve to stimulate new thinking and inform personal, voluntary decision-making; while *fiqh* that has gone through appropriate processes of law-making and has become law is justiciable and can be implemented and enforced by the modern state. In fact, the very processes of *shūrā* can serve to rejuvenate *fiqh* (as ethics), particularly if new stakeholders are included in the consultative processes (for example, women and specialists in various disciplines) and participation is not limited to classically trained jurists.

Due to this ability to differentiate between the two functions of *fiqh* (law and ethics), *shūrā* has the potential of bridging the gap between *fiqh* and the modern state in contemporary ethical-legal theory. The way *shūrā* is depicted in the Qur'an suggests that it can serve to justify law and its implementation in contemporary democratic systems of governance. One should note that famous *shūrā* verse implies that the governance of a people belongs to them and that it needs to be in the form of consultation among them (verse 42:38) or, phrased differently, what makes a law legitimate is the process of consultation among the people who are subject to the law (that is, not only

---

you pay what you promised in a fair manner. Be mindful of God and know that God sees what you do.'

elite scholars).[35] One should also note that classical *fiqh* has not gone through appropriate consultative channels with all the important stakeholders (for example, women) in this day and age and should therefore not function as law in the modern state. Of course, as is well known, even democratic processes can be unjust and can serve to marginalize minority voices and women. It thus becomes the job of ethicists and other stakeholders working in the domain of a revitalized *fiqh* to determine just how ethical a particular state's processes of law-making are and to attempt to improve upon them to make them more representative and inclusive of women and other marginalized voices.

In light of the above, the proposed theory consists of four principles. Three are substantive, in that they provide source materials and methodologies to produce ethical-legal rulings and other content. The Qur'an is the main textual source in this theory; hadiths can be utilized critically, while rational sources are also deployed, including the new 'consideration of justice' tool. The last principle, *shūrā*, is procedural, describing an important step in the process of producing law and ethics.

3. SPIRITUALLY INTEGRATIVE ETHICS AND JURISPRUDENCE OF MARRIAGE AND DIVORCE

I now turn to applying the above methodology to the case of marriage and divorce. This part is organized into two sections: one dealing with marriage and one dealing with divorce. The above methodology is reflected in the following analysis in two ways: in the way the sections are organized and in the contents of each section.

Each of the sections on marriage and divorce consists of three parts: the first explores definitions, the second examines cornerstones, and the third raises the bar of ethics higher. The first two parts establish definitions and cornerstones that are broadly derived from *Surat al-Baqara* and elsewhere from the Qur'an, while the third part develops these constructs based on the higher values and processes described in *Surat al-Nisā'*. In the spiritually integrative approach, as hinted above and discussed elsewhere (Reda, 2019a; 2019b), *Surat al-Baqara* establishes the basic foundations of the Islamic faith

[35] Note the pronouns in the *shūrā* verse: *amruhum* (*their* affairs) are conducted through mutual consultation *baynahum* (among *them*). For more, see Reda (2015).

tradition, while *Surat al-Nisāʾ* focuses on internal relationships within the faith community, each sura having its place within this organized pathway and building on previous suras. In terms of content, each subsection relies heavily on the Qurʾan, but key hadiths are also examined, as well as rational principles, mainly consideration of justice. The intent here is to construct a basic framework for marriage and divorce, drawing broad outlines, without going into too much detail, due to lack of space. Procedurally, these preliminary ideas would need to be fleshed out and undergo *shūrā* before they could be considered either ethics or law.

3.1 Marriage

3.1.1 *Defining marriage and its purpose*

The Qurʾan utilizes two terms in connection with marriage: *nikāḥ* (sexual intercourse, marriage) and *zawj* (partner, spouse). *Nikāḥ* invariably refers to marriage in verb or noun form, that is, the act of marrying or the marriage.[36] *Nikāḥ* and its derivatives are never used to designate marriage partners, which hints that the Qurʾan does not affirm social hierarchies dependent on who gets penetrated and who does the penetrating in marriage.[37] In contrast, *zawj* and its derivatives are always used to designate marriage partners, but never marriage in noun or verb form, except on rare occasions when it refers to God joining two people together in marriage.[38] Both marriage partners are termed *zawj*, a word which occurs in the singular, dual and plural in the Qurʾan. The feminine form *zawjah* does not occur in the Qurʾan; in fact, the Qurʾan does not differentiate linguistically between husband or wife, who are both designated as *zawj*, which hints at equality in the union. Beginning with *Surat*

[36] Verses 2:221, 230, 232, 235, 237; 4:3, 6, 22, 25, 127; 24:3, 32–3, 60; 28:27; 33:49–50, 53; 60:10.

[37] Al-Shāfiʿī argues that a woman 'is married' whereas a man 'marries', a play on words since the word *nikāḥ* means both marriage and intercourse. He uses this argument to justify inequalities in marriage. For al-Shāfiʿī, sex was one way of affirming social hierarchies: penetrating meant one was higher up on the social hierarchy than if one was being penetrated (see Ali, 2010, pp. 178–9). Although this linguistic differentiation exists in the context of sexual relations (without the hierarchies) in the case of marriage, the Qurʾan also describes women as the ones who 'marry' (*yankiḥna*), not only men (verse 2:230).

[38] See, for example, verses 2:25, 102, 230–4, 240. God is described as joining a couple in marriage in this life (verse 33:37) or the next (verses 44:54, 52:20, 81:7) or as giving both male and female offspring to partners (verse 42:50).

al-Baqara, from a purely linguistic perspective the terminology suggests that marriage is a union of two equals for the purposes of licit sexual intercourse (see, for example, Mir-Hosseini, 2008). Finer spiritual values, such as love and kindness, are added later on, for example, verse 30:21. In contrast, the Qurʾan strongly prohibits *zinā* (verses 24:2–3; 25:68; 60:12), which is not associated with these higher spiritual values.

Classical jurists point to the marriage contract, with certain cornerstones (*arkān*) without which a union is not deemed an ethical-legal marriage. As Ziba Mir-Hosseini, Kecia Ali and others have demonstrated, they patterned it after the contract of sale model: the husband provides *ṣadāq* and *nafaqa* (marriage gift and financial maintenance) in return for the wife's *tamkīn* (sexual availability), sometimes using the language of purchasing access to and domination of *al-buḍʿ* (vagina, *arvum mulieris*) (see, for example, Mir-Hosseini, 2012). This language recalls another, negative model for men-women relationships in the Qurʾan: that of prostitution (verses 19:20, 28; 24:33); thus, legally, a wife is conceptualized as a kind of personal prostitute, which is a distinct disadvantage of this model. Kecia Ali has studied the development of the 'contract of sale' conceptualization of marriage in its formative period (c. ninth century), showing how it parallels and is affected by slavery – which was a common phenomenon at the time (Ali, 2010; see also Mir-Hosseini, 2008, pp. 80–3). In this model, a man 'buys' access to sex, in that he acquires a material exchange from the woman in return for his money. Sex is not something reciprocal: a woman does not have an equal right to sex from her husband. The inequality in this construct finds expression in a man's right to unilateral divorce and polygyny, sometimes subject to moral sanctions but not legal ones (Al-Sharmani, 2018, p. 83).

This construction of marriage undergirds much of modernist and reformist Islamic thinking, which suggests that women must give up their Qurʾan-mandated right to financial support in order to be treated equally in a marriage; in other words, human dignity is dependent on the ability to pay for it. While proponents of formal equality want to remove the few financial advantages women have retained from medieval constructs of marriage – thus disadvantaging women even more – traditionalists sacramentalize the medieval constructs, thus enshrining their inherent injustices in the law and in the practice of the community and allowing for the continuation of male privilege. This construct is not only demeaning to women, but it also fails the above-mentioned bar of *ʿadl* or minimal formal equality, venturing into gender discrimination (*tatfīf jinsī*). At the same time, its modernist renditions do not account for women's vulnerabilities in marriage, thus stripping away *qisṭ* from the medieval construct. Needless to say, neither the modernist nor the traditionalist positions can be considered 'just' from a Qur'an-inspired 'consideration of justice' perspective.

Despite these drawbacks, the contractual aspect has its advantages, three of which stand out. First, it delineates marriage as a civil contract as opposed to a sacrament, and thus under the control of the community and not the religious elite. Second, it can be reimagined to remove the 'sex in return for money' nuances, for example, in the form of a partnership (*shirāka*), since the intellectual infrastructure exists for it in various manuals of *fiqh* (although it will need reworking) (see, for example, Ibn Rushd, 2004, vol. 3, pp. 35–9).[39] Third, it has legal claws, in that it can be enforced in a court of law.

There are two other relationships in the Qur'an upon which classical (and contemporary) jurists could have patterned their construction of marriage but did not: 1) charity, which similarly entails a giving of money but with a spiritual reward as opposed to a material return; and 2) covenant, termed *'ahd* or *mīthāq* in the Qur'an. The charity aspect is essential in countering the 'prostitution' nuances of classical constructions, because it demonstrates that not all spending must have a material return for the giver; rather, spending (*infāq, nafaqa*) is a foundation for spiritual advancement, second only to salat (worship, ritual prayer), as indicated right at the beginning of *Surat al-Baqara* (verse 2:3). In fact, spending is a pillar of a believer's practice, as outlined in this verse and elaborated further in the rest of the Qur'an. The terminology occurs in a variety of contexts, including support for family members (verse 2:215). Spending should not be accompanied by reminders of one's generosity and by harm to the beneficiary (*al-mann wa al-adhā*), which can cancel out such generosity (verse 2:264). Women give abundantly of themselves during childbirth, suckling and otherwise providing care for their loved ones, and thereby develop certain spiritual potentialities of love, caring and generous giving; men thereby also have an opportunity for similar spiritual development. The Qur'an's instruction for men to spend on their womenfolk becomes their pathway to activate these latent potentialities. Just as requiring material return would neutralize charity, so too would legally requiring spousal obedience, unilateral right to sex or other material exchange in marriage.[40] Men's

---

[39] Al-Jazīrī, al-Gharawī and Māziḥ (1998) also have treatments of *shirka*. These ideas, however, would need to be developed to fit marriage. See also Quraishi-Landes (2021).

[40] In countries where charitable giving provides a tax refund, one could make an argument that spousal spending also warrants a tax refund.

spending on women in marriage is an expression of *qisṭ* and an important aspect of their spiritual journey and does not require a material return.

The covenantal aspect is also useful since it describes the relationship between human beings and God as well as human beings and each other. It entails responsibilities and expectations that guide the development of these relationships, as individuals learn within their frameworks and grow on their spiritual journey. *Mīthāq* also happens to be the term used to describe the marriage relationship in *Surat al-Nisāʾ* (verse 4:21), although *nafaqa* describes an aspect of it (verse 4:34). In fact, marriage is the only human–human relationship in the Qurʾan that is described by the term *mīthāq ghalīẓ* (firm covenant) (verse 4:21), just like the God–human relationship (verse 4:154). No other human–human relationship is described in this manner.[41]

The importance of marriage for spiritual growth is also asserted in a hadith in which the Prophet describes marriage as 'half your religion'.[42] 'Half your religion' is an indication of just how important the marriage relationship is to help deepen our understanding of the God–human covenant and perhaps also of the breadth of the latent divine qualities that marriage can help actualize, more so than any other practice. Rather than slavery, one can liken marriage to a school where both men and women learn to develop faithfulness, fidelity (*ikhlāṣ*), loyalty, love, kindness, generosity and other latent divine qualities that enable them to draw closer to God and reach their full potential as human beings. Marriage nurtures the internal infrastructure that can help people better relate to God and draw closer to God mentally, emotionally, physically and spiritually. The conceptualization of marriage as a kind of 'slavery' is not compatible with the notion of marriage as an institution that helps in spiritual growth; rather, 'slavery' has connotations of oppression and stands in opposition to notions of *ʿadl* and *iḥsān* (kindness, beauty, spiritual growth) that are important values to learn on the path to God. Marriage is also the building block of the social infrastructure, ontologically the first human relationship (as noted in the story of Adam and Eve) and where subsequent relationships are built and a society's young are

[41] Abou-Bakr, Lamrabet and Al-Sharmani in this volume have termed it a 'solemn bond' of ethical and spiritual significance and as serious as the relationship between God and His prophets.
[42] 'When a servant marries, he has completed half the religions, so let him be mindful of God in the remaining half' (al-Bayhaqī, 2003, vol. 7, pp. 340–1, no. 5100). Other narration and versions exist, such as Islamweb.net, '*Hal al-zawāj nisf al-dīn ḥadīth ṣaḥīḥ am qawl maʾthūr?*', no. 195617, www.islamweb.net/ar/fatwa/195617/

nurtured. Accordingly, from a spiritually integrative perspective, marriage is a school, not slavery.

One should note that the Catholic Church and other Christian and Jewish traditions also envision marriage as a covenant, though it is one that is sacramentalized and thus under the control of the religious elite. In the Qurʾan, despite the spiritual importance that is given to marriage, the civil nature of marriage (and the marriage contract) is indicated in the use of the plural, implying the involvement of the entire community in the act of contracting a marriage.[43] Accordingly, marriage is not a sacrament that is ratified by religious scholars, but a civil contract that needs to be recognized by the community and its mechanisms, for example, the law. The term 'covenant' suggests that the spiritual aspects of marriage are not justiciable, but are God's domain, although the law can provide a minimal framework for marriages to be healthy, so spiritual growth can take place.

In light of the above, from an ethical-legal perspective, marriage can be defined as a civil contract with financial and sexual implications and a covenant for the purpose of spiritual advancement. Its contractual aspects are justiciable, while its spiritual aspects are not; however, the law serves to regulate marriage in ways that best enable this institution to fulfil its spiritual purpose and that best achieve *ʿadl* and *qisṭ* within its particular contexts and jurisdictions. It is not a sacrament, that is, the religious elite cannot validate or invalidate a marriage or a divorce; rather, it is the community who has this power, exemplified in the mechanisms of the modern state.

3.1.2 *Cornerstones of an ethical-legal marriage*

Classical constructions of marriage identify five cornerstones for a marriage contract to be ethical-legal: wording (*ṣīgha*),[44] contracting partners (*ʿāqidān*), the bride-gift (*ṣadāq*), witnesses (*shuhūd*) and the male guardian of the bride (*walī*). In conversation with classical constructions, I propose three cornerstones for modern Muslim marriages: suitable partners, bride-gift and registration. As I elaborate below, registration is what makes a marriage legal; choosing suitable marriage partners and the bride-gift give it a basic ethical foundation for marriage to do its work and for spiritual growth.

---

[43] The wording of the Qurʾanic text, particularly the use of the grammatical plural, suggests that marriage needs to be recognized by society and women's financial and divorce rights guaranteed in it. See, for example, verses 2:221, 242; 4:3, 15–26; 65:1–6. See also verse 2:235, which forbids secret engagements and unions.

[44] In the Ḥanafī *madhhab*, this is the only cornerstone of marriage.

As mentioned above, the Qurʾan uses the language of *zawj* to refer to marriage partners, which points to two contracting partners. Legal requirements for who these two persons may be varies from country to country; however, the Qurʾan further narrows down who a Muslim may or may not marry from an ethical perspective. It is noteworthy that these injunctions occur in four suras, each with a related theme and spiritual growing edge, which further underscores the spiritual dimension of marriage and the need for a suitable marriage partner who can assist one on the journey of spiritual advancement (Reda, 2019b). The first exclusion occurs in *Surat al-Baqara*: Muslims may not marry partners who associate other deities with God (verse 2:221). The reason given is important: it is because polytheists call to the fire, whereas God calls to the Garden and forgiveness (verse 2:221). Thus, it is not because of concern over prospective children's religious identification; rather, it is for the role a marriage partner plays in the spirituality of the other. The second exclusion occurs in *Surat al-Nisāʾ*. Verse 4:6 seems to suggest a minimum age of marriage[45] and verses 4:22–23 exclude incestuous marriages: Muslims may not marry their parents, offspring or siblings, or their uncles, aunts, nephews, nieces, stepmothers, stepfather, stepdaughters, stepsons, mothers-in-law, fathers-in-law, daughters-in-law, sons-in-law, or mothers or siblings through nursing relationships. *Surat al-Māʾida* has a further clarification with regard to marriage to People of the Book (Jews and Christians): marriage to People of the Book is permissible for Muslims. Although the wording specifies marriage to women from the People of the Book, marriage to men is also implied, since it indicates that People of the Book do not necessarily call to the fire and thus Muslims may marry them.[46] *Surat al-Nūr* fine-tunes suitable marriage partners further: chaste men may only marry chaste women and vice versa. Unchaste men, those who have engaged in illicit sexual intercourse, may only marry similarly unchaste women, and vice versa (verse 24:3). A case can be made for exceptions in cases of repentance (verse 24:5), although Muslims who want to adhere to the highest standards of ethics would wish a truly repentant unchaste man or woman to marry a similarly repentant unchaste woman or man due to the use of the expression, '*ḥurrima dhālika ʿalā al-muʾminīn*' ("This has been declared forbidden to believers'), which carries very strong nuances of prohibition (verse 24:3). When taken

[45] For more on child marriage, see Amin (2020).

[46] Marriage of a Muslim woman to a non-Muslim man has also been allowed in certain circumstances in *fiqh al-aqalliyāt* (see Ali, 2006, pp. 17–19).

together, these four suras suggest that suitable marriage partners are other chaste (or repentant) Muslims or other monotheists who are of age[47] and are not closely related by blood or through nursing.

The bride-gift is an important cornerstone of marriage, one which is clearly commanded in the Qur'an (verse 4:4). It formalizes the marriage contract, initiates the practice of marital giving (*infāq*) and balances some of the historical and inherent inequalities in marriage, thus contributing to social justice (*qisṭ*).

Here, registration replaces the remaining three cornerstones of classical constructions: wording, witnesses and male guardian. It ensures intentionality and legal recognition of both marriage and divorce in the modern state. Not registering a marriage hints at ill intentions, since it prevents the partner from suing for their rights, as specified in the Qur'an, such as spousal maintenance and divorce settlements. Marriage is not generally a private or secret union between two people, but needs communal recognition, which in a modern state means the law of the land. In pre-modern times, jurists deemed two witnesses and a correctly worded verbal or written agreement to be enough; however, this is no longer the case.[48] The main benefit of the male guardian requirement – that of the bride having someone to pursue her rights in cases of recalcitrant husbands – is today accomplished by registering a marriage and the mechanisms of the modern state. Accordingly, a marriage or a divorce that is not fully recognized as such in the court system of the country and thus guarantees full legal rights is not an ethical-legal marriage or divorce, for example, *ʿurfī* 'marriages' in Egypt, polygynous 'marriages' in Canada, *misyār* 'marriages' in Saudi Arabia, and spoken, unwitnessed and unregistered pronouncements of 'divorce' anywhere. Rational principles can also be used to argue for the registration cornerstone in the contemporary context. Such principles include custom and blocking the means of harm, as well as the related maxims 'Custom is the basis of judgement' (*al-ʿāda muḥakkama*) and 'Harm must be eliminated' (*al-ḍarar yuzāl*), among others.[49]

[47] The minimum age of marriage varies from country to country. In most countries, the minimum age of marriage for both girls and boys ranges between 16 and 18 (with parental consent).

[48] Two or more witnesses are specified in the writing of debts (verse 2:282) and when finalizing divorce (verse 65:2), but they are not specified for marriage. Requiring two witnesses was a solution of classical jurists to guarantee the recognition of the marriage by society and a court of law, one which is only accomplished today through registration.

[49] Translation of legal maxims by Kamali (2008, pp. 144–5), unless otherwise stated.

3.1.3 *Raising the bar: ethical challenges and vulnerability in marriage*
While the above three cornerstones make a marriage legal and provide a modicum of ethics, the Qurʾan provides far more for self-critical individuals and communities on the path of building their ethical foundation and advancing spiritually. It identifies three toxic behaviours which stand out, not only for the potential harm that they can do to a marriage, but also for the quality and wisdom of the ethical intervention strategies that are deployed to deal with them. All three occur in *Surat al-Nisāʾ*: polygyny, home imprisonment and domestic violence.

In the case of polygyny, monogamy is presented as the norm and polygyny as the exception, subject to three ethical imperatives: social justice to widows and orphans (*qisṭ*), good pleasure of the women (and men) involved (*ṭīb al-nafs*), and equality (*ʿadl*) (verses 4:1–4).[50] As noted above, social justice and equality are in tension with one another, this tension introducing Muslims to the notion of competing ethical imperatives as well as competing vulnerabilities. Thus, if the need for social justice to vulnerable women and children outweighs the need for equality, polygyny becomes an option. This was the case in the early Muslim community when many men lost their lives as a result of war. Today, however, in non-exceptional circumstances, the ever-present need for equality outweighs the demands of social justice to widows and orphans and thus points to monogamy, particularly due to the welfare system that provides for vulnerable members of the community. Lawmakers and those engaged in ethical reasoning would need to pay attention to context when weighing between these ethical imperatives and vulnerabilities in order to determine the most ethical outcome. Verse 4:3 thus challenges jurists and Muslims more generally to take ethical reasoning to a more complex, sophisticated level.

Surat al-Nisāʾ also addresses the problem of controlling husbands curtailing their wives' mobility and preventing them from going out of their homes. Historically and today, this oppression is often justified by men's fear of women's promiscuity or spousal infidelity (which could be a projection of

[50] The Qurʾanic text specifies *mā ṭāba lakum min al-nisāʾ*, which suggests that the women need to feel good to the men, but also towards the men, thus requiring the free consent of all parties involved. Verse 4:4 further affirms the importance of women's free agreement and good pleasure when giving up some of their rights, in this case some of the marriage gift, using the same verb. Equality (*ʿadl*) here is envisioned as a general value that encompasses equality between husband and wife and other forms of equality. For more see Reda (2020, pp. 81–2).

their own behaviour).[51] The Qur'an challenges such men to come up with four eyewitnesses to such indiscretions prior to imprisoning women in their own homes (verse 4:15). It thereby introduces Muslims to the notion of the presumption of innocence within family relationships, which developed into the legal maxim '*al-bayyina ʿalā al-mudda ʿī*' ('The burden of proof rests on the accuser').[52] This notion is revolutionary in the history of scripture; in the Hebrew Bible, for example, when a husband suspects a wife of adultery, the onus was on her to prove her innocence, not on him to prove her guilt.[53]

In the case of domestic violence, this sura provides three ethical intervention strategies to help self-critical individuals and communities combat domestic violence. The first is a positive intervention strategy that relies on establishing positive behavioural norms of men giving to women and depicting women positively as devoutly humble before God and as guardians of the spiritual dimension (verse 4:34). The second two are negative intervention strategies that work with negative emotions and prohibitions: the first evokes the fear that men may have of women leaving them and the second forbids the oppression of women (verse 4:34). Like a carrot and a stick, both positive and negative intervention strategies work together to stop domestic violence (verse 4:34) (see Reda, 2019a).

In light of the above, *Surat al-Nisā'* identifies three vulnerabilities for women in marriage relationships and provides novel, ethical guidelines, pushing individuals and communities to raise the bar of ethics and think in sophisticated ways. Depending on the ethical advancement of a community and its social context, it may decide to introduce legal interventions to protect the vulnerable, for example, by criminalizing or providing other legal deterrents against polygyny, home imprisonment and wife-beating. Such measures would be one way of guarding against abuse, especially in societies that take these ethical guidelines seriously.

---

[51] See, for example, the work of Abū al-Faraj ibn al-Jawzī (1987, p. 57; 1989, pp. 14–16; 1992, pp. 62–3), who asserts men's right to have multiple sexual partners and frowns upon women's jealousy, while at the same time counselling men to seclude a wife in the home, prevent her from talking to other females or looking out of the window, and to have an elderly woman gatekeeper to discipline her, instruct her in the exaltation of the husband (*tulaqqinuhā ta'ẓīm al-zawj*), and teach her his rights.

[52] Translation mine. This maxim is based on a hadith.

[53] Numbers 5:11–31; Deuteronomy 22:13–19. See also Qur'anic verses 24:2–25 for the punishment for falsely accusing a woman without four witnesses to the physical act of penetration and how a wife's word trumps a husband's when he accuses her of adultery.

3.2 Divorce

3.2.1 *Redefining divorce*

In the Qur᾿an, the term for divorce is *ṭalāq*.[54] The terms *khul*ʿ (extraction) and *faskh* (termination) do not occur in the Qur᾿an; rather, they are juristic constructs that were employed specifically to refer to women-initiated divorce.[55] Classical jurists saw fit to define *ṭalāq* as a purely male prerogative and to deny it to women; however, since the phenomenon of women-initiated divorce existed at the time of the Prophet and was affirmed by him, they needed to find alternative terminology to refer to it. Here, I redefine *ṭalāq* as both a male and female right, utilizing the appropriate Qur᾿anic terminology for divorce: *ṭalāq*. I begin by examining the Qur᾿anic verses, follow with evidence from the Hadith corpus, and end with rational sources, showing why women have equal right to divorce an unwanted spouse.

Divorce verbs occur almost exclusively in the plural in the Qur᾿an,[56] indicating that divorce is a collective undertaking that needs to be recognized by the community and its legal instruments. While the *ʿadl* imperative (*istiʿdāl*) points to both men and women having the right to unilaterally divorce, a close inspection of the divorce verses in the Qur᾿an indicates that *qisṭ* is paramount. Examples of *qisṭ* in divorce include providing women with extra financial resources, prohibiting men from preventing them from remarrying, letting them stay in the marital home during their waiting periods, counselling *maʿrūf* (good) and *iḥsān* and otherwise delineating compassionate treatment of divorced women (verses 2:226–237, 239–242; 33:49; 65:1–7; 66:5). Not once do the verses privilege men or otherwise disadvantage women; in fact, they clearly prohibit men from preventing women from remarrying and taking away any of their possessions (except when both the wife and the husband freely agree due to fear of transgression and the community ratifies this agreement (verses 2:229–232)). Denying women an equal right to divorce constitutes preventing them from remarrying and allows abusive husbands the leverage they need to negotiate with their estranged spouse for financial

---

[54] Related terms include *īlā*᾿ (locational separation), *ẓihār* (sexual separation) and *sarāḥ* or *tasrīḥ* (letting go). *Nushūz* (locational separation), *shiqāq* (split between the couple) and *firāq* (parting of ways) are discussed below.

[55] *Khul*ʿ is borrowed from pre-Islamic (*jāhiliyya*) anecdotes. See Ibn Ḥajar al-ʿAsqalānī (n.d., hadith no. 4971).

[56] Two exceptions address specific cases: once when explaining the details of triple divorce and the second time in connection with the Prophet (verses 2:230; 66:5).

benefits to which they have no right. The use of the plural verb form ensures that the entire community is addressed and thus culpable, not only the abusive husband. Accordingly, it is the entire community's responsibility to ensure that women are not denied their right to divorce.

The Hadith tradition preserves a memory of three women who unilaterally divorced unwilling husbands: Ḥabība bint Sahl, Jamīla (or Zaynab) bint ʿAbd Allāh ibn Ubayy ibn Abī Salūl and Barīra,[57] ʿĀʾisha's freedwoman. The hadith evidence seems to confuse the first two, as can be noted in the similarities and differences in their depictions. Both had reasonable grounds – Jamīla's husband beat her and broke her hand, whereas Ḥabība found her husband repulsive because of his looks. Jamīla's husband was at fault and her brother took her case to the Prophet, while Ḥabība's husband was not at fault, which explains why she returned his orchard to him (al-ʿAsqalānī, n.d., no. 4971). It seems that both Ḥabība and Jamīla (or Zaynab) were known for their beauty – Jamīla means 'beautiful' and could be a description – hence the confusion. In oral traditions like the hadiths and *āthār*, it is not unusual for such confusion to take place. However, it is also possible that jurists chose to keep one tradition alive – the one where a woman had to pay her husband for her freedom – and chose to confuse it with the other one, since it was unpalatable to them for a woman to divorce her husband without paying him for her freedom. Someone who beats his wife to the point of breaking her hand can hardly be described as being 'faultless in character (*khuluq*) and religion'; in fact, her brother even complained to the Prophet about it (al-ʿAsqalānī, n.d., no. 4971).

The third woman, Barīra, is well known for divorcing her husband Mughīth, despite his love for her (al-ʿAsqalānī, n.d., hadith no. 4979). In this instant, al-Bukhārī was unable to utilize the term *khulʿ*, since Barīra did not pay Mughīth anything, so al-Bukhārī retained the term *ṭalāq* in his subheading. Barīra divorced Mughīth (*ṭalāq*), despite his unwillingness and devastation to the point that the Prophet Muhammad sought to intervene on his behalf. Barīra was able to divorce Mughīth because ʿĀʾisha freed her from slavery, which means that a free woman should be able to divorce her husband, despite his refusal, and have this divorce recognized by society and the highest

[57] Barīra is a very important figure for Islamic feminism, but is understudied. She rose to become one of the foremost scholars of her age, yet little of her *fiqh* remains. One of her students was al-Sayyida Sukayna bint al-Ḥusayn, the Prophet Muhammad's great-granddaughter. She was well known for her intelligence and wit, for insisting on attending male-dominated gatherings, and for having divorced several husbands, dragging them to court (to the entertainment of onlookers). Barīra and her students are well worthy of study.

authority of the land (the Prophet), even if this authority sympathized with the ex-husband. However, medieval jurists, who conceptualized divorce in a slave-owning context, could not see beyond social hierarchies. Just as, for them, women ranked below men, slaves ranked below free persons. Although this particular hadith does not state that Mughīth was a slave, jurists explained away Barīra's ability to divorce him on the basis that he was; thus, only a newly freed slave woman could divorce her slave husband, since he was below her in rank (see al-ʿAsqalānī, n.d., commentary on hadith no. 4980). For jurists, the concept of *kafāʾa* (worthiness, social suitability, social equivalence) comes into play. However, the hadith is clear that Barīra divorced Mughīth because she hated him; she did not divorce him because he was socially inferior and thus not *kufʾ* (worthy). In fact, some *āthār* (reports) traced back to ʿĀʾisha state that he was free and thus, not a slave. There is a contradiction in the *āthār*: while some state he was free, others surmise that he was a slave, probably to limit a free woman's ability to divorce a free man. If one removes the lens of social hierarchies, as is more appropriate to Islam's egalitarian message, this incident demonstrates that free women should be able to divorce their husbands without their consent and without recourse to a court, although, of course, a court is necessary to settle financial disputes.

Several rational principles can also be used to argue for women's equal right to *ṭalāq*, including consideration of justice, *qiyās*, blocking the means of harm, custom in some countries and consideration of the common good. Several legal maxims can also be used to make the argument, such as 'the norm in relation to things is that of permissibility', which supports the permissibility of women divorcing their husbands without their permission or consent. Another is 'harm must be eliminated', which similarly suggests that the harm that is inflicted upon women by denying them divorce and keeping them hanging, neither married nor able to remarry, must be eliminated. The related maxim 'removal of harm takes precedence over the bringing of benefits' also applies, as it suggests that the removal of harm to women takes precedence over the benefit to men from using divorce to try to wring money out of their abused spouse. Likewise, 'hardship begets facility' supports a woman's right to be able to divorce an unwanted husband without recourse to a court. 'Acts are judged by their objectives', and the objectives of the protection and preservation of a woman's life and her offspring's (in cases of abusive husbands), her wealth, honour/dignity and intellect (from mental illness due to abuse) all support women being given the legal right to end their marriages without recourse to a court, just like men.

3.2.2 *Cornerstones of divorce*

Here, I point to three cornerstones in divorce: registration, financial provision and waiting periods. As in marriage, registration is what makes a divorce legal; financial provision and waiting periods are what make it ethical. In order for a divorce to be ethical-legal, all three cornerstones must be in evidence.

Registration has been discussed above in relation to marriage and divorce, so there is no need to repeat it here. Suffice to say that, just as in the case of marriage, a divorce that is not registered does not constitute a divorce, whether it is a single or triple *ṭalāq* (in one sitting or interspersed).

Financial provision to divorced women is a right, irrespective of who initiates the divorce (verses 2:228–237, 241; 65:1–7). Minimum requirements are specified in the Qurʾan; however, divorce settlements vary from country to country and can reach half a couple's joint possessions, including the marital home, which is an expression of *ʿadl*. Husbands do not have a right to a wife's possessions, even to the bride-gift he may have given her, unless it is freely given (verse 4:4). Ethicists, jurists and/or the couple will need to weigh between the competing ethical imperatives of *ʿadl* and *qisṭ*, the Qurʾanic stipulations, and the laws of the land when coming to a decision as to who gets what.

Waiting periods are also specified in the Qurʾan: if a woman is pregnant, until she delivers and, if not, three menstrual cycles or three months for those who are menopausal or who have amenorrhea (have not received their period due to malnutrition, physical stresses, or other reasons) (verses 2:228; 65:1–7) (see Amin, 2020). Waiting periods allow for couples to resolve their differences, particularly if a woman is pregnant. Since divorce is not yet final, it is not ethical-legal for either the husband or the wife to remarry during the waiting period.

3.2.3 *Raising the bar: mutual agreement*

Just as *Surat al-Nisāʾ* raises the bar when it comes to the ethics of marriage (above), so too for divorce. Indeed, the sura depicts divorce as a process with stages and associated intervention strategies, the final parting of ways as one by mutual agreement. To this end, the sura introduces three new terms: *nushūz* (separation), *shiqāq* (splitting) and *firāq* (parting of ways), all of which have different nuances that depict different stages in the breakdown of a marriage. It is noteworthy that these unusual terms occur in two contexts: once, when a woman initiates the separation and another time when a man initiates the separation, further affirming a woman's equal right to initiate divorce. In both contexts, the Qur᾿an encourages *iṣlāḥ* (reparation, reconciliation, peacemaking) and points to mediation. These occurrences hint at equality in divorce and at the importance of mediation and reparation when marriages hit a rocky patch (verses 4:34–35, 128–130).

Occurrences of *nushūz, shiqāq* and *firāq* elsewhere in the Qur᾿an can help affirm and further clarify their meaning. The word *nushūz* (to rise, get up and leave, protrude) always denotes a physical displacement.[58] In *Surat al-Mujādila* (verse 58:11), the word occurs in the meaning of bodily rising from a seated position and leaving the gathering area, in order to make room for others to sit down with the Prophet Muhammad or to go perform other duties (al-Zamakhsharī, n.d., vol. 4, p. 359).[59] In *Surat al-Baqara* (verse 2:259), God raises the bones from the dead (*nunshizuhā*), that is, God physically erects them from a lying down position, and then clothes them in flesh, in readiness to walk away. *Shiqāq* has numerous occurrences in the Qur᾿an, sometimes in connection with the splitting or splintering of earth, sky and other geological phenomena, but more importantly in relation to people splitting with God and/or the Prophet, which denotes a break in another kind of covenantal relationship.[60] *Firāq* also occurs multiple times, most notably in verse 18:78 in connection with al-Khiḍr parting ways with Moses and in verse 65:2 referring to a husband and wife parting ways at the end of the waiting period. A close reading thus suggests that *nushūz* refers to the stage when a spouse is getting ready to walk away from the marriage, but when mediation is still possible, and *shiqāq* and *firāq* to more advanced stages: a break in the covenantal relationship and a parting of ways that is more or less final. This three-stage description and the reference to mediation suggests that divorce is a process, not a spur-of-the-moment decision by one partner without consulting the other. In fact, in the case when the husband is the one who distances himself from his wife, the Qur᾿an describes the final break-up as 'if the two of them part ways (*yatafarraqā*), God will provide for each from His bounty', the use of the dual active verb form suggesting that it is a mutual decision (verses 4:128–130).

[58] One should note that both classical and modern jurists seem to have been uncomfortable with the notion that a woman can leave her husband (but not that a man can leave his wife), so they interpreted this term figuratively as 'arrogance' or similar meanings, since physically rising is a form of elevation. For more, see Reda (2019a).

[59] For the various meanings of *nushūz*, see also al-Zabīdī (1994, vol. 8, pp. 159–60). See al-Zabīdī (1994, vol. 2, p. 374) for the heel defined as protruding bone.

[60] See verses 2:137, 176; 4:115; 8:13; 11:89; 16:27; 22:53; 38:2; 41:52; 47:32; 59:4. Derivatives of the same root are also used to denote a split in or splintering of the earth, sky, moon and rocks (verses 2:74; 54:1; 19:90; 25:25; 50:44; 55:37; 69:16; 80:26; 84:1).

The wording of the verses and the detailed process that they describe suggest that an ethical-legal divorce is by mutual agreement, after attempts at reconciliation have failed, not a single partner's unequivocal, unilateral right to rid himself of the other. Accordingly, the laws of countries that allow a husband to unilaterally repudiate his wife, sometimes even irrevocably in a spur-of-the-moment decision, fall short of Qurʾanic ethical-legal instruction and need to be revisited.

CONCLUSION

This chapter has re-envisioned Muslim marriage and divorce in a more egalitarian direction, as a civil contract and covenant between two equals, constructing a new methodology of *uṣūl al-fiqh* to do so. Although just a brief outline, this chapter contends that this new, spiritually integrative methodology is well suited to the needs of the time, responding to the growing spiritual turn on one hand, and to the emergence of the modern state on the other. It respectfully critiques and reconstructs the four main principles of *uṣūl al-fiqh*, demonstrating both continuity and change with the work of past and present scholars, in conversation with the tradition in its entirety. The biggest change is to the principle of consensus, which is reconstructed in the form of the more realistic *shūrā*, thereby providing a theoretical foundation for dealing with the mechanisms of the modern state, while, at the same time, allowing for the continuation of the collective, deliberative character of consensus. In the realm of reason, it has introduced a new principle – consideration of justice – to ensure gender and other justice in processes of ethical reasoning. Sunna continues to be an important resource, albeit to indicate the Prophet's example, but not as an independent source capable of overruling the Qurʾan. The Qurʾan is the mainstay of the methodology and the inspiration for all its principles, but interpreted in more linguistically accurate ways and more holistically.

The timeless words of al-Shāfiʿī succinctly describe the experience of the Qurʾan for scholars of old, as well as new:

> Everything that He has sent down – may His praise be glorified – is a mercy and an authoritative proof. Whoever knows it [the Qurʾan], knows this; and whoever is ignorant of it, is ignorant of this. Whoever is ignorant of it [the Qurʾan], doesn't have knowledge; and whoever

knows it, is never ignorant ... No problematic ethical-legal issue may occur to one of the people of the religion of God except that in the book of God is a proof-text that guides to ways to resolve it. (al-Shāfiʿī, 1938, pp. 19–20; brackets mine)

REFERENCES

Abou-Bakr, Omaima. 2015. 'The Interpretive Legacy of *Qiwamah* as an Exegetical Construct'. In *Men in Charge? Rethinking Authority in Muslim Legal Tradition*, edited by Ziba Mir-Hosseini, Mulki Al-Sharmani and Jana Rumminger, pp. 44–64. London: Oneworld.

Afsaruddin, Asma. 2020. 'Reading the Qurʾan through a Gendered, Egalitarian Lens: Revisiting the Concept of *Wilāya* in Q. 9:71'. In *Islamic Interpretive Tradition and Gender Justice: Processes of Canonization, Subversion, and Change*, edited by Nevin Reda and Yasmin Amin, pp. 100–24. Montreal: McGill-Queen's University Press.

Ahmad, Nehaluddin. 2009. 'A Critical Appraisal of "Triple Divorce" in Islamic Law'. *International Journal of Law, Policy and the Family* 23 (1): pp. 53–61.

Ali, Kecia. 2006. *Sexual Ethics and Islam*. Oxford: Oneworld.

Ali, Kecia. 2010. *Marriage and Slavery in Early Islam*. Cambridge, MA: Harvard University Press.

Al-ʿAlwānī, Zaynab Ṭāhā. 2012. *Al-Usra fī Maqāṣid al-Sharīʿa: Qirāʾa fī Qaḍāyā al-Zawāj wa-l-Ṭalāq fī Amrīkā*. Herndon, Virginia: International Institute of Islamic Thought.

Amin, Yasmin. 2020. 'Revisiting the Issue of Minor Marriages: Multi-disciplinary *Ijtihād* on Contemporary Ethical Problems'. In *Islamic Interpretive Tradition and Gender Justice: Processes of Canonization, Subversion and Change*, edited by Nevin Reda and Yasmin Amin, pp. 314–63. Montreal: McGill-Queen's University Press.

Al-Asadabādī, Al-Qāḍī Abū al-Ḥasan ʿAbd al-Jabbār. 1963. *Al-Mughnī fī Abwāb al-Tawḥīd wa-l-ʿAdl*, edited by Amīn al-Khūlī. Cairo: al-Muʾassasah al-Miṣriyyah al-ʿĀmmah.

Al-ʿAsqalānī, Ibn Ḥajar. n.d. *Fatḥ al-Bārī bi-Sharḥ Ṣaḥīḥ al-Bukhārī, Kitāb al-Nikāḥ, Bāb mā Yuttaqā min Shuʾm al-Marʾa*.

Al-ʿAsqalānī, Ibn Ḥajar. 1968. *Tahdhīb al-Tahdhīb*. Beirut: Dār Ṣādir.

Al-Azri, Khalid. 2011. 'One or Three – Exploring the Scholarly Conflict over the Question of Triple *Talaq* (Divorce) in Islamic Law with Particular Emphasis on Oman'. *Arab Law Quarterly* 25 (3): pp. 277–96.

Al-Azri, Khalid. 2012. *Social and Gender Inequality in Oman: The Power of Religious and Political Tradition*. London: Routledge.

Al-Baghdādī, al-Khaṭīb. 2012. *Al-Kifāya fī ʿUlūm al-Riwāya*, edited by Zakariyyā ʿUmayrāt. Beirut: Dār al-Kutub al-ʿIlmiyya.

Barazangi, Nimat Hafez. 2015. *Woman's Identity and Rethinking the Hadith*. Farnham, Surrey: Ashgate.

Baugh, Carolyn G. 2017. *Child Marriage in Early Islamic Law*. Leiden: Brill.

Al-Bayhaqī, Abū Bakr. 2003. *Al-Jāmiʿ li-Shuʿab al-Īmān*, edited by Mukhtār Aḥmad al-Nadwī. Riyadh: Maktabat al-Rushd.

Brown, Jonathan. 2009. *Hadith: Muhammad's Legacy in the Medieval and Modern World.* Oxford: Oneworld.

Constitution of the Arab Republic of Egypt (*Dustūr Jumhūriyyat Miṣr al-ʿArabiyya*). 2014. www.sis.gov.eg/Newvr/consttt%202014.pdf

Al-Dārimī, ʿAbd Allāh ibn ʿAbd al-Raḥmān. 1978. *Sunan al-Dārimī.* Beirut: Dār al-Kitāb al-ʿArabī.

Al-Ghazālī, Abū Ḥāmid Muḥammad ibn Muḥammad. n.d. *Al-Mustaṣfā min ʿIlm al-Uṣūl*, edited by Ḥamza ibn Zuhayr Ḥāfiẓ. Jeddah: Sharikat al-Madīna al-Munawwara li-l-Nashr.

Hallaq, Wael. 1984. 'Was the Gate of Ijtihad Closed?' *International Journal of Middle East Studies* 16 (3): pp. 3–41.

Hallaq, Wael. 1986a. 'Authoritativeness of Sunni Consensus'. *International Journal of Middle East Studies*, 18 (4): pp. 427–54.

Hallaq, Wael. 1986b. 'On the Origins of the Controversy about the Existence of Mujtahids and the Gate of Ijtihad'. *Studia Islamica* 63 (1): pp. 129–41.

Hallaq, Wael. 2009. *Sharīʿa: Theory, Practice, Transformations.* Cambridge, UK: Cambridge University Press.

Harvey, Ramon. 2019. *The Qurʾan and the Just Society.* Edinburgh: Edinburgh University Press.

Ibn al-ʿArabī, Abū Bakr. n.d. *Aḥkām al-Qurʾān.* Beirut: Dār Ṣādir.

Ibn al-Jawzī, Abū al-Faraj. 1987. *Ṣayd al-Khāṭir*, edited by Ādam Abū Sunayna. Amman: Dār al-Fikr.

Ibn al-Jawzī, Abū al-Faraj. 1989. *Aḥkām al-Nisāʾ*, ed. ʿAbd al-Qādir Aḥmad ʿAbd al-Qādir. Al-Manṣūra, Egypt: Dār al-Wafāʾ.

Ibn al-Jawzī, Abū al-Faraj. 1992. *Al-Ṭibb al-Rūḥānī*, edited by Abū Hājar Muḥammad al-Saʿīd ibn Basyūnī Zaghlūl. Cairo: Maktabat al-Thaqāfa al-Dīniyya.

Ibn Ḥazm, ʿAlī ibn Aḥmad ibn Saʿīd and Taqī al-Dīn Aḥmad ibn Taymiyya. 1357 AH. *Marātib al-Ijmāʿ wa-Yalīh Naqd Marātib al-Ijmāʿ.* Maktabat al-Qudsī li-Ṣāḥibihā Ḥusām al-Dīn al-Qudsī.

Ibn Qayyim al-Jawziyya. 1423 AH. *Iʿlām al-Muwaqqiʿīn min Rabb al-ʿĀlamīn*, edited by Abū ʿUbayda Mashhūr ibn Ḥasan Āl Salmān. Riyadh: Dār Ibn al-Jawzī.

Ibn Rushd, Abū al-Walīd. 2004. *Bidāyat al-Mujtahid wa-Nihāyat al-Muqtaṣid*, edited by Farīd ʿAbd al-ʿAzīz al-Jindī. Cairo: Dār al-Ḥadīth.

Al-Jazīrī, ʿAbd al-Raḥmān, Muḥammad al-Gharawī and Yāsir Māziḥ. 1998. *Al-Fiqh ʿalā al-Madhāhib al-Arbaʿa wa-Madhhab Ahl al-Bayt.* Beirut: Dār al-Thaqalayn.

Juynboll, G. H. A. 1989. 'Some Isnād-analytical Methods Illustrated on the Basis of Several Women-demeaning Sayings from Ḥadīth Literature'. *Al-Qantara* 10 (2): pp. 343–84.

Kamali, Mohammad Hashim. 2008. *Shariah Law: An Introduction.* London: Oneworld.

Kamali, Mohammad Hashim. 2009. 'Law and Ethics in Islam—the Role of the *Maqāṣid*'. In *New Directions in Islamic Thought: Exploring Reform and Muslim Tradition*, edited by Kari Vogt, Lena Larsen and Christian Moe, pp. 23–46. London: I.B. Tauris.

Kaʿwāsh, Maylūd. 2009. *Ḥaqq al-Zawja fī al-Kadd wa-l-Siʿāya; Dirāsa fī al-Turāth al-Fiqhī al-Mālikī.* Rabat: al-Rabiṭa al-Muḥammadiyya li-l-ʿUlamāʾ.

Mir-Hosseini, Ziba. 2008. 'Classical *Fiqh*, Contemporary Ethics, and Gender Justice'. In *New Directions in Islamic Thought: Exploring Reform and Muslim Tradition*, edited by Kari Vogt, Lena Larsen and Christian Moe, pp. 77–88. London: I.B. Tauris.

Mir-Hosseini, Ziba. 2012. 'Sexuality and Inequality: The Marriage Contract in Muslim Legal Tradition'. In *Sexuality in Muslim Contexts: Restrictions and Resistance*, edited by Anissa Hélie and Homa Hoodfar, pp. 124–48. London: Zed Books.

Musawah. 2017. 'Islam and the Question of Gender Equality'. Knowledge Building Brief no. 3. www.musawah.org/wp-content/uploads/2019/02/KnowledgeBuildingBriefs-3-Islam-and-the-Question-of-Gender-Equality-EN.pdf

Al-Nawawī, Abū Zakariyya Yaḥyā ibn Sharaf. n.d. *Shurūḥ al-Nawawī ʿalā Muslim, Kitāb al-Salām, bāb lā ʿAdwā, wa-lā Ṭayra wa-lā Hāma*.

Noor, Zanariah and Nazirah Lee. 2014. 'The Conflict among Hadrami Arab Community in Malaysia Regarding the Issues of Kafā'a in Muslim Marriage'. *Hawwa: Journal of Women of the Middle East and the Islamic World* 11 (2–3): pp. 252–74.

Al-Qaraḍāwī, Yūsuf. 1991. *Kayfa Nataʿāmal maʿ al-Sunna al-Nabawiyya: Maʿālim wa-Ḍawābiṭ*. Riyadh: Maktabat al-Muʾayyad.

Quraishi-Landes, Asifa. 2021. 'A Meditation on *Mahr*, Modernity, and Muslim Marriage Contract Law'. In *Half of Faith: American Muslim Marriage and Divorce in the Twenty-First Century*, edited by Kecia Ali, pp. 52–67. Boston: OpenBU.

Al-Qurṭubī, Muḥammad in Aḥmad. 2006. *Al-Jāmiʿ li-Aḥkām al-Qurʾān*, edited by ʿAbd Allāh ibn ʿAbd al-Muḥsin al-Turkī. Beirut: al-Risāla.

Reda, Nevin. 2004. 'Women in the Mosque: Historical Perspectives on Segregation'. *American Journal of Islamic Social Sciences* 21 (2): pp. 77–97.

Reda, Nevin. 2013. 'From Where Do We Derive "God's Law"? The Case of Women's Political Leadership: A Modern Expression of an Ancient Debate'. In *Feminism and Islamic Perspectives: New Horizons of Knowledge and Reform*, edited by Omaima Abou-Bakr, pp. 119–35. Cairo: Women and Memory Forum.

Reda, Nevin. 2015. 'From the Canadian Sharia Debates to the Arab World: Developing a Qurʾan-Based Theology of Democracy'. In *Religion and Democracy: Islam and Representation*, edited by Ingrid Mattson, Paul Nesbitt-Larking and Nawaz Tahir, pp. 78–100. Newcastle upon Tyne: Cambridge Scholars Publishing.

Reda, Nevin. 2018. 'What is Islam: The Importance of Being Islamic in Christian Theological Schools'. *Journal of Islam and Christian-Muslim Relations* 29 (3): pp. 309–29.

Reda, Nevin. 2019a. 'The Qurʾan and Domestic Violence: A Spiritually Integrative Reading of Verse 4:34'. *International Journal of Practical Theology* 23 (2): pp. 257–73.

Reda, Nevin. 2019b. 'What is the Qurʾan? A Spiritually Integrative Perspective'. *Journal of Islam and Christian-Muslim Relations* 30 (2): pp. 127–48.

Reda, Nevin. 2020. '*Tafsīr*, Tradition, and Methodological Contestations: The Case of Polygamy'. In *Islamic Interpretive Tradition and Gender Justice: Processes of Canonization, Subversion, and Change*, edited by Nevin Reda and Yasmin Amin, pp. 67–99. Montreal: McGill-Queen's University Press.

Al-Ṣawwāṭ, Muḥammad ibn ʿAbd Allāh ibn ʿĀbid. 2001 (1422 AH). *Al-Qawāʿid wa-al-Ḍawābiṭ al-Fiqhiyya ʿinda Ibn Taymiyya fī Fiqh al-Usra*. Taif: Maktabat Dār al-Bayān al-Ḥadītha.

Al-Shāfiʿī, Muḥammad ibn Idrīs. 1938. *Al-Risāla*, edited by Aḥmad Muḥammad Shākir. Cairo: Muṣṭafā al-Bābī al-Ḥalabī.

El Shamsy, Ahmed. 2013. *The Canonization of Islamic Law: A Social and Intellectual History*. New York: Cambridge University Press.

Al-Sharmani, Mulki. 2013. 'Reforming Egyptian Family Laws: The Debate about a New Substantive Code'. In *Feminist Activism, Women's Rights and Legal Reform*, edited by Mulki Al-Sharmani, pp. 73–100. London: Zed Books.

Al-Sharmani, Mulki. 2014. 'Legal Reform, Women's Empowerment, and Social Change: The Case of Egypt'. In *Feminisms, Empowerment and Development: Changing Women's Lives*, edited by Andrea Cornwall and Jenny Edwards, pp. 32–48. London: Zed Books.

Al-Sharmani, Mulki. 2018. 'Marriage in Islamic Interpretive Tradition: Revisiting the Legal and the Ethical'. *Journal of Islamic Ethics* 2 (1–2), pp. 76–96.

Ṭayfūr, Abū al-Faḍl Aḥmad ibn Abī Ṭāhir. 1908. *Balāghāt al-Nisā'*, edited by Aḥmad al-Alfī. Cairo: Maṭba'at Madrasat Wālidat 'Abbās al-Awwal.

Wadud, Amina. 1992. *Qur'an and Woman*. Kuala Lumpur: Penerbit Fajar Bakti Sdn. Bhd.

Al-Zabīdī, Muḥammad Murtaḍā. 1994. *Tāj al-'Arūs min Jawāhir al-Qāmūs*. Beirut: Dār al-Fikr.

Al-Zamakhsharī, Maḥmūd ibn 'Umar. n.d. *Al-Kashshāf 'an Ḥaqā'iq al-Tanzīl wa-'Uyūn al-Aqāwīl fī Wujūh al-Ta'wīl*, edited by Yūsuf al-Ḥammādī. Al-Fajjālah, Cairo: Maktabat Miṣr.

Ethics and Gender Equality in Islam: A Constructivist Approach

Mariam Al-Attar

Patriarchal religious discourses, juristic rulings and modern *fiqh*-based family laws are often justified on the grounds that they are implementation of Shariʿa, which is commonly understood by Muslims to be divine and just. While we can agree that within the framework of Islamic faith Shariʿa is divine and just, the problem is that it is often erroneously conflated with the body of legal rulings (*fiqh*) formulated by pre-modern jurists.

Islamic Shariʿa, as many modern Muslim scholars have persuasively argued, is first and foremost an ethical paradigm that presents the totality of the moral teachings and norms found in the Qurʾan and Sunna. However, the understanding of Shariʿa as an ethical paradigm (and the implications of this) remains a perspective that is not widely shared. Even if that understanding is to successfully take root, there are still further important questions with which we need to grapple. Such questions have been largely ignored by contemporary Muslim scholars. They include: What is the nature of morality and what sources of moral knowledge could inform egalitarian Muslim gender norms? Are norms simply to be discovered from textual sources or the natural world? What is the role for human reasoning and specifically ethical reasoning in these processes? And what shapes and characterizes the kind of ethical reasoning that can unmask patriarchy and lay the foundation for gender equality? These questions, although theoretical in nature, are important for establishing a philosophical foundation for ethical thought. They cannot be disregarded, especially in a time when the ethical perspective is being prioritized by many Muslims. The main aim of this chapter is to engage with these questions and attempt to arrive at reasonable answers based on classical Islamic theories that pertain to ethics and recent developments in moral philosophy.

The first section of the chapter reviews how various issues related to ethics (as a discourse with distinct questions) have been discussed under different genres of Islamic disciplines including *kalām* (speculative theology), *fiqh* and *uṣūl al-fiqh* (law and jurisprudence), *taṣawuf* (Islamic mysticism) and *falsafa* (philosophy). It explicates the challenges and implications of the fragmental and piecemeal approach to ethics and the hegemony of Islamic jurisprudence over other genres in the course of the history of this intellectual tradition. It also presents modern developments related to the study of ethics in Islamic tradition and the potentialities for a systematic inquiry in ethics as a field of knowledge. However, this section by no means attempts to provide a comprehensive review of the present status of works on ethics or examine all ethical issues in different Islamic disciplines in detail, since this is beyond the objectives of this chapter.

The second section focuses on the nature of moral values (the foundations of morality) and the nature and formation of moral judgements (*aḥkām*). In this section, I argue for a set of rational criteria for evaluating moral judgements, by building on the theory of rational obligation (*al-taklīf al-ʿaqlī*) and the presuppositions of moral judgements (*shurūṭ ḥusn al-taklīf*) introduced by the earliest Muslim theologians, the Muʿtazilites.

My inquiry into the nature of moral judgements and the foundations of morality is in fact motivated by the ideas and arguments that I encountered in the works of *kalām*, especially in *al-Mughnī fī Abwāb al-Tawḥīd wa-l-ʿAdl* by the tenth/eleventh-century scholar ʿAbd al-Jabbār ibn Ahmad (d. 415 AH/1025 CE). It prompted me to search for a refinement and elucidation of some rudimentary ideas that are present in his work like those related to the rationality and objectivity of moral judgements. I could not find what I was looking for in the works of his successors or his opponents. I found it elsewhere, in the later developments made in the field of contemporary moral philosophy.

In this chapter, I also develop an understanding of two of those presuppositions that were not fully elaborated in the past, namely rationality and objectivity. In doing so, I build upon some contemporary understandings of the rules of practical reason, rules that any moral judgement needs to abide by in order to be true. I argue that moral judgements (*aḥkām*) are, in fact, constructed rather than discovered or invented and that by adopting a form of constructivism we can avoid both ethical relativism according to which anything goes, and moral absolutism which implies that moral judgements, rules and regulations are static and absolute. I contend that by embracing universal Qurʾanic moral values and the rules of practical reason, we can develop criteria for assessing judgements, for example in relation to gender relations and rights. I conclude with some reflections on the implications of my argument for the question of norm making and gender justice.

1. ETHICS IN THE ISLAMIC DISCIPLINES

The importance of ethics has been emphasized by many Muslim reformers who have argued that the classical juristic tradition must be examined and interrogated through what Khaled Abou El Fadl (2017, p. 9) calls 'the probative lens of ethical and moral theory'. In the context of religious societies, the cultivation of ethos or an ethical dimension also 'prevents the emergence of religious radicalism, based on ignorance, exclusiveness, intolerance and even violence', as noted by Raid al-Daghistani (2018, p. 2). Ebrahim Moosa also rightly maintains that 'Muslims today must work to make the ethical apparatus the lens through which one evaluates practices' (2020, p. 245) and that 'ethics cannot be beyond reason and rationality' (2017, p. xiv).

I believe that trying to understand or develop Islamic ethics based only on divine texts, without scrutinizing textual and historical contexts and ontological and epistemological assumptions, is an impossible mission. Indeed, pretending that one can construct ethics from the sacred texts without taking into consideration Muslim thought is tantamount to denying the very philosophical premises of a culture or a tradition, as argued by Zahra Ayubi (2019, p. 278). Different theo-philosophical, ontological and epistemological premises, including the conception of human being, divinity and moral values, informed and will always inform interpretations of the sacred text and the understanding of morality.

Asma Barlas, amina wadud, Kecia Ali and other scholars who engage with gender and Islam have focused on critiquing the theological presuppositions related to the God–human relationship that informs how law is created and discussed (Ahmed, 2019, p. 126). Nevertheless, theological and philosophical presuppositions about the meaning of moral judgements and the nature of moral values, including justice, are among the foundational assumptions of Islamic thought that also need to be critiqued in a way that challenges the patriarchal assumptions that permeate judgements related to gender.

Ethics or moral philosophy as understood today[1] has never been a separate domain of inquiry in traditional Islamic disciplines. This does not mean that morality was not a concern to classical Muslim scholars. On the contrary, all the religious science disciplines were pervaded by moral concerns. Contemporary scholars writing on Islamic ethics investigate issues that pertain to ethics in different classical works that belong to the established field of religious disciplines, and thus classify ethical issues according to the discipline under which it is discussed. Therefore, we have ethics in *kalām*, *fiqh*, *taṣawuf* and of course *falsafa* (philosophy).[2]

Questions related to metaethics, that is the meaning of obligation, right and wrong, good and evil, and the sources of our moral knowledge, were mainly dealt with in *kalām* and *uṣūl al-fiqh*. *Fiqh* is mainly focused on rules and regulations derived from the sources established in *uṣūl al-fiqh*. Thus, we can say that it is closer to normative ethics and practical or applied ethics. Of course, *fiqh*, *uṣūl al-fiqh* and *ʿilm al-kalām* are not disciplines that are exclusively concerned with ethics. Yet, among contemporary scholars, Kevin Reinhart argues that *fiqh* and *uṣūl al-fiqh* must be the focus of the discussion of Islamic ethics since ethics is basically a practical science that studies normative actions (Reinhart, 1983, p. 186). Other scholars, contending the hegemony of *fiqh* over all other Islamic disciplines, argue for the need of a clear demarcation between what is legal and what is ethical (Rahman, 2021). Nevertheless, to understand any normative action, talk or thought we need to understand what it assumes and presupposes. Presuppositions of normative judgements,

[1] Ethics or the philosophy of morality investigates and questions the prevailing moral values and norms and seeks a deeper understanding of the nature of morality. It is now usually divided into three branches: normative ethics, metaethics and applied ethics. While normative ethics investigates norms, principles and rules that should guide human behaviour and can include deontological, consequentialist, virtue ethics or a combination of these, metaethics investigates the meaning and the foundations of those norms and principles. Examples of metaethical theories include natural law theory, divine command theory, intuitionism, prescriptivism and other theories that ground normative ethics. See Sayre-McCord (2014). Applied ethics is the field of inquiry that applies moral theories and norms to various human activities like medicine, business, engineering, finance, environment, etc.

[2] For example, see Ansari (1989) and Subḥi (1969), who was one of the first Arab thinkers to study ethics in the *kalām* tradition and in Sufism in his book on moral philosophy in Islamic thought.

including psychological, epistemological and metaphysical, are mainly discussed in the works of *kalām*, as we will see below. George F. Hourani rightly maintained that '*kalām* is the second major occurrence in history of a profound discussion on the meanings and general content of ethical concepts. The first being that of the ancient Greek philosophers' (Hourani, 1985, p. 21).

In the works of the Sufis and the philosophers who produced the classical works of *akhlāq* literature, the focus is mainly on virtue ethics, that is, the moral virtues and the refinement of individual character. This diverse literature, known traditionally as *akhlāq*, also includes teachings of Prophet Muhammad and other religious figures and philosophical reflections. In what follows, I briefly examine the ethical questions tackled in *kalām*, *fiqh* and *uṣūl al-fiqh* and *falsafa* tradition.

1.1 Speculative theology (*kalām*)

In the field of *kalām*, as mentioned above, various issues pertaining to metaethical questions were discussed, such as human free will and capacity for action, the nature of moral values, moral ontology and moral epistemology. This does not mean that *kalām* has mainly been about ethical and metaethical issues. It is primarily concerned with establishing true religious belief. Thus, it was sometimes called *uṣūl al-dīn*, which literally means 'the foundations of religion', as it seeks to understand and defend basic Islamic beliefs, including the nature and the meaning of divine attributes, the relation between God and the world, and the implication of this relation. In *kalām*, discussions about the divine attribute of justice build upon justice as understood in this world. The discussion of the divine attribute of goodness also starts by exploring the value of goodness and what it means for something or for an action to be good. Important ideas and theories that are related to metaethical issues can be reconstructed from the views of the classical Muslim scholars, since a guiding principle in the development of early *kalām* was the analogy from the seen to the unseen (*qiyās al-ghā'ib 'ala al-shāhid*).

Three schools of *'ilm al-kalām* emerged in Islam: the Mu'tazilites, the Ash'arites and the Māturidis. The first two schools often held opposite views regarding different issues, including those pertaining to ethics, while the Māturidi school witnessed developments and varieties of positions advocated by various Māturidi scholars. The views of al-Māturidi (the epitome of the school) that are related to different ethical concerns were closer to the

Muʿtazilites than the Ashʿarites (Harvey, 2018, p. 38). The Muʿtazilite views were later incorporated in the Shiʿite schools of thought, while the Ashʿarite and Māturidite views prevailed in the Sunni thought (see Kadivar in this volume). The Muʿtazilites lost their popularity in Sunni Islam for political reasons that are beyond the concern of this chapter. However, they represent the school of thought that prevailed in Sunni Islam from the early eighth century until the end of the tenth century. It seems that it is only after the integration of *kalām* and *fiqh* in the eleventh century by Imām al-Ḥaramayn al-Juwaynī (d. 419 AH/1085 CE) that the Ashʿarite theology was integrated into the body of Sunni orthodoxy (Widigdo, 2019, p. 166). But it is important to mention that not all Sunnis are Ashʿarites and that most ordinary Muslims today do not identify with any school of *kalām*. This is partly due to the fact that the prevailing discourse does not favour engagement in *kalām*, and partly because the polemics between different schools are seen as matters of the past that are not relevant to today's concerns.

Ashʿarite theologians adhered to a position known today as 'theological voluntarism', which is in fact a metaethical theory that is disputed by the more rationally minded scholars in the present and by those who are said to have Muʿtazilite tendencies among the early jurists and theologians. Theological voluntarism is a metaethical theory that centres divine absolute will rather than God's justice or goodness in determining moral and ethical concepts. Hence, goodness or justice, for example, are whatever God wills and cannot be defined or understood otherwise. However, how do we determine God's will and intentions? Our understandings of God's will and intentions were in fact constructed by religious scholars ('ulama') who had a system of values and interests that reflected their times and customs. Their context influenced the way they understood the divine message and the ethical concepts they derived from that understanding. Thus, ethical or theological voluntarism calls upon God's authority to sanctify human-made interpretations and understandings.

Although held by scholars who presumably had good intentions, this theory has been utilized to justify political and social oppressions in the name of God. This is similar in other religions and traditions. As noted by J. B. Schneewind (2010, p. 206), the 'fear that voluntarism had unacceptable political implications was never out of sight and voluntarism seemed to pose a problem for anyone who shared moral and political concerns'. Voluntarism, as argued by contemporary Muslim scholar Ramon Harvey, clearly 'gives the opportunity for political authority to be held in God's name' (2018, p. 83). Theological voluntarism was held so strongly that when it came to the question of the objectives of the Shariʿa (*al-maqāṣid al-sharīʿa*), justice for and in the society was not included among the five universal necessities (*al-kulliyāt al-khamsa*) that were considered the divine purposes (Askari and Mirakhor, 2020, pp. 17–18). This has been noted by many contemporary scholars. The divine purposes were articulated in the works of *uṣūl al-fiqh* and *kalām*. The theory of *maqāṣid* will be briefly discussed in the next part.

1.2 Islamic jurisprudence (*fiqh* and *uṣūl al-fiqh*)

A large number of *fiqh* rules and regulations are related to morality, as they tend to regularize human actions and behaviour. One can say that it is indeed the closest discipline to normative ethics. Classical Muslim jurists referred to *fiqh* manuals when passing their judgements. However, not all *fiqh* rules and principles are legal in nature. Some are moral and cannot be sanctioned by law and others are related to dietary obligations and rituals. The sources of law and ethics that are traditionally accepted by the majority of classical Muslim scholars include the Qurʾan, the Sunna, *qiyās* (reasoning by analogy) and *ijmāʿ* (consensus). Islamic normative ethics is a combination of different discourses merging duty-based rules of *fiqh* (which can be compared to deontological (duty-based) ethics) with a teleological or a consequentialist (results-based) approach of *maṣlaḥa* (public well-being or interest) and *maqāṣid*.

For the early jurists, who accepted *istiḥsān* (reason and preference) as a source for deriving moral and legal judgements, the criteria for the rightness of an action were related to *maṣlaḥa*. Later, the principle of *istiḥsān* as a source of law was disputed by jurists who were eager to ground all the judgements and rules in revelation and the prophetic tradition. This was the position of al-Shāfiʿī (d. 820 CE), who is often considered to be the founder of legal theory or *uṣūl al-fiqh*. *Al-qiyās* (reasoning by analogy) and *al-ijmāʿ* (consensus) allowed the jurists to extrapolate the law and apply it to all aspects of life while still tracing it back to a divine foundation. Many of the legal norms were thus considered and are still considered divine, immutable and absolute.[3] Laws and regulations of *fiqh* are generally considered by the jurists and the common people to be 'discovered not produced' (Reinhart, 1983, p. 188), which is

[3] For a critique of the methodology of *uṣūl al-fiqh* (the principles of jurisprudence), see Nevin Reda's contribution to this volume. For an approach to *fiqh* that operates within the framework of 'rational ethics', see Mohsen Kadivar's chapter in this volume.

disputed by many Muslim and non-Muslim scholars. Neither all law nor all morality is discovered, as will be argued in the second part of this chapter.

Many modern and contemporary Muslim scholars find the theory of *maqāṣid al-sharīʿa* an adequate tool that can help in amending some outdated *fiqh* rules constructed by medieval Muslim scholars. The *maqāṣid* theory, notably, has become one of the 'main religious frameworks guiding contemporary Islamic ethical deliberations' (Abou-Bakr and Al-Sharmani, 2020, p. 36). However, these *maqāṣid* or purposes, as articulated by medieval Muslim jurists, represent the 'interests' of a religio-political community who wished to preserve religion, life, intellect, property and family. These interests, as stated by Ebrahim Moosa (2017, p. xiv), are not moral imperatives. Traditionally the *maqāṣid* were articulated by the Ashʿarite theologians, who derived these aims or purposes through the induction process from specific legal rules and judgements. However, there is also a realization that *fiqh*-based *ijtihād* alone is no longer adequate to assess modern developments, and that there exists a 'dire need to move from a juristic towards an ethical approach in dealing with emerging issues' (al-Khaṭīb, 2019, p. 5).

Also, it is important to emphasize that judgements (*aḥkām*) in Islamic thought, whether moral or legal, include the obligatory (*wājib*), recommended (*mustaḥab*), permissible (*mubāḥ*), discouraged (*makrūh*) and prohibited (*maḥẓūr*). These judgements are the judgements of actions or behaviours of rational agents (*al-mukallafīn*). In theory, all Islamic laws are divided into two categories – *ʿibādāt* (concerning ritual worship) and *muʿāmalāt* (concerning interactions between humans) – and it is within the latter that 'innovations or creative determinations are favored' (Abou El Fadl, 2016, p. 26). Moreover, the earliest Muslim theologians, the Muʿtazilites, distinguished between what they called rational obligation (*taklīf ʿaqlī*) and religious obligation (*taklīf samʿī*) (Al-Attar, 2010, p. 77). Any reconstruction of moral theories that are compatible with contemporary morality and relevant to current moral concern thus belongs to the realm of *muʿāmalāt* and *al-taklīf ʿaqlī* and is mainly concerned with what is obliged by reason without contradicting what is obliged by revelation.

1.3 Ethics (*ʿilm al-akhlāq*)

Akhlāq refers to ethics or moral philosophy. However, '*akhlāq*' in Arabic, like 'ethics' in English, is often used to refer to a diverse genre of literature, including moral philosophy or philosophical ethics. The literature of *akhlāq* 'spans materials as diverse as sayings of the Prophet and other pious figures, philosophers' classification of virtue and Sufi descriptions of personal and spiritual development' (Vishanoff, 2020, p. 12). But it is *akhlāq* that deals with questions that are both profound and philosophically interesting which is the focus of this chapter. *Akhlāq, falsafat al-akhlāq* or *'ilm al-akhlāq* are often used synonymously to refer to moral philosophy, which is evident from the works written by Ahmad Amin (1953), Tawfīq al-Ṭawīl (1979) and many others who focused on philosophical ethics in Islam like Ahmad Maḥmoud Subḥi (1969) and Muhammad Yusef Mousa (1963). Philosophically interesting questions are those about the nature and foundations of morality, whether they are tackled in *kalām, fiqh, akhlāq* or elsewhere.

However, when we talk about the *akhlāq* tradition in early Islamic culture we are referring to the works written by early Muslim philosophers such as al-Kindī (d. 256 AH/870 CE), al-Farabi (d. 338 AH/950 CE) and Ibn Miskawayh (d. 421 AH/1030 CE), who is labelled as the chief moral philosopher of Islam. These and many other Muslim philosophers who followed in the Greek tradition since the middle of the ninth century developed a version of virtue ethics in the tradition of Aristotle. The *akhlāq* tradition is sometimes singled out as 'the philosophical' tradition in Islamic ethics, but that is only because it was developed by those who were recognized as philosophers because they engaged with the Greek philosophical tradition.

What both virtue ethics in the *akhlāq* tradition and Sufi ethics have in common is the preoccupation with the individual and the refinement of character. No doubt one's character contributes to one's well-being in this world and salvation in the Hereafter, as well as to the establishment of better social relations. As described by Cyrus Zargar (2017, p. 301), virtue ethics in both Islamic philosophy and Sufism 'responds to the profoundest of human desires, a desire that lies at the heart of what it means to be human, the desire for self-perfection'. Virtue ethics also persisted as the dominant approach in western moral philosophy until at least the Enlightenment. It suffered a momentary eclipse during the nineteenth century, but re-emerged in Anglo-American philosophy in the late 1950s. But it is currently one of three major approaches in normative ethics (Hursthouse and Pettigrove, 2018). It is important to mention that each of the above-mentioned approaches to normative ethics can make room for virtues, consequences and rules. Indeed, any plausible normative ethical theory will have something to say about all three (Hursthouse and Pettigrove, 2018). Yet, one of the main criticisms raised against virtue ethics is that it is, in principle, unable to provide action-oriented guidance. It seems to me that ethical theories which are able to provide action-guidance should be the focus of ethics that aspires to make a change and ultimately result in institutional reform.

Recently, Zahra Ayubi (2019) critically investigated texts that belong to the *akhlāq* tradition, unveiling the hierarchical nature and biases that prevail in them. She concluded that these texts are clearly written for the elite men of the time, excluding women and other less fortunate men. Ethics in the works studied by Ayubi has been constructed as an exclusively male tradition, which is not surprising, given the fact that the authors of those texts lived in an era when patriarchy was still the dominant norm everywhere and was approved by all cultures and religious traditions (Al-Attar, 2013, p. 73).

1.4 Contemporary developments

Over the course of history of Islamic intellectual tradition, *fiqh* became the dominant discourse, with detrimental consequences for the question of gender. For example, the common understanding of Shariʿa as divine law and synonymous with *fiqh* has become widespread. This understanding furthermore conceals the patriarchal contexts and social norms of early jurists, which influenced their processes of norm and law-making. It also results in conflating ethics with law, with little reflection on the former (that is, what is legal according to the jurists is by definition ethical since it is assumed to represent the Shariʿa). However, some scholars have recently pointed out that 'with the weakening of the classical dominant religious worldview that used to govern the entire society, ethics became an independent and interdisciplinary philosophical field' (Hashas and al-Khaṭīb, 2020, p. 3).

A number of recent developments in Islamic intellectual thought that emphasize ethics are promising. First, there is resurgence of the Muʿtazilite ethical views, which is evident in the works of many modern and contemporary Muslim scholars and reformers starting with Muḥammad ʿAbduh (d. 1905), Tahar al-Haddad (d. 1935) and Ahmad Amin (d. 1953), among others. Second, there is growing scholarship that investigates the Qurʾan as an ethical text (for example, Draz (2008, originally published in 1951), Rahbar (1960), Izutsu (1959), Rahman (1980) and many others).[4] Additionally, classical

[4] For a thematic and structural analysis and critique of these attempts, see Rashwānī (2017).

works and manuscripts in theology, philosophy and Sufism that are attentive to ethics are being published and translations and engagement with contemporary western ethical theories have appeared. Moreover, there is now a growing trend of engagement with different fields of applied ethics such as bioethics, business ethics, environmental ethics, etc.[5] Also, a growing number of scholars identify with Islamic feminism. They are challenging and exposing outdated patriarchal legal postulates, such as *qiwāma* and *wilāya*, that allow for discrimination against half of the society (see, for example, Mir-Hosseini et al., 2015). Their insights into the meaning of religious texts prioritize ethics and ethical reasoning over slavish adherence to the prevailing legalistic discourses. Books are being published under the rubric of Islamic ethics that include different sections looking into the ethical dimension of various Islamic disciplines.[6] Such recent intellectual efforts reveal a growing awareness of the significance of ethics and ethical reasoning.[7] However, that does not compensate for the true engagement with ethics as an important field of inquiry, with its own questions, concepts, theories and problems.[8]

I believe that if one is concerned with questions related to ethics rather than the history of ethical thought in Islam, then identifying and discussing different normative and metaethical theories in Islamic thought might be the more fecund approach. Also, classical Islamic disciplines are usually themselves classified according to sectorial affiliations. Needless to say, ethics and ethical reasoning transcend sectorial affiliations and polemics found in many

[5] See the *Journal of Islamic Ethics* first published by Brill in 2017.

[6] For example, through correspondence with editors I am aware of two edited volumes being prepared that will include parts on Qur᾿anic ethics, theological ethics, Sufi ethics, legal ethics and practical ethics. They will be published by Routledge under the title *The Routledge Handbook of Islamic Ethics* and by Bloomsbury under the provisional title of *Islamic Ethics*. The classification of ethics into scriptural, theological and philosophical partly follows Fakhry (1991).

[7] For a more comprehensive review of the main works that contributed to the development of Islamic ethics, see Hashas and al-Khaṭīb (2020).

[8] Examples of works that engage with ethics as a field of inquiry in classical Islamic thought include Hourani (1985), which contains sixteen articles published between 1960 and 1982. Most of the articles, including the article on al-Juwaynī, al-Ghazāli and Ibn Hazm, are centred around the controversy about the ontological status of moral values and the source of our knowledge of them. Hourani's *Islamic Rationalism: The Ethics of ʿAbd al-Jabbār* (1971) is a pioneering work and the first systematic attempt in the English language to engage with philosophical ethics found in the work of *kalām*. The ninth Giorgio Levi Della Vida Conference in 1983, which focused on 'Ethics in Islam', marks a turning point in studying Islamic ethics (proceedings available at Hovannisian, 1985), in addition to articles of Richard M. Frank (2005; 2007; 2008) related to ethics in the work of *kalām*. An important article related to the nature of moral values in Islamic thought was written by the Lebanese scholar Michael E. Marmura (1994).

works of *kalām*. Valid ethical arguments trump any sectorial affiliations and do not properly belong to the realm of any of the above-mentioned disciplines.

A serious engagement with questions of ethics requires, I contend, developing theories that connect and build on the ethical theories and norms found in the above-mentioned genres of Islamic disciplines in light of contemporary notions of justice and developments in moral philosophy. After all, we need to remember that some of the great scholars of the past fully engaged with the Hellenistic world. They assimilated philosophical theories and ideas from Greek philosophy that prevailed at the time. Such scholars include not only philosophers such as al-Farabi (d. 339 AH/950 CE), Ibn Sina (d. 427 AH/1037 CE) and Ibn Rushd (d. 595 AH/1198 CE), but also theologians and jurists such as Abū Hamīd al-Ghazāli (d. 505 AH/1111 CE) and Fakhr al-Dīn al-Rāẓī (d. 606 AH/1209 CE), among others.[9] Indeed, contemporary Muslim scholars need to engage with different philosophical and scientific traditions and keep up to date with the latest fruits of humans' endeavours while staying faithful to their own tradition.

An important development in contemporary ethical thought is a set of theories that adopt a constructivist approach. It likely developed in response to the critiques raised against different versions of deontological and consequentialist theories in ethics, and the assumptions that underlie these theories, most importantly absolutism. The term 'constructivism' itself entered debates in moral theory with John Rawls' seminal Dewey Lecture 'Kantian Constructivism in Moral Theory' (1980). Constructivists 'aim to develop a non-skeptical, non-realist account of normative truth' (Barry, 2018, p. 386). Moral constructivism is 'a significant view in metaethics that is often contrasted with moral realism[10] and expressivism,'[11] as argued by Muhammad Legenhausen (n.d.). This indicates that morality is not absolute and static, nor is it relative to individuals or societies. Moral norms do not exist independently but are constructed by human deliberation, taking into consideration universal moral values such as, for example, the Qur'anic values of *ʿadl* and *iḥsān* and also the

[9] For more on Islamic philosophy in general, see Khalidi (2005), Adamson (2016), López-Farjeat (2021).

[10] Moral realism is the view that there are objective, mind-independent facts of the matter about which actions are right and which wrong, and which things are good and which bad.

[11] Expressivism is a theory about the subject matter of morality, about the nature of moral thought and about the meaning of moral language. It 'suggests that the function of moral language is to express desire like attitudes.' Thus, it is a version of ethical relativism. See van Roojen (2015).

relevant social context. It is true that traditionally, most religious thinkers in the West and in the Islamic tradition have been moral realists. However, this is no longer the case today. As Kevin Jung notes, 'Contemporary religious ethicists often implicitly, if not explicitly, endorse antirealism' (2018, p. 8).

I first came across the concept of constructivism when I was working on a paper on food ethics in Islam and read a chapter by Ebrahim Moosa (2009) in which he argued for a constructivist approach to ethics. I was reminded of the concept again while reading '*Al-Akhlāq wal 'Aql*' or *Ethics and Reason: A Critique of Western Philosophy* by Adel Daher (1990), the Lebanese Arab philosopher who is mainly concerned with ethics and political philosophy. Daher does not mention constructivism, but it seems obvious that his views are compatible with a version of constructivism that is close to John Rawls' interpretation of Kant.

Similarly, I have found that contemporary Islamic feminists and reformers often talk of 'constructing' norms and moral values that build upon both Islamic principles and universal human rights. For example, different derivatives of the word 'construct' (including constructing, constructed, construction) are used more than 150 times in amina wadud's *Inside the Gender Jihad* (2006) and 125 times in *Men in Charge?* edited by Mir-Hosseini et al. (2015). As far as I know the term was popularized by the late Indian thinker and reformer Muhammad Iqbal, who wrote *The Reconstruction of Religious Thought in Islam* (1934). The key word 'Reconstruction' in the title has connotations of rebuilding and renewing, using a mixture of pre-existing and new materials. In this work Iqbal makes substantial reference to German thinkers, including Kant, Hegel, Goethe and Schopenhauer, as well as French thinkers such as Bergson and Descartes.

2. ANCHORING MORALITY AND ASSESSING CONSTRUCTED JUDGEMENTS

In our deliberations we usually seek to be objective, which mainly indicates seeking an unbiased, true judgement. However, whether there is such a thing as objective morality is often disputed. In what follows I defend the view that we can construct objective moral principles and judgements, which is a view that opposes subjectivist ethics and different kinds of ethical relativism.[12]

---

[12] Subjectivist ethics is the view that morality is grounded in individuals' preferences and that there are no other grounds for morality. Some theories that tend to explain morality endorse

To develop an understanding of objectivity and what it means for a moral judgement to be objective, we need to look into the nature of value judgements, good and bad (*al-ḥusn wal qubḥ*). This is because moral judgements, whether obligatory (*wājib*), recommended (*mustaḥsan*), permissible (*mubāḥ*), discouraged (*makrūh*) or prohibited (*maḥẓūr*), are grounded in value judgements that can be classified as good (*ḥusn*) and bad (*qubḥ*). Thus, value judgements, good and bad, provide the foundations of any moral judgements. Grounding moral judgements in value judgements allows for rationalization in the field of ethics. As such, one could argue that what is forbidden is forbidden because it is bad, and that what is obligatory is obligatory because it is good and necessary to prevent evil, and so on.

2.1 The grounds of normative judgements – anchoring morality[13]

Classical Islamic scholars looked into the nature of value judgements good (*ḥusn*) and bad (*qubḥ*) and developed different views about the nature of good and bad. This means that they developed different understandings of the foundations or grounds of moral judgements. ʿAbd al-Jabbār, a Muslim theologian from the late tenth century, said that:

> Acts known by reason to be evil (*al-qabīḥ al-ʿaqlī*) such as 'wrongdoing' and 'lying' have to be discerned from other things by something characteristic to it (*li-amr yakhtaṣu bihi*) ... The reason for their being evil must be intelligible such as having a peculiar state (*ḥāl*), or a determinant cause (*maʿnā*) or due to the state of their agent. For there is no difference between saying that they are evil for an unintelligible reason, and saying that they are evil for no reason at all. (ʿAbd al-Jabbār, 1958–65, vol. 6, part 1, p. 57)

In other words, ʿAbd al-Jabbār distinguished between three positions regarding the ultimate grounds of goodness or badness. The first position is of

this view, arguing that good and evil only mean that one is perceived with aversion or attraction and that there is no objective truth behind our moral judgements. Subjectivism in ethics is a type of moral relativism and moral relativism is a very problematic position to endorse. Most of the philosophers in western and Islamic traditions came up with theories that would explain the objective nature of morality.

[13] This section is partly based on the sixth chapter of my book *Islamic Ethics* (2010), particularly the section 'Grounds of Normative Judgments: Good and Evil' (p. 123–35).

those who grounded morality in a determinate natural cause (*ma ʿnā*) inherent in things and actions. If good and bad depends on some intrinsic property of the action, then it is necessarily objective as it does not depend on the perceiver. ʿAbd al-Jabbār criticized this view, which is ascribed to some earlier Muʿtazilites. For him good and bad are not attributes that are added to the attributes of the action or to an event related to it. Value is not something that inheres in actions. An example given by ʿAbd al-Jabbār considers *sujūd* prostration. *Sujūd* is good when performed to God but evil when performed to Satan. So, there is nothing intrinsically good or bad in the action of *sujūd* itself that makes it good or bad. The goodness or the badness themselves do not inhere in the action. The objectivity of moral values is not related to the intrinsic nature of the actions. For simplicity, let us call this position the 'naturalist position' akin to moral realism as defined earlier.

The second position is of those who grounded good and bad in the state of the agent, which clearly implies that it is relative to the individual. ʿAbd al-Jabbār said: 'Some people say that the evilness (*qubḥ*) of wrongdoing is just like the ugliness (*qubḥ*) of ugly pictures and there is no difference between the two cases' (1958–65, vol. 6, part 1, p. 20). He considers those who hold such views to be mistaken, as rational people who look at a picture may disagree among themselves – some might see it as beautiful, and others might see it as ugly. Thus, beauty or ugliness depends on the state of the person, his desire (*al-shahwa*) or aversion (*al-nufūr*). Even the same person might view something differently at different times. This is not the case with moral values, such as wrongdoing or injustice, as all rational people agree on the evilness of such acts (ʿAbd al-Jabbār, 1958–65, vol. 6, part 1, p. 19). This view is compatible with ethical relativism. Let us call this a 'relativist position'.

Third is the position that grounds morality in the state of the action (*ḥāl*). The state of an action is determined by its circumstances and consequences. For example, according to ʿAbd al-Jabbār the ground of evil '*wajh qubḥ*' of the action of 'inflicting pain' is it being wrongdoing (*ẓulm*). 'Inflicting pain' is a perceived entity or a physical feature of an action, thus an intrinsic property '*ma ʿnā*', that determines the genus (*jins*) of an action. Whereas *ẓulm* is an attribute of the action of inflicting pain necessitated by the state (*ḥāl*) of the action. The state of the action is determined by certain conditions and by the consequences that the action brings about or is thought to bring about. Therefore, it is not an intrinsic property of an action that qualifies it as good or evil, but the aspects of an action that provide good reasons for certain judgements, expressed by ʿAbd al-Jabbār as *wajh al-qubḥ* and *wajh al-ḥusn*. Let us call this view a 'constructivist position'. Since, according to this position, the truth of a moral judgement, as in constructivism, is not simply there waiting to be discovered, since it depends on the circumstances and the consequences of the action that is evaluated. The truth of the moral judgement, according to this view, is akin to a version of constructivism that also depends on the outputs of our reasoning procedures that take into consideration different factors.

In addition to the three possible grounds of morality mentioned above, we should include the view that grounds morality in divine commands and prohibitions or in the will of God. This is the position that we can refer to as 'theological voluntarism'. According to this view, good and evil are ultimately based on revelation. Moral values, good and bad (*al-ḥusn wa al-qubḥ*), are established and known to us only through divine commands and prohibitions.

The last view is usually mistaken for being the *truly* religious one. But it is important to clarify that referring to a text in a case of disagreement on a legal matter is one thing, while holding the view that moral values exclusively depend on scripture is another. After all, there is no legal tradition that is not ultimately based on a certain text that is considered authoritative by the community that adheres to it. But holding that moral values exclusively depend on scripture is a very problematic view.[14] It allows for 'social norms and practices to be sanctified and turned into fixed entities' (Mir-Hosseini, 2018, p. 108).

What the last position, which is 'ethical voluntarism', has in common with the first one, which we call a 'naturalist position', is that both views assume that good and evil and right and wrong need to be discovered rather than constructed. According to ethical voluntarism, normative values are grounded in divine commands and prohibitions, while according to the natural position values are grounded in nature. Thus, both views are compatible with a version of 'moral realism'. Moral realists hold that there are objective, mind-independent facts and properties (Lutz and Lenman, 2021), which can only be discovered 'as they actually are'. Also, moral realism, like voluntarism and naturalism, implies that moral truth is absolute and static. In other words, both the naturalist and voluntarist positions imply that there are objective criteria of correctness for moral judgements only if such judgements represent matters of fact about the way the world is. Nevertheless, it is worth mentioning that in practice, the classical medieval scholars and Muslim jurists did not discover real and true moral judgements that represent matters of fact or

[14] For arguments against this position, which is also sometimes called divine command theory, see Al-Attar (2015).

absolute divine judgements. Indeed, they 'constructed, rather than discovered, God's law', as argued by Ziba Mir-Hosseini (2003).

The constructivist view entails that there are objective criteria of moral judgement insofar as there are objective criteria about how to reason about practical matters. For example, there are objective reasons that prohibit deceiving and manipulating others, but such reasons are the result of moral reasoning. Accordingly, moral judgements can be true or false without representing mind-independent normative facts about the world (Bagnoli, 2021), since 'moral judgments have no ontological connotations' (Daher, 1990, p.367). However, it must be strongly emphasized that 'stripping ethics from any ontological grounds does not mean stripping it from any rational grounds' (Daher, 1990, p. 385). Also, objectivity does not require any version of moral realism that would render morality static and absolute. Yet it requires the fulfilment of certain conditions which, to use the Arabic Islamic terminology, are called the 'conditions of moral obligations' (*shurūṭ ḥusn al-taklīf*) or better the 'presuppositions of normative judgements', as discussed in the section that follows.

2.2 Presuppositions of normative judgements (*shurūṭ ḥusn al-taklīf*)

Classical Muslim scholars developed what can be considered 'morally neutral' principles for evaluating moral judgements under the title of *shurūṭ ḥusn al-taklīf*, which can be translated as 'conditions of valid obligations' or 'the presuppositions of moral judgements'. The importance of studying the presuppositions of moral judgements is explained by contemporary philosopher Neil Cooper, who stated that 'if one finds out what moral judgments imply or presuppose, he/she shall be in a position to shoot holes in any moral judgment which implies or presupposes what is false, impossible, or otherwise unacceptable' (1966, p. 46). The late professor of ethics at the University of Jordan, Sahban Khalifat, indicated that the *mutakallimūn* (scholars of *kalām*) have articulated such presuppositions in great detail, which indicates that they were aware of the importance of such conditions in evaluating normative judgments (2004, vol. 3, p. 1079).

The Muʿtazilite ʿAbd al-Jabbār al-Asadābādī (d. 1025 CE) proposed and defended some 'morally neutral' principles for evaluating moral judgements. These conditions can be divided into two. First, conditions related to the agent, including her/his intellectual, physical and psychological abilities.

These include, for example, the ability to understand the meaning of a judgement and the ability to act independently of any deterministic factors. In other words, normative judgements presuppose certain qualities in the agent which, if not present, would undermine the validity of any judgement. ʿAbd al-Jabbār says: 'A responsible human being (*mukallaf*) is the one who is able to act (*qādir*), knowing (*ʿālim*), living (*ḥayy*) and willing (*murīd*)' (ʿAbd al-Jabbār, 1958–65, vol. 11, p. 309) and any obligation imposed on a *mukallaf* should take that into consideration. Thus, if an obligation includes what is impossible or intolerable it should be considered irrational (*taklīf mā lā yutāq qabīh*) (ʿAbd al-Jabbār, 1958–65, vol. 11, p. 367). Moral judgement is irrational unless it presupposes a certain physical and mental capacity on the part of the addressee that makes him/her responsible for the choice and action.

The second set of conditions relate to the judgement itself. For a judgement to be moral it needs to satisfy some 'conditions of valid obligation', which include purposefulness, rationality, objectivity, impartiality and universality. For example, a moral judgement must be purposeful and not arbitrary. Thus, if one had no purpose in assigning an obligation, then the assignment of the obligation would be irrational. A moral judgement, in order to be valid, needs to apply to everyone, including 'the atheists who know the evilness of injustice, although they do not know the divine commands or the commander' (Mānkdīm, 1965, p. 309). A rational human being or an adult with a sound mind (*al-ʿāqil*) 'should do what is obligatory by reason (*wājib fī ʿaqlihi*) for its goodness' (ʿAbd al-Jabbār, 1958–65, vol. 11, p. 489). The impartiality of ethical judgements is exemplified in ʿAbd al-Jabbār's thought, when he said: 'An action if considered evil for occurring in a certain way, then it must be evil from any agent if it occurs in the same way' (ʿAbd al-Jabbār, 1958–65, vol. 6, part 2, p. 244). Moreover, ʿAbd al-Jabbār holds that 'being obliged by God is not a condition for obligation'.[15] This implies that not all obligations and rules are mentioned in the Qurʾan. Moral obligations and moral rules should then be constructed taking into consideration the core Qurʾanic moral values.

The Qurʾan emphasizes a core of universal values that are shared by all human beings. But morality encompasses not only abstract universal values such as justice and mercy, it also includes codes of practice and rules that determine duties, obligations and rights. These are constructed by taking

[15] For a detailed discussion of the presuppositions of ethical judgements based on the work of the Muʿtazilite scholar ʿAbd al-Jabbār (d. 415 AH/1025 CE), see my chapter: 'Ethics of ʿAbd al-Jabbār: Presuppositions of Ethical Judgments', in Al-Attar (2010, pp. 63–98).

into consideration not only the core moral values but also advancements in psychology, neurology, anthropology and other fields of knowledge. In addition to that, any judgement, rule or principle must satisfy rules of practical reason[16] to be considered a true moral judgement, as will be argued below. To use ʿAbd al-Jabbār's terminology, to be a 'rational obligation' (*taklīf ʿaqlī*), any obligation must conform to the rules of practical reason.

The rules of practical reason (formal as opposed to substantial) distinguish the ethical discourse from any other type of discourses. These rules of practical reason as articulated by contemporary Muslim philosopher Adel Daher include several points. First, a rule should entail that acting according to it is absolutely mandatory. This can be interpreted as saying: do not treat others (or do not accept treating others) except in a way that you want to be treated if you were occupying the same position that the other occupies (Daher, 1990, p. 405). It has also been called the universalizability principle.

It should be clear that rejecting the absolute character of normative ethics does not include rejecting the absoluteness of moral perspective (Daher, 1990, p. 386). For example, the norms and the application of the norms in certain situations can vary, following certain details and circumstances which require the application of the norm. Thus, a normative rule such as 'one should never steal' or 'stealing is wrong' is not absolute, as there are situations when stealing to feed a dying person is the right thing to do. Rejecting the absoluteness of such rules does not mean rejecting the absoluteness of a moral perspective, as moral considerations of *ʿadl* (justice) and *iḥsān* (beauty and goodness) are the reasons behind breaking such rules.[17]

Second, what is required by a moral rule cannot be overruled by considerations that do not belong to the domain of ethics, like legal considerations or considerations of self-interest. Ethical considerations have the priority over any other considerations (Daher, 1990, p. 408). A good example is when Muslim jurists in the past wondered what to do with the divine moral injunction revealed in verse 16:90 of the Qurʾan: 'God commands *ʿadl* (justice) and *iḥsān* …' They were aware that the concept of justice requires equality, but they found that problematic. Thus, the Muslim jurists and exegetes restricted

[16] Practical reason is a term with main roots in Kantian philosophy and it indicates the ability of moral reasoning. 'It is the general human capacity for resolving, through reflection, the question of what one is to do' (Wallace, 2020).

[17] Constructivism rejects the absolute character of normative ethics and that includes Kant's 'categorical imperative'. That means that there are no absolute moral rules that must be followed regardless of the context and the consequences.

equality by reference to *al- shar*ʿ or what they considered divine injunctions. Al-Qarafi, for example, defined *ʿadl* (justice) as *al-taswiya bil shar*ʿ (equality according to revelation) (al-Khaṭīb, 2017, p. 106). This allowed the jurists to give priority to specific verses and miss 'a great deal of the original intended moral message by God in the Qurʾan – that of shaking patriarchal culture and enslavement and putting Muslims on the road to equal human dignity and emancipation' (Abou-Bakr, Lamrabet and Al-Sharmani in this volume). Indeed, as stated by Abou-Taleb also in this volume, exegetes adopted 'a practical approach that translates the verses into legal injunctions (*aḥkām*), mostly shaped by the norms of their contexts'.

The third rule of practical reason articulated by the philosopher Adel Daher is that of consistency. For example, the absence of consistency can be the result of a rule that requires us to do something and not to do it in the same time or requires us to do what leads to a situation that contradicts with the same rule, like, for example, saying that 'everyone has to prioritize her own interest and abide by her obligations towards others' (Daher, 1990, p. 409). Such a rule requires one to prioritizes her own interest and not to do so at the same time.

The fourth rule that any judgement must satisfy is the applicability to all individuals without exception. Accordingly, any rule that discriminates against women, including those related to marriage and divorce, is not a moral rule, as it clearly fails to satisfy this condition.

The fifth states that a moral rule should be for the good of all equally. Indeed, all Muslim jurists agreed – in theory – that well-being (*maṣlaḥa*) is the ultimate aim of revelation and this includes, of course, the well-being of all men and women.

It is important to mention that any judgement must satisfy these rules of practical reason in order to be considered an objective true moral judgement. These rules are therefore the necessary conditions of moral judgements. Necessary, but not sufficient as they do not preclude other conditions that also need to be satisfied for a judgement to be considered true, like the ones articulated by ʿAbd al-Jabbār and conditions derived from other fields of knowledge. These conditions should be taken into consideration when constructing any moral judgement or moral code and in assessing any previously constructed rule or judgement.

Therefore, the question of objectivity, as argued above, is not whether the moral value that we ascribe to a judgement or an action inheres in that action, but whether it satisfies the presuppositions of moral judgements articulated by ʿAbd al-Jabbār and the rules of practical reason as explained by Adel Daher.

CONCLUDING REMARKS

Understanding ethics and appreciating its significance is of paramount importance in the contemporary Islamic reformers' discourse. In the first part of this chapter, I shed light on some recent contributions to the field of Islamic ethics, highlighting the importance of ethical thought in the works of *kalām*. The second part is an attempt to develop an understanding of ethics along the lines of constructivism, which is a recent development in moral philosophy that is, in my view, compatible with objective, universal, rational and Islamic views of morality. I argue, building upon the arguments of ʿAbd al-Jabbār, that for any ruling (*ḥukm*) or ethical judgement to be truly moral, it must satisfy certain necessary conditions of moral judgements.

The implications of the chapter's approach for the question of Muslim gender justice are multifaceted. While there is a core set of universal values shared by all human beings and emphasized in the Qurʾan, morality and its related duties and obligations include rules, codes of practice and moral judgements that go beyond these broad and abstract values. The rules, codes of practices and moral judgements are constructed based on the universal values as well as contextual understandings and intellectual advancements in any given time and place. In addition, to be considered a true and valid moral judgement, any judgement, rule or principle must satisfy certain rules of practical reason.

In other words, norms and values that can guide egalitarian gender relations are not simply to be discovered as monolithic and fixed teachings from sacred texts. Nor are they merely reducible to context-determined worldviews and discourses. Rather they are constructed through human reasoning in dynamic processes where the sacred texts and social historical contexts play a role, but *do not* negate or replace ethical reasoning that can evaluate moral judgements independently with its own rational tools.

REFERENCES

ʿAbd al-Jabbār, ʿImād al-Dīn Abū al-Hasan b. Aḥmad. 1958–65. *Al-Mughnī fi Abwāb al-Tawḥīd wa-l-ʿAdl* (20 vols, of which 16 are extant). Cairo: Ministry of Education.

Abou-Bakr, Omaima and Mulki Al-Sharmani. 2020. 'Islamic Feminist *Tafsīr* and Qurʾanic Ethics: Rereading Divorce Verses'. In *Islamic Interpretive Tradition and Gender Justice: Processes of Canonization, Subversion, and Change*, edited by Nevin Reda and Yasmin Amin, pp. 23–67. Canada: McGill-Queen's Press.

Abou El Fadl, Khaled. 2016. 'What Type of Law is Islamic Law'. In *Routledge Handbook of Islamic Law*, edited by Khaled Abou El Fadl, Ahmad Atef Ahmad and Said Fares Hassan, pp. 11–39. London and NY: Routledge.

Abou El Fadl, Khaled. 2017. 'Qur'anic Ethics and Islamic Law'. *Journal of Islamic Ethics* 1 (1): pp. 7–28.

Adamson, Peter. 2016. *Philosophy in the Islamic World*. Oxford: Oxford University Press.

Ahmed, Rumee. 2019. 'Islamic Law and Theology'. In *The Oxford Handbook of Islamic Law*, edited by Anver Emon and Rumee Ahmed, pp. 105–32. Oxford: Oxford University Press.

Amin, Ahmad. 1953. *Al-Akhlāq*. 6th edn. Cairo.

Ansari, Abdul Haq. 1989. 'Islamic Ethics: Concept and Prospect'. *The American Journal of Islamic Social Sciences* 6 (2): pp. 81–91.

Askari, Hossein and Abbas Mirakhor. 2020. *Conceptions of Justice from Islam to the Present*. New York: Palgrave Macmillan.

Al-Attar, Mariam. 2010. *Islamic Ethics: Divine Command Theory in Arabo-Islamic Thought*. London: Routledge.

Al-Attar, Mariam. 2013. 'Women and Violence in Light of an Islamic Normative Ethical Theory'. In *Gender and Violence in Islamic Societies: Patriarchy, Islamism and Politics in the Middle East and North Africa*, edited by Zahia Smail Salhi, pp. 62–81. London: I.B. Tauris.

Al-Attar, Mariam. 2015. 'The Ethics and Metaphysics of Divine Command Theory'. In *The Routledge Companion to Islamic Philosophy*, edited by Richard C. Taylor and Luis Xavier López-Farjeat, pp. 315–25. New York: Routledge.

Ayubi, Zahra. 2019. *Gendered Morality: Classical Islamic Ethics of the Self, Family, and Society*. New York: Columbia University Press.

Bagnoli, Carla. 2021. 'Constructivism in Metaethics'. In *Stanford Encyclopedia of Philosophy* (Spring 2021 edn), edited by Edward N. Zalta.

Barry, Melissa. 2018. 'Constructivism'. In *The Routledge Handbook of Metaethics*, edited by Tristram McPherson and David Plunkett. New York: Routledge.

Cooper, Neil. 1966. 'Some Presuppositions of Moral Judgments'. *Mind* 75 (297): pp. 45–57.

Al-Daghistani, Raid. 2018. 'Ethics in Islam: An Overview of Theological, Philosophical and Mystical Approaches'. *ANNALES* 28 (1): pp. 1–12.

Daher, Adel. 1990. *Al-Akhlāq wa al-ʿAql: Naqd al-Falsafa al-Gharbiyya* (Ethics and Reason: A Critique of Western Philosophy). Amman: Dār al-Shurūq.

Draz, Muhammad Abdullah. 2008. *The Moral World of the Qur'an*, translated by Danielle Robinson and Rebecca Masterton. London: Bloomsbury.

Fakhry, Majid. 1991. *Ethical Theories in Islam*. Leiden: Brill.

Frank, Richard M. 2005. *Philosophy, Theology and Mysticism in Medieval Islam: Texts and Studies on the Development and History of Kalam, Vol. I*, edited by Dimitri Gutas. Burlington and Aldershot: Ashgate.

Frank, Richard M. 2007. *Early Islamic Theology: The Muʿtazilites and al-Ashʿarī. Texts and Studies on the Development and History of Kalām, Vol. II*, edited by Dimitri Gutas. Burlington and Aldershot: Ashgate.

Frank, Richard M. 2008. *Classical Islamic Theology: The Ashʿarites. Texts and Studies on the Development and History of Kalām, Vol. III*, edited by Dimitri Gutas. Burlington and Aldershot: Ashgate.

Harvey, Ramon. 2018. *The Qur'an and the Just Society*. Edinburgh: Edinburgh University Press.

Hashas, Mohammed and Mutaz al-Khaṭīb. 2020. 'Modern Arab-Islamic Scholarship on Ethics: A Reflective Contextualization'. In *Islamic Ethics and the Trusteeship Paradigm Taha Abderrahmane's Philosophy in Comparative Perspectives*, edited by Mohammed Hashas and Mutaz al-Khaṭīb, pp. 1–31. Leiden and Boston: Brill.

Hourani, George F. 1971. *Islamic Rationalism: The Ethics of ʿAbd al-Jabbār*. Oxford: Clarendon Press.

Hourani, George F. 1985. *Reason and Tradition in Islamic Ethics*. Cambridge: Cambridge University Press.

Hovannisian, Richard G. (ed.). 1985. *Ethics in Islam: Ninth Giorgio Levi Della Vida Conference, 1983, in Honour of Fazlur Rahman*. Malibu, CA: Undena Publications.

Hursthouse, Rosalind and Glen Pettigrove. 2018. 'Virtue Ethics'. In *Stanford Encyclopedia of Philosophy* (Winter 2018 edn), edited by Edward N. Zalta.

Iqbal, Muhammad. 1934. *The Reconstruction of Religious Thought in Islam*. Oxford: Oxford University Press.

Izutsu, Toshihiko. 1959. *The Structure of the Ethical Terms in the Qurʾan*. Tokyo: Keio University.

Jung, Kevin. 2018. 'Introduction'. In *Religious Ethics and Constructivism: A Metaethical Inquiry*, edited by Kevin Jung. York: Routledge.

Khalidi, Muhammad Ali. 2005. *Medieval Islamic Philosophical Writings*. Cambridge: Cambridge University Press.

Khalifat, Sahban. 2004. *Manhaj al-Taḥlīl al-Lughawī al-Manṭiqī fī al-Fikr al-ʿArabī al-Islāmī (al-Naẓariyya wa-l-Taṭbīq)* (The Logical and Linguistic Analysis Methodology in the Arab Islamic Thought (Theory and Practice)), vol. 3. Amman: University of Jordan.

Al-Khaṭīb, Mutaz. 2017. 'Ayāt al-Akhlāq: Suʾāl al-Akhlāq ʿInda al-Mufassirīn' (Verses in Ethics: The Question of Ethics in Qurʾanic exegesis). *Journal of Islamic Ethics* 1 (1): pp. 83–121.

Al-Khaṭīb, Mutaz. 2019. 'Contemporary *Ijtihād*, Ethics and Modernity'. *Journal of Islamic Ethics* 3 (1–2): pp. 1–7.

Legenhausen, Muhammad. n.d. 'Constructivist Elements in the Ethical Philosophy of Mulla Sadra'. Available at www.al-Islam.org

López-Farjeat, Luis Xavier. 2021. *Classical Islamic Philosophy: A Thematic Introduction*. New York and London: Routledge.

Lutz, Matthew and James Lenman. 2021. 'Moral Naturalism'. In *Stanford Encyclopedia of Philosophy* (Spring 2021 edn), edited by Edward N. Zalta.

Maḥmoud, Ahmad. 1992. *Subḥi Al-Falsafa al-Akhlāqiya fī al-Fikr al-Islami*, 3rd edn. Beirut: Dar al-Nahḍa al-ʿArabiyah.

Mānkdīm, Shāshdīw Aḥmad b. al-Ḥusayn. 1965. *Sharḥ al-Uṣūl al-Khamsa*, edited by ʿAbd al-Karīm ʿUthmān (ascribed to ʿAbd al-Jabbār). Cairo: Maktabat Wahbah.

Marmura, Michael E. 1994. 'A Medieval Islamic Argument for the Intrinsic Value of the Moral Act'. In *Corolla Torontonensis: Studies in Honour of Ronald Morton Smith*, edited by Emmet Robbins and Stella Sandahl, pp. 113–31. Toronto: TSAR.

Mir-Hosseini, Ziba. 2003. 'The Construction of Gender in Islamic Legal Thought and Strategies for Reform'. *Hawwa* 1 (1): pp. 1–28.

Mir-Hosseini, Ziba. 2018. 'Women's Equality'. In *The Shariʿa: History, Ethics and Law*, edited by Amyn B. Sajoo. London: I.B. Tauris.

Mir-Hosseini, Ziba, Mulki Al-Sharmani and Jana Rumminger (eds). 2015. *Men in Charge? Rethinking Authority in Muslim Legal Tradition*. London: Oneworld.

Moosa, Ebrahim. 2009. 'Genetically Modified Food and Muslim Ethics'. In *Acceptable Genes, Religious Traditions and Genetically Modified Food*, edited by Conrad D. Brunk and Harold Coward, pp. 135–58. Albany: SUNY Press.

Moosa, Ebrahim. 2017. 'Foreword'. In *The Imperatives of Progressive Islam*, edited by Adis Duderija. New York: Routledge.

Moosa, Ebrahim. 2020. 'The Ethical in Shariʿa Practices: Deliberations in Search of an Effective Paradigm'. In *Pathways to Contemporary Islam: New Trends in Critical Engagement*, edited by Mohamed Nawab Mohamed Osman, pp. 235–64. Amsterdam: Amsterdam University Press.

Mousa, Muhammad Yusef. 1963. *Falsafat al-Akhlāq fī al-Islam*. 3rd edn. Cairo.

Rahbar, Daud Rahman. 1960. *God of Justice: A Study in the Ethical Doctrine of the Qurʾan*. Leiden: E.J. Brill.

Rahman, Amilah Awang Abd. 2021. 'Demarcation of Ethics and Law: A Theoretical Framework that Recaptures the Primary Role of *Akhlāq Islamiyyah*'. *The Islamic Quarterly*, June.

Rahman, Fazlur. 1980. *Major Themes of the Qurʾan*. Chicago: Bibliotecha Islamica.

Rashwānī, Samir. 2017. *'Al-Dars al-Akhlāqī fī al-Qurʾān: Qirāʾa fī Baʿḍ al-Muqārabāt al-Hadītha'* ('The Ethical Lesson of the Qurʾan: Review of Some Modern Approaches'). In *Journal of Islamic Ethics* 1 (1–2): pp. 158–94.

Rawls, John. 1980. 'Kantian Constructivism in Moral Theory'. *The Journal of Philosophy* 77 (9): pp. 515–72

Reinhart, A. Kevin. 1983. 'Islamic Law as Islamic Ethics'. *The Journal of Religious Ethics* 2 (1): pp. 186–203.

Sayre-McCord, Geoff. 2014. 'Metaethics'. In *Stanford Encyclopedia of Philosophy* (Summer 2014 edn), edited by Edward N. Zalta.

Schneewind, J. B. 2010. *Essays on the History of Moral Philosophy*. New York: Oxford University Press.

Subḥi, Ahmad Maḥmud. 1969. *Al-Falsafa al-Akhlāqiya fī al-Fikr al-Islami: al-ʿAqliyūn wa-l-Dhawqiyūn, Aw al-Naẓar wa-l-ʿAmal*. Cairo: Dar al-Maʾarif.

Al-Ṭawīl, Tawfīq. 1979. *Falsafat al-Akhlāq: Nashʾatuha wa Taṭawuruha*, 3rd edn. Cairo: Dar al-Nahḍa al-ʿArabiya.

Van Roojen, Mark. 2015. 'Expressivism'. In *Routledge Encyclopedia of Philosophy*. Taylor and Francis.

Vishanoff, David R. 2020. 'The Ethical Structure of Imām al-Ḥaramayn al-Juwaynī's Legal Theory'. In *Islamic Law and Ethics*, edited by David Vishanoff, pp. 1–33. London: International Institute of Islamic Thought.

Wadud, Amina. 2006. *Inside the Gender Jihad: Women's Reform in Islam*. London: Oneworld.

Wallace, R. Jay. 2020. 'Practical Reason'. In *Stanford Encyclopedia of Philosophy* (Spring 2020 edn), edited by Edward N. Zalta.

Widigdo, M. S. A. 2019. 'Jadal and the Integration of *Kalām* and *Fiqh*: A Critical Study of Imām Al-Ḥaramayn Al-Juwaynī's Application of Islamic Dialectic'. *Analisa: Journal of Social Science and Religion* 4 (2): pp. 165–85.

Zargar, Cyrus Ali. 2017. *The Polished Mirror: Storytelling and the Pursuit of Virtue in Islamic Philosophy and Sufism*. London: Oneworld.

LAW AND PRACTICE

Historicizing Muslim Marriage Practices in Pre-Modern Islamic Egypt

Hoda El Saadi

There is tension between the Qur'an's message of equality and justice and the hierarchical model of marriage and gender relations in Islamic jurisprudence (*fiqh*). Many modern Muslim family laws are based on this *fiqh*-based model, hence perpetuating gender-based inequalities. Important textual studies are being conducted to critically examine the foundations of Islamic legal theory and jurists' rulings on marriage and gender relations (see, for example, Kadivar and Reda in this volume). However, it is also critical to revisit the prevalent understanding of Islamic law that locates it solely in doctrine, but not in practice, in the manuals of early jurists, but not in the lived realities. We need to delve into Islamic history and the lived experiences of law. What can marriage practices of medieval and pre-modern Muslims teach us about the nature of Islamic law and its sources? What can they teach us about the strategies and agency of women as they navigated marriage and family life? How can the insights from such historical inquiry inform present-day efforts to reform modern Muslim family laws?

This chapter engages with these questions through a study of marriage practices in Egypt from the seventh to the sixteenth centuries CE. I show that the construction of Muslim marriage norms has taken place throughout history not only through the writings of Muslim jurists but also the lived realities of gender relations, which are 'the product of the historical development of human experience, a relationship that changes, evolves and adapts in rhythm with a changing society' (Tucker, 2000, p. 10).

Recent scholarship has highlighted the importance of studying how the law takes shape and develops through its applications in local and time-bound contexts.[1] In other words, we have to contextualize Islamic legal tradition, as it did not appear and develop in a vacuum but in a context bound to a specific time and space. The scholarship has shown that understanding the historical cultural contexts in which Islamic law functions can help explain why a certain form of legal transformation happened at a particular juncture in history, and why the resulting legal system took the form that it did. Yet when people talk about Muslim marriage and divorce today, they often invoke a notion of ahistorical fixed Islamic law, ignoring the historical context and the social reality that changed from one period to another and from one geographical location to another.

In this chapter, I examine rulings concerning marriage practices and marital relations in Islamic jurisprudence (*fiqh*) and in daily lived experiences of women and men as recorded in diverse documents. I explore a variety of legal and historical sources to determine whether or not juristic rulings reflected the lived realities of men and women in marital relations and to shed light on the complexity of Islamic law and how it intersects with social, political and economic factors. I argue against the claim that the construction of marital relations is only found in the writings of Muslim jurists and that the Islamic law governing marriage is a set of stagnant rules having only one source of authority. I highlight the responsiveness of Islamic law to the social norms and customs, and argue that this important feature of the legal tradition can facilitate modern efforts towards gender-sensitive reform in *fiqh*-based Muslim family laws.

The lived experience of the law has been studied by a number of scholars in recent years. Most of this kind of research focuses on the Ottoman empire because of the wealth of court records that survived from this period.[2] Very

[1] In the last two decades, legal historians, anthropologists and sociologists have written articles on qadi courts in different countries of the Arab world, all shifting their focus from the legal doctrine to local practice (Masud et al., 2006, p. 4).

[2] For Ottoman historians using court records for the study of socio-legal history, see Jennings (1975), Sonbol (1996; 2003; 2005), Peirce (2003) and Ergene (2003). Sonbol uses court records as a source for the study of gender and to understand the legal status of women in pre-modern Islamic history. She has published and edited many essays and books exploring different aspects of marriage, divorce and child custody.

few studies focused on the topic in the pre-Ottoman period because of the complete absence of the court archives. This study is an attempt to fill that gap and contribute to our understanding of marriage practices and marital relations within the broader context of early medieval Islamic socio-legal history.

The chapter has three sections. The first focuses on the methodological framework and the sources used in this study. It illustrates the different methods and techniques that I use to understand the complexity of Islamic law. It also discusses the diversity and complexity of the historical sources for the period under study, highlighting the importance of juxtaposing legal and historical sources to better understand the dynamics of the early and medieval Islamic societies. It evaluates the sources by discussing their benefits and limitations.

The second section examines marriage contracts belonging to early and medieval Islamic Egypt. I compare them to marriage contracts of other religions and to those of earlier periods before Islam in an attempt to understand the development of marriage practices in the country, and to identify the impact of the socio-cultural context in shaping Muslim marriage practices and rules across the historical periods studied. My analysis demonstrates the importance of *ʿurf* (custom) in the formulation of the law.

The third section highlights the plurality of the legal scene in Islamic Egypt showing how such plurality and diversity worked in favour of women. The absence of consensus among scholars on many issues gave room to the sultans and military men to interfere in the legal scene and issue rules regulating the domestic sphere and marital relations. To shed further light on this plurality, I also explore the tension between the jurists as formulators of the law and the qadis as the implementers of the law. The written word was in many cases stricter than the application and was usually a reaction to women's empowerment and economic independence.

1. METHODOLOGY

I undertake a gender-sensitive reading of Islamic textual traditions. My focus is not on just events, hard facts and historical figures, but also on historical sources as social and cultural discourses on marriage norms and practices. I follow an approach that turns the lens from the doctrine to the practice of the law. In other words, I move from an idealized model of Islamic law to its manifolds in particular times and specific places. I situate my study in the academic literature interested in the lived realities of Islamic law as a social cultural phenomenon. In what follows, I describe my methodology and its key elements:

- **Contextualization:** Rather than approaching Islamic law simply as written texts, I examine how it actually functioned in early and medieval Islamic Egypt. I show how gender relations were determined by the interplay of politics, religion, culture and change in the modes of production in the society. I shed light on how juristic doctrines on marriage developed over the years as jurists proved their willingness and ability to adapt the legal traditions to the lived experiences and social practices of the pre-modern Islamic societies.
- **Examining multiple and diverse sources:** I consult diverse data sources. Islamic civilization was never monolithic with a singular all-embracing gender paradigm. It was a diversified rich civilization shaped by the blending and mixture of Arabic, Persian, Turkish, African, Andalusian and South Asian histories and cultures. One must expect to find different attitudes towards women arising at various historical epochs in a Muslim civilization that reached from Atlantic to the Pacific for over fourteen centuries.

  Even though women were well represented in Islamic historiography, they did not represent themselves. We do not have any chronicles or biographical dictionaries written by women. As a result, we only read marriage and divorce from the perspective of the husband. Therefore, in order to hear the voices of women, I use diverse sources, and particularly non-traditional sources.[3] With non-traditional material, I do not look through the lens of a particular historian who belonged to a specific local and time-bound context, but rather engage directly with data sources that recorded the social realities of the people of various backgrounds.

  There are countless records and documents of different types surviving from early and medieval Islamic societies in the region in their original form. They provide us with a different image of gender relations and marital practices in these societies. For the

[3] These are documents that were not produced to record history but for different purposes of daily life such as notarizing agreements, recording a dispute, contracting a marriage, personal communication, etc.

purposes of this chapter, I draw on fatwa compilations; *waqf* documents; *Ḥaram al-Sharīf* collections; Geniza documents; pre-Islamic marriage contracts; and marriage contracts that are available from the period under study.[4] The fatwa compilations[5] and the *waqf* documents,[6] which survived from the late-fourteenth and fifteenth centuries, give us a good sense of the texture of the life of medieval Islamic societies. The *Ḥaram al-Sharīf* collections, named after the location where they were found, are hundreds of documents that mostly emanated from a fourteenth-century qadi court in Jerusalem when it was under Mamluk rule.[7] The Geniza papers are a vast trove of Jewish documents found in the document depository (*'geniza'* in Hebrew) of a synagogue in Fustat, which is now a part of Cairo. They are important historical sources related to Islamic law because Muslims, Jews and Christians – despite the difference in their legal traditions – shared some marriage and divorce practices and held common views regarding the 'ideal family'. The scholar Goitein states that the Jewish community shared many of the practices, assumptions and lifestyles of the broader Muslim society of the day (Goitein, 1967, vol. III, pp. 142, 147).[8] This also applies to the Coptic or Greek papyri documents that were produced before Islam. Comparing the pre-Islamic papyri documents of marriage and divorce to the ones of early Islamic Egypt reveals a lot about the marriage tradition as practiced after Islam and shows how it was affected and shaped by the pre-Islamic traditions (Grohmann, 1934–62; Abbott, 1941). These diverse non-traditional sources are a source of rich data. However, one needs to note that they also

---

[4] Most court records pertaining to marriage date only from the Ottoman period, the sixteenth to nineteenth centuries CE.

[5] According to Tucker (2000; 2005) fatwas (legal opinions) 'provided the critical link between legal theory and lived human experience' (2005, p. 166). She uses fatwas to challenge the prevalent views on Islam and gender, showing how Islamic law had always been an open, flexible system, adapting to the demands of different social settings.

[6] Fay (1997) approached *waqf* as a source for unlocking women's history and for understanding the dynamics of the Mamluk household.

[7] The *Ḥaram al-Sharīf* collections have been catalogued by Little (1984). They were also the subject of a monograph by Lutfi (1985), who paid special attention to the question of gender. Even though the *Ḥaram* collections emanate from a qadi court in Jerusalem, they are valuable for studying Mamluk Egypt as Jerusalem during this time was under the Mamluk rule.

[8] Goitein (1967) discusses in length how 'the social customs of a majority are apt to be accepted by a minority'.

could have their own limitations as well, similar to written history texts, since they also could have been manipulated by people in power.

- **Linking different sources:** I explore how different sources may speak to one another. When legal information is supplemented by archival information from endowment trust deeds, court registers, transactions, *fatāwa*, or biographical dictionaries, we find that a different social image of both genders appears. This also reveals a discrepancy between the theoretical prescriptions of the law found in legal manuals, that is, what could be called doctrines and the practice of the law in the courts. Muslim jurists' writings make us believe that women were dependent on their husbands, yet the significant number of divorce cases in medieval courts forces us to rethink if that juristic construction of spousal roles was true to real life then. The image of the secluded and dependent woman that is constructed in legal manuals is at odds with the active independent woman we see in sources such as court records or endowment deeds. However, this does not mean that normative discourses were completely detached from social realities or that they existed in an abstract space unaffected by the religious scholars' interactions with the world around them. Rather than presuming that scholars unilaterally dictated behavioural norms that were unquestionably carried out by the ordinary women and men, I argue that legal norms were in a more complex dialogic relationship with practices on the ground. The strictest rules on women were produced in contexts where women were highly visible and vocal about their rights.
- **Classification and analysis:** I classify and analyse the different documents and texts with which I am working. Then I dissect the key information to organize the data and relate it to one another. I try to systematize the historical information. I then use this organized historical data to counter check other literary and historical sources in order to offer a more comprehensive balanced picture of the topic under study.

These methodological processes are significant because they help demonstrate the array of sources available, and reveal the rich stories between the lines and beyond the assumptions that are usually made about women's lives and roles in Muslim societies.

2. THE ROLE OF CONTEXT AND *'URF* IN SHAPING MARRIAGE PRACTICES

Legal rules and decisions pertaining to marriage practices and marital relations must be understood in context. Law is not an autonomous set of rules and principles standing outside the social world. It is not detached from the social realities but is rather profoundly entrenched within the society.

The context examined here is early and medieval Islamic Egypt. At the end of 639 CE or the beginning of 640 CE, the Arabs launched their first attack on Egypt. They defeated the Roman Byzantines and took control of the country. From this time Egypt became a province of the Islamic empire with a governor, *wali,* ruling in the name of the Caliph in Medina. Egypt continued to be a province of the Islamic empire under the rule of the Umayyad and later the Abbasid caliphate. However, the country became an independent centre of power and the capital of the empire with the coming of the Fatimid Shiʿi caliphate (969–1171 CE) and later the Mamluks (1258–1517 CE). Eventually Egypt moved back to the position of a periphery state with the rule of the Ottoman empire in 1517 CE.[9]

In what follows I examine marriage contracts in early and medieval Islamic Egypt, from the seventh to sixteenth centuries. I compare such contracts to marriage contracts of other religions and to those of earlier periods before Islam in an attempt to understand the development of marriage practices, and to shed light on the impact of the socio-cultural context on marriage rules and practices in the time period under study.

The papyri marriage contracts preserved from early Islamic Egypt all included the same information. They are contracts outlining the terms by which spouses agree to live together. They convey rights and obligations to each spouse. They include basic information of the name of the bride and her father, the groom and his father and the names of their guardians or deputies if present at that time as well as the names and signatures of the witnesses. They also include information on the date and place of the marriage and give details on whether the bride is a virgin or has been married before. Some contracts include the profession of the groom and that of his father and of the father of the bride. As discussed in the following sections, marriage contracts also detail a marital gift from the groom to the bride (*ṣadāq,* now often known as *mahr*) and conditions or stipulations inserted by either of the prospective

[9] See Petry (1998) for more information on the history of Islamic Egypt.

spouses to delineate conditions that are considered a necessity for his or her well-being in the marriage.

2.1 The *ṣadāq*

A common striking feature among all marriage contracts in early and medieval Islamic Egypt is the fact that in all of them the groom gives a gift called *ṣadāq* to the bride. This *ṣadāq* was always divided into advanced portion and a deferred portion, which were written in the contract as *muqaddam* and *muʾakhkhar* (Rapoport, 2000, pp. 5–10; Tucker, 2000, p. 207; 2012, p. 229). Deferring a portion of the *ṣadāq* was a common practice in Egypt. It featured in all marriage contracts going back to the second century Hijri. Husbands did not pay the full sum of the *ṣadāq* at the time of the marriage; some of it remained as a debt against them. It was to be paid only at the termination of the marriage by death or divorce (Grohmann, 1934, vol. 1, pp. 83, 86, 92, 97, 109, 119, 121).

Many contemporary jurists of the researched era raised objections against the practice of deferring part of the *ṣadāq*. The famous Medina jurist Mālik ibn Anas (711–95 CE/93–179 AH) and other jurists in the city did not accept this practice (Mālik ibn Anas, 1997, vol. 2, pp. 30–5). They argued that the entire *ṣadāq* was to be paid immediately following the marriage contract. In case of divorce, the woman had the right to the compensation, *mutʿat al-muṭallaqa*, that is stated in verse 2:241 in the Qurʾan. Moreover, the Mālikī school of law stated clearly that a *ṣadāq* deferred until death or divorce was an innovation (*bidʿa*) as it was not mentioned in the Qurʾan or the prophetic Hadith. Additionally, they argued that marriage contracts that do not specify the due time of the payment of the *ṣadāq* are ambiguous and usually lead to uncertainty in the marriage. Mālik's teachings reflected the practices of the early Islamic community of Medina. His position was that the practice of Medina was binding and that all his scholar students should adhere to the consensus of Medina (Rapoport, 2000, p. 8).

The local Egyptian customs, however, clashed with the *ṣadāq* practices of Medina. The Mālikī jurists of Egypt, headed by al-Layth ibn Saʿd, rejected the practice of Medina and challenged Imam Mālik. They insisted on the division of the *ṣadāq* into advance and deferred payments. In doing so they were trying to adapt the Mālikī legal doctrine to the local practice in Egypt. Deferring a portion of the bridal gift was a common practice in Egyptian society over the years (al-Jawziyya, 1347 AH, vol. 3, pp. 556–61).

Comparing marriage contracts from earlier periods such as Greek papyri from the Byzantine period (30 BCE–640 CE) clearly shows that during this historical period, it was important for the groom to give the bride a gift. The gift is known as the *hedna*.[10] It is interesting to note that the bride did not get the *hedna* at the time of marriage. It was a promise, a vow taken by the husband and was to be paid when divorce took place or in case of death. It was one of the strong means of deterring husbands from the unilateral action of divorce against their wives (Rapoport, 2000, pp. 29–31).

The *hedna* also appears in Coptic marriage contracts of the seventh and early eighth centuries under the name *shkhaat*. It is a gift that the groom gives to the bride or to her guardian but retains for himself the legal right to use and derive profit from this property. The bride could only claim the financial pledge of the groom at the termination of the marriage (Rapoport, 2000, pp. 30–1).

Linking the marriage gift to the time of divorce or the death of the husband was also a common practice among the Jewish community in Egypt before Islam. The custom of the bridal gift was known as the *mohar*. The *mohar* or groom's payment was divided into two parts: advanced (given at the time the marriage takes place) and delayed (to be paid to the bride at the termination of the marriage, through either divorce or the husband's death) (Friedman, 1976).[11]

Later Geniza marriage contracts of the Jewish community in medieval Islamic Egypt showed clearly that the marriage gift was paid in instalments. In some marriage contracts, the delayed marriage gift to be paid at a divorce or the husband's death was identified as debt owed from the husband (Goitein, 1967, vol. III, p. 104). Similarly, later Coptic contracts of the second/eighth centuries continued to share the same financial settlements of deferring the part of the nuptial gift. These Coptic marriage contracts were written in Arabic and referred to advance and deferred portions of the *ṣadāq* (Abbott, 1941, pp. 61–5).[12]

[10] *Hedna* or '*eedna*' are the valuables given by the groom to the bride's family in many Homeric marriages (Sealey, 1990, p. 11), and are documented in Greek marriage contracts from the fourth century CE and a Jewish marriage contract from early in the fifth century CE (Rapoport, 2000, p. 29).

[11] Friedman (1976) discusses how the 'delayed mohar became a fundamental phenomenon of Jewish marriage law at a rather early period' (p. 32).

[12] In a marriage contract of the year 378 AH/989 CE, the Copt Tudor gave his bride an extravagant gift of ninety gold dinars. He paid fifteen dinars up front and promised the balance within a year (Abbott, 1941, pp. 61–5, 70).

Thus, the practice of deferring the marital gift was strongly enmeshed in Egyptian society throughout different ages. Arab Muslims who came to settle in the country after the conquest also adopted this custom. Accordingly, Arab Muslim jurists in Egypt integrated this practice into their marital laws in an attempt to fit into their Egyptian environment.[13]

By rejecting the practice of Medina and insisting on deferring the *ṣadāq*, the Mālikī jurists of Egypt were observing and respecting a long tradition. They were adapting the legal theory to the local tradition and context. As mentioned above, the Mālikī Imām of Egypt al-Layth ibn Saʿd strongly supported the position of the Egyptian jurists. In a long correspondence with Imām Mālik, he argued that the practice of Medina should not be binding as not all the Companions of the Prophet agreed with it. To make his point on the importance of the local practice, al-Layth mentioned many other practices in which the Companions of the Prophet in different states departed from the custom in Medina. It was common for the Companions to disagree on different issues since they were met with many practices and matters that the Qurʾan did not address in the states they moved to. Al-Layth always highlighted the importance of context and *ʿurf* in the shaping and development of legal tradition.

In terms of social realities, turning the marital gift into a debt on the husband was an attempt by the men of law to make it easier for poor grooms to marry without immediate monetary expenditure. It was a means to lift the financial burden from the shoulders of the groom. As much as deferring the marital gift served the husband, it also gave the wife a good bargaining position in the marriage and provided the widow and divorcee with a measure of financial security. The *hedna*, the *shkhaat*, the *mohar* and the deferred *ṣadāq* were similar to a loan with the wife as creditor and the husband as debtor, giving the wife power in the marriage through her strong negotiating position and discouraging husbands from unilateral actions.

Legal theory was not only shaped by local traditions, but it also reshaped them. Later Mālikī scholars of Egypt gradually reshaped the local traditions of the country and succeeded in eliminating this practice of deferring the *muʾakhkhar al-ṣadāq* to the time of divorce or death. Later marriage contracts written down between the third/ninth and the fifth/eleventh centuries

---

[13] Paying the nuptial gift in instalments goes very well with the seasonal nature of the Egyptian agrarian economy. It was common in Egypt for debts to be paid at the harvest time in the months immediately before the inundation of the river Nile (Müller, 2020, p. 232).

included fixed dates for the payment of the deferred portion. Contrary to local custom until then, the payment of the deferred portion was now being set at a specific time (for example, one year, five years, and even one day).[14] In other words, rulings on the *ṣadāq*, as applied in early and medieval Islamic Egypt, were shaped through the interplay and interaction of the growing Islamic law and local practice. It was through this interaction that both elements adjusted, adapted and transformed over the years.

In short, *ʿurf* and religion were intertwined and played an important role in defining marriage in Egypt during this early period of Islam. The analysis above challenges the normative view that Islamic law is a fixed law. On the contrary, what is revealed is a dynamic legal tradition with marriage practices being shaped and reshaped, and interpretations and rulings changing not only from place to place and era to era but also from scholar to scholar within the same time period.

2.2 Conditions in marriage contracts

Marriage contracts in early and medieval Islamic Egypt included conditions that favoured the wife and gave her the right to dissolve the marriage and get out of it if the husband did not abide by these stipulations. Judith Tucker (2000, pp. 62–3) and Amira Sonbol (2007) argue in many of their studies that the contractual stipulation was a common technique for expanding the bride's rights in the Ottoman era. In what follows I focus on the conditions and stipulations inserted in the pre-Ottoman marriage contracts in Egypt, illustrating the trajectories of evolution and change of the marriage contract in different historical contexts. Examining such conditions helps us better understand marriage and gender relations in these past communities.

Husbands were not interested in setting conditions within marriage contracts since they had the unquestionable right to unilaterally divorce their wives. The conditions in the marriage contracts therefore defined the wives' expectations; they tell us how things worked in past Egyptian marriages and what women expected from their husbands. For example, in one Muslim marriage contract, a wife asked for the right to have the authority to divorce

[14] See Grohmann (1934–62, vol.1, pp. 97–8; vol. 2, pp. 212–13, 220–1) for contracts signed in the fifth and sixth centuries Hijri showing how the deferred *ṣadāq* was paid at a due date or in instalments.

any second wife that her husband took and to sell any concubine he purchased. Stipulations against polygamy in marriage contracts were always common and increased particularly in fifteenth-century Egypt. To avoid the repercussions of breaking the conditions of the marriage contract, husbands resorted to clandestine marriages *(nikāḥ al-sirr)*, which became a common practice during this time. The idea that husbands feared their wives and married in secret reveals a lot about the shift in power relations in the family from husbands having absolute authority to wives holding some negotiating power (Rapoport, 2007, p. 32).

It was also common for some wives to insert conditions regarding their living arrangements. For example, some stipulated that they live close to their families and that the husband did not have the right to move them away. Others inserted conditions such as obligating the husband not to prevent the wife from visiting her parents or to prevent her parents from visiting her. Such conditions were common in Islamic (Rapoport, 2000, p. 13) and Jewish (Goitein, 1967, vol. III, p. 152) marriage contracts.

Another condition obligated the husband not to drink wine. It is interesting here to see the power held by the wife in demanding exemplary behaviour and good conduct from the future husband.[15]

Another common condition was the husband's good treatment of the wife. If the husband did not treat the wife in a good way (*bil maʿrūf*) she had the right to get a divorce. Such conditions allowed women a way out of marriage when things did not go the way they wanted or expected (Abu Ghazi, 1998, p. 124).

The use of conditions in marriage contracts presents us with an image of women with great agency. They depict the image of women who had the ability to negotiate their marriages and sue husbands or dissolve marriages if their conditions were not fulfilled. The deferred portion of the *ṣadāq* gave women an upper hand in these negotiations. This counters the stereotypical image of the passive submissive woman of early Muslim societies who followed her husband's orders and had no say in her marriage. Highlighting a past when women claimed rights and had high expectations also casts doubt on the assumption that women's status improved only in modern eras.

[15] Wives demanding exemplary behaviour from husbands was a common practice in different religious communities in Egypt during the medieval period. In a Jewish marriage contract from medieval Cairo a wife demands that her husband would no longer associate with disreputable members of society (Goitein, 1967, vol. III, p. 157).

The practice of inserting conditions in the marriage contract also shows that the permanency of the marriage was not a given. If the husband did not fulfil the conditions, then divorce would take place and the husband would pay the deferred portion of the *ṣadāq* (the *mu'akhkhar*). In some cases, the husband refused to give the wife divorce, yet she was still able to get out of the marriage through giving up all her rights and paying the husband for the divorce. This is referred to as either *ibra' or khul'*.[16] There was an interesting case in the papyri documents where a Coptic wife gave up her financial rights and compensated the husband financially in return for being divorced (Abbott, 1941, pp. 77–80). In this divorce deed the term *ibra'* was used for severing the marriage. Besides giving up all her financial rights, the wife gave the husband a house she owned in Aswan and her trousseau (*shiwār*), which were the household possessions that she had brought into marriage.[17]

The term *shiwār* does not seem to appear in marriage contracts; I only found it in divorce deeds. None of the marriage contracts examined had a list of what the bride brought into the marriage. This could be because in Islamic jurisprudence anything that the bride brings into the marriage remains her private property and does not pass on to the husband or any other family relative. Most likely the norm was whatever the wife brought to the marriage she took with her if the marriage was dissolved.

It is notable that through marriage contracts and practices we can also learn a lot about the economic position of the wife and her property rights. It is clear from the marriage and divorce contracts under study that the husband and the wife were separate entities and that the woman had economic independence and full control over her money or property.

Divorce seemed to have been an acceptable practice in medieval and premodern Egypt. The society did not frown on divorced women and hence women were not pressured to remain in undesirable marriages. Even the Copts whose Christian belief forbade divorce dissolved their marriages like their Muslim counterparts. This is demonstrated by the case of the Coptic woman discussed above who ended her marriage through *ibra'*. Therefore, we can deduce that some Copts made use of Islamic divorce doctrines, although

[16] *Ibra'* is an act by which a wife absolves her husband of all financial obligations in return for divorce. In practice this may involve the wife waiving (*ibra'*) any outstanding financial rights (including her deferred dower and any remaining maintenance entitlement). In *khul'* divorce, the woman relinquishes the dower and post-divorce waiting period (*'idda)* maintenance (Welchman, 2004).

[17] See the Appendix of Abbott (1941) for a copy of the contract.

these doctrines contravened the very basis of Christian marriages (Afifi, 1996, pp. 205–7). Thus, by examining marriage settlements in early Islamic Egypt we gain much information about the interaction of Islam with other religions and the relations between the three Abrahamic religious communities at that time. It shows us how the social practices of the three communities were shaped by common customary norms and interactions with one another in a shared context (Frantz-Murphy, 1981, p. 206).[18]

2.3 Reflections

This brief historical overview of marriage practice in Islamic Egypt sheds light on two significant facts about the nature of Islamic legal tradition. First, this tradition was shaped by local contexts and customs, and in turn shaped them. In relation to this, Islamic, Coptic and Jewish legal similarities resulted not from 'borrowing', but from shared customs and contexts. Second, Islamic legal tradition is plural. It was not produced by a static monolithic entity; jurists spoke in different voices. In the next section, I elaborate on this plurality and how it created space for women's agency.

3. PLURALITY OF ISLAMIC LAW AND WOMEN'S AGENCY

The *fuqahā'* were not the only source of authority of Islamic law in medieval Muslim contexts. The rulers were also involved in the development of Islamic law, acting in their capacity as the protectors of the believers and the defenders of the faith. The ruler's legal and political authority, known as *siyāsa* or *siyāsa shar'iyya* (governance according to the Shari'a), also held significant weight in the formulation of the law. Furthermore, the plurality of opinions among *fuqahā'* and their disagreement and debates between them, known as *ikhtilāf*, opened the space for the rulers to issue binding decrees, resulting in legal plurality that remained compatible with religious teachings. Therefore, we should not equate Islamic law with *fiqh*. The former is broader than the

[18] Note that the Coptic marriage contracts written in Arabic, as discussed in Frantz-Murphy (1981), provide useful information about the relations between Muslims and Copts in early Islamic society.

latter, for it comprised the sum total of laws issued by both scholars and rulers as well as some local customs which were incorporated into the legal system.

The state interfered on a wide scale in the personal affairs of the people, including in the private domain of husbands and wives, leading to a shift in the judicial policy that worked in favour of women. The Mamluk sultans, facing political decline and chaos in the mid-fourteenth century, tried to consolidate their position and control their subjects by regulating society and dominating the domestic domain. This was a continuation of the practice of the Mamluk sultans, as since their early days, royal justice was their way to get the support of the public and gain legitimacy.

There was direct competition between the sultan and jurists over the legal system, culminating in the expansion of state courts at the expense of the qadi courts in the mid-fourteenth century. The jurisdiction of the state courts expanded to include payment of debts and marital disputes.[19] Military officials encroached on the realm of the qadis' jurisdiction by adjudicating family law cases to protect the rights of abused wives. This shift in judicial policy was advantageous to women as these military courts had more procedural flexibility and were able to issue different types of sentences to hold guilty husbands accountable. For example, women resorted to these courts to claim unpaid financial dues from their husbands, or have abusive spouses held accountable by imprisonment, fines or physical punishment. Women were also able to bring complaints to the court when husbands forfeited oaths that were conditioned on repudiation of the wife. With their new and strong hold on the domestic domain, these military courts challenged and undermined the authority of husbands (Rapoport, 2007, p. 35). This makes us question and rethink the dominant understanding of the dynamics and relations of power in Muslim gender and marital relations. The image of the domineering husband and the obedient wife was not always the case.

Just as the politics of fifteenth-century Egypt had a direct impact on the position of women in the household and marital relations, the economy of the age also greatly affected the dynamics of power in late Mamluk households.

---

[19] Al-Maqrīzī (2002, vol. 3, pp. 713–14) tells us that the jurisdiction of the state and military courts expanded after a case concerning commercial debt in Cairo in the year 1352, when the Ḥanafī qadis did not punish local merchants who would not pay the sale price to Persian merchants, as they had proclaimed themselves bankrupt. The Persian merchants appealed to the sultan, who interfered directly and gave orders to the chamberlain to oversee the case and cancel the ruling of the Ḥanafī qadis. From that day on, the debt cases and marital financial disputes were handed over to the military courts.

The end of the fourteenth and early fifteenth centuries witnessed great expansion in the textile industry of Mamluk Egypt. The draw loom and spinning wheel were introduced during this period, allowing for rapid and cheap production of textiles. Women benefited greatly from the expansion of this industry since they were the main participants in it; spinning was the most common occupation open to them in medieval Islamic societies. The more the industry expanded, the more employment opportunities opened up for women. The number of women earning wages was growing tremendously. Rapoport mentions in *Marriage, Money and Divorce in Medieval Islamic Society* (2006, pp. 31–50) that the number of female-headed households increased considerably during the late Mamluk age. Many women became decision-makers in the family, boosting their position in relation to their husbands and gaining a better bargaining position in cases of divorce.[20]

The monetization of marriage further enhanced the position of women (Rapoport, 2005, p. 53). During this period, everything became centred around money. The debasement of the currency, inflation and rising prices led to higher expenditure on the purchase of necessities, which in turn created a considerable need for cash. Accordingly, both husbands and wives started to evaluate several aspects of their relationship on monetary bases. Instead of waiting for the termination of the marriage to get their money, many wives forced their husbands to pay them the marriage gifts and support in cash during the marriage years. Many wives in the Mamluk period managed to secure their right to receive the deferred portion of the *ṣadāq* during the marriage years. This was a shift from deferring the payment of the *ṣadāq*, as was the custom in early Islamic Egypt as discussed earlier. However, as mentioned above, the practice of deferred *ṣadāq* was not eliminated altogether. Rather, fixed dates were set for the payment of the deferred portion, which were recorded in the marriage contract. Sometimes, the clause 'payment upon request' was added. If the husband did not pay the owed money, the wife would take him to court. Qadis who were presented with contracts that had the clause of 'payment upon request' forced the husband to pay the deferred portion to the wife. Husbands who refused to pay were subject to a jail sentence. Women demanded not only to receive the deferred portion of *ṣadāq* upon request, but also that their husbands pay them maintenance – food and clothing – in cash rather than in kind as was the practice before.

[20] Rapoport (2005) dedicates chapter 2 of his book to working women and how their mere presence was a challenge to the patriarchal ideal of the medieval family.

Paying the maintenance in cash became a common practice in the fifteenth century. In an account of his visit to Egypt in the late 1400s, a German traveller named Arnold von Harff referred to this practice and described how the wives when not given their monetary allowance would go to court to file a complaint against their husbands. If the complaint was found to be true, the husband was beaten, and the wife could secure a divorce from him (Letts, 2010, p. 112).

The marriage contract thus became like a business transaction and qadis attempted to enforce its resulting financial obligations. The jurists, by contrast, voiced alarm over this new practice and denounced the wives and the qadis for doing so. They believed that this monetization of marriage was reversing the spousal hierarchy. Jurists such as Ibn Taymiyya and Ibn Qayyim al-Jawziyya were among those who were most critical.[21] They argued that the qadis, in supporting the claims of the wives and punishing the husbands, disrupted the 'natural' power dynamics in marriage. They compared the position of the wife in the household to that of the slave who is supported and fed by the master in kind, not in cash. By punishing the husband and putting him in prison for not paying his wife a cash allowance, the qadi would therefore be making the husband a slave and prisoner to his wife, thus reversing and challenging the patriarchal ideal of the household.[22] The jurists in their criticism of the cash payment for the wife's support were in fact reacting to the changing social reality in fifteenth-century Mamluk Egypt. Marriage in this medieval Islamic society was very clearly a business transaction. It was a contract between two partners often leading to court litigation, in which both parties held power.

The practices of claiming the full *ṣadāq* upon request and spousal maintenance in cash continued to be the norm during the Ottoman rule of Egypt beginning in 1517. Thus, the sight of the creditor wife and the debtor husband continued to be common in society. Also, adding conditions to the marriage contract remained a common practice.[23]

---

[21] For example, Ibn Taymiyya (1997, vol. 32, pp. 124–5) stated that the husband should not be forced to pay the deferred portion of the *ṣadāq*. Ibn Qayyim al-Jawziyya (n.d., vol. 1, p. 163) said that imprisoning the husband for not paying the deferred portion of *ṣadāq* is a corrupt, evil act.

[22] Both Ibn Taymiyya (1998, p. 124) and Ibn Qayyim al-Jawziyya (1347 AH, vol. 3, p. 527) compared the position of the wife to that of a slave.

[23] The Ottoman period is beyond the scope of this chapter and already well studied, hence it will not be covered in this analysis.

Taken collectively, the studied sources show that far from being obedient wives subject to their husbands' authority, women in early and medieval Islamic Egypt had agency and were able to negotiate favourable marriage and divorce terms through a number of legal options and mechanisms. These mechanisms were shaped and facilitated by interconnected social and economic factors in the local context.

CONCLUSION

This historical analysis of marriage practices in early and medieval Islamic Egypt reveals the plural and dynamic nature of Islamic law. It shows that it is not sufficient to look at only the doctrine of the law; the practice is significantly important. This analysis also shows that studying diverse data sources gives us a better understanding of the lived realities of past communities. These sources show that women in the studied time periods were living under a dynamic plural legal system that gave them legal and social space to voice their demands and rights in a marriage. I acknowledge that the experiences of these active vocal women in the sources might not necessarily reflect the reality of all women. The records document stories of women who had the means to go to court, file cases and record their marriages. There were definitely other women who did not have the means to do so and were economically marginalized. Yet the mere fact that these cases existed in society – no matter how small their number – is striking. These cases did not appear in a vacuum; there were factors in society that were conducive to these practices. This suggests that perhaps there is a lot more to learn about the women of those times if we had more documented data. Stipulations inserted by the wife in marriage contracts, such as demanding her husband not to take a second wife or demanding exemplary behaviour and good conduct from her husband, are significant in an early and medieval society, especially because they were largely enforceable and not just vague or preachy didactic words.

On the whole, the researched sources suggest that Islamic legal tradition – despite its patriarchal doctrines – has mechanisms and processes that have enabled women to claim rights and negotiate more equitable marriages and divorces. This tradition was dynamic, plural and eclectic. The role of human interpretation in the law-making process resulted in differences in juristic opinions (*ikhtilāf al-fuqahā'*). The difference between the Mālikī scholars of Egypt and Medina over the issue of the *ṣadāq* and the mode of its payment was a clear example of how jurists were ready to adapt to their local context and to social change. The analysis also shows the interplay between Islamic, Coptic and Jewish marriage and divorce practices. This overlap helps us better understand the development in matrimonial practices as well as gender and social relations in early and medieval Islamic Egypt. In particular, the similarities between Muslim and non-Muslim marriage contracts challenge the normative view that Islamic law is unchanging and monolithic.

Furthermore, the role of sultans and military elites in the development and application of the law, by issuing of binding decrees and establishing military courts, contributed to the plurality and complexity of Islamic legal tradition. *Fiqh*, *siyāsa shar'iyya* and rulers' edicts were all sources of Islamic legal authority, and both jurists and rulers were constantly competing over the legal system. Such competition worked in favour of women as it gave them options and different means of litigation, leading to changes in family dynamics.

We can conclude that women in early and medieval Islamic Egypt had agency and were able to negotiate flexible and more just marriages and divorces in comparison to Egyptian women of today. It is interesting that while those women could easily opt out of a marriage and challenge the authority of their husbands through the monetization of dower and maintenance, contemporary Egyptian women's access to divorce remains difficult. It was only in 2000 that women got the legal right to petition for judicial *khul'*, and only after a difficult struggle against conservative forces in the state and the religious institution.

In short, this historical study of Islamic law in an Egyptian context affirms that Islamic law is plural in its sources of authority and can be responsive to social norms and customs. Esteemed jurists agreed and disagreed on matters large and small. These features can be the foundation for producing new egalitarian jurisprudence today. The *ṣadāq* could be a tool for the empowerment of women, as it allows for financial independence and can provide women with a degree of economic security and leverage in marital negotiations. In addition, the researched marriage contracts of the past demonstrate how the deferred *ṣadāq* was closely tied to the conditions added to the contract to check and limit the husband's prerogatives (Rapoport, 2000, p. 12). I believe that strategic use of the *ṣadāq* can enable women to negotiate more favourable terms for their marriages.

Inserting stipulations in marriage contracts could be another tool to negotiate more just marriages. Many women today are not aware of their right to add conditions to their marriage contracts or mistakenly think that marriage conditions are against the Shariʿa. The prevailing opinion, specifically among males, condemns the use of stipulations in marriage contracts. As a result, although the Egyptian legislators issued a new marriage contract in 2000 which allows both parties to enter stipulations, this right is rarely exercised.[24] Interestingly, Egyptian activists and feminists invoked the historical precedent of the marriage contract of Sukayna bint al Hussein when advocating for this new marriage contract. Sukayna, the granddaughter of Prophet Muhammad, was able to negotiate egalitarian marriages with her husbands through the use of stipulations.

To conclude, history is an empowering tool for women. This study highlights the importance of in-depth knowledge of the history of Muslim marriage practices as a means to inform present day efforts to advocate for gender-sensitive Egyptian family laws. Historical evidence can challenge arguments that depict Islamic law as sacred, monolithic and unchanging. Furthermore, it gives us insight into historical precedents that activists and lay women can draw on in their pursuit of egalitarian marriage and divorce rights.

REFERENCES

Abbott, Nabia. 1941. 'Arabic Marriage Contracts among Copts'. *Zeitschrift der Deutschen Morgenländischen Gesellschaft*, 95(n.F. 20) (1): pp. 59–81.

Abu Ghazi, Emad. 1998. *Qiraʾa Jadīda fi Wathʾiq Qadima: Hawāmish ʿala baʿad al-Wathʾiq al-ʿArabiya fi Misr', Zaman al-Nissa' wal dhakira al-Badila.* Cairo: Women and Memory Forum.

Afifi, Muhammad. 1996. 'Reflections on the Personal Laws of Egyptian Copts'. In *Women, the Family and Divorce Laws in Islamic History*, edited by Amira El-Azhary Sonbol, pp. 202–18. Syracuse, NY: Syracuse University Press.

Ergene, Boğaç. 2003. *Local Court, Provincial Society and Justice in the Ottoman Empire: Legal Practice and Dispute Resolution in Çankırı and Kastamonu, 1652–1744.* Leiden: Brill.

Fay, Mary Ann. 1997. 'Women and *Waqf*: Toward a Reconsideration of Women's Place in the Mamluk Household'. *International Journal of Middle East Studies* 29 (1): pp. 33–51.

Frantz-Murphy, Gladys. 1981. 'A Comparison of the Arabic and Earlier Egyptian Contract Formularies, Part I: The Arabic Contracts from Egypt (3d/9th–5th/11th Centuries)'. *Journal of Near Eastern Studies* 40 (3): pp. 203–25.

Friedman, Mordechai A. 1976. 'The Minimum Mohar Payment as Reflected in the Geniza Documents: Marriage Gift or Endowment Pledge?' *Proceedings of the American Academy for Jewish Research*, vol. 43: pp. 15–47.

[24] In a recent study on marriage practices and family law in Egypt, only four women in a sample of one hundred women and men (fifty each) inserted stipulations in their marriage contracts (Al-Sharmani, 2017, p. 134).

Goitein, S.D. 1967. *A Mediterranean Society. Vol. III: The Family: The Jewish Communities of the Arab World as Portrayed in the Documents of the Cairo Geniza, The Family*. Berkeley: University of California Press.

Grohmann, Adolf. 1934–1962. *Arabic Papyri in the Egyptian Library*. Vols. 1–6. Cairo: Egyptian Library Press.

Ibn Taymiyya. 1997. *Majmu' al-Fatawa*, edited by Amer el Gazzar and Ahmad el Baz. Mansoura, Egypt: Dar al-Wafa.

Ibn Taymiyya. 1998. *Ahkām al Zawaj*. edited by Mohamad Abdel Qadir 'Atta. Beirut: Dar al-Kutub al-'Ilmiyya.

Al-Jawziyya, Ibn Qayyim. 1347 AH. *I'lām al-Muwaqqi'īn 'an Rabb al-'Ālamīn*, edited by Mohamad 'Aziz Shams. Mecca: Dar 'Alam al Fawa'id.

Al-Jawziyya, Ibn Qayyim. n.d. *Al-Turuq al-Hukmiya fī al-Siyāsa al-Shar'iya*, edited by Nayef el Hamad. Jeddah.

Jennings, Ronald C. 1975. 'Women in Early 17th Century Ottoman Judicial Court Records –The Sharia Court of Anatolian Kayseri'. *Journal of the Economic and Social History of the Orient* 18 (1): pp. 53–114.

Letts, Malcolm (ed.). 2010. *The Pilgrimage of Arnold Von Harff, Knight, from Cologne: Through Italy, Syria, Egypt, Arabia, Ethiopia, Nubia, Palestine, Turkey, France and Spain, Which He Accomplished in the Years 1496–1499*. London: Hakluyt Society.

Little, Donald. 1984. *A Catalogue of Islamic Documents from al-Ḥaram al-Sharīf in Jerusalem*. Beirut and Wiesbaden: Franz Steiner.

Lutfi, Huda. 1985. *Al-Quds Al-Mamlūkiyya: A History of Mamlūk Jerusalem Based on the Ḥaram Documents*. Berlin: Klaus Schwarz Verlag.

Mālik ibn Anas. 1997. *Al-Muwatta'*, edited by Bashar Ma'ruf. Beirut: Dar al-Gharb al-Islami.

Al-Maqrīzī, Aḥmad ibn 'Alī. 2002. *Al-Mawā'iẓ wa-l-I'tibār fī Dhikr al-Khiṭaṭ wa-l-Āthār*, edited by Ayman Fu'ād Sayyid. London: Mu'assasat al-Furqān lil-Turāth al-Islāmī.

Masud, Muhammad Khalid, Rudolph Peters and David Stephan Powers (eds). 2006. *Dispensing Justice in Islam: Qadis and their Judgements*. Leiden: Brill.

Müller, Matthias. 2020. 'Andreas, Son of Petros, and the Monastery of Dayr al-Rūmī: An Usurious Monk? or a Monastic Record Vault?' In *Living the End of Antiquity Individual Histories from Byzantine to Islamic Egypt*, edited by Sabine R. Huebner, Eugenio Garosi, Isabelle Marthot-Santaniello, Matthias Müller, Stefanie Schmidt and Matthias Stern. Berlin and Boston: Walter de Gruyter GmbH.

Peirce, Leslie. 2003. *Morality Tales: Law and Gender in the Ottoman Court of Aintab*. Berkeley: University of California Press.

Petry, Carl (ed.) 1998. *The Cambridge History of Egypt, Vol. 1: Islamic Egypt 640–1517*. Cambridge, UK: Cambridge University Press.

Rapoport, Yossef. 2000. 'Matrimonial Gifts in Early Islamic Egypt'. *Islamic Law and Society* 7 (1): pp. 1–36.

Rapoport, Yossef. 2005. *Marriage, Money and Divorce in Medieval Islamic Society*, Cambridge, UK: Cambridge University Press.

Rapoport, Yossef. 2007. 'Women and Gender in Mamluk Society'. *Mamluk Studies Review* 11 (2): pp. 1–47.

Sealey, Raphael. 1990. *Women and Law in Classical Greece*. Chapel Hill: UNC Press.

Al-Sharmani, Mulki. 2017. *Gender Justice and Legal Reform in Egypt: Navigating Muslim Family Law*. Cairo: The American University in Cairo Press.

Sonbol, Amira El-Azhary (ed.). 1996. *Women, the Family, and Divorce Laws in Islamic History*. Syracuse, NY: Syracuse University Press.

Sonbol, Amira El-Azhary. 2003. 'Women in Shariʿah Courts: A Historical and Methodological Discussion'. *Fordham International Law Journal* 27 (1): pp. 225–53.

Sonbol, Amira El-Azhary (ed.). 2005. *Beyond the Exotic: Women's Histories in Islamic Societies*. Syracuse, NY: Syracuse University Press.

Sonbol, Amira El-Azhary. 2007. 'Shariʿah and State Formation: Historical Perspective'. *Chicago Journal of International Law* 8 (1): pp. 59–84.

Tucker, Judith E. 2000. *In the House of the Law: Gender and Islamic Law in Ottoman Syria and Palestine*. Berkeley: University of California Press.

Tucker, Judith E. 2005. '"And God Knows Best": The Fatwa as a Source of History of Gender in the Arab World'. In *Beyond the Exotic: Women's Histories in Islamic Societies*, edited by Amira El-Azhary Sonbol, pp. 165–79. Syracuse, NY: Syracuse University Press.

Tucker, Judith E. 2012. *Women, Family, and Gender in Islamic Law*. Cambridge, UK: Cambridge University Press.

Welchman, Lynn. 2004. 'Egypt: New Deal on Divorce'. *The International Survey of Family Law*, 2004 edition, edited by Andrew Bainham, pp. 123–41.

Muslim Family Laws: Trajectories of Reform

Lynn Welchman, Zahia Jouirou and Marwa Sharafeldin

What are the different pathways through which Qur'anic ethics of equality, justice and care can be and have been incorporated today into the texts and practices of Muslim family laws? This chapter considers this question through an initial consideration of 'Muslim family law' and its 'trajectories of reform', then an exploration of three approaches to reform: substantive reform of family laws through a combination of religious, human rights and other arguments; procedural or administrative reform; and enactment or reform of laws outside but intimately connected with family law.

Substantively, 'Muslim family law' as a term covers the spousal relationship (marriage, how it is conducted and its termination by death or divorce), the parental relationship (rights and obligations arising in that relationship, also child custody and guardianship), succession and other family relationships insofar as they give rise to rights and obligations such as maintenance of and responsibility for minors. Muslim family law matters to mothers, grandmothers, daughters, sisters, aunts and wives, as well as their male relatives, because it governs our most intimate relationships. It also configures relations with the world outside the family, including the worlds of education, work, property, politics and resource distribution (Htun, Jensenius and Nelson-Nuñez, 2019). This is the case whether we are referring to 'Muslim family law' in statutory form, that is, in individual laws issued by Muslim majority states such as those considered here, or less tangibly, as part of a 'normative repertoire' that for Baudouin Dupret exists alongside other normative repertoires, interacting and competing with them. The use of 'normative repertoire' according to Dupret (1999, p. 34) aims 'to account for the discursive forms used in the construction of an action claiming to be founded on a norm (a justificatory norm) and expressed in a norm (a prescriptive or regulatory norm)': that is, the way things actually *are* (and somehow have always been) and also the way things *should be*. Considering the 'religious normative referent' to 'the Shariʿa' in the Egyptian Constitution, Dupret (1999, p. 39) observes that:

> without prejudice to its content, the fact that it [the Shariʿa] presents and combines a conception of the world and a system of values, and is perceived to do so, make it fertile ground for ideological exploitation ... Every (or nearly every) protagonist in the political arena projects his[/her] own representation of it and the use [s/]he intends to make of it in that area, where it is supposed to be seen as the expression of a self-evident fact. In reality, of course, this is anything but the fact – each actor's relationship with the norm is highly strategic in nature.

The idea of the Shariʿa (in this case, governing Muslim family relations) as a normative repertoire frames the debates on family law reform mostly through the discourses of Islamic jurisprudence (*fiqh*), which shaped the promulgation of these laws. The fact that the meanings of repertoire differ according to who is invoking it is shown in our consideration below. Ideas of justice, equality and care, for example, which may be associated with the Shariʿa by those expecting its protection, may be perceived to be undermined or contradicted by the *fiqh* articulations that are developed in statutory family laws. This understanding underpins our use of these terms in this paper and supports the distinction made by Musawah and others between Shariʿa ('the way', as revealed in Islam's sacred texts) and *fiqh* (legal science and juristic rulings), a distinction which the movement views as critical in order to 'pierce the veil of sanctity surrounding the classical law' and to counter the notion of Shariʿa as 'immutable and not open to negotiation or to contestation from within' (Mir-Hosseini, 2012, p. 300).[1]

[1] For a more detailed argument as to the significance of making the distinction between *fiqh* as the human result and Shariʿa as the original message, in the specific context of arguments for Muslim family law reform, see Mir-Hosseini (2009, pp. 25–7); Ali (2003).

In this chapter, we proceed from the findings of many scholars and activists that Muslim family laws as currently codified remain largely the result of patriarchal interpretations of the source texts and situated contexts, and that the formulations of male authority in these interpretations stand in contrast to the normative principle of human equality. The normative principle of human equality has not been fully achieved anywhere in the world. But for the purposes of Musawah's work and for this chapter, key among the formulations of male authority in classical and current expressions of Muslim family law – and therefore key among the challenges – are the juristic and legislative articulations of *qiwāma* and *wilāya* as, respectively, male authority in the spousal relationship and male guardianship over females in the family (Welchman, 2015). Such constructions of male authority in the family are by no means particular to dominant articulations of Islamic jurisprudence (*fiqh*) or indeed to Muslim family laws, but there are particular challenges in addressing how they might give way to the principle of equality and the Qur᾽anic ethics of justice, equality and care. That is because these two concepts (*qiwāma* and *wilāya*) may be understood as 'legal postulates' in the sense given by Masaji Chiba, a Japanese scholar of comparative law: 'A *legal postulate* is a value principle or value system specifically connected with a particular official or unofficial law, which acts to found, justify and orient the latter' (1986, p. 7).

Chiba's work was developed by Werner Menski first into a triangle and subsequently into a kite to illustrate Menski's theory of the constituent elements of 'living law' (Menski, 2012, p. 79). Menski's four-pointed kite has four different sources of normative ordering in each of its corners: 'Nature' (religion/ethics/morality); 'Society' (socio-legal approaches); 'State Law'; and 'International Law'. Each corner of the kite is itself plural, and a complicated numbering system is used to further develop the theory. Menski explains that the kite image 'seems useful also to convey the dynamic nature of all law' (Menski, 2012, p. 79; see further 2006, p. 595). We can picture the four corners of a kite, each representing different sources of normative authority, overlapping and competing with each other, contesting and confirming, pushing and pulling, and all this in specific, situated contexts.

Menski's thinking may help in framing the approach already articulated by Musawah at its launch in 2009. The 'Musawah Framework for Action' (2009, p. 2) outlines four focuses of attention in Musawah's struggle for gender equality: Islamic teachings, universal human rights, national constitutional guarantees of equality and other national legislation, and lived realities. These correspond to Menski's 'Nature', 'International Law', 'State Law', 'Society', with 'Nature' articulated by Menski as religion/ethics/morality, and which – depending on context – we might also identify as the *shar'i* (Islamic legal) normative repertoire.

It is possible that for Musawah the kite may help to illustrate two different overarching ideas in the struggle for equality and justice. First, it could demonstrate how, from all four corners and the many interstices, there are practices and principles that come together to uphold 'equality, fairness and justice'. Second, it may help to show how legal postulates – such as, for example *qiwāma* and *wilāya* – in some states come together with state law and judicial practice to frustrate these goals or to uphold them through gender-sensitive reforms and practices in cases where successful efforts for change have combined advocacy and actors in more than one corner.

The issue of 'equality of the spouses' in a Muslim marriage has been increasingly prominent during the last fifty years, largely in synchronicity with the 1979 adoption of the UN Convention on the Elimination of All Forms of Discrimination Against Women (CEDAW) and associated feminist activism – international, regional and national/local – around the idea of gender equality and related implications of human rights discourse. Legislators, commentators and scholars discussing Muslim personal status laws in different parts of the world frequently invoke their strategic understanding of the Shari'a as a normative repertoire that requires codification of particular *fiqh* interpretations within family laws. These interpretations often enforce norms that are premised on concepts such as *qiwāma* and *wilāya*. Such norms are at odds with ever-evolving international equality and non-discrimination norms (see Freeman, Chinkin and Rudolf, 2012), with the lived realities of many Muslim families and the exigencies that challenge them, and with the fundamental values of equality and dignity found in Islam's sacred texts and identified by Musawah and others as underpinning Muslim moral and legal impetus. Hence, such laws may be met with counter arguments based on an understanding of the Shari'a that invoke norms of justice and equality, which can combine with successful advocacy efforts to achieve or at least lay a foundation for change.

We try to bear these dynamic configurations in mind in this chapter, examining how, in the interstices of the kite's corners, multiple factors come together to create change in the direction of gender justice and equality in Muslim family laws. There are many different paths to effecting such change, often intersecting and coinciding. In their work on family law reform in Palestine, Johnson and Hammami (2014, p. 19) cite the

UNIFEM 2008/2009 *Progress on the World's Women* report (2008, pp. 72–3), which identifies

> three types of changes in gendered access to justice: the normative (changes in constitution and legal framework), procedural (implementation of changes and more equitable and fair procedures of judiciary, police and other state authority), and cultural (changes in attitudes of those responsible for protecting women from arbitrary exercises of power).[2]

We will focus on three approaches to change that to some extent mirror these categories, namely substantive changes to family laws themselves through a diversity of arguments balanced to fit the political, religious and social context; procedural or administrative reform; and enactment or reform of laws outside family laws that nevertheless address family and cultural practices – in this case, violence against women.

Advocates have employed a number of broadly defined strategies besides the three outlined here. Such strategies include reorganization of the judicial system (for example, to include specialized family courts, where family-related claims may be considered together and quicker progress made to settlement, or family guidance departments attached to the courts that have officials trained in areas other than law or *fiqh* such as sociology, child welfare, etc.); judicial interventions through court rulings that are anti-discriminatory and pro-equality (such as courts in Tunisia ruling that a Muslim woman's marriage to a non-Muslim man is valid, and an appeals court in Morocco recognizing the existence of marital rape); and judicial training and increasing diversity in the judicial body, including through the appointment of women judges. Running beside all of these is the technique of *takhayyur*, the 'selection' among the vast body of rulings that comprise *fiqh* on Muslim personal status issues to include some but not others in the laws enforced by the state.

These strategies or approaches have not yet resulted in comprehensive change that Musawah advocates and others are seeking. But they have often achieved results that may be seen as important cumulative milestones towards this kind of change, which requires vigilant monitoring and follow-up. It is also evident that change to the statutory narrative of the family is insufficient

[2] Johnson and Hammami expand 'cultural' to include 'community and society attitudes' for their work.

to achieve change in family life – and particularly women's lives – without supportive institutional input such as socio-political and economic policies that take an intersectional approach especially for marginalized, rural and poor women.

First, we focus on strategies involving reform of substantive laws through arguments based on religion, constitutional law, human rights, socio-economic realities and other sources. We then examine approaches to legal change through procedural or administrative regulation. Finally, we look at efforts to influence family dynamics and practices by enacting or reforming legislation outside family or personal status laws, such as in the enactment of laws related to domestic violence or revision of penal codes. In conclusion, we consider the strengths and weaknesses of these approaches and reflect on how, regardless of the approach, it is essential to have women's groups and other civil society actors engaged in sustained action that can be amplified when political opportunities for reform arise.

Given space limitations, the explanations of each strategy and the examples are broad and illustrative, and do not comprehensively cover the diverse tactics employed in different contexts. In addition, the examination is limited to the Middle East and North Africa (MENA) region, though examples of reform can be found throughout Muslim majority and minority contexts.

1. SUBSTANTIVE FAMILY LAW REFORM USING MULTIPLE FRAMES OF REFERENCE

The most direct approach to reforming Muslim family laws is advocating for changes to the texts of the laws themselves. Changing the legal texts, either through amending individual provisions in a piecemeal fashion or by introducing an entirely new law, establishes new standards for family relations, and over time affects family dynamics through impacting the types of recourse that may be accessed through the courts and the kind of behaviour that will be supported or sanctioned by the judiciary.

Yet reform of laws in general, and family laws in particular, is not easy. Mala Htun and Laurel Weldon's research demonstrates that a state's relationship with religion shapes the degree of inequality within its family laws (Htun and Weldon, 2015; 2018). In countries where religion is institutionalized by the state and an alliance between the state and religious authorities exists, family laws may be both more discriminatory and more resistant to change. Htun and Weldon state:

> When religion is institutionalized, patriarchal interpretations – and interpreters – of family law gain greater authority and more immunity to contestation. They become increasingly insulated from external influences and more closely linked to the public status of religion. Challenges to particular versions of family law are seen as challenges to the entire church-state relationship. (2015, pp. 452–3)

This makes it difficult for women's movements and other reformers to call for changes in family law, as such calls are viewed as direct threats to the alliance's power interests. Htun and Weldon conclude: 'When state power and religious power are fused, particularly in highly devout societies, it is difficult to reform family law toward greater equality, and patriarchal norms endure' (2015, p. 471). They are careful to note that this analysis is not linked to one particular religion, but to the institutionalization of religion within state power. At the same time, they note that religion is not fixed, but is a field of contestation that must be responsive to remain relevant.

Where a nexus of state and religious power has led to discriminatory family laws that are difficult to reform, those arguing for change must challenge that power and demonstrate how religious interpretations can incorporate change, and why social and political factors make that change so essential. It is for this reason that many successful reform efforts in recent years have been crafted around an advocacy strategy that relies on different reference points for reform, often related to the corners of the four-pointed Menski or Musawah 'kite'. Reformers combine a variety of arguments to challenge the state-religion nexus. This includes arguments from within Islam itself, showing how concepts from Muslim legal tradition can embrace greater gender equality. Constitutional and legal requirements in the state laws are brought into play, with advocates as citizens who are equal under the law and entitled to equal constitutional rights and protections. Similarly, activists refer to international human rights standards within conventions that have been ratified by the state, and that the state is thus obligated to fulfil. Finally, activists offer evidence of how laws affect people's lives based on data. Because each national context is different, with various political, social, religious and economic elements and actors creating a delicate balance, reform strategies in one country may vastly differ from those in another, depending on what concepts resonate more.

This section considers three examples of advocacy efforts in which a variety of arguments were used to push for substantive changes to family laws or personal status codes: the 2004 comprehensive family law reform in Morocco that included the concept of equality between spouses as well as changes to the rules on child marriage, marriage guardianship and other areas of family law; the 2000 reform of divorce laws in Egypt; and the recent inheritance reform debates in Tunisia.

1.1 Morocco: comprehensive family law reform

In February 2004, the Moroccan parliament unanimously enacted a new Law of the Family, commonly called the *Moudawana*,[3] that established equal status and shared responsibility for women and men within the family while reconciling Islamic principles, human rights and lived realities in contemporary Moroccan society. This reform was a ground-breaking victory for women in Morocco, who struggled for years to promote the reform. It continues to present a model for other Muslim-majority countries around the world, despite criticisms of parts of the law as implemented in practice over the years since its promulgation.[4] A diverse consultative commission established by King Mohammed VI drafted the law. King Mohammed VI introduced the importance of this new code in a speech that referenced the Qurʾan, *fiqh* principles and Hadith.[5]

The campaign for reform of the *Moudawana* involving coalition building, research, articulation of demands and arguments, a comprehensive advocacy and communications strategy to reach decision-makers and the public, and

[3] '*Moudawana*' is the Moroccan transliteration of the Arabic *Mudawwana*, meaning Code. Morocco's original Personal Status Code (*mudawwanat al-ahwal al-shakhsiyya*) of 1957/8 was substantively amended in 1993 and then replaced in 2004 by the current Family Code (*mudawwanat al-ʿusra*).

[4] These criticisms are made by Moroccan women's rights advocates and scholars; see in summary Nour-Assaoui (2020).

[5] This section, including the description of arguments made by Moroccan advocates, is written based on the following sources: Collectif 95 Maghreb-Égalité, 1995; 2003; presentations by Rabéa Naciri and Amina Lemrini at Sisters in Islam and Musawah meetings in Kuala Lumpur, Malaysia, in March 2006 and February 2009; Pittman and Naciri, 2007; El Hajjami, 2013; Nour-Assaoui, 2020.

the development of international support for reform. Moroccan women's rights advocates worked together with activists from Tunisia and Algeria in a regional women's coalition called Collectif 95 Maghreb-Égalité, which produced a number of advocacy documents that used international human rights provisions side-by-side with arguments based on Islamic jurisprudence, guarantees of equality in the national constitution and laws and sociological trends relating to the status of women and realities of Maghrebi families.[6] The comprehensive approach allowed the Moroccan women's rights groups to engage multiple audiences (the king, the government, religious groups, the judiciary, the media, the public), all of whom had different perspectives and interests, and provide convincing arguments for reform of the discriminatory law from a variety of angles.

Multiple aspects of the new law might serve as a model for advocates from other countries in Muslim contexts as they seek to address discriminatory provisions within their own laws. For example:

- **Raising the minimum age of marriage:** The new *Moudawana* raised the minimum age of marriage to 18 years for all from 15 for girls and 18 for boys.[7] Moroccan advocates used a variety of religious arguments to push for raising the minimum age of marriage in addition to international human rights standards and evidence of the harm child marriage causes. They noted that the Qurʾan and Hadith do not specify an age of marriage, so this is an area for interpretation by *fuqahāʾ* that can evolve based on societal changes. Proponents of child marriage often cite verse 65:4 regarding the ʿ*idda* for divorced women, noting that it contains a category for women who have not menstruated, which they interpret as pre-pubescent girls. But this could also mean women who do not menstruate because of a health condition. Proponents also mention ʿĀʾisha's age when she married Prophet Muhammad, but advocates against child marriage noted that his marriages were unique to him, and there are questions around ʿĀʾisha's actual age

[6] Musawah's Framework for Action (2009) was inspired by the Collectif 95 Maghreb-Égalité approach.

[7] The final law allowed judges to grant exceptions to this minimum age and did not specify an absolute minimum age below which children may not marry. Women's groups have been lobbying to abolish these exceptions for several years. See further in Section 2.2 below; Y.J.(2019).

at the time of the marriage and consummation. Moroccan advocates also argued strongly that child marriage is against the *maṣlaḥa* (well-being) of all the parties concerned – the wife, husband and their offspring – because of the physical, emotional and social harm it brings to girls who marry, the anxiety it adds to the marital relationship and the health concerns for children born by young mothers.

- **Elimination of matrimonial guardianship requirement:** The new Law of the Family explicitly allows women who are of age to contract their own marriages without a matrimonial guardian (*walī*). Advocacy for this change involved human rights standards, the constitutional principle of equality, and sociological arguments that matrimonial guardianship relegates women to the position of minors and is detrimental for women and society. Advocates used juristic arguments, such as those of Mālikī jurist Ibn Rushd, that disputed the necessity of a guardian as a condition for marriage. They pointed out differences in interpretation between the *fiqh* schools, with jurists using verse 2:232 to argue both for and against the requirement of marriage guardianship. There are also questions about the authenticity of the hadiths that support the role of a matrimonial guardian. The Ḥanafī school does not demand a marriage guardian for a woman of age as long as she marries a man who is compatible to her (*kufʾ*) and receives the same dower as her peers. The Moroccan commission and legislators adopted the Ḥanafī doctrine and eliminated these two latter conditions.
- **Establishment of equality in marriage:** The law defines marriage as a partnership and specifies the 'mutual rights and duties' between spouses, which include: 1) cohabitation, mutual respect, affection and preservation of the family interest; 2) both spouses assuming responsibility of managing and protecting household affairs and children's education; and 3) consultation on decisions concerning the management of family affairs. Moroccan advocates again combined arguments to promote the idea of restructuring marriage as an equal partnership instead of viewing the male as the head of household. The reformers observed that mainstream principles on the issues of obedience and male authority, including readings of verse 4:34, are matters of interpretation. They noted the ques-

tionable authenticity of many hadiths related to obedience and discussed how interpretations of verse 4:34 around maintenance focus wrongly on authority instead of the idea of taking care of one another. They pointed to other verses of the Qur'an that can support the idea of mutual partnership within a family, such as 30:21 and 2:187. Advocates pointed to the equality clause in the constitution and provisions in various human rights conventions that Morocco has ratified. They also shared sociological data which show that men and women in Morocco already share household responsibilities – from income to chores to parental roles – and data and arguments about how equalizing such roles could lead to greater marital harmony.

1.2 Egypt: expanding women's options for divorce

In the early 2000s, after a multi-year advocacy campaign by a coalition of women's rights activists, lawyers and NGOs, the Egyptian parliament adopted three new laws related to the family: a new marriage contract, a new procedural law (Law No. 1 of 2000), and another new procedural law that established family courts (Law No. 10 of 2004). One of the major successes of Law No. 1 of 2000 – and one of the provisions that brought about intense opposition – was article 20, which allows a wife to initiate a *khul'* divorce without consent of her husband by agreeing to forfeit certain financial rights. Previously, women had to prove ill-treatment or harm by the husband to apply for divorce, a process that could take years, while a husband could unilaterally repudiate his wife.[8]

The Egyptian advocacy coalition prepared a series of arguments grounded in religious, sociological and human rights terms of reference. The advocates argued that *khul'* is a form of divorce that has always been practised in Islamic history. It is based on verse 2:229 and a hadith concerning a woman who came to the Prophet seeking divorce even though her husband had done her no wrong. The report states that the Prophet granted the woman divorce in exchange for her giving up her dower and without securing the consent of the

---

[8] This can happen in the absence of the wife; the divorce is considered legally valid if the husband registers it.

husband.[9] The Egyptian advocates argued that the new law was true to the Qur'anic verse and the hadith, unlike the preponderant opinion in most juristic schools that the consent of the husband was necessary in a *khulʿ* divorce. Advocates also argued that the new Egyptian *khulʿ* provision ensured equality of all citizens as stipulated in the country's constitution by granting women access to judicial divorce without needing to prove harm or go through lengthy court proceedings. This would help address the problem of discrimination and hardship women suffer in seeking divorce. Thus, the new law helped create a more conducive environment for justice, stability and harmony in Egyptian families (Sonneveld, 2012).

Al-Azhar supported the new provision, and the Sheikh of Al-Azhar stated that the *khulʿ* provision was in accordance with Islamic sources. However, there was fierce opposition from religious scholars, parliamentarians and other figures in society. These opponents made patriarchal arguments that were couched in religious and sociological terms. Some argued that the law, by making the husband's consent irrelevant, diminishes his claim to *qiwāma*. Other counter arguments included that such a law would benefit rich women who could afford to give up their financial rights and that women would abuse the access to divorce and break up their families while their husbands were diligently working as migrants in faraway countries to provide for them and their children. Regardless, the law passed due to the multidimensional and successful advocacy work of women's rights groups and the support of the government and the religious establishment.[10]

1.3 Tunisia: equal inheritance

Articles 85 to 152 of Tunisia's Code of Personal Status codify classical inheritance rules in which distribution of shares are laid out for men and women based on their relationship with the deceased.[11] While women receive equal or more shares in certain circumstances, in four significant situations men receive

[9] In some narrations, the wife's name was Jamīla while in others it was Ḥabība. The husband was named Thabit ibn Qays.

[10] This advocacy work included working closely with supportive religious scholars; co-hosting workshops to educate the public about the benefits of the new law and its (religious) legitimacy; media campaigns; lobbying parliamentary members from the ruling party and from Al-Azhar.

[11] The current text of the Tunisian Code of Personal Status is available in Arabic (https://tinyurl.com/TunisiaCodeArabic) and in French (https://tinyurl.com/TunisiaCodeFrench).

a double share and women a single share (Elbalti, 2018, p. iii). After decades of advocacy by Tunisian women's rights activists, lawyers and NGOs, the Tunisian cabinet approved a bill proposed by the president outlining equality in inheritance for men and women in November 2018 and forwarded it to parliament for approval (Sadek, 2018). However, Ennahda, the party with the parliamentary majority, rejected the president's proposal when it was first announced, and Tunisian society is reported to be quite divided on the issue (Bajec, 2019; Sadek, 2018). While there have been two parliamentary discussions on the topic, as of August 2021 the Tunisian parliament had not yet enacted the bill into law (Jouirou, 2021).

The struggle for equality in inheritance goes as far back as the early twentieth century, when the Tunisian religious scholar Tahir al-Haddad argued that inheritance rules can be interpreted to allow equal rights between men and women and especially for children of the deceased. He argued that rules in Islam were introduced and gradually adapted based on changes in society, and that inheritance rules can do the same (al-Haddad, 2011, pp. 30ff; English translation Husni and Newman, 2007, pp. 47–8). Discussions and debates over these ideas continued in Tunisian history. *Tafsīr* by religious scholar Muḥammad al-Ṭāhir Ibn ʿĀshūr supported a thesis that the so-called 'inheritance verses' in the Qurʾan[12] are not definitive, and that there are many differences in interpretation (Ibn ʿĀshūr, 1978). He also introduced justice as one of the main purposes of Shariʿa in his *Treatise on Maqāṣid al-Sharīʿah* (Ibn ʿĀshūr, 2011; English translation 2013). In 1973, President Habib Bourguiba unsuccessfully proposed that sons and daughters should have equality in inheritance. Since 1995, feminist organizations Association des Femmes Tunisiennes pour la Recherche sur le Développement [AFTURD], Association Tunisienne des Femmes Démocrates [ATFD], and the regional coalition Collectif 95 Maghreb-Égalité have developed arguments and organized campaigns separately and together on equality in inheritance laws and published volumes that included sociological, cultural, religious and juristic arguments for equality.[13]

The 2011 revolution resulted in a new constitution in 2014 that incorporated several equal citizenship provisions in part based on civil society interventions (Mekki, 2014). After this, Tunisian civil society and some political

[12] These verses include 2:180, 240; 4:7–9, 11–12, 19, 33, 176; 5:105–108.

[13] See, for example, AFTURD, 2006; Collectif 95 Maghreb-Égalité, 1995, pp. 27–9, 34–5; Collectif 95 Maghreb-Égalité, 2003, pp. 131–40, 199–200; ATFD, 2018; Collectif 95 Maghreb-Égalité, 2014.

parties began to focus more on establishing equality in the family and for the harmonization of inheritance legislation with constitutional provisions (see, for example, FIDH, 2015). The Committee for Individual Freedoms and Equality (COLIBE) was created by former president Beji Caid Essebsi in August 2017 to ensure that the country's legislation is consistent with the new 2014 Constitution and its equal rights clause (article 21), and with Tunisia's international human rights obligations. Three sets of actors were involved in the discussions. The first is those who resist all reform on the grounds that inheritance laws are immutable (mainly preachers, traditionalist scholars, conservative thinkers). The second is those who argue for equal inheritance based purely on secular human rights and constitutional arguments (mainly secular feminist associations and human rights organizations, as well as intellectuals and politicians). The third group is those who argue for equal inheritance using a holistic approach, including religious, constitutional, sociological and human rights arguments, and who try to show that reform from within the Islamic frame of reference is possible (Islamic and secular intellectuals and some feminist and human rights organizations). In 2018, COLIBE issued a report in support of inheritance reform as well as a number of other issues such as equality in nationality law and equality in the family (COLIBE, 2018). It was in accordance with this report that the cabinet approved a bill on inheritance reform to send to parliament.

The COLIBE report took up justifications for equal inheritance that had been made by progressive Islamic scholars and feminist organizations based on Islamic precepts. The report suggested the adoption of the principle of equality in the law, while leaving individuals the option of adopting the traditional Shariʿa rulings, provided that this is stated in a will written by the deceased before death. The commission took the approach that Islamic precepts must be understood within a social and historical context, and that interpretations of religious texts, including the inheritance texts, can change as society changes. Religious and jurisprudential arguments for equal inheritance included:

- **Ontological equality of all humans in the Qur'an**: This is exemplified in verses such as 49:13.
- **Historical trajectory**: Before Islam, heirs were defined under tribal rules rather than by filiation. With the advent of Islam, customary succession rules were reformed in favour of women, with women represented in the categories of those who can inherit (Jouirou,

2018, pp. 59–78). The succession rules should continue to evolve based on the needs of the current time and place and social roles (AFTURD, 2006, Tome 1). This is similar to laws related to slavery evolving when the social situation changed.

- **Diversity of *fiqh* approaches:** *Fiqh* rulings on inheritance are not sacred but human interpretations, flexible and evolving; there have always been differences in *tafsīr* between the *fiqh* schools (Youssef, 2018, pp. 9–18).
- **The concept of testamentary will (*wasiya*):** The Qur᾿an allows the use of the *wasiya* to freely bequeath possessions in ways that are more in line with equality and justice.
- **Reformist interpretations of the Qur'an:** Reformist thinkers such as Tahir al-Haddad, Mahmoud Mohamed Taha, Muhammad Iqbal, Muhammad Shahrur and Nasr Hamid Abu Zayd provided arguments and interpretations that allow for equality in inheritance. These include ideas such as how the principle of ontological equality of all humans should govern all interpretations and rules derived from the Qur᾿anic verses, and that the Qur᾿anic rule of the double share for men and single share for women in certain situations can be seen simply as a recommendation, rather than a command (see El Hourri, 2015). Reformist thinkers stress the importance of applying *ijtihād* in light of the *maqāṣid al-shari῾a* (objectives of the Shari῾a) to derive rulings that speak to contemporary needs. If equality is God's final purpose in the sacred text, inheritance rules should shift towards that goal.

In addition, civil society arguments for inheritance reform rested on the state's legal obligations to ensure equality, including the constitutional guarantee of equality for all citizens under article 21 and commitment to protect women's rights under article 46; international human rights standards (particularly ICCPR and CEDAW) (see, for example, Ashihi, 2015); and article 21 of the regional Protocol to the African Charter on Human and Peoples' Rights on the Rights of Women in Africa (the Maputo Protocol), which Tunisia ratified in August 2018.

Civil society and the COLIBE report also relied on numerous economic and sociological arguments to support law reform (Collectif 95 Maghreb-Égalité, 2003, pp. 136–8). For instance, double shares for men are justified based on the idea that men are responsible for providing for their families, but this does not represent reality. Women materially contribute to their families through paid employment as well as domestic work and caregiving, in some cases as sole providers. The structure of families has also changed, and new economic and social realities should be recognized in the laws. Furthermore, the fact that many families are trying to circumvent inheritance rules through a variety of strategies, particularly with the goal of providing equally for their daughters, demonstrates that there is a sense that these rules are unjust.

The Tunisian Coalition for Equality in Inheritance (*Coalition tunisienne pour l'égalité dans l'héritage*), a coalition of associations and NGOs, has organized major events to support reform such as a national march and a civil and cultural event titled 'Tunis Congress on Individual Liberties and Equality'; videos by Tunisian public figures broadcast on social networks; the formation of a committee of 'Ambassadors of Equality and Individual Freedoms' composed of many Tunisian public figures; and more than 90 associations and NGOs signing the 'Tunisian Covenant for Equality and Individual Freedoms'.

In February 2019, without providing reasons, the parliament's Health and Social Affairs Committee suspended discussions on this initiative. Since then, until the time of writing (August 2021), civil society, women's associations and a significant number of academics, intellectuals and artists have been working to urge parliament to bring the bill to a vote and to develop societal awareness of the need to achieve equality (Jouirou, 2021). Despite the delays, the Coalition remains hopeful that the bill will soon be enacted into law.

1.4 Reflections

The reform processes in the Moroccan, Egyptian and Tunisian cases teach us that substantive reforms in family laws that aim at gender equality can be successfully pursued through multiple strategies combining religious, social, economic and historical arguments, as well as seeking to work with different stakeholders. Muslim laws vary considerably in the rights they grant women, as influenced by a combination of differences in *fiqh* schools, interactions with other sources of law – including both internal (customary) and external (imperial, colonial, international) influences – and the context's specific social, economic, cultural and historical evolution. Similarly, law reform processes differ considerably between contexts, especially in terms of the balance between different forces within the living law.

2. PROCEDURAL AND ADMINISTRATIVE REFORM

One of the most common approaches to Muslim family law reform consists of implementing measures that can broadly be described as procedural or administrative.[14] These measures can be presented to the public as regulatory rather than judgemental or prohibitive, and as securing rights that command considerable support through state oversight rather than taking on the substance of *fiqh*-based principles. As with the case of substantive law reform, procedural and administrative reform efforts often combine arguments from different frames of reference such as the religious tradition, state or constitutional law, international human rights requirements and socio-economic data.

This section will consider the following procedural and regulatory approaches: a) marriage registration requirements; b) judicial scrutiny of intended acts for their compliance with preconditions identified in the law or attached regulations; and c) notification requirements. These approaches will be considered in relation to the efforts to eliminate or reduce the incidence of child marriage and of polygyny and to protect women's access to their inheritance rights. The goals around each of these issues ultimately aim to ensure the principle of equality.

2.1 Marriage registration requirements

Registration requirements and related measures (such as court scrutiny over issues such as age of marriage or conditions for permission for a polygynous union) play a key role in determining the validity of a marriage contract and the legally enforceable rights and obligations arising from that contract and throughout the union. Through registration requirements, the state can expand its knowledge of the private lives of its citizens and at the same time give effect to identified objectives of codified law, such as regulating and reducing the incidence of polygyny and early marriage. The CEDAW Convention in article 16(2) requires formal registration and links this with preventing child marriage, and the CEDAW Committee in its 1994 'General Recommendation 21' linked registration requirements with 'equality between

[14] See for example Alim and Yassari (2016, p. 113), where the authors identify three broad categories of reform 'devices': codification of substantive family law, 'private autonomy, reflected in the emergence of stipulations in marriage contracts', and 'procedural devices'.

partners, a minimum age for marriage, prohibition of bigamy and polygamy and the protection of the rights of children' (para. 39).

States and legislatures may justify the obligatory registration of a Muslim marriage on grounds of *siyāsa shar ʿiyya* (a concept usually translated as 'governance according to the Shariʿa') and public interest (*maṣlaḥa*).[15] Penal law may be relied upon to encourage compliance with registration requirements, with penalties (usually fines) for violation, though analysis of the effectiveness of such penalties in promoting registration is limited. On the other hand, proponents of child marriage and polygyny may successfully appeal to established *fiqh* to support their case. Governments and judiciaries may not want to reject the legal validity of a marriage contract that meets *fiqh* terms and the state's legal requirements (for example, minimum age of marriage or constraints on polygyny) by the time it comes to the attention of the authorities, especially for marriages that have resulted in pregnancy or childbirth.

Unregistered marriages continue in different parts of the Muslim world. A considerable amount of scholarship has focused on the legal and social motivations and implications of marriages conducted outside the state system, such as the lack of judicial remedy. There are also discussions on how the public and the judiciary react to the statutes, particularly in Egypt but also in Morocco, Syria and the UAE (see, for example, Carlisle, 2008; Fawzy, 2004; Hasso, 2011; Shaham, 1995). In Indonesia, Bedner and van Huis (2010) argue from a pragmatic perspective against proposals to more strictly enforce existing rules on marriage and divorce registration. But civil society groups generally argue for tighter state control over and scrutiny of the conclusion of marriage, as further discussed below.

2.2 Court scrutiny and associated interventions

As noted above, requirements to register marriages are included in family laws or civil codes as a mechanism for state control over marriage and pursuit of its other social objectives. In some states, the effort to reduce child marriage or the incidence of polygyny combines these registration requirements with procedural processes of scrutiny for compliance, such as a set of preconditions that may be included in regulations supplementing the family law.

[15] See for example the position of the Palestinian Supreme Fatwa Council in 1996, as described in Welchman (2003, p. 60).

A recent debate around the minimum age for marriage took place in Jordan in the lead up to the enactment of the 2019 Law of Personal Status (Law No. 15 of 2019).[16] The issue has engaged the attention of legislators, civil society, the general public and officials from the Supreme Justice Department,[17] which is responsible for the Shariʿa court system, over a sustained period. The standard age of capacity for marriage is 18 years for both males and females, which was implemented in the 2001 amendments by decree (in proposals drafted by the country's Royal Commission for Human Rights) and in the 2010 Temporary Law (in a process led by the Supreme Justice Department) after vibrant civil society campaigns.[18] Debates around the 2019 law focused on exceptional cases that are ruled by special Regulations. In the end, the 2019 law did not result in a change to the already established absolute minimum age of marriage, except in wording from those who have 'completed their 15th year' (aged 15), to those who have 'reached their 16th year' (aged 15) in the 2019 wording.[19]

The 2019 law is the first new Jordanian family law to be passed by parliament and then signed by the king, rather than issued by decree as a Temporary Law as in the case of the laws of 1976 and 2010 (during lengthy periods when Jordan's legislature was suspended), or as amendments in the meantime. In welcoming the new law in 2019, the *Qāḍī al-Quḍāh* stressed that civil society, the public and both parliamentary houses had engaged in extensive examination and discussion of the law and emphasized the fact that it had gone through all the proper legislative stages.[20] Shaykh ʿAbd al-Karim al-Khasawnah invoked the repertoire of reform methodologies that had been

---

[16] The 2019 Law of Personal Status (Arabic text) is available from the Supreme Justice Department at: https://sjd.gov.jo/Pages/viewpage.aspx?pageID=197

[17] This is the official English translation for the *Da'irat Qāḍī al-Quḍāh* in Jordan.

[18] JLPS 2019 article 10(a). The age of capacity was first set at 18 in 2001 amendments by decree that failed to pass when brought to parliament for subsequent approval, but remained in force until passed by decree in the 2010 amendments to the 1976 JLPS. See in detail on the debates on the 2001 amendments Welchman (2009, pp. 128–30 and 132–5). See also, including on the 2010 debates, Engelcke (2019, pp. 117–32). For civil society interventions see, for example, those by the Nujud Coalition to Combat Child Marriage at www.sigi-jordan.org/?p=5168

[19] JLPS 2019 article 10(b). Under the JLPS 1976, the 'standard' age of capacity for marriage was set at 16 for males and 15 for females, under the lunar calendar (see Welchman, 2000, pp. 108–21).

[20] *Qāḍī al-Quḍāh* Interview, 2019. Similar claims of transparency and consensus (although no parliamentary process was included) were made around the passage of the 2010 temporary law (Englecke, 2019, p. 126). Our thanks to Shereen Abbady for directing us to this interview and to the on-line parliamentary debate.

employed to construct the law, including *ikhtiyar* or 'selection' (critics might say 'picking and choosing') among the different *fiqh* schools with the intention of realizing the 'manifest interest' in accordance with the *maqāṣid al-sharīʿa* (objectives of the Shariʿa) and 'as befits the needs of the age and developments of the time'; the inclusion of modern scientific methods, such as the use of DNA to establish paternity; and the deployment of *ijtihād* in certain inheritance matters. Later contextual references invoke 'lived reality' as supporting certain interventions in the law.

The *Qādī al-Qudāh* noted that after the House of Deputies had agreed on the 328 articles of the bill, the Senate approved all but three provisions which were duly considered in a joint meeting of the two houses (the *majlis al-umma*). One of these contested provisions was on the exceptional minimum age of marriage, which the lower house had voted to keep as in the existing law and the Senate wished to increase by one year. As noted above, the joint meeting changed the wording while retaining the substance and approved the addition of a reference to the principle of offering courses for those embarking upon marriage, optional in the law but mandatory in the Regulations for the Granting of Permission for those aged under 18 and over 15.[21] While arguments for retaining the exceptional minimum age at 15 included references to Islamic *fiqh* as considering 'minors' to refer to children before they reach puberty, many interventions during the April 2019 debates in the joint session were made against foreign actors (embassies, organizations, etc.) for their perceived interference in and attacks on Jordanian values and society.[22] The debate can be compared to earlier discussions in Jordan on minor marriage that were framed in terms of national identity and fixed gender relations, describing a valorized notion of 'family' presented as integral to that identity and distinctively Jordanian.

The decision on retaining the exceptional age of marriage at 15 did not meet the demands of the Jordanian National Commission for Women, an official body, which proposed to raise it to 16 (Jordanian National Commission for Women, 2018). Nor yet did it meet the aspirations of civil society and non-governmental women's rights groups who had been advocating against

[21] Ta'limat no.1/2017 issued in accordance with art. 10 (b) of Law of Personal Status no.36/2010 by *Qādī al-Qudāh* Shaykh 'Abd al-Karim akl-Khasawnah, 20 June 2017. (*Official Gazette* 5472 16 July 2017 pp. 4500–2).

[22] Compare analysis of the debates on the 2001 amendments when brought to parliament for review in Welchman (2009, pp. 132–5); and Engelcke (2019, pp. 120–2, and pp. 158–9 on the 2010 debates).

child marriage for some years, highlighting the negative impact of this practice on young girls' health and education as well as the rates of divorce and of mortality in childbirth resulting from child marriage (see, for example, Tadamun – SIGI Jordan, 2019a).

Although the exceptional minimum age of marriage remains at 15 years, there has been incremental strengthening of procedural safeguards, for example through regulations. In his address to the Jordanian public just after the 2019 Law was passed, the *Qāḍī al-Quḍāh* emphasized that his department continually issues regulations to govern procedures for approval of an application for marriage of an underage party. The regulations were last updated in 2017 with application beginning in 2018, the year before the new family law was passed.[23] The *Qāḍī al-Quḍāh* claimed that underage marriage had already been reduced during the first year of the new regulations.[24]

In the regulations, the court must find there is a 'necessity required by an interest' in the proposed marriage, and then is required to observe several factors before granting permission. These include ascertaining consent and choice of the underage parties and the 'realisation of a benefit or the prevention of a corruption', as phrased in the very first iteration of these Regulations in 2002 (see Welchman, 2007, p. 162). One new element includes specification that the age difference between the engaged couple should not exceed fifteen years, a reduction from the twenty-year age gap that had since 1951 required the judge's attention. The 2011 Regulations had required only that the age difference be 'appropriate'.[25] There is a requirement that the fiancé is not already married – potentially a significant protection against the polygynous marriage of underage girls – and that the marriage not be a reason to drop out of school, which again addresses a significant concern of those campaigning

---

[23] Previous versions of the regulations include those of 2002 (see Welchman, 2007, p. 162) and 2011.

[24] The Supreme Justice Department *Annual Statistical Reports* for 2017 and 2018 give percentages out of all marriages concluded that year involving females marrying under the age of 18 as 13.4 per cent and 11.63 per cent respectively. The 2019 report was not yet available at the time of writing.

[25] See Welchman (2000, pp. 113–15) for the history of this provision in Jordanian law, which prohibited an age difference of more than twenty years without further examination of the fiancée's consent and choice (as the younger party). This was interpreted as being constrained to cases of marriage under the age of full capacity under the JLFR and was specified as meaning that in the JLPS 1976; the amendments of 2001 removed this constraint and left the twenty-year gap as requiring the judge's attention no matter what the age of the woman as the younger party. Article 11 of the 2019 law maintains this position.

against early marriage.[26] Protection of an underage bride's economic position is envisaged in the requirement that the fiancée's dower is not to be less than the proper dower (*mahr al-mithl*), so that at least technically some financial rights are secured for her; and the court is to explain to the fiancée that she has the right to insert stipulations into the marriage contract in accordance with the law. Again, this opens the space for a supportive discussion of further potential protections and rights to be secured at the time of the contract, should those involved in drawing it up take the opportunity as such. These matters (the dower, any stipulations) and others are all to be recorded in the deed of permission for the marriage to be concluded, should the court decide to grant it. The couple are also required to present a certificate that shows they attended a course for those intending to marry organized by the Supreme Judge Department or any other authorized party.[27] In 2019, the *Qāḍī al-Quḍāh* also pointed to an increase in penalties for involvement in a marriage below the age of 15 and for not officially documenting a marriage contract as part of the effort to reduce or eliminate early marriage.

Shortly after the interview with the Supreme Justice and at the end of a National Week to Combat Child Marriage, Jordanian women's research and activism group Tadamun welcomed the apparent reduction in marriages of those aged under 18, but insisted that it was impossible to tell from the available statistics whether the clause regarding a girl's education was having any effect – 'we don't know how many married girls are in school' (Tadamun – SIGI Jordan, 2019b). They posed questions for the Ministry of Education about the statistics, the role of the Supreme Justice Department in following up on this clause, and the consequences for the condition being broken and the girl prevented from continuing her school education. The apparent lack of a monitoring and remedy mechanism for this clause in the Regulations clearly undermines their potential, and active follow-up by non-governmental groups is ongoing.

Some of the concerns reflected in the preconditions for early marriage in the Jordanian Regulations are echoed in different efforts in Morocco, where ongoing advocacy to set an absolute minimum age of capacity for marriage (for exceptions below the standard age of 18) have not yet been successful.

[26] These were first introduced in the 2011 Regulations.

[27] As noted above this is referred to in the 2019 law as optional for all engaged couples. See Hasso (2011, pp. 153–66) on 'family instruction' in the UAE and Egypt; Engelcke (2019, pp. 199–224) considers the conduct of training by different parties in Morocco in a reflection on 'the prevalence of multiple normativities'.

Here again arise opportunities for engagement by actors beyond the narrow court sphere: what Engelcke terms 'street-level bureaucrats' whose direct involvement at different stages of a process contribute to 'multiple normativities' in implementing the law. Engelcke reports that 'social assistants' are increasingly engaged with investigating whether, for example, permission is being sought for an underage marriage because of financial pressures on the girl's family (rather than in the specific interest of the girl) and whether the marriage will lead to the interruption of her education. Certain judges are reported to have rejected applications where 'families wanted to marry off their daughters for financial reasons' (Engelcke, 2019, p. 207).[28] Nevertheless, this again seems to remain a potential impact: figures from the Ministry of Justice reproduced by Engelcke appear to show that from 2006–10, the courts approved 86.8 to 92.2 per cent of the applications for minor marriage. Morocco's National Human Rights Commission, the Conseil National des Droits de l'Homme (CNDH), in its report on ten years of the implementation of the 2004 *Moudawana*, expressed grave concern at the statistics on early/child marriage and at the abuse of the provisions on documenting out of court unregistered marriages in order to avoid legal constraints on minor marriages (CNDH, 2015, pp. 10, 13).

2.3 Notification requirements

This form of procedural approach is based on ensuring all those considered involved in or implicated by a particular act are in possession of the relevant information to allow an informed choice. This type of requirement may be used as a marriage requirement generally, for regulation of child marriage or polygyny, in divorce cases, and in cases related to distribution of property and inheritance.

Notification requirements are often used in efforts to regulate polygyny, and most commonly require the court to ensure that the female party – the fiancée – is aware that her husband-to-be is already married. Less commonly, the court is also required to notify the existing wife or wives that the husband is marrying again. Further contention arises over whether this notification is

[28] See also p. 199 note 5 regarding statistics from the Minister of Justice and the impossibility of knowing whether the increased number of minor marriage registrations is because of the requirement to register, rather than an increase in the numbers per se.

to be made before or after the polygynous contract is concluded. In at least two Arab League member states, notification requirements legislated in one statute have been reduced or removed in subsequent legislation, relaxing constraints that such notification requirements place upon the prospect of a man's polygynous marriage.[29]

The Jordanian National Commission for Women had sought full disclosure to the existing wife or wives and an examination with all spouses of various financial implications of the intended marriage. However, the 2019 Jordanian law kept the existing provision (dating from 2001), which requires the judge to inform the fiancée that her husband-to-be is already married, and to inform the existing wife or wives after conclusion of his new contract of marriage. There had previously been objections from Jordanian Islamist and other figures – including parliamentarians – even to this requirement of *ex post facto* notification. Resistance to such measures (see also in Qatar for example) can be seen at least partly as an acknowledgement of the substantial challenge that could be posed to a man's decision if his wife (and in turn her family and others) are empowered with prior knowledge before the polygynous marriage is concluded: this is at least in some part to do with other forms and nodes of power (Welchman, 2007, p. 82).

In Morocco, Engelcke reports that 'social assistants' (mostly young women) in some cities are charged with investigating 'whether the first wife is sick, whether she is informed about the second marriage, and whether the husband is financially capable' of supporting another family, including through home visits. Their findings are significant to the judge responsible for giving permission for the polygynous union. Engelcke notes that 40 per cent of the applications to conclude a polygynous union were rejected over the period 2006–10, and suggests that overall, 'the conditions for polygyny ... might become subject to greater scrutiny once the position of the social assistant is well operationalized' (2019, pp. 200, 206, 207). The CNDH reported figures from the Ministry of Justice showing that in 2010, only 43.5 per cent of applications for permission for a polygynous marriage were approved, although its critique of the government for not tackling known abuses of the transitional period provisions included avoidance of the polygyny restrictions and its recommen-

[29] Yemen's 1992 law included notification of existing and intended wives before the contract was completed, but amendments in 1998 withdrew the first requirement. The notification requirements in Bahrain's 2009 law for its Sunni community were significantly softened in the 2017 unified family law that regulates both Sunni and Jaʿfarī communities.

dations included abrogating permission for polygynous marriage (CNDH, 2015, pp. 12, 13, 16).

In Palestine there is a history of judicial activism and high profile leadership on Muslim family law issues from the Department of the Palestinian Chief Islamic Justice even before the sustained absence of a functioning legislature (since 2006/2007).[30] Faced with different laws in the Gaza Strip and the West Bank at the start of Palestinian Authority rule, combined with the continuing absence of a Palestinian family law to replace them, successive Chief Islamic Justices have made considerable use of Circulars and Directives to institute or amend procedural requirements. A 2013 study from Birzeit University documented a 'key shift in local legal reform strategies from a focus on normative justice' to one more focused on 'procedural and cultural issues', following the interim years after the Oslo Accords (1995–2000) (Johnson and Hammami, 2014, p. 10). Among these procedural strategies was a 2011 circular to Shariʿa court judges requiring them to ensure, before carrying out the marriage contract of a married man, that the fiancée is apprised that he is already married to someone else, and that the existing wife or wives is notified that the husband is intending to marry again.[31]

In a slightly different take on the notification approach, the Palestinian Shariʿa court establishment (the Department of the Chief Islamic Justice) has also acted to protect women's access to their *fiqh* inheritance rights. A first administrative directive in 1999 sought to ensure that all entitled heirs were to be made aware of the monetary value of their portions and the implications of the division of the estate, before signing a final settlement on the division of the estate (Welchman, 2000, p. 375). A 2011 circular instituted a waiting period before female heirs were allowed to renounce their inheritance entitlement (Johnson and Hammami, 2014, pp. 10, 48).[32] Here, a combination of notification and administrative procedure requirements aims at protecting women from feeling pressured into renouncing their inheritance portions, and

[30] Women's groups and wider civil society have a strong role in Palestinian society and there has been sustained engagement with the issue of family law.

[31] Supreme Judge Department Circular 48/2011 from the Chief Islamic Justice. For a review of earlier procedural initiatives taken in this way and clearly reflecting concerns raised in a major civil society campaign on family law reform in the late 1990s, see Welchman (2000, pp. 374–5).

[32] These two issues (concerning renouncement of inheritance entitlements) are also included in the relevant Jordanian Regulations issued in 2011 in accordance with the 2010 Law (Engelcke, 2019, p. 176).

to ensure women have full information as to the value of their entitlement should they indeed choose to waive it in favour of another family member. The procedural approach is in place in advance of other possible future discussions on the applicability of the established *fiqh* positions such as those discussed above.

2.4 Reflections

The examples in this section demonstrate how procedural and regulatory approaches such as registration requirements, court scrutiny and notification requirements can be used to promote equality when substantive law reform fails or is not possible in a particular climate. Such interventions may be built on and expanded through incremental iterations after reviews for effectiveness and changing circumstances. These features arguably make them more realistically attainable than more absolute approaches to substantive parts of Muslim personal laws and less liable to be dismissed as 'West-imposed' or 'against Shariʿa' in invocations of this normative repertoire. The hope is that through incremental absorption of the expectations disseminated through such measures, expectations which resonate with wide sections of the populace (such as girls' education, for example), the targeted practices and attitudes themselves will change, permitting further approaches towards the egalitarian Qurʾanic ethics. Procedural and administrative measures however are not cost-free: they require effective enforcement and oversight mechanisms, institutionalized and funded by the state, to achieve their objectives. This in turn may need further targeted advocacy and creative proposals, building iteratively on lessons learned across the region and indeed the world by communities working towards the same objective.

3. ADDRESSING FAMILY MATTERS THROUGH OTHER LEGISLATION

In some cases, reformers choose to enact new laws or amend existing laws that relate to family issues, while avoiding the historically difficult process of reforming actual Muslim family laws. Reformers in different Muslim contexts have frequently chosen this approach around the issue of violence against women (VAW), which is a major source of injustice for women in family laws and practices.[33] A number of Muslim-majority and minority countries have enacted new domestic violence laws or reformed their penal codes, resulting in significant legal developments that may help curb violence against women.[34] Yet it may also bring about the paradoxical situation in some countries where a law combatting domestic violence applies side by side with a Muslim family law that tolerates it, at least by giving a violent husband impunity.[35]

Violence against women is not unique to the Muslim world. Globally, 50,000 women were intentionally killed by a family member in 2017. Some 30 per cent of women who have been in an intimate relationship have been subject to physical and/or sexual violence (UN Women, 2019a). The World Health Organization (2013, pp. 17–18) estimates that its Eastern Mediterranean and Southeast Asia regions have the highest levels of violence in the world, with 37 and 37.7 per cent of ever-partnered women having experienced physical and/or sexual violence at the hands of intimate partners. There are reports that percentages may be higher in some places (UN Women Arab States, n.d.). The economic cost of domestic violence in some countries amounts to 3.7 per cent of the country's GDP, which is more than double what most governments spend on education (World Bank, 2019). These are serious numbers, affecting not just women but entire societies.

The 1993 UN Declaration on the Elimination of Violence against Women explains that violence is rooted in unequal relations between the sexes. It defines VAW as 'any act of gender-based violence that results in, or is likely to result in, physical, sexual or psychological harm or suffering of women, including threats of such acts, coercion or arbitrary deprivation of liberty, whether occurring in public or in private life'. This definition therefore helps us see locations of violence in Muslim contexts and how violence is normalized in both private and public spheres. For instance, physical harm could include 'disciplining' the wife, child marriage, 'honour' killing; sexual harm includes marital rape; psychological harm can include unilateral divorce, requiring women's

---

[33] Successfully combatting violence against women in the family requires changes in the social structures and behaviours in any given society, as well as in the law. This chapter's focus is confined to law reform as one of those avenues of change.

[34] The chapter includes penal codes in its scope because violence is generally addressed through penal codes as opposed to family laws (whether those laws are religious or secular). In the contexts studied here, family and penal laws often share similar assumptions about gender roles grounded in patriarchal norms, which affect the gendered rights and obligations of different family members.

[35] This clearly crystallizes what Mir-Hosseini (2016, p. 67) calls an epistemological crisis facing Islamic jurisprudence and the laws based on it.

obedience, threat of polygyny; and threats, coercion, or deprivation of liberty can include requiring the husband's permission to work, go out, travel and have equal guardianship over children.

There have long been and will continue to be debates about the role of Islamic law in allowing, restricting, or prohibiting domestic violence and similarly different understandings of how Islamic law has played a role in reforms addressing domestic violence in Muslim contexts.[36] Many family and penal laws in MENA and other Muslim majority states not only contain provisions that promote an unequal relationship between the spouses,[37] but also condone the varying levels of violence mentioned above even if the countries have domestic violence legislation.

Penal codes in some Muslim contexts also often reflect a patriarchal understanding of a man's *qiwāma* (authority) over his female kin. Some of these codes allow for varying degrees of violence against women – wives and other female relatives – if committed in 'good faith' within the bounds of Shariʿa for the purpose of 'disciplining'.[38]

It is important to note, however, that family laws and penal codes are not the main reason we have such high rates of domestic violence in these countries. It is the patriarchal system with its socio-economic and political arms that uses the frame of Muslim family law as a tool to fulfil patriarchy's interests and condone violence within the family institution. Nonetheless, inequality and male guardianship instituted in family laws undoubtedly skew the power relation between men and women, rendering these laws an important contributing factor to the phenomenon of violence.

Given the historical difficulty in reforming Muslim family law, states have recently moved to address domestic violence issues in a variety of other ways, including enacting or reforming laws other than the family law. Many factors came together to allow a change in laws related to domestic violence; these

---

[36] A major focus of these debates is the dominant hierarchical interpretation of verse 4:34 that justifies authority of men over women and related 'disciplining' of wives. This debate is beyond the scope of this chapter; for discussions of it see Mir-Hosseini et al. (2015) and Stowasser (1998).

[37] See the discussion on *qiwāma* in the introduction to this chapter as well as Mir-Hosseini et al. (2015).

[38] For example, article 41 of the Iraqi Penal Code (Law No. 111 of 1969) states: 'There is no crime if the act is committed while exercising a legal right. The following are considered in exercise of a legal right: (1) The punishment of a wife by her husband.' The Libyan Penal Code's article 375 allows a man to beat wife, daughter, or sister if they are found committing unlawful sexual intercourse, as long as he does not cause serious harm (UNDP Arab States, 2019, p. 44).

can be seen to originate in all four corners of Menski's kite of living law as discussed in the introduction to this chapter. These factors can be understood through examples of new laws combatting violence against women and reform of penal code provisions related to exoneration of rapists through marrying their victims.

3.1 Laws combatting violence against women

Countries in the MENA region predominantly have Muslim family or personal status laws; eight such countries have recently passed laws combatting domestic violence or violence against women: Algeria (2015), Bahrain (2015), Jordan (2008, updated in 2017), Lebanon (2014), Morocco (2018), Saudi Arabia (2013), Tunisia (2017), the Kurdistan Region of Iraq (2011), and most recently Kuwait (2020). Egypt, Iraq and Palestine have all prepared draft laws on domestic violence that are yet to be enacted. These laws fulfil the international standards of due diligence on prevention, protection, prosecution, punishment and the provision of reparations to varying degrees.[39] Some include access to services such as medical and psychological care. They also vary in the scope of the definition of domestic violence, generally including physical, sexual, psychological and economic violence. Some such as Tunisia's go further by adding moral and political violence as well as discrimination against women within their definition of domestic violence (UNDP Arab States, 2019, p. 46).

The Tunisian feminist movement began advocating for a law combatting violence against women as far back as the 1990s. The necessity of a law protecting women became apparent after the movement witnessed the level and extent of violence against women from its work on the ground.[40] This work included conducting research and field surveys on the nature and extent of the violence; collecting stories of victims; building safe shelters; providing psychological rehabilitation services; creating alliances with organizations,

---

[39] There are important critiques that most of these newly passed laws in the region were not in compliance with State obligations for due diligence nor with the UN model law on violence against women. For more see ESCWA (2017, p. 14).

[40] More recently, the national survey on violence against women of 2010 estimated that nearly 50 per cent of Tunisian women had experience one form of violence or the other during their lifetime (UN Women, 2017b). This is significantly higher than the global rate of 30 per cent (Bailey, 2018; UN Women, 2019a).

human rights activists, judges and lawyers; working with UN agencies; raising public awareness; and working collectively to draft and advocate for a law against VAW.[41]

In addition to the work of the feminist movement, several significant steps paved the way towards the law, including state action around recognition of the problem as well as the occurrence of noteworthy public incidents involving VAW. According to scholar-activist Monia Ben Jemia, the feminist movement struggled for decades to push the state to officially recognize that VAW is indeed a serious problem in Tunisian society, after the Ben Ali regime's initial denial of it. This culminated in 2002 with a national strategy to combat VAW followed by a 2004 law to combat sexual harassment that arose from both state and civil society efforts (Arfaoui and Moghadam, 2016, p. 642; Ghalib and Ghoneim, 2017).

In 2012 a woman was raped by two policemen who justified their crime by what they saw as her 'immodest behaviour' with her boyfriend. The case created an outcry and Tunisian feminists organized protests, petitions and workshops to galvanize public support against this violence. In 2014, the appeals court doubled the policemen's sentences from the court of first instance to fifteen years in prison (Arfaoui and Moghadam, 2016, p. 644). In 2016, after the Law on Eliminating Violence against Women had already made it to parliament and before its final passing in 2017, a 13-year-old girl living in a village was found to be pregnant outside wedlock. The family of the girl and the man who impregnated her agreed on marriage to hide the pregnancy and managed to obtain a judicial licence for the marriage from the court. When the news spread, the women's movement immediately took action, issuing statements and organizing protests against the marriage of the girl child. Following this, the Minister of Justice ordered the review of the judicial authorization in this case as well as all laws predating the 2011 revolution to align them with the 2014 Constitution (UNDP Arab States, 2019, p. 37). This incident is cited as one of the reasons that helped speed the passing of the law in parliament in 2017, combatting violence against women.[42]

Under the new law, the police are obliged to refer violence cases to hospitals for forensic examinations.[43] Doctors in hospitals are reporting a rise in

[41] Interview with Dr Zahia Jouirou, 17 September 2020. For more details about these activities see Arfaoui and Moghadam (2016).

[42] Interview with Dr Zahia Jouirou, 17 September 2020.

[43] Historically police forces were part of the problem, as they would discourage women from filing complaints. The 2017 law now punishes members of the police force who commit this act with imprisonment. It is interesting to see this very same punishment in article 13 of the most

cases from two to six patients per week as police deal with these cases more appropriately and women feel more empowered to come forward. Some lawyers using the law in court also report that judges are slowly taking these cases more seriously now as opposed to before when they would encourage women to go back home quietly. However, challenges to the realization of the full potential of the law remain, such as dedicating sufficient state funds for its implementation and building of shelters; changing cultural mindsets of society, judges and other state actors who oppose the law; and raising women's awareness of their new rights. Indicating how passing new laws is not enough, Ahlem Belhadj, a psychiatrist and activist involved in this work from its early days, stated: 'It took thirty years of campaigning to get this law. But it might take us another thirty to really change the situation for women' (Bailey, 2018).

3.2 Exoneration of rapists upon marriage

Besides enacting specific laws combatting violence against women in the family, countries have also pursued amendments in the penal code as a route for reform. For example, in 2015 Algeria made notable amendments to its Penal Code, increasing penalties for violent offences involving spouses (Law No. 15-19 of 2015, articles 266 *bis*, 266 *bis* 1, 330, 330 *bis*). Several MENA countries have recently repealed provisions in their penal codes that exonerated rapists from punishment if they marry their victims (UNDP Arab States, 2019, pp. 37–9). In Tunisia, Penal Code articles 227 *bis* and 239 (exonerating rapists from punishment upon marriage) were eventually abolished by the adoption of Law No. 58 of 2017 on the Elimination of Violence Against Women. In Jordan, after intensive advocacy efforts, the equivalent article 308 of the Penal Code was abrogated by the Jordanian parliament (UN Women, 2017a). A month later, and again after a widely supported civil society campaign, Lebanon abolished article 522 of its Penal Code on the same issue. In 2018, the President of the Palestinian Authority repealed article 308 in its Penal Code in the West Bank.

Progress in some of these countries stemmed from civil society activism taking advantage of tragic, well-publicized incidents of violence or other political opportunities:

---

recent Kuwaiti law combatting domestic violence, evidence that recent laws are better taking into consideration the enabling or disabling role that state actors play in the perpetuation of VAW.

- **Morocco**: Against the backdrop of the progressive 2004 Muslim family law, an incident took place that spurred nationwide action against a provision in the Penal Code exonerating a rapist from punishment upon marrying the victim. In 2012 a 16-year-old girl, Amina El Filali, was raped and later made to marry the perpetrator[44] who, through a court judgement, was exempted from punishment by marrying her based upon article 475 of the Penal Code.[45] She was subjected to physical abuse at his hands for seven months during their marriage; this eventually led to her suicide. The case generated unprecedented public criticism and spurred protests in various cities around Morocco (BBC, 2014). Both national and international media widely covered the case and its developments. The government then organized a round table including prominent women's rights organizations, the Minister of Family and Women's Issues, the Minister of Justice and a government spokesperson. In January 2014, the Moroccan parliament unanimously abrogated the second clause of article 475 of the Moroccan Penal Code.
- **Jordan**: Progress on this issue began with a political opportunity instead of a widely publicized incident. In October 2016, King Abdullah II ordered the reform of the Penal Code. Campaigners who were already working on the issue, including civil society activists, the Jordanian National Commission for Women, parliamentarians, justice sector professionals and journalists, seized this opportunity and started campaigning intensively for the repeal of article 308 of the Code (UN Women, 2019b). Campaigners publicized Ministry of Justice numbers that 159 rapists avoided punishment based on this article between 2010 and 2013. They highlighted similar reforms that took place in Egypt in 1999 and Morocco in 2014, even organizing an exchange between Moroccan and Jordanian parliamentarians to understand the Moroccan experience in repealing a similar provision. They rooted their

[44] See Mesbahi (2018) for a nuanced presentation of this story that portrays the complexity of the incidents composing it.

[45] This article does not come from Islamic legal tradition nor from local traditional practices. Rather, it was copied almost verbatim from the Napoleonic code that was imposed on Morocco in 1913 (Mesbahi, 2018, p. 52). See Dupret (2001) on the case of Egypt repealing a similar provision traced to French law.

campaign in real stories of women to show that the suffering is real and that the campaign was not merely a western feminist agenda. Through analysis of twenty-two court cases in which the rapist eventually married the victim, they showed how these marriages usually ended in violence or divorce, indicating that the article does not provide for the basis of a healthy marriage and family. They attended parliamentary discussions on the issue and collected signatures on petitions for change two days prior to parliament's voting to increase pressure. Finally, on 4 August 2017, the Jordanian parliament repealed the Penal Code article (UN Women, 2019b).

- **Lebanon:** Around the same time, activists in Lebanon also seized the regional momentum and organized a campaign to repeal a similar legal provision in the Lebanese Penal Code. They traced the roots of this article to the Napoleonic code showing that it is not part of local traditions or values. They also conducted a survey that showed that only 1 per cent of the Lebanese public know about this provision. ABAAD, a prominent Lebanese women's rights organization, led a visually impactful campaign entitled 'A White Dress Doesn't Cover the Rape' to push for the repeal of this provision. This campaign used social media, videos and protests in front of parliament depicting battered women wrapped in bandages that eventually morph into wedding dresses (ABAAD, 2016). In August 2017, the Lebanese government voted to repeal article 522 (UN Women, 2019b).[46]

While these are all important legal advancements, they do not represent the end of the practice or even its persistence in other provisions of the law.[47] More needs to be done to change public perceptions around honour and women carrying the weight of the family's honour on their shoulders.

---

[46] For the wider sphere of gendered violence in Lebanon also see Mikdashi (2015).

[47] For more on the complexities of the predominant 'culture of rape-marriage' that still persists in rural Morocco in spite of this law reform, see Mesbahi (2018, p. 54). In Jordan, other articles on the perception of honour can still be addressed, such as article 340 that still allows for reduced penalties if a man murders or injures his wife or female relative when caught in the act of adultery. In Lebanon, articles 505 and 518 of the Penal Code that are still in effect and have similar implications as the repealed article 522. For the text and a description of these articles, see UNDP (2018, p. 14); International Commission of Jurists (2019, p. 15).

3.3 Reflections

In the experiences above of passing new legislation on domestic violence or amending penal code provisions, as opposed to reforming the family law, there is an interplay between different factors – such as religious precepts, human rights norms, state laws and particularly lived realities – in each country's reform playing field. Different actors involved in this process managed these interactions in ways dictated by a particular context's givens and constraints. However, in every case, it was women's groups who helped push for law reform through extensive and varied advocacy efforts. They based their work on real life stories of women or families who were suffering, lobbying around tragic stories, as in Morocco and Tunisia; gathering data; conducting surveys and publicizing this information, as in Tunisia on domestic violence and in Lebanon and Jordan on the issue of rapists escaping punishment by marrying their victims; and familiarizing decision-makers with the issues. They showed that problematic practices and legal provisions that institutionalized violence either did not reflect local values and beliefs or had foreign colonial roots. They built on previous similar reforms in countries with similar cultures and religions, creating a ripple effect of reforms. They also seized political moments that could open the door to successful reform.

In light of the serious difficulties facing direct reforms of the substantive Muslim family law, reforms to penal code provisions and adoption of laws combatting domestic violence present an alternative to spur needed change. These particular pathways to change shape public discourses on gender relations in the Muslim family and contribute towards changing the meta-narrative justifying domestic violence. As such, these legal changes – and the cultural shifts they help foster – form part of a cumulative effort that can eventually influence the family law reform trajectory. However, the potential of such reforms will be restricted if the legal framework is not harmonized with this new conception of gender relations. This includes reforming other provisions in the penal code and other laws, but more importantly family law itself, which is an important location reproducing gender inequality and potential for violence in the family. The patriarchal understanding of *qiwāma* and *wilāya* that informs these laws and legitimates men's authority over women needs to be directly addressed and changed. Without this, recent efforts to combat domestic violence, through the approach of reforming other laws or passing new ones, can be seriously undermined.

CONCLUSION

This chapter demonstrates how reformers can use a multitude of different approaches or pathways to address family issues in Muslim contexts. Such pathways are both selected for and affected by the context in terms of the types of reform needed and the political and social constraints and opportunities. This is why, for example, Morocco was able to adopt major substantive family law reforms, while other countries have focused primarily on procedural changes or enacting stand-alone domestic violence laws.

Each country has its own law reform arena in which the four corners of Menski's 'kite' of living law – the national, international, religious and social – interact and engage with each other. Additionally, the four corners affect one another, with religious jurisprudence changing as a result of the conversation with human rights, human rights adapting to local contexts, and state law changing in response to the realities of people's lives. Not every corner of the kite is in play in every case. One or two corners may be more of a force in any given situation, or may look different depending on the situation. In a similar way, equality and justice do not hold fixed meanings in this process, but also evolve and respond to the context and the various sources of law.

While this chapter provided examples only from the MENA region, Muslim family law reform fuelled by one or more of the three approaches has occurred in other regions as well. For instance, provisions around minimum age of marriage were changed in Indonesia in 2019 based on extensive advocacy using knowledge and arguments from religious, domestic, international and social perspectives (Muthmainnah, 2018; UNICEF, 2019).[48] In Malaysia an administrative directive allowed single mothers to sign official documents even though they are not the legal guardians of their children (Shah, 2003, pp. 63–4). Laws relating to intimate partner violence have been enacted in many Muslim-majority countries around the world such as Gambia, Indonesia and Malaysia (UN Women Global Database, n.d.), and the marital rape exemption was recently repealed for both Muslims and non-Muslims in multi-ethnic and multi-religious Singapore after extensive advocacy by civil society, input from Muslim scholars, and political will from the government (Neo, 2019).

[48] This change in law took part after a fatwa on child marriage was issued by a congress of women ulema in 2017, advocacy by women's groups, and success in a Supreme Court case filed by a civil society coalition. For more information on the fatwa-making process, see Nur Rofiah's chapter in this volume.

One of the most important lessons is the highly significant role of women's groups, who develop and maintain campaigns over many years in order to seize opportunities for political action. No matter how restrictive or open the democratic space was in each of the countries examined, women's movements often felt the problem on the ground and translated it to advocacy campaigns pushing for reform. Indeed, Htun and Weldon (2013) demonstrated through analysis of VAW measures in seventy states from 1975–2005 that 'the most important and consistent factor driving policy change is feminist activism'. The wider the networks, the greater the opportunity for differently placed actors to exchange and together identify short term and longer strategic objectives in family law reform.

Excitingly, the advocacy efforts do not influence only law reform itself, but can have significant ripple effects. Debates about religious arguments for and against particular reforms can create incentive and space for the production of new religious knowledge that challenges patriarchal interpretations condoning inequality in family laws. For example, in the case of Egypt, just before the *khulʿ* law was promulgated, Abdel Moty Bayoumy published a series of articles about *khulʿ* and its basis in the Qurʾan, Hadith and Islamic jurisprudence (2001; 2010). Then in 2007, as a result of discussions with civil society organizations, he published a book on *qiwāma* and *wilāya*. Zeinab Radwan, an Egyptian scholar of Islamic religious sciences and member of the now-dissolved National Democratic Party, and female Islamic scholar Amna Noseir, gained knowledge and conviction from Bayoumi's articles and hence researched and published studies on similar issues (Radwan, 2007). After the 2011 Egyptian revolution, these publications and the scholarship of Omaima Abou-Bakr, Amany Saleh and others were used in advocacy work for new family laws and for inclusive societies, as well as workshops with other activists, scholars and even religious preachers.[49]

Legal reforms, of course, are not the end of the story; energy and resources are needed to ensure the reforms do in fact change reality.[50] In addition to socio-economic and cultural work that lies outside the remit of this chapter, states must proactively work to implement the laws and ensure consistency within and between the laws. It is not enough to add a provision in the penal code to prevent violence while the family law still sets up conditions

---

[49] Examples include the work of the Center for Egyptian Women's Legal Assistance (CEWLA) or the Mada Foundation in Egypt (Al-Sharmani, 2016; 2017, chapter 5).

[50] For an exploration related to violence against women, see Klugman (2017).

that enable it to happen, or to guarantee equality in the constitution but ignore it in the family law. The whole legal framework must be revised and harmonized.[51]

Activists and reformers working towards law reform must study the field, the opportunities, challenges and resources available, and use this analysis to choose strategies and pathways to reform. In the process, they must question what impact the reforms have on the lives of women, and how change can happen in a holistic way. Though it may take many years of persistent, consistent work, there are multiple pathways to law reform based on the opportunities presented in a given context. Efforts at reform can lead to changing laws or adopting new ones, changing processes and expectations, and hopefully bringing about real equality within families in the process.

REFERENCES

ABAAD. 2016. 'A White Dress Doesn't Cover the Rape'. www.abaadmena.org/programmes/advocacy-and-policy-development/project-58748b6fa56f85-59472059

AFTURD. 2006. *Égalité dans l'Héritage: Pour Une Citoyenneté Pleine et Entière*. Tome 1: *Histoire, Droits et Sociétés*; Tome 2: *Plaidoyer pour l'Égalité dans l'Héritage*. Tunis.

Ali, Kecia. 2003. 'Progressive Muslims and Islamic Jurisprudence: The Necessity for Critical Engagement with Marriage and Divorce Law'. In *Progressive Muslims: On Justice, Gender, and Pluralism*, edited by Omid Safi, pp. 163–89. Oxford: Oneworld.

Alim, Nora and Nadjma Yassari. 2016. 'Between Procedure and Substance: A Review of Law Making in Egypt'. In *Changing God's Law: The Dynamics of Middle Eastern Family Law*, edited by Nadjma Yassari, pp. 113–30. London and New York: Routledge.

Arfaoui, Khedija and Valentine Moghadam. 2016. 'Violence Against Women and Tunisian Feminism: Advocacy, Policy, and Politics in an Arab Context'. *Current Sociology* 64 (4): pp. 637–65.

Ashihi, Muhammad. 2015. *'Ad-Din wa 'Alaqatuhu bi-Ahkam al-Mawarith fi Thil raf' at-Tahafuthat 'an Itifaqiyat "CEDAW" wa "Dastaret Huriyat ad-Damir"'*. *Nawaat*. 18 March.

ATFD. 2018. *20 Arguments pour l'Égalité dans l'Héritage*, Tunis: Dar Nuqush 'Arabia.

Bailey, Charlotte. 2018. 'One Year Ago, Tunisia Passed a Groundbreaking Law to Protect Women. Has It Worked?' *Time*. 26 July.

Bajec, Alessandra. 2019. 'How a Win in Tunisia's Inheritance Law Could Contribute to Ending Gender Inequality'. *The New Arab*. 3 March.

Bayoumy, Abdel Moty. 2001. *'Risala ila Majlis al-Sha'b: Dars fi Alif ba' al-Usul'*. *Al-Musawar*. 28 January.

---

[51] For specific recommendations on further reforms see Musawah (2019); UNDP Arab States (2019, pp. 85–7).

Bayoumy, Abdel Moty. 2010. *Min Qaḍāya al-Mar'a: al-Wilāya wa-l-Wisāya, al-Qiwāma fī al-Islam, Ta'adud al-Zawjāt, al-Talāq al-Ghiyābī, Shahadat al-Mar'a*. Cairo: Center for Egyptian Women's Legal Assistance.

BBC. 2014. 'Morocco Amends Controversial Rape Marriage Law'. 23 January.

Bedner, Adriaan and Stijn van Huis. 2010. 'Plurality of Marriage Law and Marriage Registration for Muslims in Indonesia: A Plea for Pragmatism'. *Utrecht Law Review* 6 (2): pp. 175–91.

Carlisle, Jessica. 2008. 'From Behind the Door: a Damascus Court Copes with an Alleged Out of Court Marriage'. In *Les Metamorphoses du Mariage au Moyen-Orient*, edited by Barbara Drieskens, pp. 59–74. Beirut: Institut Français du Proche-Orient.

Chiba, Masaji. 1986. 'Introduction'. In *Asian Indigenous Law in Interaction with Received Law*, edited by Masaji Chiba, pp. 1–9. London and New York: KPI.

COLIBE. 2018. *Taqrir Lajnat al-Huriyat al-Fardiya wa-l-Musawa*. Tunis.

Collectif 95 Maghreb-Égalité. 1995. *One Hundred Steps, One Hundred Provisions for an Egalitarian Codification of Family and Personal Status Laws in the Maghreb*, English version translated and published by Women Living Under Muslim Laws.

Collectif 95 Maghreb-Égalité. 2003. *Guide to Equality in the Family in the Maghreb*. English version translated and published by Women's Learning Partnership in 2005.

Collectif 95 Maghreb-Égalité. 2014. *Egalité dans l'Héritage et Autonomie Économique des Femmes*. www.observaction.info/wp-content/uploads/2016/05/Egalit%C3%A9-dans-lheritage.pdf

Conseil National des Droits de l'Homme [CNDH]. 2015. *Wad'iyat al-Musawa wa-l-Munasafah fī al-Maghrib* (Gender Equality and Equity in Morocco). Rabat: CNDH.

Dupret, Baudouin. 1999. 'Introduction'. In *Legal Pluralism in the Arab World*, edited by Baudouin Dupret, Maurits Berger and Laila Al-Zwaini, pp. 29–40. The Hague: Kluwer Law International.

Dupret, Baudouin. 2000. 'Normality, Responsibility, Morality: Virginity and Rape in an Egyptian Legal Context'. *Yearbook of the Sociology of Islam*.

Economic and Social Commission for Western Asia (ESCWA). 2017. *Status of Arab Women Report 2017. Violence against Women: What is at Stake?* Beirut: ESCWA.

Elbalti, Béligh. 2018. 'Translator's Foreword'. In *Equality between Men and Women in the Islamic Law of Inheritance*, by Abdelmagid Zarrouki; translated from Arabic by Béligh Elbalti.

Engelcke, *Dörthe*. 2019. *Reforming Family Law: Social and Political Change in Jordan and Morocco*. Cambridge: Cambridge University Press.

Fawzy, Essam. 2004. 'Muslim Personal Status Law in Egypt: The Current Situation and Possibilities of Reform through Internal Initiatives'. In *Women's Rights and Islamic Family Law. Perspectives on Reform*, edited by Lynn Welchman, pp. 17–94. London and New York: Zed Books.

Fédération Internationale des Ligues des Droits de l'Homme (FIDH). *2015. Droits Humains Garantis: de la Constitution à la Legislation.*

Freeman, Marsha, Christine Chinkin and Beate Rudolf (eds). 2012. *The UN Convention on the Elimination of All Forms of Discrimination Against Women: A Commentary*. Oxford: Oxford University Press.

Ghalib, Ghada and Rida Ghoneim. 2017. '*Al-Haraka al-Niswiya al-Tunisiya: Tarikh Hafil min an-Nidal*'. *Al-Masry al-Youm*.

Al-Haddad, Tahir. 2011. *Imra'atuna fi'l-Shari'a wa'l Mujtama' (Muslim Women in Law and Society)*. Cairo: Dar Al-Kitab Al-Masri.

El Hajjami, Aicha. 2013. 'The Religious Arguments in the Debate on the Reform of the Moroccan Family Code'. In *Gender and Equality in Muslim Family Law: Justice and Ethics in the Islamic Legal Tradition*, edited by Ziba Mir-Hosseini, Kari Vogt, Lena Larsen and Christian Moe, pp. 81–106. London: I.B. Taurus.

Hasso, Frances. 2011. *Consuming Desires: Family Crisis and the State in the Middle East*. Stanford: Stanford University Press.

El Hourri, Abdelali. 2015. 'Héritage. De Tariq Ramadan à Asmaa Lamrabet, des savants favorables à l'égalité'. *Medias24*. 23 October.

Htun, Mala, Francesca R. Jensenius and Jami Nelson-Nuñez. 2019. 'Gender-Discriminatory Laws and Women's Economic Agency'. *Social Politics* 26 (2): pp. 193–222.

Htun, Mala and S. Laurel Weldon. 2013. 'Feminist Mobilisation and Progressive Policy Change: Why Governments Take Action to Combat Violence Against Women'. *Gender and Development* 21 (2): pp. 231–47.

Htun, Mala and S. Laurel Weldon. 2015. 'Religious Power, the State, Women's Rights, and Family Law', *Politics and Gender* 11 (3): pp. 451–77.

Htun, Mala and S. Laurel Weldon. 2018. *The Logics of Gender Justice: State Action on Women's Rights Around the World*. New York: Cambridge University Press.

Husni, Ronak and Daniel L. Newman. 2007. *Muslim Women in Law and Society: Annotated Translation of Al-Ṭāhir al-Ḥaddād's Imra'tunā fī 'l-Sharī'a wa'l-Mujtama'*. London: Routledge.

Ibn 'Āshūr, Muḥammad al-Ṭāhir. 1978. *Tafsīr al-Taḥrīr wa-l-Tanwīr*. Tunis: Dar al-Tunisiya li'l-Nashr.

Ibn 'Āshūr, Muḥammad al-Ṭāhir. 2011. *Maqāṣid al-Sharī'a al-Islamiyya*. Cairo: Dar al-Kitab al-Masri.

Ibn 'Āshūr, Muḥammad al-Ṭāhir. 2013. *Treatise on Maqāṣid al-Sharī'a*, translated from the Arabic and annotated by Mohamed El-Tahir El-Mesawi, abridged by Alison Lake. Herdon, VA: International Institute of Islamic Thought.

International Commission of Jurists. 2019. *Gender-Based Violence in Lebanon: Inadequate Framework, Ineffective Remedies*. Geneva: ICJ.

Qāḍī al-Qudāh Interview. 2019. *'Qāḍī al-Qudah Yuwaḍih li'l-Urduniyyīn Abraz al-Ta'dilāt 'ala Qanūn al-Ahwāl al-Shakhsiyya'*. 10 April. https://royanews.tv/news/179362

Johnson, Penny and Rema Hammami. 2014. *Change & Conservation: Family Law Reform in Court Practice and Public Perceptions in the Occupied Palestinian Territory*. Birzeit: Institute of Women's Studies, Birzeit University.

Jordanian National Commission for Women. 2018. *'Mulahaẓāt 'ala Qararāt al-Lajna al-Qanūniyya fi Majlis an-Nuwwāb Hawla Qanūn al-Ahwāl al-Shakhsiyya al-Mu'aqqat'* ('Observations on the decisions of the legal committee of the House of Deputies on the temporary law of personal status'). 12 December.

Jouirou, Zahia. 2018. *Mawarith al-Nisa', al-Naṣ wa-l-Tārīkh, ḍimn Mu'alaf Jamā'i: Al-Musāwa fi-l-Mirāth bayn al-Rajul wa-l-Mar'a*.

Jouirou, Zahia. 2021. *'Al-Khalfiya al-Dīniya li-l-Jadal hawla al-Musāwa fi-l-Mirāth'. In Al-Hurriyāt al-Fardiya wa-l-Musāwa bi Tunis bayn al-Tanwir wa-l-Takfīr*. Tunis.

Klugman, Jeni. 2017. 'Gender Based Violence and the Law'. World Bank Background Paper. Washington, DC: World Bank.

Mekki, Nidhal. 2014. *Tunisia: Equality in Gender and Constitution*. Arab Forum for Citizenship in Transition.

Menski, Werner. 2006. *Comparative Law in a Global Context: The Legal Systems of Asia and Africa*. 2nd edn. Cambridge: Cambridge University Press.

Menski, Werner. 2012. 'Plural Worlds of Law and the Search for Living Law'. In *Rechtsanalyse als Kulturforschung*, edited by Werner Gephart, pp. 71–88. Frankfurt am Main: Vittoria Klostermann.

Mesbahi, Nima. 2018. 'The Victimization of the "Muslim Woman": The Case of Amina Filali, Morocco'. *Journal of International Women's Studies* 19 (3): pp. 49–59.

Mikdashi, Maya. 2015. 'The Politics of Gendered Violence in Lebanon'. *Jadaliyya*. 1 June.

Mir-Hosseini, Ziba. 2009. 'Towards Gender Equality: Muslim Family Laws and the *Shari'ah*'. In *Wanted: Equality and Justice in the Muslim Family*, edited by Zainah Anwar, pp. 23–63. Kuala Lumpur: Sisters in Islam.

Mir-Hosseini, Ziba. 2012. 'Women in Search of Common Ground: Between Islamic and International Human Rights Laws'. In *Islamic Law and International Human Rights Law: Searching for Common Ground?* edited by Anver M. Emon, Mark S. Ellis and Benjamin Glahn, pp. 291–303. Oxford: Oxford University Press

Mir-Hosseini, Ziba. 2016. 'Moral Contestations and Patriarchal Ethics: Women Challenging the Justice of Muslim Family Laws'. In *Shari'a and Modern Ethics*, edited by Robert Hefner, pp. 65–82. Indianapolis: Indiana University Press.

Mir-Hosseini, Ziba, Mulki Al-Sharmani and Jana Rumminger (eds). 2015. *Men in Charge? Rethinking Authority in Muslim Legal Tradition*. London: Oneworld.

Musawah. 2009. 'Musawah Framework for Action'. Kuala Lumpur: Sisters in Islam.

Musawah. 2019. 'Positive Developments in Muslim Family Laws'. www.musawah.org/resources/positive-developments-in-muslim-family-laws/

Muthmainnah, Yulianti. 2018. 'Why Women Ulema Reject Patriarchy'. *Jakarta Post*. 28 December.

Neo, Rong Wei. 2019. 'Criminal Law Reform Bill: A Look at Key Changes in the Penal Code'. *Today*. 6 May.

Nour-Assaoui, Karima. 2020. 'The Current Debate on the Moroccan Family Code Mudawwanat al-Usra in Morocco'. *Electronic Journal of Islamic and Middle Eastern Law* 8 (1): pp. 77–85.

Pittman, Alexandra and Rabéa Naciri. 2007. 'Cultural Adaptations: The Moroccan Women's Campaign to Change the Moudawana'. Institute of Development Studies.

Radwan, Zeinab. 2007. *Al-Mar'a bayn al-Mawruth wa-l-Tahdith*. 3rd edn. Cairo: al-Hay'a al-Masriya al-'Ama li-l-Kitab.

Sadek, George. 2018. 'Tunisia: Cabinet Approves Bill Requiring Equal Inheritance Shares for Men and Women'. *Library of Congress – Global Legal Monitor*. 4 December. www.loc.gov/law/foreign-news/article/tunisia-cabinet-approves-bill-requiring-equal-inheritance-shares-for-men-and-women/

Shah, Nik Noriani Nik Badli. 2003. *Islamic Family Law and Justice for Muslim Women*. Kuala Lumpur: Sisters in Islam.

Shaham, Ron. 1995. 'Custom, Islamic Law and Statutory Legislation: Marriage Registration and Minimum Age at Marriage in the Egyptian Shari'a Courts'. *Islamic Law and Society* 2 (3): pp. 258–81.

Al-Sharmani, Mulki. 2016. 'Contemporary Egyptian Islamic Feminism: Possibilities and Challenges'. *Afriche e Orienti* 18 (1): pp. 58–77.

Al-Sharmani, Mulki. 2017. *Gender Justice and Legal Reform in Egypt: Negotiating Muslim Family Law*. Cairo: American University in Cairo Press.

Sonneveld, Nadje. 2012. *Khul' Divorce in Egypt: Public Debate, Judicial Practices, and Everyday Life*. Cairo/New York: American University in Cairo Press.

Stowasser, Barbara Freyer. 1998. 'Gender Issues and Contemporary Quran Interpretations'. In *Islam, Gender and Social Change*, edited by Yvonne Yazbeck Haddad and John Esposito, pp. 30–44. Oxford: Oxford University Press.

Tadamun – SIGI Jordan. 2019a. 'Nujud Coalition to Combat Child Marriage Calls on Majlis al-Umma to Raise the Exceptional Age of Marriage from 15 to 16.' 7 April. www.sigi-jordan.org/?p=5168

Tadamun – SIGI Jordan. 2019b. 'Statement on the Rate of Child Marriage', 24 April. www.sigi-jordan.org/?p=5214

UNICEF. 2019. 'UNICEF Welcomes Recent Amendment of Indonesia's Marriage Act', 19 September.

UNDP. 2018. *Lebanon: Gender Justice & the Law*. New York: UNDP.

UNDP Arab States. 2019. *Gender Justice and Equality Before the Law: Analysis of Progress and Challenges in the Arab States Region*. New York: UNDP.

UNIFEM. 2008. *Progress of the World's Women 2008/2009: Who Answers to Women? Gender and Accountability*. New York: UNIFEM.

UN Women. 2017a. 'Jordanian Parliament Abolishes Law that Allowed Rapists to Avoid Prosecution by Marrying their Victims'. 4 August.

UN Women. 2017b. 'Tunisia Passes Historic Law to End Violence Against Women and Girls'. 10 August.

UN Women. 2019a. 'Global Factsheet' (summary of the *Progress of the World's Women 2019-2020: Families in a Changing World* report).

UN Women. 2019b. 'Reforming the Laws that Forced Women to Marry their Rapists'. 16 July.

UN Women Arab States. n.d. 'Facts and Figures: Ending Violence against Women and Girls'. https://arabstates.unwomen.org/en/what-we-do/ending-violence-against-women/facts-and-figures

UN Women Global Database on Violence Against Women. n.d. https://evaw-global-database.unwomen.org/en

Welchman, Lynn. 2000. *Beyond the Code. Muslim Family Law and the Shar'i Judiciary in the Palestinian West Bank*. The Hague: Kluwer.

Welchman, Lynn. 2003. 'In the Interim: Civil Society, the *Shar'i* Judiciary and Palestinian Personal Status Law in the Transitional Period'. *Islamic Law and Society* 10 (1): pp. 34–69.

Welchman, Lynn. 2007. *Women and Muslim Family Laws in Arab States: A Comparative Overview of Textual Development and Advocacy*. Amsterdam: Amsterdam University Press.

Welchman, Lynn. 2009. 'Family Gender and Law in Jordan and Palestine'. In *Family, Gender and Law in a Globalizing Middle East and South Asia*, edited by Kenneth M. Cuno and Manisha Desai, pp. 126–44. Syracuse, NY: Syracuse University Press.

Welchman, Lynn. 2015. '*Qiwamah* and *Wilayah* as Legal Postulates in Muslim Family Laws'. In *Men in Charge? Rethinking Authority in Muslim Legal Tradition*, edited by Ziba Mir-Hosseini, Mulki Al-Sharmani and Jana Rumminger, pp. 132–62. London: Oneworld.

World Bank. 2019. 'Gender-Based Violence (Violence against Women and Girls)'. www.worldbank.org/en/topic/socialsustainability/brief/violence-against-women-and-girls

World Health Organization. 2013. 'Global and Regional Estimates of Violence against Women: Prevalence and Health Effects of Intimate Partner Violence and Non-partner Sexual Violence'. https://apps.who.int/iris/bitstream/handle/10665/85239/9789241564625_eng.pdf

Y. J. 2019. 'Réforme de la Moudawana: l'UAF relance le débat'. *Médias24*. 26 February. www.medias24.com/l-uaf-relance-le-debat-sur-la-reforme-de-la-moudawana-456.html

Youssef, Olfa. 2018. *Qir'a Hijajiya min ajl al-Musawa fi al-Mirāth bayn al-Rajul wa-l-Mar'a, min al-Fiqh ilā al-Akhlāq, ḍimn Mu'alaf Jama'i*. Tunis: Manshurat al-Kridif.

Justice, Refinement and Beauty: Reflections on Marriage and Spirituality

Sa'diyya Shaikh

This chapter presents the perspective that marriage for a believer, like all other relationships, constitutes a workshop for human–divine encounters. These reflections emerge from my life experiences and observations, as well as from the valuable lessons I acquired from spiritual teachers and varied Muslim textual traditions of wisdom.

Throughout the Qur'an, believers are encouraged to engage all aspects of reality, including interpersonal and social interactions, as an opportunity for spiritual refinement. Islamic tradition provides rich resources for the cultivation of the self, which is organically connected to the social good. Through every sphere of a person's being and life, including intention, thought, awareness and action, the seeker of God is encouraged to align herself to the higher divine qualities. This requires a process of refinement and cultivation based on a particular understanding of the God–human relationship.

The human being in an Islamic cosmology is a constellation, a combination, an embodiment of divine attributes – the divine qualities provide humanity with our existential archetype.[1] We were created to reflect and

[1] Some central sources for this religious anthropology are the Qur'anic verse 'God taught Adam all the names' (2:31) and the hadith that God created Adam in God's own form, where Adam

personify the divine qualities, that is, Allah's names and attributes, and our life journeys provide an opportunity to cultivate and refine these interrelated divine names harmoniously within ourselves. Muslim thinkers have placed the divine names into two groups, broadly categorized into names of beauty (*jamāl*) and majesty (*jalāl*), with a priority given to the *jamāli* qualities both within the divine and the human being. This integration is central to the development of *iḥsān* as integrating forms of goodness that encompass virtue, which are best reflected when human beings distil the varying divine qualities into a balanced equilibrium, a *mizān*. Such a *mizān* or balance is both premised on and is intended to reflect justice. Justice thus is intrinsic to a *jamāli* mode of existence. Spiritual refinement emerges on the basis of an organic interrelationship between *jamāl* and *jalāl* and between *ʿadl* and *iḥsān*.

Following the lead of the Qurʾan and Muslim teachings, I suggest that the very mode of refining divine qualities is through *raḥma* and a related *jamāli*-based ethics. The Qurʾanic vision of Allah presents us with an overriding emphasis on the divine quality of *raḥma*, a term that is best translated as the combination of divine love and compassion (verses 17:110; 6:12). We are informed that God has inscribed on Godself *raḥma* (verse 6:12). God says, 'My *raḥma* extends over and embraces all things' (verse 7:156) and 'My Mercy prevails over My wrath' (al-Tirmidhī, n.d., vol. 6, no. 3543).[2] Even more significantly, of the 114 chapters of the Qurʾan, 113 commence with the *basmalah*: 'In the name of Allah, the Most Lovingly Compassionate, the Most Merciful.' This invocation guides and echoes in the heart of a receptive reader, connecting Allah repeatedly with the divine names *al-Raḥmān* and *al-Raḥīm* (the Lovingly Compassionate and the All-Merciful). The reverberation of *raḥma* captured within the *basmalah* reiteratively threaded through the Qurʾan seeks to imprint these divine *jamāli* qualities on the hearts, minds and beings of its readers. Here, Qurʾanic scholar Ghazala Anwar (2022) presents us with a powerful spiritual insight when approaching the Qurʾan: 'Invoking the *basmalah* over the Qurʾan, we commit ourselves to reading with a *raḥmanic* bias, to prioritize the understanding that is most *raḥmanic* in its attribution

represents the inclusive human archetype in all these discussions. For a detailed description of these ideas see Shaikh, 2012, pp. 75–81.

[2] This is a hadith *qudsī*.

to the Divine and its consequences for creation.'[3] Thus through opening one's recitation of the Qur᾿an with *basmalah*, we are directed, steered and guided to a *jamāli* mode of meaning making and interpretations of revelation. To ensure that we don't miss this central teaching, the Qur᾿an more directly and explicitly describes itself as a source of healing and a *raḥma* for believers (verse 17:82).[4]

Furthermore, our beloved teacher and messenger of the Qur᾿an, Prophet Muhammad, the superlative exemplar of a *jamāli* mode of being, was described by his wife ʿĀ᾿isha as the living embodiment of the Qur᾿an. It is worth pausing to reflect on the fact that the description of the Prophet as the living Qur᾿an was articulated by his wife and intimate partner. Some of the deeper questions that this poses for each of us within intimate relationships, and indeed in all relationships are: What might it take to embody the Qur᾿an? How can we best exemplify the divine *jamāl*? How do we learn to reflect and reverberate beautiful qualities such that those we are closest to, and with whom we engage on an everyday basis, can see living evidence of the beauty, love, kindness and justice of the Divine? The fact that ʿĀ᾿isha makes this comment also helps us to recognize a related teaching – that spiritual cultivation and religious ethics must always bear fruit not only in the public sphere but must resonate beauty and justice in spaces of our intimate interpersonal relationships.

Moreover, the continuous resonance of *jamāli* ethics is reflected in God's unambiguous instruction to the Prophet that he is sent to be a mercy for all realms of existence (*raḥmatan lil ʿalāmīn*).[5] This verse also provides guidance to the followers of Muhammad that all understandings, readings and invocations of the Prophet and his Sunna are to be circumscribed by this divine teaching of *raḥma*. Believers, as lovers of God, the Qur᾿an and the Prophet, are thus invited to inscribe upon ourselves loving compassion and mercy in all that we are and do, how we engage and embody faith and tradition in the world, and in all that we seek to become. As such I propose a *jamāli* ethics

[3] For a luminous theological reflection on *raḥma* as a four-arched portal to the Divine, see Anwar (2022).

[4] Verse 17:82: 'We send down in the Qur᾿an healing and *raḥma* for the faithful ...'

[5] Verse 21:107: 'And We have not sent you [Oh Muhammad] except as *raḥmatun lil ʿalamīn* (*raḥma* for all realms of existence).' See Ghazala Anwar's (2022) powerful contemporary theological reflections and Omid Safi's (2009) compelling thoughts on the Prophet as *raḥmatun lil ʿalamīn*.

to nourish our marital journeys in attaining increasingly deeper and higher forms of virtue or *iḥsān*.

Having framed my overall approach as a *jamāli* ethics to marriage, I proceed to focus on three areas of application and praxis.[6] First, I present some reflections on the nature of the *nikāḥ* (marriage) ceremony and creation of a *nikāḥ* contract, elements that each require careful consideration prior to a wedding. Second, I present deliberations on the spiritual dynamics within everyday marital life that might support growth, learning and transformation, as well as ways to deepen love, justice and beauty within marriage. Third, I end with a prayer that I originally prepared for the *nikāḥ* ceremony of my sister, reflecting the aspirational possibilities for healthy, loving relationships that justice-seeking Muslims might seek. Together, I hope that these reflections present a constructive Islamic feminist imaginary that might contribute to cultivating spiritually nourishing forms of love and marriage to which justice is absolutely integral.

1. *NIKĀḤ* CEREMONIES AND CONTRACTS

The performance of *nikāḥ* rituals constitutes the crucial rite of passage that marks a couple's transition into the social institution of marriage. The forms that these rituals take reflect and shape a community's religious imagination. They comprise a social mirror for how power is culturally and symbolically constructed within marriage. The *nikāḥ* ceremony contributes to a broader 'habitus' or set of socialized norms that believers internalize and that consciously and unconsciously structure feelings, dispositions and approaches guiding their expectations and behaviour in relation to marital roles.[7] Given that the rites of entry into marriage symbolize deeper levels of expectations both for the couple and the larger community, it is important to explore the related gender dynamics reflected in these ceremonies and the extent to which they demonstrate ideals of justice and beauty. Attentiveness to the ways in which gender and authority function at this level allows us to clearly identify and assess prevailing practices for sexism.

---

[6] Previously I have presented some of these ideas as part of a *nikāḥ* khutbah or as an invited speaker at a wedding. I first presented the *du'ā'* at the end of the chapter at my sister's wedding.

[7] For a brief and accessible definition of habitus as conceptualized by Pierre Bourdieu, see www.powercube.net/other-forms-of-power/bourdieu-and-habitus/, and for an academic discussion on gender and habitus see McLeod (2005).

We need to create alternative ritual forms that imbibe the inner spiritual essence and reflect the egalitarian aspirations of marriage that we seek to embody.

In my South African context, the dominant local custom in Muslim communities is that on the day of the wedding, the father of the bride, accompanied by two male witnesses, asks the daughter for her consent to the marriage in the family home. The men then go to the mosque, where a male imam officiates the ceremony between the bride's father (who represents her) and the groom. Generally, the woman is not physically present at that critical moment of entering into the religious covenant of marriage.[8] The religious ceremony is officiated between men, without the presence or voice of the woman who is entering into the marriage.[9]

It is only after this defining religious moment that the family and community all gather for a reception to celebrate the marriage, where everyone arrives, dressed-up smartly. Much of the energy, excitement and attention of the bride and the women in the family prior to the wedding is focused on clothing and the food to be served at the celebration after the *nikāḥ*.

While the creation of physical beauty and aesthetics are joyful aspects of a marriage celebration to be embraced, it is equally if not more important to prioritize women's presence and the bride's active participation in the religious ceremony, and prior to that, also in the creation of the marital contract. These enable the social beauty of engaged presence, full awareness, active participation and just relations. A bride's absence or silence at the crucial moment of entering into a marriage contract reflects androcentric cultural traditions that have entangled themselves around the *nikāḥ* ceremony. Such outer ritual forms of the *nikāḥ* ceremony, dictated by dated patriarchal cultural customs and norms, render women invisible in the most crucial moment of a sacred covenant with her partner. As such, the androcentric *nikāḥ* rituals present the community and the couple with a patriarchal imaginary for marriage – they prefigure, structure and enable marital expectations based on gender hierarchy within our individual and communal consciousness. This certainly does

[8] Even if, as in some rarer cases more recently, she is present at the mosque, she is generally silent during the ceremony and is represented by her father or another male member of her family who speaks on her behalf. I have attended less than a handful of *nikāḥ* ceremonies locally where a Muslim woman speaks on her own behalf during the ceremony.

[9] A number of gender sensitive and nourishing *nikāḥ* khutbahs by Muslim women that present an alternative Islamic feminist imaginary are included in a forthcoming edited collection (Shaikh and Seedat, 2022).

not reflect the egalitarian spiritual and religious ideals that many of us hold close. It is time to initiate changes and transformations to the form of the *nikāḥ* ceremony to better reflect more inclusive ideals.

Within my community, women are generally not encouraged to participate in setting out clear and informed marriage contracts that outline mutually agreed understandings about the expectations of each spouse during the marriage relating to issues such as property regime, childcare, work and maintenance, potential polygamy, and how to exit the marriage whether through death or divorce.[10] If these rather unromantic but real issues are not explicitly engaged with and rendered transparent for discussion, negotiation and informed consent between the spouses, reigning patriarchal *fiqh* norms will likely de facto come into effect, at the expense of just and *iḥsāni* forms of conduct.

Here the insights of feminist legal scholar Fatima Seedat (2022) are incisive:

> … to complete the sentence 'in Islam, marriage is a contract', we must add 'the ultimate test of which lies in the ethics of the more powerful partner at the end of that contract'. To realise the contractual nature of the relationship is also to know and teach our children how to disagree and leave relationships ethically and with dignity.

It is problematic that women in many Muslim contexts are often physically absent or silent during the *nikāḥ* ceremony, and not encouraged to actively participate in the formulation and creation of *nikāḥ* contracts stipulating just and equitable terms for marriage. All of this reflects insidious and 'normalized' cultural forms of patriarchy which must be critically interrogated: we must explicitly recognize how, as individuals and communities, we have internalized hierarchical forms of authority. We have been conditioned to unquestioningly accept and perpetuate these norms and it is time to question and reconstruct them.

Women who express discomfort with these norms are often castigated as 'trouble-makers' or said to be 'difficult'. But women should not repress or dismiss their inner unease when there is no transparency or a lack of willingness to create a fair *nikāḥ* contract – many women ignore their apprehension because they want to keep the peace in the family or with future in-laws. A

[10] Fatima Seedat's 'Not a Nikah Khutbah' in Shaikh and Seedat (2022) presents lucid and incisive feminist reflection on this process of marital contracts.

discomfort with injustice is spiritually vital and psychologically healthy. In fact, I suggest that such discomfort is a *fiṭrī* discomfort, that is, an uneasiness with injustice that arises from one's inner moral compass and God-given nature (*fiṭra*). Such discomfort in my view reflects an inner refinement, and one should welcome this type of discomfort as a messenger of the higher self. It demands a 'conscientious pause' so we can sit with and process the discomfort through reflection, mediation and conversation.[11] Validating our discomfort with injustice can be revelatory – it allows us to identify injustice as spiritually and emotionally damaging and prompts us to envision alternative modes of engagement.

Since marriage in Islam is a contract, it is open to negotiation, rethinking and reconstruction in ways that remove patriarchal accretions and create more spiritually nourishing alternatives for justice-seeking Muslim communities and individuals. Indeed, there are large spaces for innovating and constructing more egalitarian and justice-based ethics and rituals through producing non-discriminatory *nikāḥ* contracts and imaginative ceremonies. Central questions we need to reflect on as we do such reconstructions include: What rituals enable us to relish and appreciate the full personhood, equality and presence of each partner entering into this union? What kinds of language, soundscapes, visualscapes and outer forms materialize a spirit of equality, egalitarianism and mutuality both contractually and ceremonially? What candid and difficult conversations are needed prior to marriage that allow potential spouses and their families to create *nikāḥ* rituals and contracts that reflect an ethics of justice and beauty? Given that there are minimal legal requirements for a marriage to be lawful within Muslim tradition, how do we create, animate and authorize new cultural forms of celebration and covenant-making as well as contractual formulations that embody *mawadda* and *raḥma* (love and compassion), *ʿadl* (justice) and *iḥsān* (beauty)? Tradition is, after all, a dynamic, living and ongoing process.

In light of these broader considerations of how to cultivate love and compassion, justice and beauty, I now turn to the second part of this chapter which focuses on the more intimate dynamics of everyday marital relationships and ways to foster the deepening of love and justice between spouses.

---

[11] Khaled Abou El Fadl (2001, p. 433) suggests a conscientious pause as a way to stop and allow space for personal grappling and reflection when one finds a conflict between the apparent meaning of a religious text (or, I would suggest, a religious norm) and one's inner conscience and faith-based conviction.

2. MARRIAGE AS A JOURNEY OF SPIRITUAL TRANSFORMATION[12]

Marriage is indeed half of religion[13] because the work that goes into it can be some of the most intense inner and outer work a human being can do. Some of this work is deeply joyous, nourishing and fulfilling, some of it is just ordinary and mundane, and some of it is difficult and painful. Living and embodying love and commitment day after day, during ease and during difficulty, provides meaningful challenges and opportunities for us as human beings. While the beginning of a relationship might be wrapped in excitement and butterflies in the stomach, experiencing the glow of a heady romance, marriage in the long view requires ways of being that are hardier, earthier and deeper, and that enable a love that endures.

One of the most significant offerings of a marriage is that it creates the possibilities to see oneself in an intimate mirror. In healthy and functional relationships, our spouses can indeed be intimate mirrors, sometimes reflecting our most unique beauty and special gifts; and at other times reflecting our limitations. If spouses engage the image their partners reflect with integrity, marriage opens up possibilities for a transformative and unfolding spiritual journey of growth.

At the outset it is necessary to recognize that for marriage to function in this transformative register, it requires the basic components of justice and mutual respect. If there is a damaging power imbalance between spouses in the ways that patriarchy often creates, many of the spiritual possibilities enabled by marriage can be distorted and, in fact, abused.

The cultivation of the self in marriage is only fully possible when there is justice in the marriage, and the relationship between partners is based on respect for the full dignity of one another. The insights offered have a much more significant possibility to be useful if spouses establish as a necessary foundation that their marriage must be built on justice, deep respect, and full recognition of the integrity of one's partner as a companion and a friend. This resonates with my earlier reflection that *iḥsān* (goodness and beauty) is enabled when the foundation of justice (*ʿadl*) is securely

---

[12] See my earlier version of some of these thoughts presented in a *nikāḥ* khutbah entitled 'Divine Love, Human Love: Marriage as Heart-Cultivation', in Shaikh and Seedat (2022).

[13] The hadith tradition that states a person who marries fulfils half of religion can be found in *Mishkāt al-Maṣābīḥ* (Khaṭīb al-Tibrīzī, n.d., no. 3096).

in place. Here I am referring to a basic level of justice and respect, while I turn to deeper reflections on justice within marriage in more nuanced ways shortly.

Turning to the luminous insights of a great spiritual teacher, Shaykh Muhammad Rahim Bawa Muhaiyaddeen (*raḥmatullah ʿalayhī*), we discover profound lessons on the importance of cultivating specific qualities in our love relationships and marriages: 'Unless love is connected to God, unless it is connected to truth, to compassion, to justice, to grace, it is possible for it to break down' (1981, p. 2).

Bawa Muhaiyaddeen turns our attention to the core attributes that characterize the Divine and which human beings are urged to develop in their intimate relationships. Each of these divine attributes – truth, compassion, justice and grace – are vital spiritual nutrients that nourish love and enable it to grow, to endure and to flower into a source of mutual plenitude. In Islam, each of these attributes of God – truth, compassion, justice and grace – are integral to love, and are also the attributes that humans are meant to cultivate in themselves and in their relationships with one another. Since these qualities capture some of the most significant spiritual dimensions of an intimate love relationship in marriage, we must ponder how to embody these in everyday life.

Practically, the connection between love and truth translates into honesty and candour in a relationship – being frank and unguarded with one's partner provides an open space for the self, to let down your guard, to be authentic with fewer boundaries than you need elsewhere; when truth and love come together it frees one to 'feel comfortable in your skin'. However, we need to hold truth and honesty together with the essential quality of compassion, that genuine extension of care, sensitivity and gentleness to one's partner. Compassion provides a necessary support and balance to the quality of honesty: when honesty has the potential to become brutal and hurt one's spouse, it is compassion that holds honesty together with tenderness, and enables deeper comfort within the marriage. Through this combination of qualities, an intimate partner can raise important, tough and difficult issues without causing injury to the heart of one's beloved.

Justice is essential to harmony and balance in a marriage. Justice at the first and most basic level is to treat one's spouse fairly, to be respectful of the dignity, individuality and the full personhood of one's partner. Treating a partner fairly and respectfully, particularly in times of conflict and disagreement, allows love to deepen and mature. This is especially important when we are angry and feel justified in our anger, perhaps having brought up the same irritating behaviour or quality in a partner a hundred times before. Justice insists that we recognize, even in tense moments, other aspects of the person that are good and admirable. Justice asks us to not myopically focus on the 'bad' aspect in our spouse, to resist the impulse to constantly find fault or see the cup as half-empty, and to not reduce all of the person to one occasion or episode of having messed up. Justice invites us to rise to the sometimes difficult challenge of keeping the whole person in view, particularly remaining attentive to our partner's noble qualities during difficult times.

Justice also helps us to recognize that we are all shifting and changing, that who we were a year ago is different from who we are now, and who we were at some previous time in our relationship is not likely to be who we are in the future. We should not hold ourselves or our partners hostage to some version of themselves in the past, or some painful experience, on the condition that each has learned and changed from those struggles. Let me be clear, this is not a call to be patient with abuse of any kind, but rather a call to see that when meaningful growth and change happens, when we grow out of a limitation or heal from a painful space, that we are present to the change and the development in ourselves and in our spouses.

A couple who are friends of mine use a helpful catchphrase when there is danger of such relapsing to old wounds and injury during an argument: when one partner says, 'Don't kitchen-sink' (that is: Don't bring up issues that should have passed through already and been discarded), the other is reminded to resist the temptation to dig up old stuff. Such modes of perception and behaviour allow us to support the process of forgiving ourselves and our partners for past mistakes, of letting things that have passed genuinely leave each person. It can be seen as a form of *tawakkul* (reliance on God) where you entrust your previous pain to Allah, so that you do not have to keep negative past experiences alive within yourself. This is not only personally and spiritually liberating it can also enable a shift in negative patterns in one's relationships.

Furthermore, justice summons us to establish equality in our relations, thereby fostering greater intimacy between partners. A spiritual component of equality urges each partner to consciously rein-in the persistent inner voice that asserts self-importance or arrogance, that voice that reasons with oneself: 'I know better'; 'I am right'. We must recognize this instinctive assertion of the *nafs al-ammāra* (the commanding self/lower self) as it arises and transform it.

Here let us return to the image of a mirror that I invoked earlier, of spouses as our intimate mirrors: ironically in reflecting our flaws and sometimes even giving us a glimpse into our own ugliness, our spouses can provide us with perhaps the greatest gift of alchemy. It is only when we are able to see our own weaknesses and failings in this mirror, which our partner sometimes so sharply reflects, that we are able to attend to them, work on them, clean up the muck, cultivate and transform our character, become more beautiful, more noble, more tender, more just, more kind, more compassionate and more truthful; in sum more like our Divine potential. Embodying truthfulness, fairness, compassion, tenderness and justice, internally and externally, both in relationship to the self and one's partner, and in fact in any human relationships more broadly, enables our growth and creation of healthier human bonds within families and communities.

Finally, I want to turn to the nourishment that marriage can offer. By grounding our relationships in equality, we create the conditions for cultivating genuinely mutual relationships, and mutuality is that most beautiful dimension of marriage which verse 2:187 of the Qurʾan exquisitely captures:

> (your spouses) are a garment for you, as you are a garment for them

The profound symbolism of spouses being garments to one another invites deeper reflection. Garments sit up snuggly against our skin, alluding to the deep intimacy and closeness that marriage can bring; garments protect our bodies against the withering influence of the elements, from the bitter cold and from the harsh sun; so too, can marriage provide protection from the severity life sometimes brings. A solid marriage creates a protective layer of relationship that comforts one's heart when weathering the storms of life. Moreover, in the same way that garments cover private parts and shield them from the public, spouses hold the sanctity and vulnerabilities of each other's innermost, private being; covering one another's weaknesses and faults from the public eye, all the while gently supporting each other to overcome these. Finally, a garment also beautifies and adorns the wearer. So too, loving, compassionate partners accentuate one another's inner beauty, and that process bountifully results in more deeply cultivating the hearts of both partners in the relationship. Such is the promise and the trust of a healthy marital relationship, which the Qurʾan in verse 4:21 describes as a 'strong covenant' (*mīthāqan ghalīẓan*).

In the Qur'an, love is sublimely connected to grace:

> And among God's signs is that
> God created partners for you from yourselves
> That you may find tranquillity in them,
> And God puts between your hearts, love and compassion.
> Surely there are signs for people who reflect. (verse 30:21)

Love, tranquillity and compassion between intimate partners are gifts from God to humanity, gifted not only to make us feel good but to present us with signs (*ayāt*) for our existential reflection, signs for perceiving the Divine Beloved. Despite what might at times feel like labour within marriage, overall and for the greater part, Allah (*swt*) assures us that marriage is meant to be a source of tranquillity and existential guidance. Marriage enriches our spiritual journeying when we engage with it as a form of heart-cultivation, with self-awareness and commitment to the higher within ourselves. It is my sincere desire that we can create ever more expansive religious imaginaries that can support such transformations within marriage and, indeed, within all social interactions.

3. PRAYER AT A *NIKĀḤ* CEREMONY

I offer in this final part, a *du'ā'* (prayer) I gave at a wedding ceremony that I performed for my sister and brother-in-law, Laila and Rob.

> Laila and Rob, I wish you a life filled with love and a love filled with the most beautiful divine qualities – truth, compassion, justice and grace. God-willing, yours will be a sustaining love weathering the storms of life and marriage; indeed marriage is filled with both wonder and difficulty. My *du'ā'* for you as a couple:
>
> > Oh Allah, *Ya Wadūd*, the Loving, *Ya Raḥīm*, the Gracious, shower this union with blessings unceasing.
> >
> > Oh Allah, *Ya Wali*, the Protecting Friend, grant your loving friendship to this couple so that they each become sheltering and protective garments of the other.

Oh Allah, *Ya Nūr*, the Radiance, fill this marriage with laughter and ease so that in their togetherness is the light and lightness of Your luminous being.

Oh Allah, *Ya Karīm*, the Generous, bestow bounty in their labour so that they become a wellspring of your abundance and service for other lives.

Oh Allah, *Ya Sabūr*, the Ever-Patient, *Ya Raḥmān*, the Compassionate, grant them endurance, gentleness and perseverance in times of anger, struggle and difficulty, and when life's weariness overtakes them.

Oh Allah, *Ya Haqq*, the Source of Reality and Truth, grace these two hearts so that their love remains steadfastly connected to your most beautiful, sublime qualities, to your divine attributes of mercy, truthfulness, subtlety, integrity, compassion and justice.

Amin

REFERENCES

Abou El Fadl, Khaled. 2001. *Speaking in God's Name: Islamic Law, Authority and Women*. Oxford: Oneworld.

Anwar, Ghazala. 2022.'*Khutbah al-Muwaddah lil Ghuraba* – For the Love of the Queer Strangers'. In *The Women's Khutbah Book: Contemporary Sermons on Spirituality and Justice from around the World*, edited by Sa'diyya Shaikh and Fatima Seedat. New Haven: Yale University Press.

Khaṭīb al-Tibrīzī, Muḥammad ibn 'Abd Allāh. n.d. *Mishkāt al- Maṣābīh*. https://sunnah.com/mishkat al-*Maṣābīh*

McLeod, Julie. 2005. 'Feminists Re-reading Bourdieu: Old Debates and New Questions about Gender Habitus and Gender Change'. *Theory and Research in Education* 3 (1): pp. 11–30.

Muhaiyaddeen, M. R. Bawa. 1981. *A Book of God's Love*. Philadelphia, PA: The Fellowship Press.

Safi, Omid. 2009. *Memories of Muhammad*. New York: HarperCollins.

Seedat, Fatima. 2022. 'Not a Nikah Khutbah'. In *The Women's Khutbah Book: Contemporary Sermons on Spirituality and Justice from around the World*, edited by Sa'diyya Shaikh and Fatima Seedat. New Haven: Yale University Press.

Shaikh, Sa'diyya. 2022. 'Divine Love, Human Love: Marriage as Heart-cultivation'. In *The Women's Khutbah Book: Contemporary Sermons on Spirituality and Justice from around the World*, edited by Sa'diyya Shaikh and Fatima Seedat. New Haven: Yale University Press.

Shaikh, Saʿdiyya. 2012. *Sufi Narratives of Intimacy: Ibn ʿArabī, Gender, and Sexuality*. Durham: University of North Carolina Press.

Shaikh, Saʿdiyya and Fatima Seedat (eds). 2022. *The Women's Khutbah Book: Contemporary Sermons on Spirituality and Justice from around the World*. New Haven: Yale University Press.

Al-Tirmidhī, Muhammad b. ʿĪsā. n.d. *Jamiʿ al-Tirmidhī*. https://sunnah.com/tirmidhi

About the Contributors

Sara Ababneh is a lecturer in international relations at the Department of Politics and International Relations, University of Sheffield. Before Sheffield she was associate professor at the Center for Strategic Studies, University of Jordan. She earned her DPhil in politics and international relations from St Antony's College, University of Oxford, where she wrote her dissertation on female Islamists in Hamas in occupied Palestine and the Islamic Action Front in Jordan. She has conducted research on the Jordanian women's movement, the Arab Uprisings, Mandate Palestine, gender and Islamism, Muslim family laws and labour movements. Her research interests include class, gender and struggles for liberation and change. She was selected as the Carnegie Centennial Fellow at the Middle East Institute at Columbia University. Currently, she is working on a manuscript on the popular protest movement in Jordan.

Faqihuddin Abdul Kodir teaches Hadith and legal injunction in the faculty of Islamic Law at Syekh Nurjati State Institute for Islamic Studies (IAIN), Cirebon, and the Fahmina Institute for Islamic Studies (ISIF). He is one of the founders of the Fahmina Institute, an Indonesian NGO working on gender, democracy and pluralism from an Islamic perspective. He is the author of several books, including *Qirā'ah Mubādalah* (2019), *Sunnah Monogami* (2017) and *Hadith and Gender Justice* (2007). He is also the founder of Mubadalah.id, an Islamic portal about gender justice. He completed his Islamic boarding school (*pesantren*) education at Dar al-Tauhid Arjawinangun Cirebon, undergraduate studies at Damascus University Syria, master's degree at International Islamic University Malaysia and PhD at Universitas Gadjah Mada Yogyakarta. He is engaged with Muslim NGOs across Southeast Asia to formulate how gender justice can be culturally negotiated and adopted within Islamic perspectives. He is an advocate for progressive Islam in Indonesia, especially concerning gender justice and democracy.

Omaima Abou-Bakr is a professor of English and comparative literature at Cairo University (Egypt), a founding member of the Women and Memory Forum and a member of the Musawah Knowledge Building team. She specializes in medieval Sufi poetry and comparative topics in medieval English and Arabic literature. Her scholarly interests also include women's mysticism and female spirituality in Christianity and Islam, feminist theology, Muslim women's history and gender issues in Islamic discourse.

Amira Abou-Taleb sought to pursue her passion for examining the interplay between reason, ethics and beauty by switching from a long career in international advertising agencies to earn an MA in Islamic studies from the American University in Cairo (AUC). Following graduation, Amira designed a course titled 'Beauty & Reason in the Arab/Islamic Civilization', which became very popular at AUC for five years before it was introduced at the University of Helsinki in Finland in 2019. Amira is currently a doctoral fellow in the Faculty of Theology at the University of Helsinki researching the concept of *iḥsān* in the Qurʾanic worldview. She is keen on understanding the impact this *weltanschauung* has and can have on informing both ethics and aesthetics. She is the author of the chapter 'Constructing the Image of the Model Muslim Woman: Gender Discourse in Ibn Saʿd's *Kitāb al-Ṭabaqāt al-Kubrā*' in *Islamic Interpretive Tradition and Gender Justice: Processes of Canonization, Subversion, and Change* (2020).

Yasmin Amin is an Egyptian-German who received her PhD in Islamic studies in 2021 from Exeter University's Institute of Arab and Islamic Studies researching 'Humour and Laughter in the Ḥadīth'. She obtained a postgraduate diploma in Islamic studies in 2006 and an MA in Islamic studies in 2010, both from the American University in Cairo. Her research covers various aspects of gender issues, early Muslim society and culture as well as the original texts of Islamic history, law and Hadith. She is the author of the forthcoming *Musnad Umm Salama and the Factors Affecting Its Evolution*, co-translator of *The Sorrowful Muslim's Guide*, and co-editor (with Nevin Reda) of *Islamic Interpretive Tradition and Gender Justice: Processes of Canonization, Subversion, and Change* (2020).

Zainah Anwar co-founded two groundbreaking women's groups that engage with Islam from a rights perspective to promote the rights of women living in Muslim contexts: Sisters in Islam (SIS) in Malaysia, which she led from 1999–2008, and Musawah, the global movement for equality and justice in the Muslim family, which she led from 2009–2021. Her other work experience includes chief programme officer, Political Affairs Division, Commonwealth Secretariat, London; senior analyst, Institute of Strategic and International Studies, Kuala Lumpur; political and diplomatic writer, *The New Straits Times*, Kuala Lumpur. She was also a member of the Human Rights Commission of Malaysia from 2000–2004. Her book, *Islamic Revivalism in Malaysia: Dakwah Among the Students* (1987), has become a standard reference in the study of Islam in Malaysia. She was educated at the Fletcher School of Law and Diplomacy at Tufts University, Boston University and the MARA Institute of Technology, Malaysia, in the fields of international relations and journalism.

Mariam Al-Attar holds a PhD in Islamic Ethics from the University of Leeds. She currently teaches Arabic heritage and Islamic philosophy at the American University of Sharjah. Before that she taught courses in philosophy at the University in Jordan and various courses at King's Academy in Madaba, where she was also head of the Department of Ethics, Philosophy and Religion. Her book *Islamic Ethics: Divine Command Theory in Arabo-Islamic Thought* traces the development of ethical thought in Islam and focuses on the work of the Muʿtazilite judge ʿAbd al-Jabbār al-Asadabādī. Her more recent work includes chapters and journal articles that reflect her research interest in metaethical theories, *kalām* (speculative theology) and *uṣūl al-fiqh* (principles of jurisprudence) in a way that relates to contemporary normative concerns. Prior to her academic career, she was a physicist working as a clinical scientist. Her initial research was related to her earlier career and is reflected in her master thesis, in Arabic, that focused on the scientific methodology and philosophy of ʿAbd al-Laṭīf al-Baghdādī.

Zahia Jouirou is a professor of Islamic and religious comparative studies in the University of Manouba (Tunis) and the director of the Institute of Translation of Tunis. She specializes in family laws, *fiqh*, *fatāwā* and *uṣūl al-fiqh*. She writes and researches on the historicity of the Islamic legal and jurisprudential system; the roots of discriminatory provisions against women; and the reformist approaches to Muslim family laws, norms and practices. She has published more than twenty academic articles and four books on the status of women in *fiqh*-based laws, polygamy and inheritance rights. She is also a member of an active Tunisian network of women's groups and was engaged in the campaign to safeguard women's rights in the Tunisian constitution after the revolution. She is the recipient of several awards and distinctions related to her work on women's issues.

Mohsen Kadivar is a theologian and a leading public intellectual. He has been a research professor of Islamic studies at Duke University (Durham, NC, USA) since 2009. He was a visiting professor at Harvard Law School, University of Virginia and University of North Carolina; a global ethics fellow with the Carnegie Council; research fellow with the Institute for Advanced Study in Berlin, Germany; and a fellow of National Humanities Centre in Research Triangle Park, North Carolina. His interests span both classical and modern Islamic thought, with a special focus on Islamic philosophy and ethics, Shiʿi theology and jurisprudence, Qurʾanic studies, Shiʿi political thought and Islam and human rights. His latest publications are *Human Rights and Reformist Islam* and *Blasphemy and Apostasy in Islam* (both published by University of Edinburgh Press in 2021), and two forthcoming books: *Governance by Guardianship: Rule and Government in the Islamic Republic of Iran* (Cambridge University Press) and *Islamic Theocracy in the Secular Age* (University of North Carolina Press).

Asma Lamrabet is a haematologist at the Avicena Public Hospital in Rabat. She was director of the Center for Women's Studies in Islam in the Rabita Mohammadia des Oulémas du Maroc from 2011 to March 2018. She has studied women's issues in Islam for many years and has delivered lectures on this topic at various conferences around the world. From 2004 to 2007, she was the coordinator of a research and reflection group on Muslim women and intercultural dialogue in Rabat. She is also the founding member of the Fatéma Mernissi Chair at Mohammed V University in Rabat since 2017 and member of the Nordic Center Advisory Board since May 2020. She is currently the Gender Studies Chair in the Euro-Arab Foundation for higher studies in Granada, Spain, and a member of the scientific committee of the Moroccan Driss Benzekri National Institute for Human Rights. She is the author of several books; *Women and Men in the Qurʾan* (Palgrave

Macmillan) received the Social Sciences Awards 2013 by the Arab Woman Organization.

Sarah Marsso is a feminist and anti-racism activist engaging with the Islamic tradition to promote gender equality in Muslim contexts. She has coordinated the activities of Musawah's Knowledge Building Working Group since 2015. She co-authored two Musawah reports entitled *Women's Stories, Women's Lives: Male Authority in Muslim Contexts* (2016) and *Who Provides? Who Cares? Changing Dynamics in Muslim Families* (2018), and has contributed to many other publications. She is a graduate of SciencesPo in European studies and international relations and holds an MA in development and cooperation in the Middle East & North Africa from l'Institut d'Etudes Politiques of Lyon.

Ziba Mir-Hosseini is a legal anthropologist who specializes in Islamic law, gender and Islamic feminism. She is a founding member and current board member of Musawah. She is professorial research associate at the Centre for Islamic and Middle Eastern Law, SOAS, University of London, and Hauser Global Law visiting professor at NYU Law School, a position she has held since 2002. She has published books on Islamic family law in Iran and Morocco, Iranian clerical discourses on gender, Islamic reformist thinkers, and the revival of *zinā* laws. She is the author of *Journeys Toward Gender Equality in Islam* (2022) and the co-editor of *Gender and Equality in Muslim Family Law* (with Kari Vogt, Lena Larsen and Christian Moe, 2013) and *Men in Charge? Rethinking Authority in Muslim Legal Tradition* (with Mulki Al-Sharmani and Jana Rumminger, 2015). Ziba co-directed (with Kim Longinotto) two award-winning feature-length documentary films on Iran: *Divorce Iranian Style* (1998) and *Runaway* (2001). She received the American Academy of Religion's 2015 Martin E. Marty Award for the Public Understanding of Religion.

Nur Rofiah is a lecturer of methodology of Qur᾿anic interpretation at the graduate and postgraduate levels at the Islamic State University Syarif Hidayatullah and at the Institute for Qur᾿anic Studies (PTIQ) in Jakarta. She is also a women's rights activist who promotes gender justice within Islam as a writer, facilitator and resource person. She has authored books in Indonesian whose titles translate in English as *Breaking the Silence: Religion Hears the Voices of Women Victims of Violence, Islam as Human Religion: Reinterpreting*

Qishas and Hudud, and *Muslimah's Critical Thinking*. She is a board member of Alimat and Rahima, two of the three institutions that initiated and arranged the first Congress of Indonesian Women Ulama in 2017.

Shadaab Rahemtulla is a lecturer in Islam and Christian–Muslim relations at the School of Divinity, University of Edinburgh. A Canadian Muslim from Vancouver/Coast Salish Territories, he completed his doctorate in contemporary Islamic thought at the University of Oxford. He is the author of the book *Qur'an of the Oppressed: Liberation Theology and Gender Justice in Islam* (Oxford University Press, 2018). His primary interest lies in how religion can be (re)interpreted as a liberating force to confront contexts of oppression, including patriarchy, empire, poverty and racism. His second book project, which is tentatively titled *Islam and Native American Suffering: Decolonising Islamic Liberation Theology* (Oxford University Press), seeks to reread the Qur'an in the light of Native American rights, occupation, and indigenous struggles against settler colonialism. Before joining the University of Edinburgh, he was an assistant professor at the University of Jordan in Amman, where he taught for six years.

Nevin Reda is an associate professor of Muslim studies at Emmanuel College of Victoria University in the University of Toronto. Her research interests include the poetics and hermeneutics of Qur'anic narrative structure, Hebrew Bible and Qur'an, spiritually integrative approaches to the Qur'an, Islamic feminist hermeneutics, Islamic ethical-legal theory (*uṣūl al-fiqh*) and Islamic political theory. She has published one monograph, *The al-Baqara Crescendo: Understanding the Qur'an's Style, Narrative Structure, and Running Themes* (2017). She also co-edited (with Yasmin Amin) *Islamic Interpretive Tradition and Gender Justice: Processes of Canonization, Subversion, and Change* (2020). She has published many articles, one of the most recent of which is 'The Qur'an and Domestic Violence: An Islamic Feminist, Spiritually Integrative Reading of Verse 4:34' (2019). At Emmanuel, she teaches a variety of courses in core Islamic disciplines, including the Qur'an, the Prophet Muhammad's biography, Shari'a, Islamic spirituality and classical and modern Islamic thought.

Jana Rumminger is a legal researcher and writer whose scholarship and activism focus on human rights issues related to gender, race/ethnicity and religion. She has been involved with Musawah in a variety of roles since 2007 and as a member of the Knowledge Building Working Group since 2010. She has played a lead role in many Musawah publications, including co-editing *Men in Charge? Rethinking Authority in Muslim Legal Tradition* (with Ziba Mir-Hosseini and Mulki Al-Sharmani, 2015). She has also worked with several local and international women's rights organizations in South and Southeast Asia and non-profit organizations in the United States. She holds an AB from Princeton University and a JD and MS in law, policy and society from Northeastern University.

Hoda El Saadi is an adjunct faculty member in the Department of Arab and Islamic Civilization at the American University in Cairo (AUC) and a co-founder of the Woman and Memory Forum. She received her BA and MA from the American University in Cairo and her PhD in Islamic History from Cairo University. She specializes in early and medieval Islamic history, with a particular focus on women's changing roles and positions from pre-modern to modern history and women's presence in public life. Her aim is to use history (and its interpretations) to strengthen the position of Muslim women in the present, as well as formulate a culturally Islamic discourse that incorporates women's perspective and an awareness of gender. She considers her work to be a form of resistance against the process of exclusion and marginalization from which women suffered in various historical periods. Some of her recent publications also include: 'Islamic Feminism in Egypt: Between Acceptance and Rejection', and *Questions and Answers about Gender and Feminism* (co-authored with Aya Sami, 2016).

Saʿdiyya Shaikh is an associate professor in the Department for the Study of Religions at the University of Cape Town. Her areas of research include gender-sensitive readings of Hadith, Qurʾanic exegesis and Sufi texts; theoretical and political debates on Islam and feminism; religion and gender-based violence; contemporary Muslim women's embodied, experiential and everyday modes of understanding Qurʾanic teachings. Her books include *Sufi Narratives of Intimacy: Ibn ʿArabī, Gender, and Sexuality* (2012), *The Women's Khutbah Book: Contemporary Sermons on Spirituality and Justice from around the World* (co-authored with Fatima Seedat, 2022), and *Violence Against Women in Contemporary World Religions: Roots and Cures* (co-edited with Daniel Maguire, 2007). Her forthcoming book project is provisionally entitled *The Breath of Merciful: Jamali Ethics, Gender and Spirituality*. In her work as well as her spiritual life, Saʿdiyya draws on several contemporary Sufi teachers including Shaykh Muhammad Rahim Bawa Muhaiyaddeen (*raḥmatullah ʿalayhī*), Shaykh Fadhlalla Haeri and

Shaykha Cemal Nur Sargut. She is mother to Nuriyya, a feisty, opinionated 19-year-old woman, and Ismael, an impish, entertaining 14-year-old, and wife to Ashraf Kagee, academic, novelist and fun life partner.

Marwa Sharafeldin is an Egyptian scholar activist. She has a PhD in law from the University of Oxford and is the senior technical advisor and MENA region expert in Musawah. She is currently a visiting fellow in Harvard Law School's Program on Law and Society in the Muslim World. Her work covers the intersection between Islamic law, international human rights law and feminist activism. She has been published in several academic books and media platforms covering those topics. In addition to her work with Musawah, she co-founded and/or served on the Advisory Boards of several feminist organizations worldwide such as the Global Fund for Women, the Young Arab Feminist Network and the Network for Women's Rights Organizations in Egypt. She has contributed to publications such as the UN's flagship *Progress of the World's Women Report* and the UN's *Gender Justice and Law Arab Region Report*. She believes in the power of art for social transformation, and is a story collector, performer and writer.

Mulki Al-Sharmani is an associate professor of Islamic and Middle Eastern studies, University of Helsinki. Mulki is also a member of the Musawah Knowledge Building Working Group and coordinated the Global Life Stories Project (2011–16) as part of Musawah's 'Knowledge Building Initiative on *Qiwamah* and *Wilayah*'. Mulki's research interests include Qurʾanic ethics and Islamic feminist exegesis; contemporary Muslim women's engagements with the Qurʾan and Islamic interpretive tradition in Finland and Egypt; Muslim family laws and gender in Islamic legal tradition; and modern diasporas and gender relations in the family domain, with a focus on transnational Muslim families. She authored *Gender Justice and Legal Reform in Egypt: Negotiating Muslim Family Law* (2017); and co-authored (with Omaima Abou-Bakr) the book chapter 'Islamic Feminist *Tafsir* and Qurʾanic Ethics: Rereading Divorce Verses' (2020). She co-edited *Men in Charge? Authority in Islamic Legal Tradition* (with Ziba Mir-Hosseini and Jana Rumminger, 2015) and *Wellbeing of Transnational Muslim Families: Marriage, Gender and Law* (with Marja Tiilikainen and Sanna Mustasaari, 2019). She is currently working on a manuscript titled *Islamic Feminism: Tradition, Authority, and Hermeneutics* (Bloomsbury).

Lynn Welchman is a professor of law at SOAS, University of London, specializing in law and society, Muslim family laws, women's rights and human rights in the Middle East and North Africa. She has published widely, including the books *Al-Haq: A Global History of the First Palestinian Human Rights Organization* (2021), *Women and Muslim Family Laws in Arab States* (2007) and *Beyond the Code: Muslim Family Law and the Shar'i Judiciary in the Palestinian West Bank* (2000). Before joining SOAS, she worked in human rights, primarily with Palestinian NGOs in the West Bank, but also with international human rights organizations. She is a board member of the Euro-Mediterranean Foundation for the Support of Human Rights Defenders, a member of the International Advisory Board of the Open Society Foundations' MENA office, and a founding co-editor of the *Muslim World Journal of Human Rights* and the Oxford Islamic Legal Studies Series. At the end of 2021, she was appointed to the Independent International Commission of Inquiry on the Syrian Arab Republic by the president of the UN Human Rights Council.

Index

WITHDRAWN FROM
CARMEL CLAY
PUBLIC LIBRARY